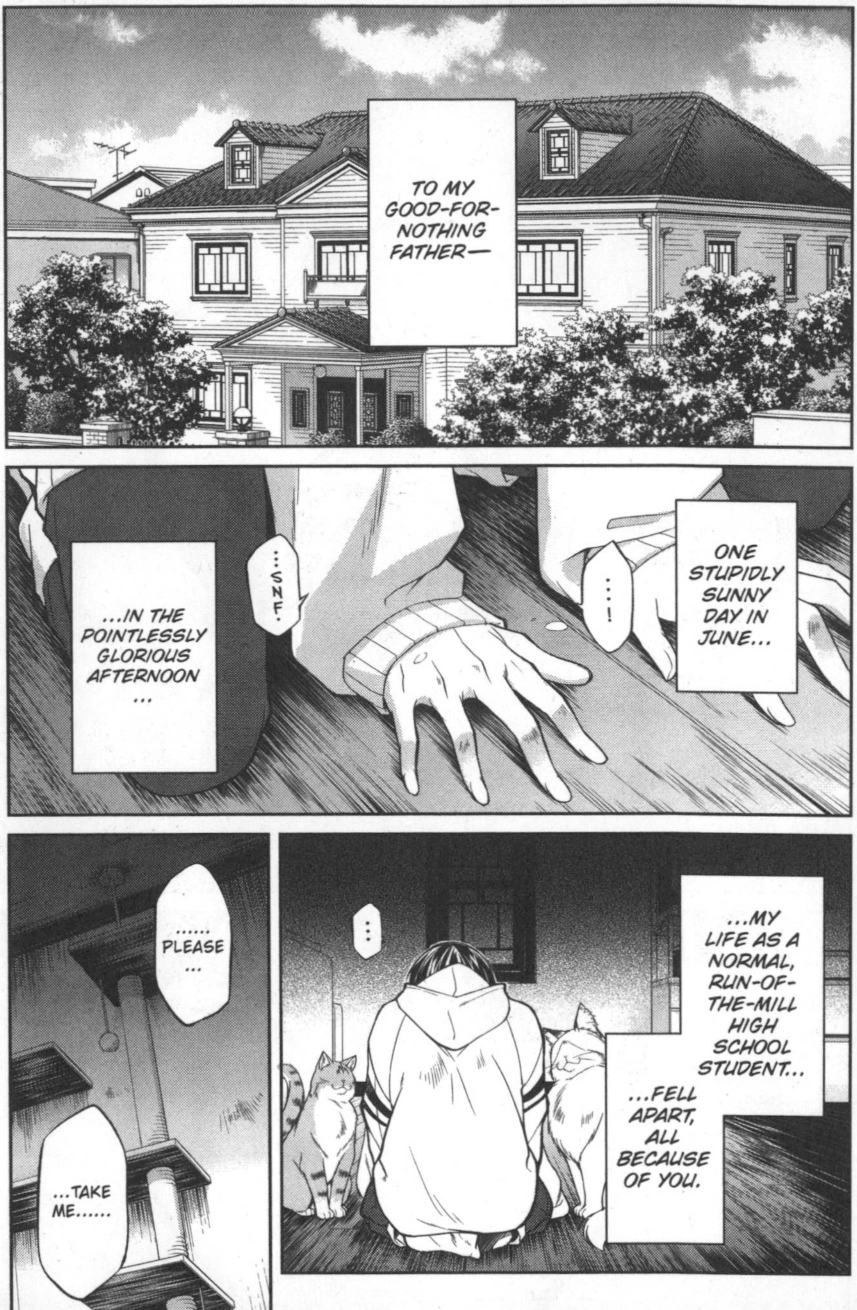
TO MY GOOD-FOR-NOTHING FATHER—
ONE STUPIDLY SUNNY DAY IN JUNE...
...!
...SNF.
...IN THE POINTLESSLY GLORIOUS AFTERNOON...
...MY LIFE AS A NORMAL, RUN-OF-THE-MILL HIGH SCHOOL STUDENT...
...FELL APART, ALL BECAUSE OF YOU.
...
......PLEASE...
...TAKE ME......

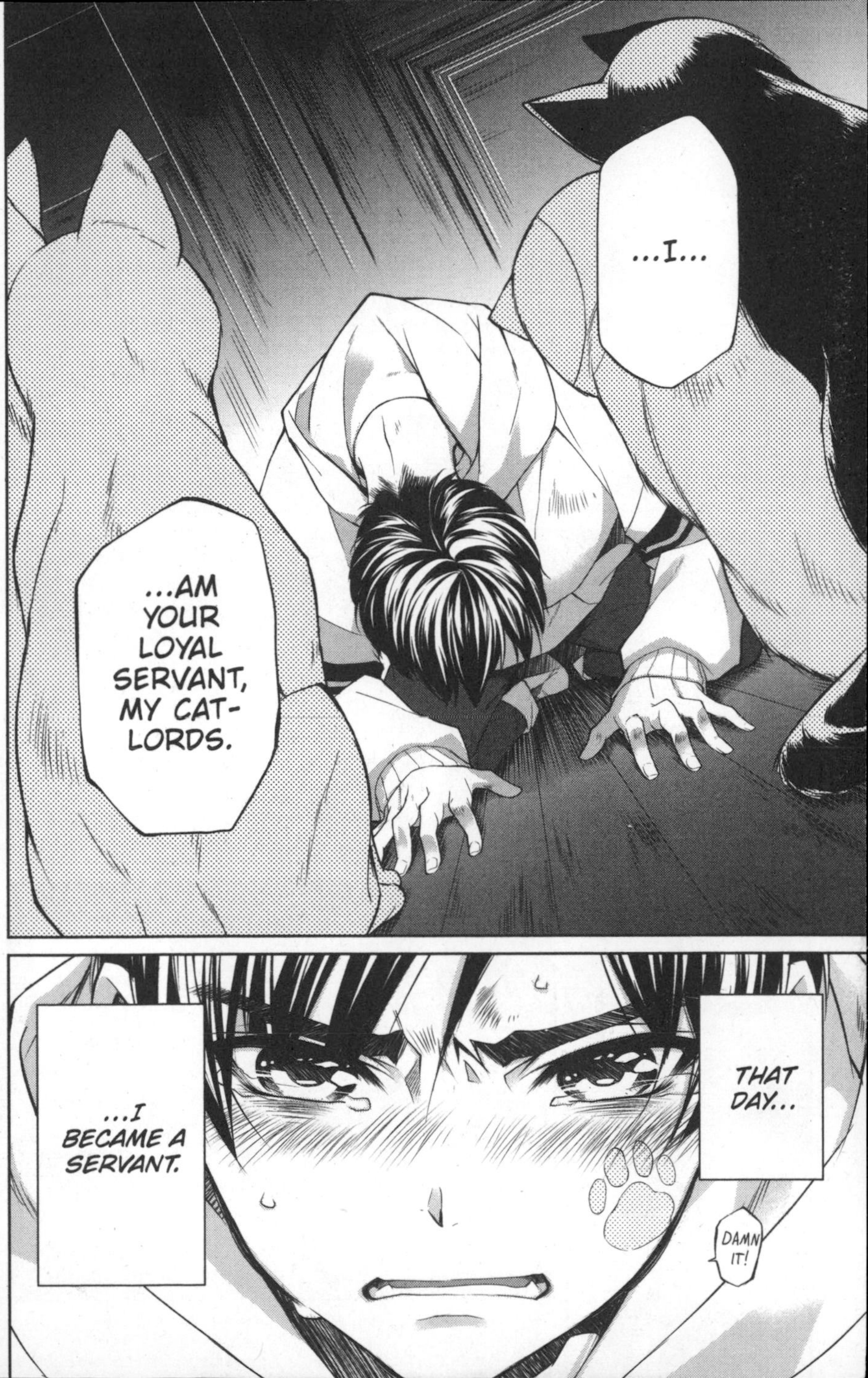
...I...
...AM YOUR LOYAL SERVANT, MY CAT-LORDS.
THAT DAY...
...I BECAME A SERVANT.
DAMN IT!

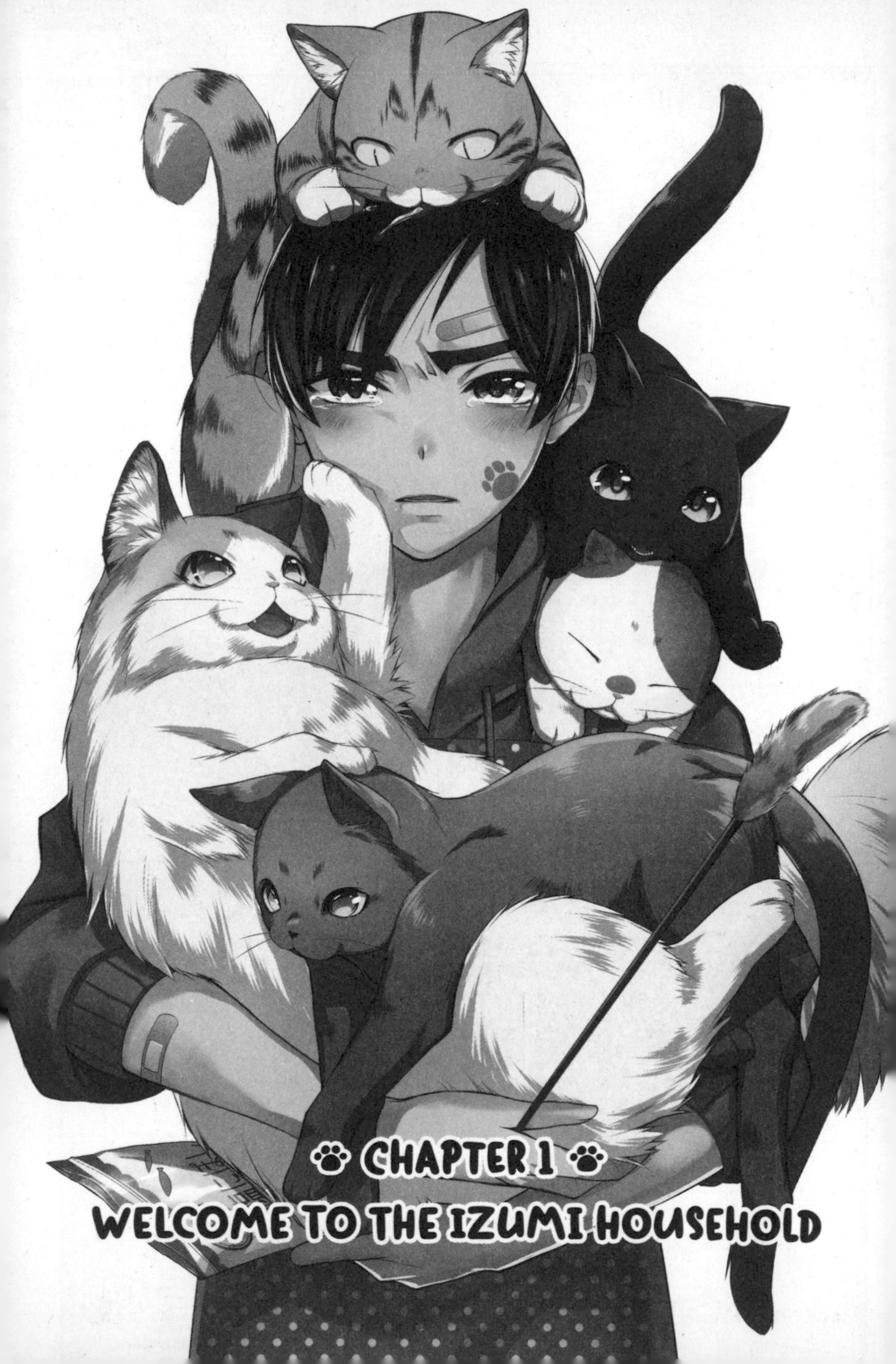
CHAPTER 1
WELCOME TO THE IZUMI HOUSEHOLD

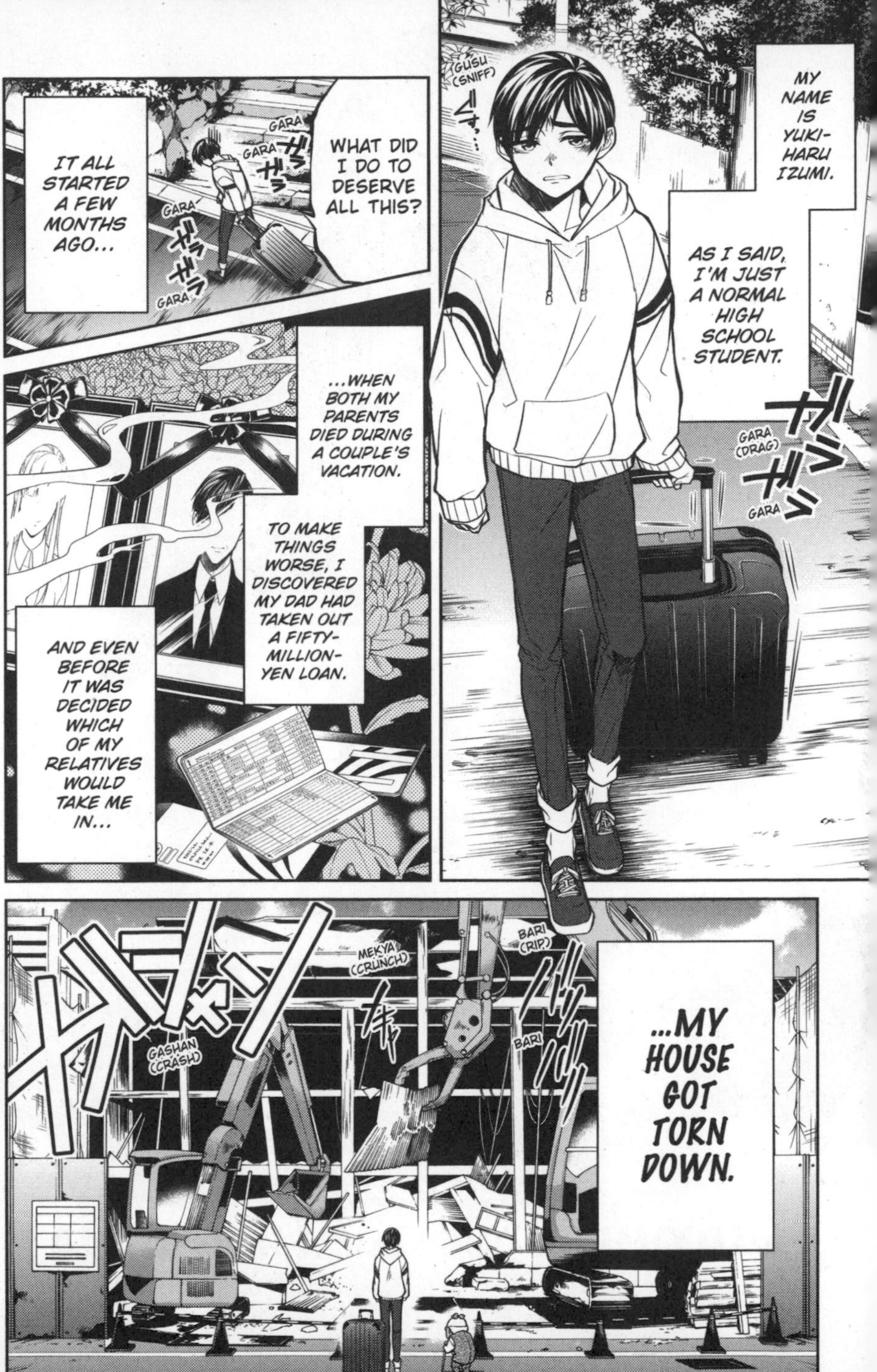
GUSU (SNIFF)
MY NAME IS YUKI-HARU IZUMI.
AS I SAID, I'M JUST A NORMAL HIGH SCHOOL STUDENT.
GARA (DRAG)
GARA
WHAT DID I DO TO DESERVE ALL THIS?
GARA
GARA
GARA
GARA
IT ALL STARTED A FEW MONTHS AGO...
...WHEN BOTH MY PARENTS DIED DURING A COUPLE'S VACATION.
TO MAKE THINGS WORSE, I DISCOVERED MY DAD HAD TAKEN OUT A FIFTY-MILLION-YEN LOAN.
AND EVEN BEFORE IT WAS DECIDED WHICH OF MY RELATIVES WOULD TAKE ME IN...
BARI (RIP)
BARI
...MY HOUSE GOT TORN DOWN.
MEKYA (CRUNCH)
GASHAN (CRASH)

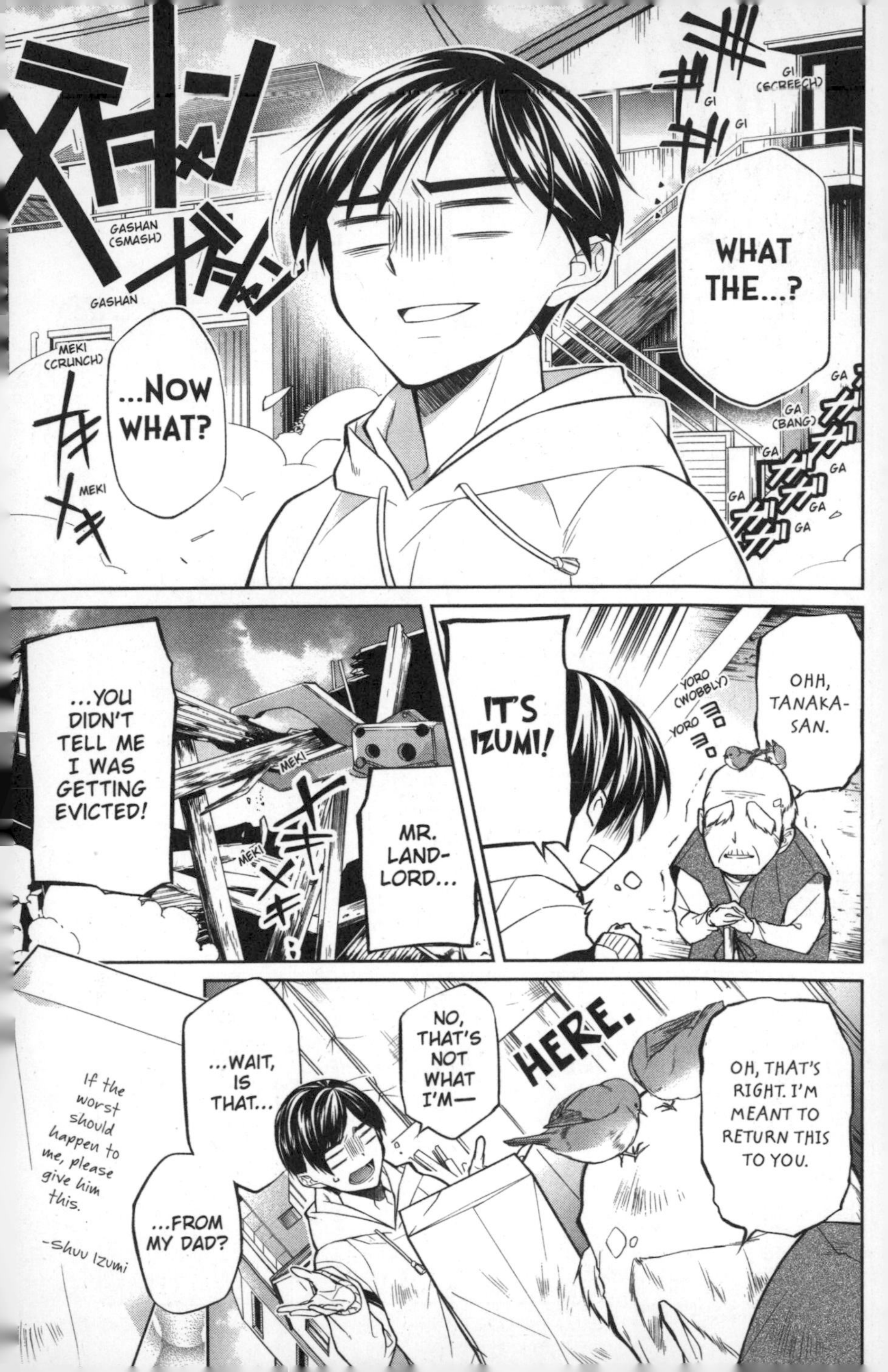
GI (SCREECH)
GI
GI
WHAT THE...?
GA (BANG)
GA
GA
GA
GA
GA
GA
GASHAN (SMASH)
GASHAN
MEKI (CRUNCH)
MEKI
...NOW WHAT?
OHH, TANAKA-SAN.
YORO (WOBBLY)
YORO
IT'S IZUMI!
MR. LANDLORD...
MEKI
MEKI
...YOU DIDN'T TELL ME I WAS GETTING EVICTED!
OH, THAT'S RIGHT. I'M MEANT TO RETURN THIS TO YOU.
HERE.
NO, THAT'S NOT WHAT I'M—
...WAIT, IS THAT...
...FROM MY DAD?
If the worst should happen to me, please give him this.
-Shuu Izumi

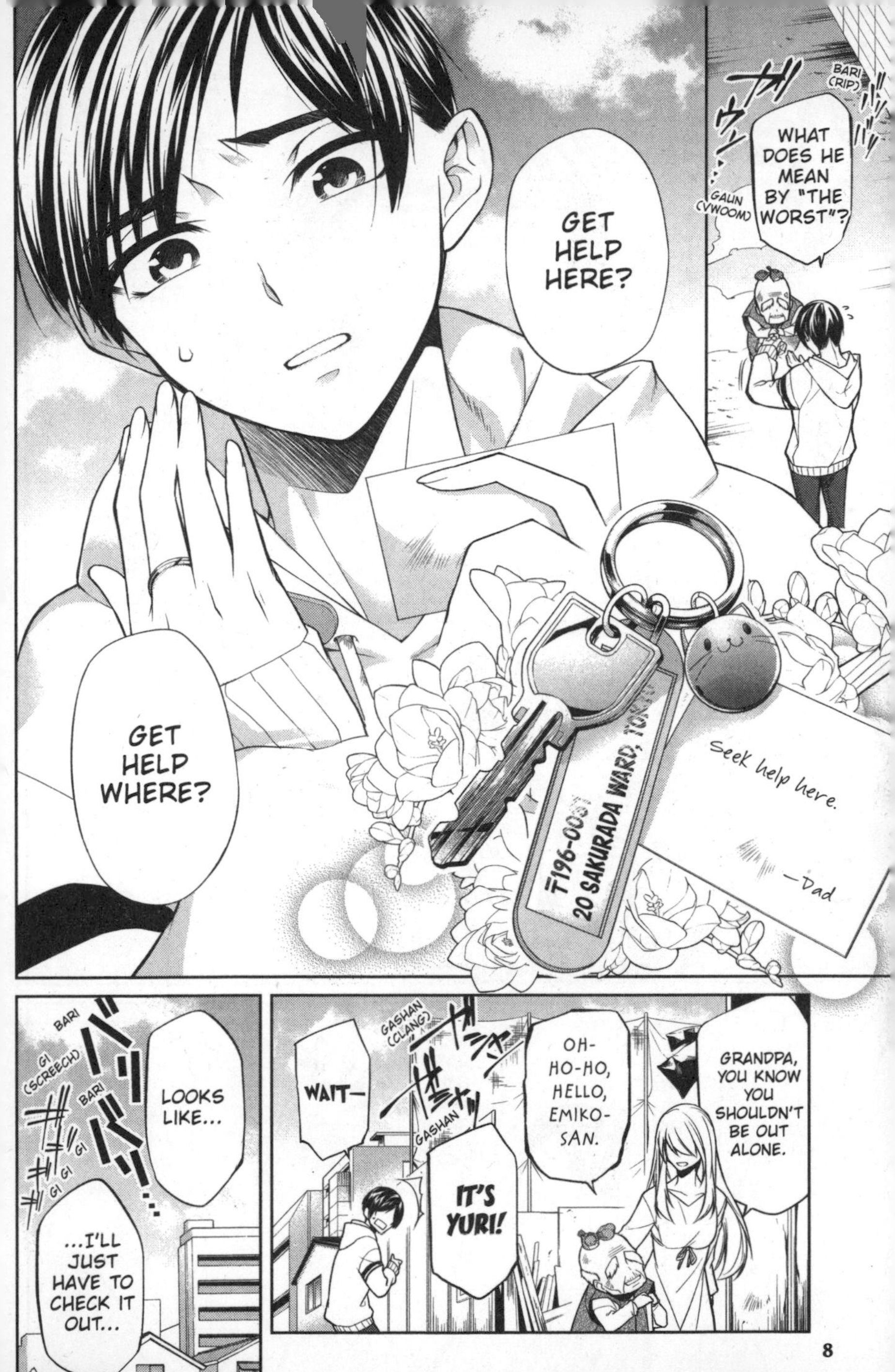
BARI (RIP)
WHAT DOES HE MEAN BY "THE WORST"?
GAUN (VWOOM)
GET HELP HERE?
〒196-008
20 SAKURADA WARD,
Seek help here.
—Dad
GET HELP WHERE?
GRANDPA, YOU KNOW YOU SHOULDN'T BE OUT ALONE.
OH-HO-HO, HELLO, EMIKO-SAN.
IT'S YURI!
GASHAN (CLANG)
GASHAN
WAIT—
BARI
BARI
GI (SCREECH)
GI GI GI
LOOKS LIKE...
...I'LL JUST HAVE TO CHECK IT OUT...

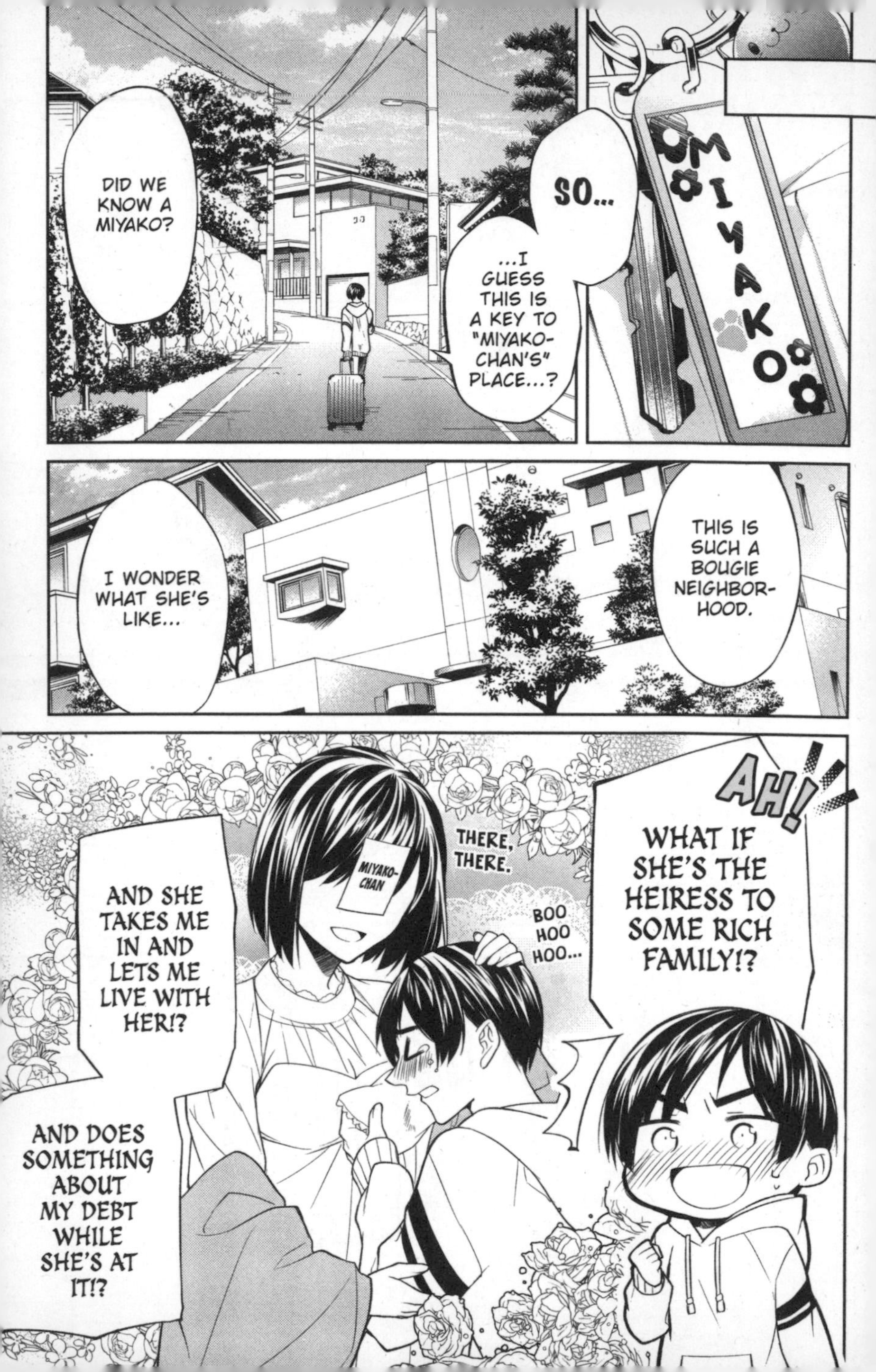
MIYAKO
SO...
...I GUESS THIS IS A KEY TO "MIYAKO-CHAN'S" PLACE...?
DID WE KNOW A MIYAKO?
THIS IS SUCH A BOUGIE NEIGHBORHOOD.
I WONDER WHAT SHE'S LIKE...
AH!
WHAT IF SHE'S THE HEIRESS TO SOME RICH FAMILY!?
THERE, THERE.
BOO HOO HOO...
MIYAKO-CHAN
AND SHE TAKES ME IN AND LETS ME LIVE WITH HER!?
AND DOES SOMETHING ABOUT MY DEBT WHILE SHE'S AT IT!?

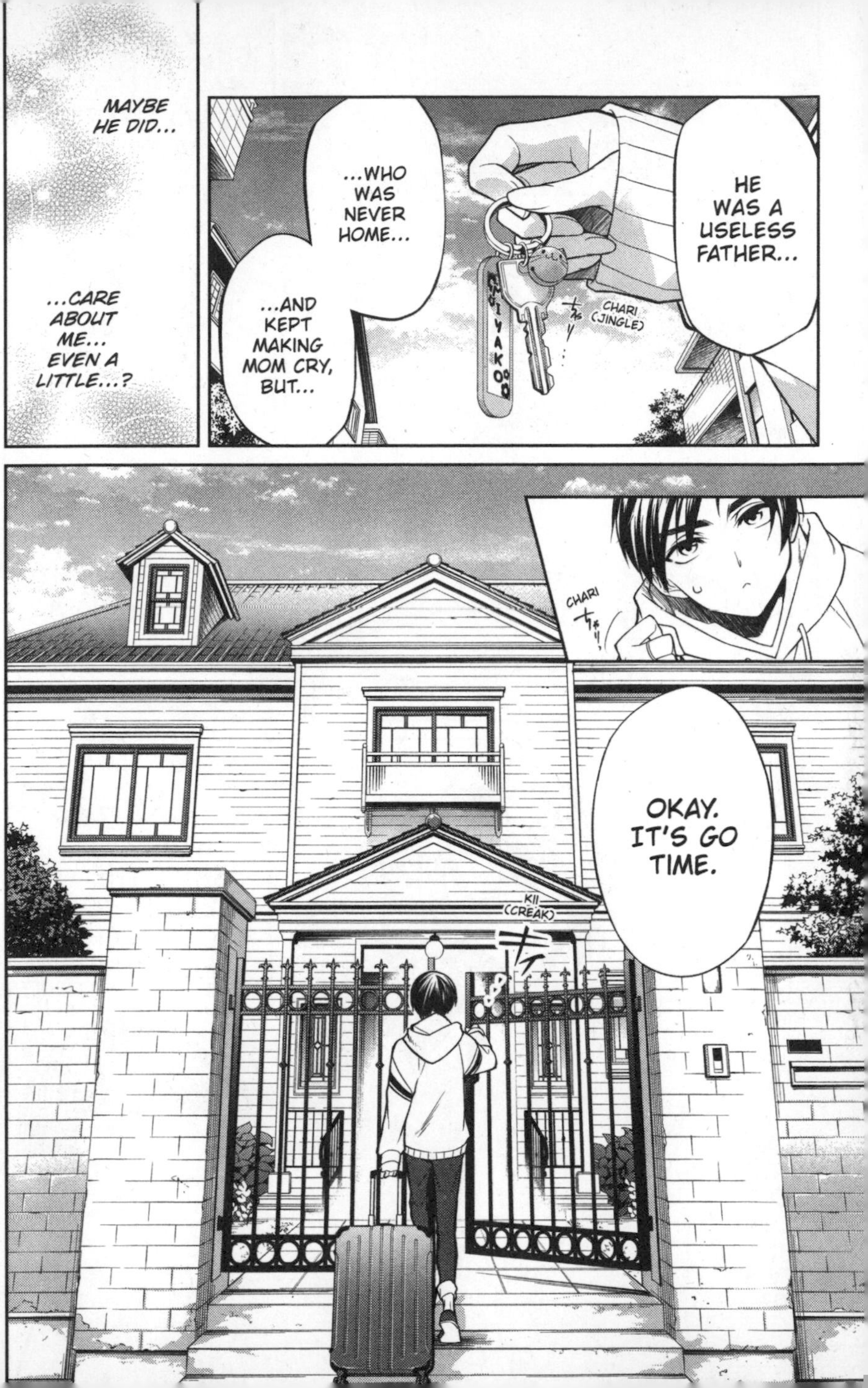
HE WAS A USELESS FATHER...
...WHO WAS NEVER HOME...
...AND KEPT MAKING MOM CRY, BUT...
CHARI (JINGLE)
MAYBE HE DID...
...CARE ABOUT ME... EVEN A LITTLE...?
CHARI
OKAY. IT'S GO TIME.
KII (CREAK)

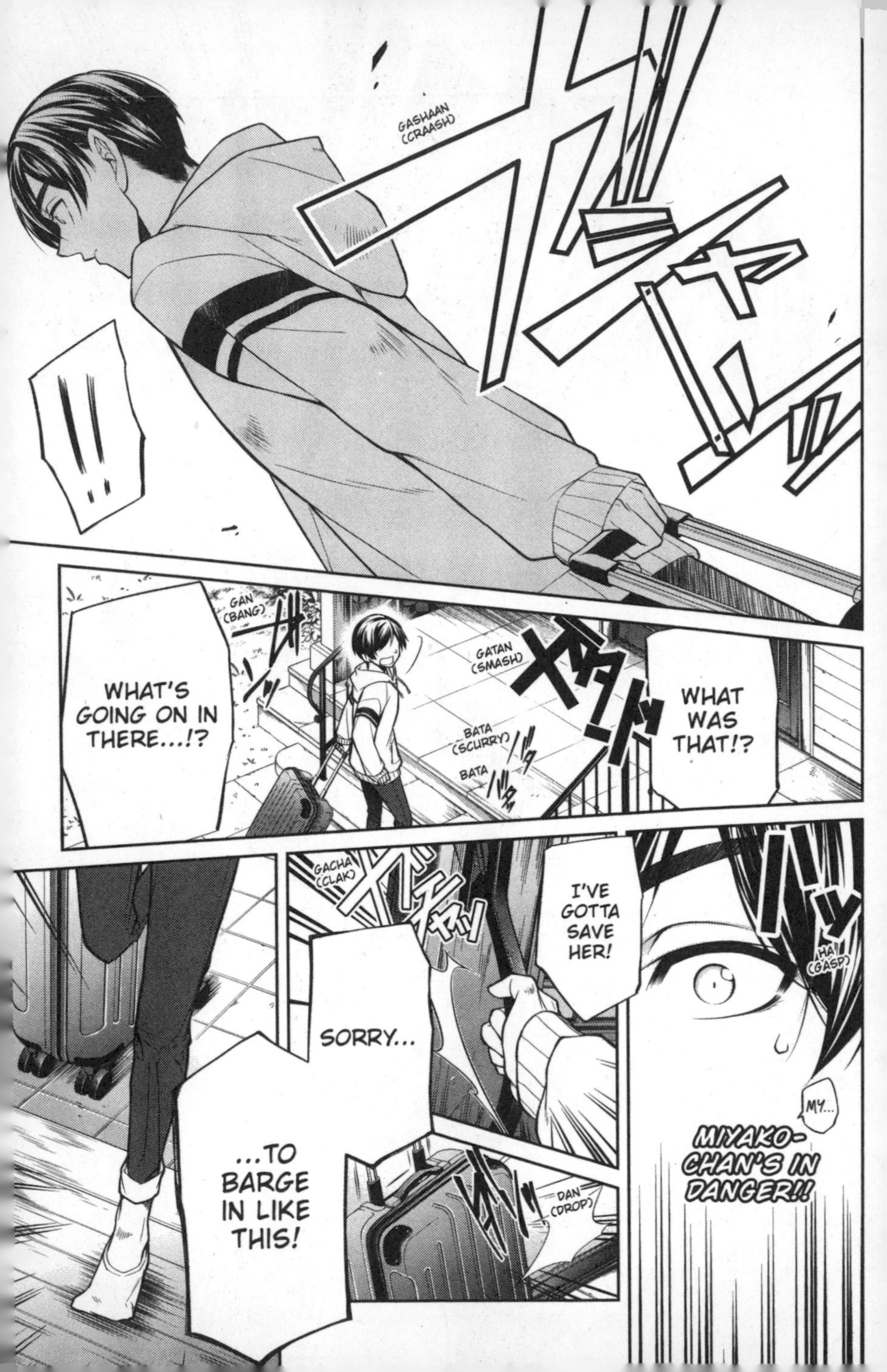
GASHAAN (CRAASH)
!!
WHAT WAS THAT!?
GATAN (SMASH)
BATA (SCURRY)
BATA
GAN (BANG)
WHAT'S GOING ON IN THERE...!?
HA (GASP)
MY...
MIYAKO-CHAN'S IN DANGER!!
GACHA (CLAK)
I'VE GOTTA SAVE HER!
DAN (DROP)
SORRY...
...TO BARGE IN LIKE THIS!

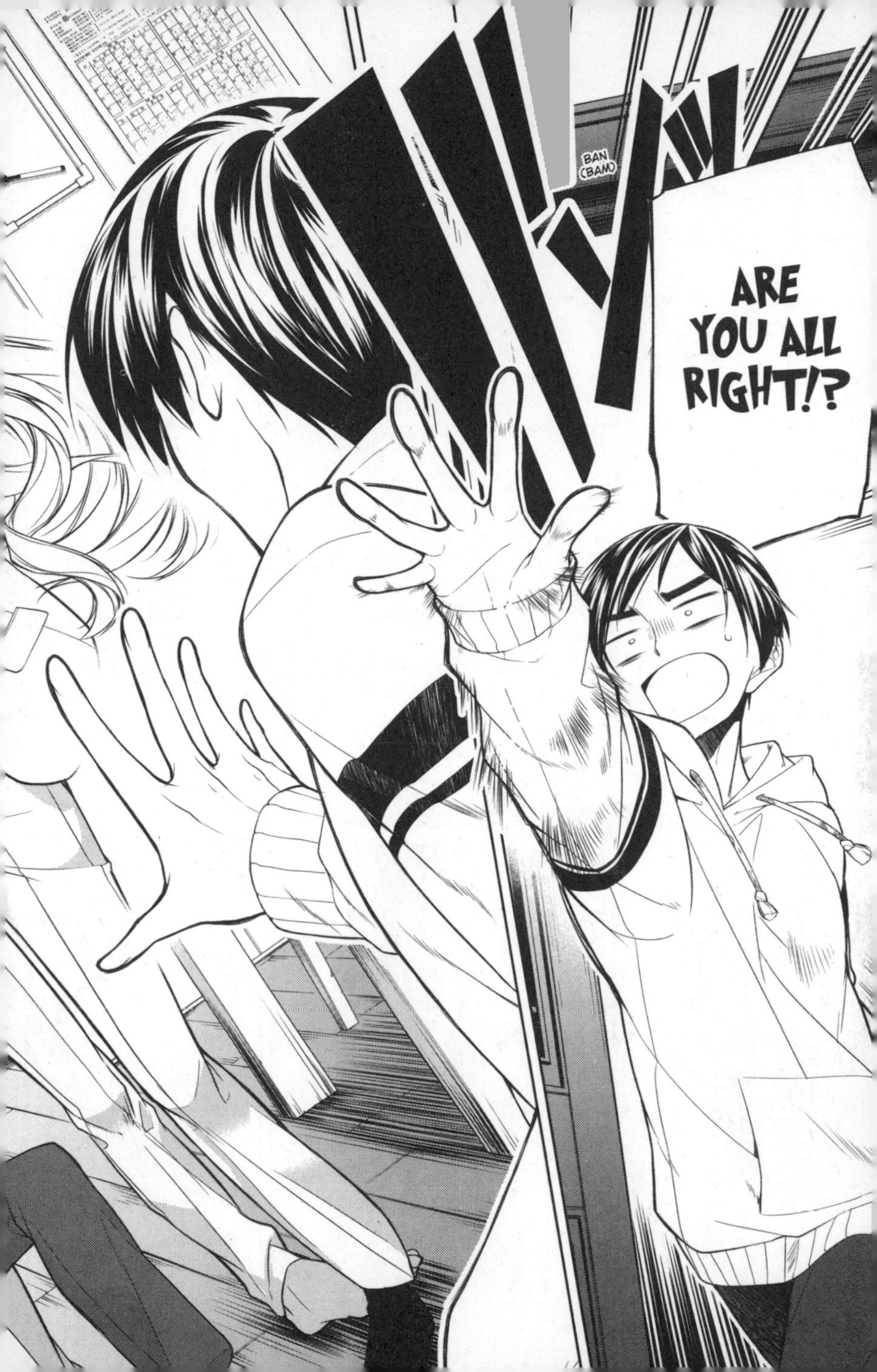
ARE YOU ALL RIGHT!?
BAN (BAM)

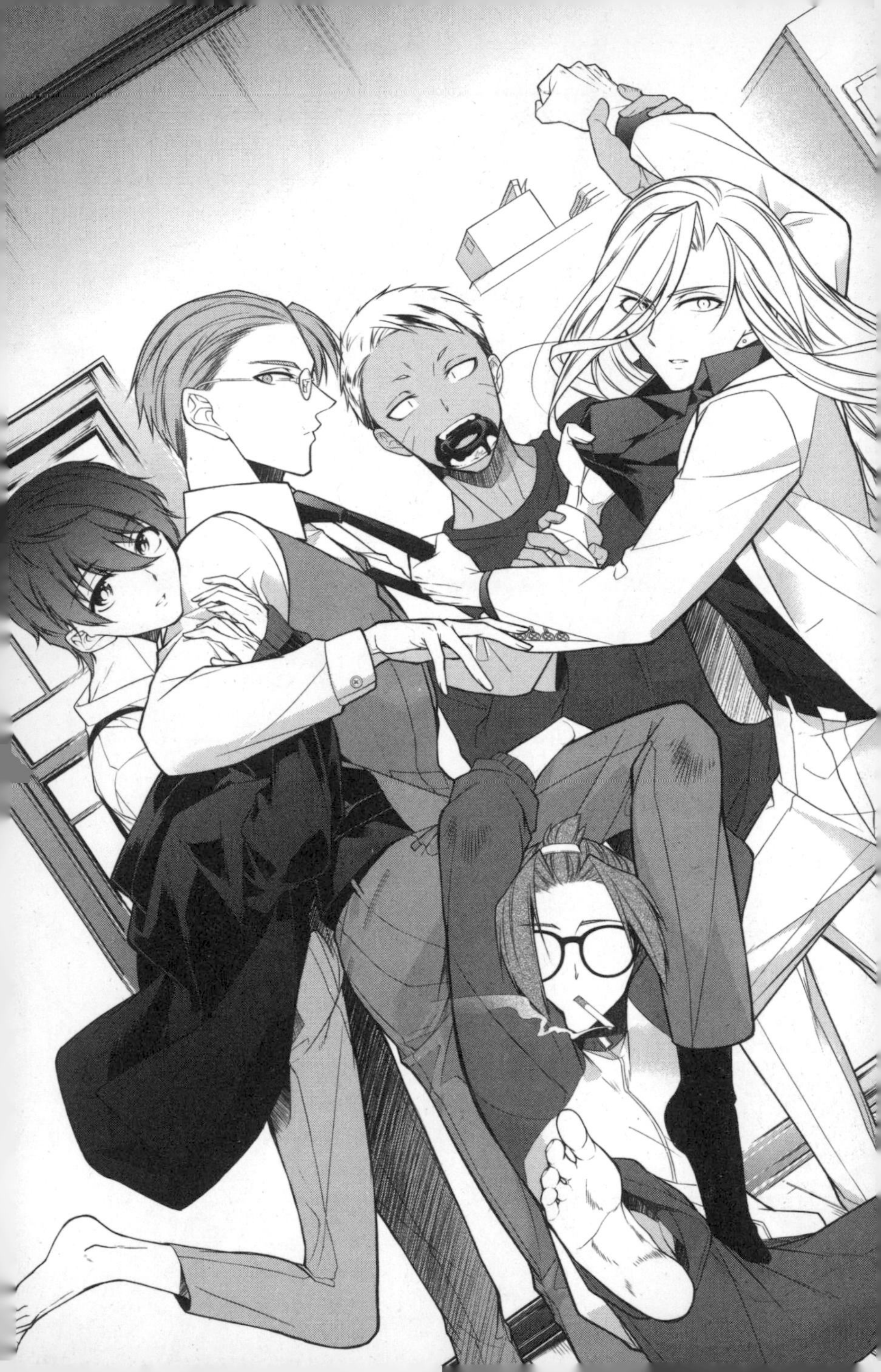

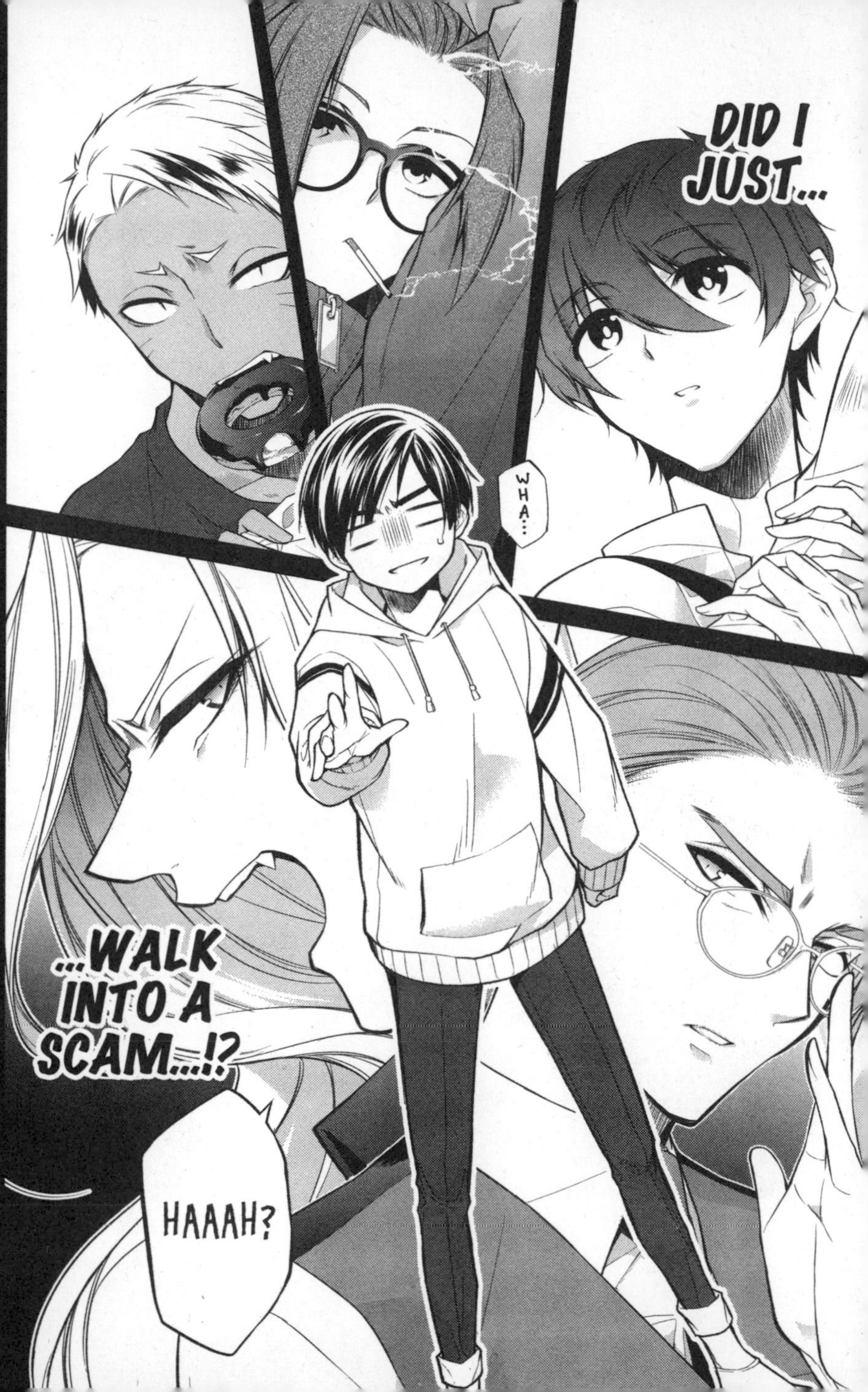
DID I JUST...
WHA...
...WALK INTO A SCAM...!?
HAAAH?

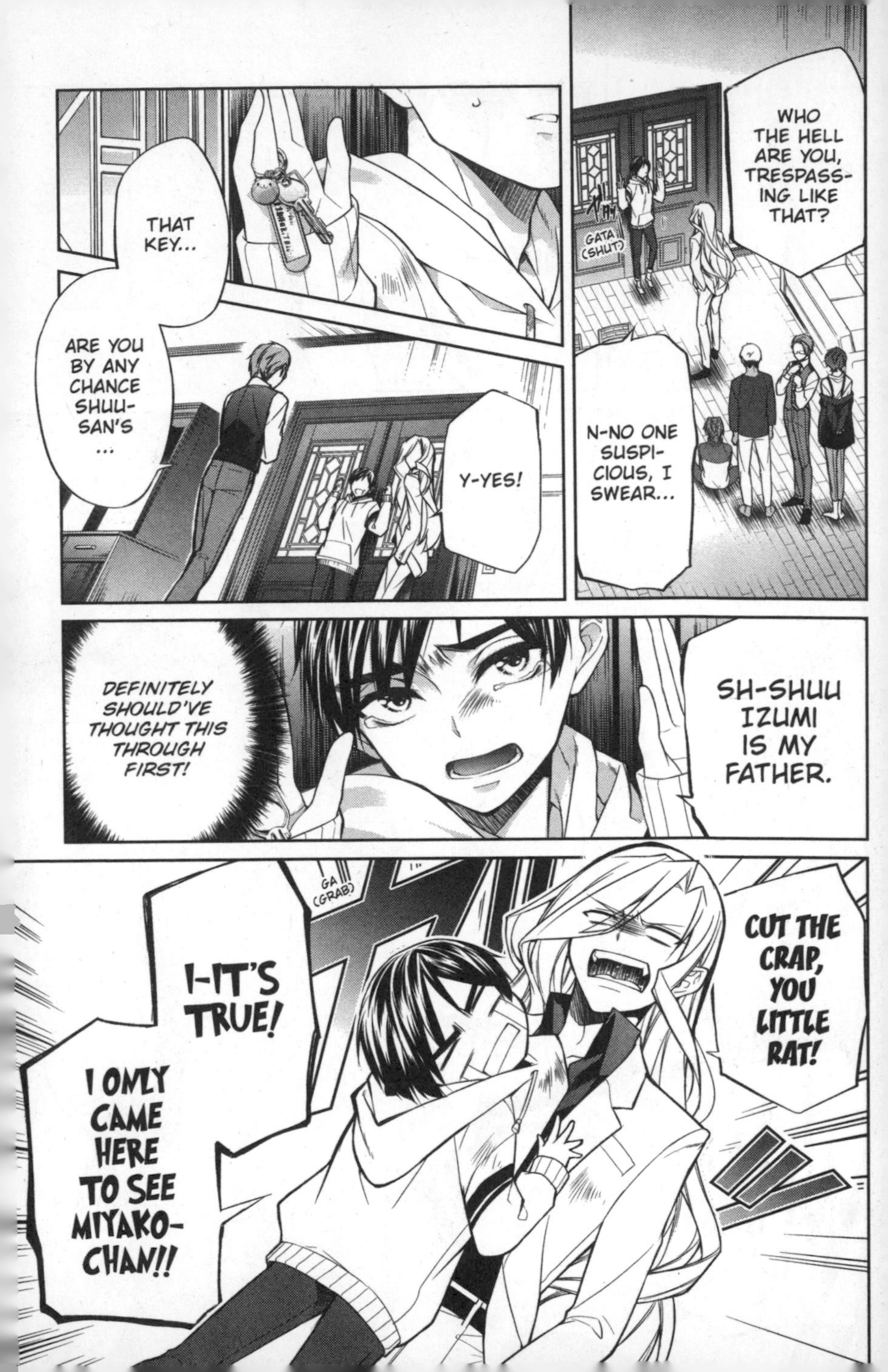

WHO THE HELL ARE YOU, TRESPASSING LIKE THAT?
GATA (SHUT)
N-NO ONE SUSPICIOUS, I SWEAR...
THAT KEY...
ARE YOU BY ANY CHANCE SHUU-SAN'S ...
Y-YES!
SH-SHUU IZUMI IS MY FATHER.
DEFINITELY SHOULD'VE THOUGHT THIS THROUGH FIRST!
CUT THE CRAP, YOU LITTLE RAT!
GA (GRAB)
I-IT'S TRUE!
I ONLY CAME HERE TO SEE MIYAKO-CHAN!!

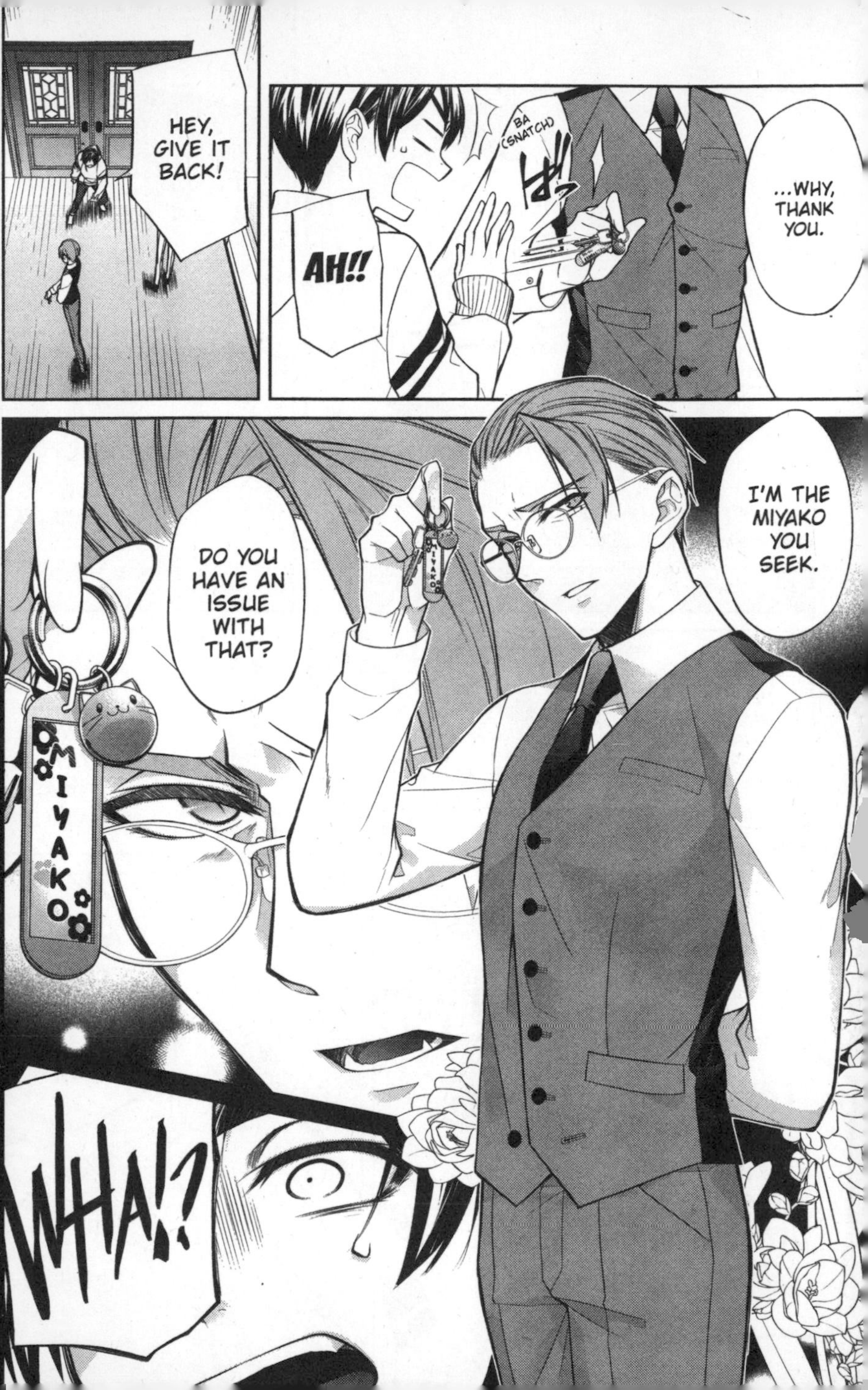
...WHY, THANK YOU.
BA (SNATCH)
ばっ
AH!!
HEY, GIVE IT BACK!
I'M THE MIYAKO YOU SEEK.
DO YOU HAVE AN ISSUE WITH THAT?
MIYAKO
WHA!?

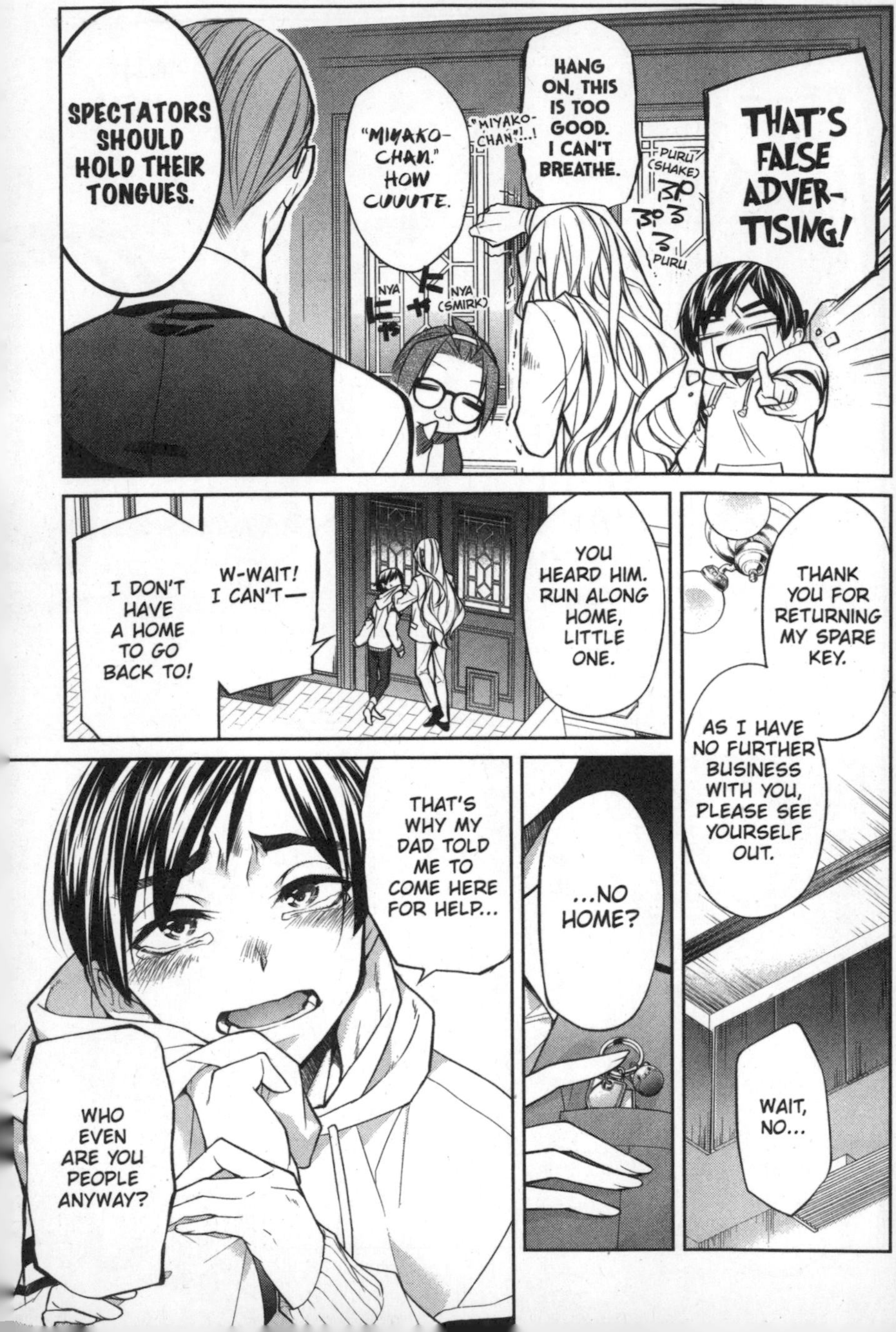
THAT'S FALSE ADVERTISING!
PURU PURU (SHAKE)
HANG ON, THIS IS TOO GOOD. I CAN'T BREATHE.
"MIYAKO-CHAN"...!
"MIYAKO-CHAN." HOW CUUUTE.
NYA NYA (SMIRK)
SPECTATORS SHOULD HOLD THEIR TONGUES.
THANK YOU FOR RETURNING MY SPARE KEY.
AS I HAVE NO FURTHER BUSINESS WITH YOU, PLEASE SEE YOURSELF OUT.
WAIT, NO...
YOU HEARD HIM. RUN ALONG HOME, LITTLE ONE.
W-WAIT! I CAN'T—
I DON'T HAVE A HOME TO GO BACK TO!
...NO HOME?
THAT'S WHY MY DAD TOLD ME TO COME HERE FOR HELP...
WHO EVEN ARE YOU PEOPLE ANYWAY?

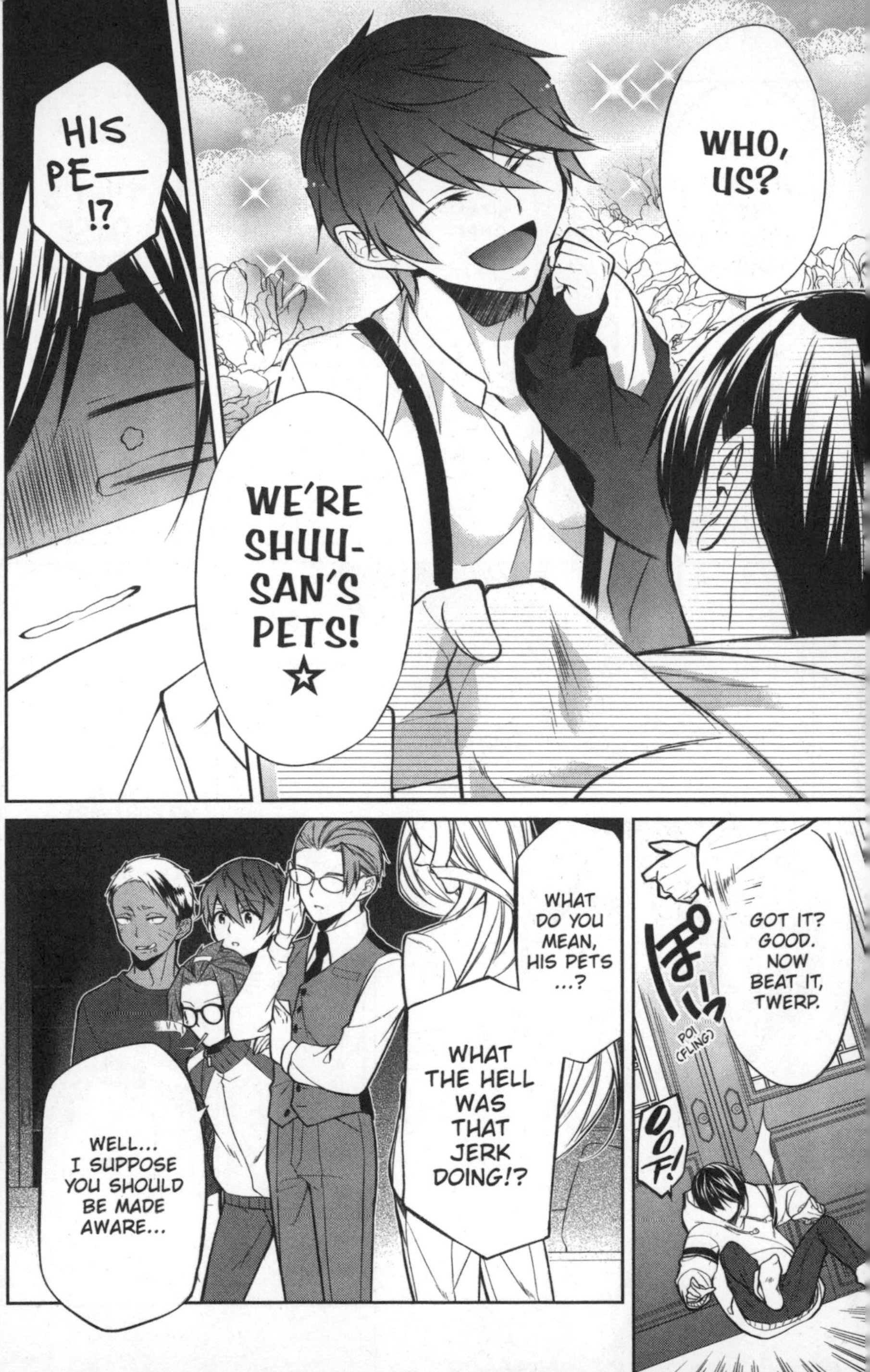
WHO, US?
WE'RE SHUU-SAN'S PETS! ☆
HIS PE—!?
GOT IT? GOOD. NOW BEAT IT, TWERP.
ぽいっ
POI (FLING)
OOOF!
WHAT DO YOU MEAN, HIS PETS ...?
WHAT THE HELL WAS THAT JERK DOING!?
WELL... I SUPPOSE YOU SHOULD BE MADE AWARE...

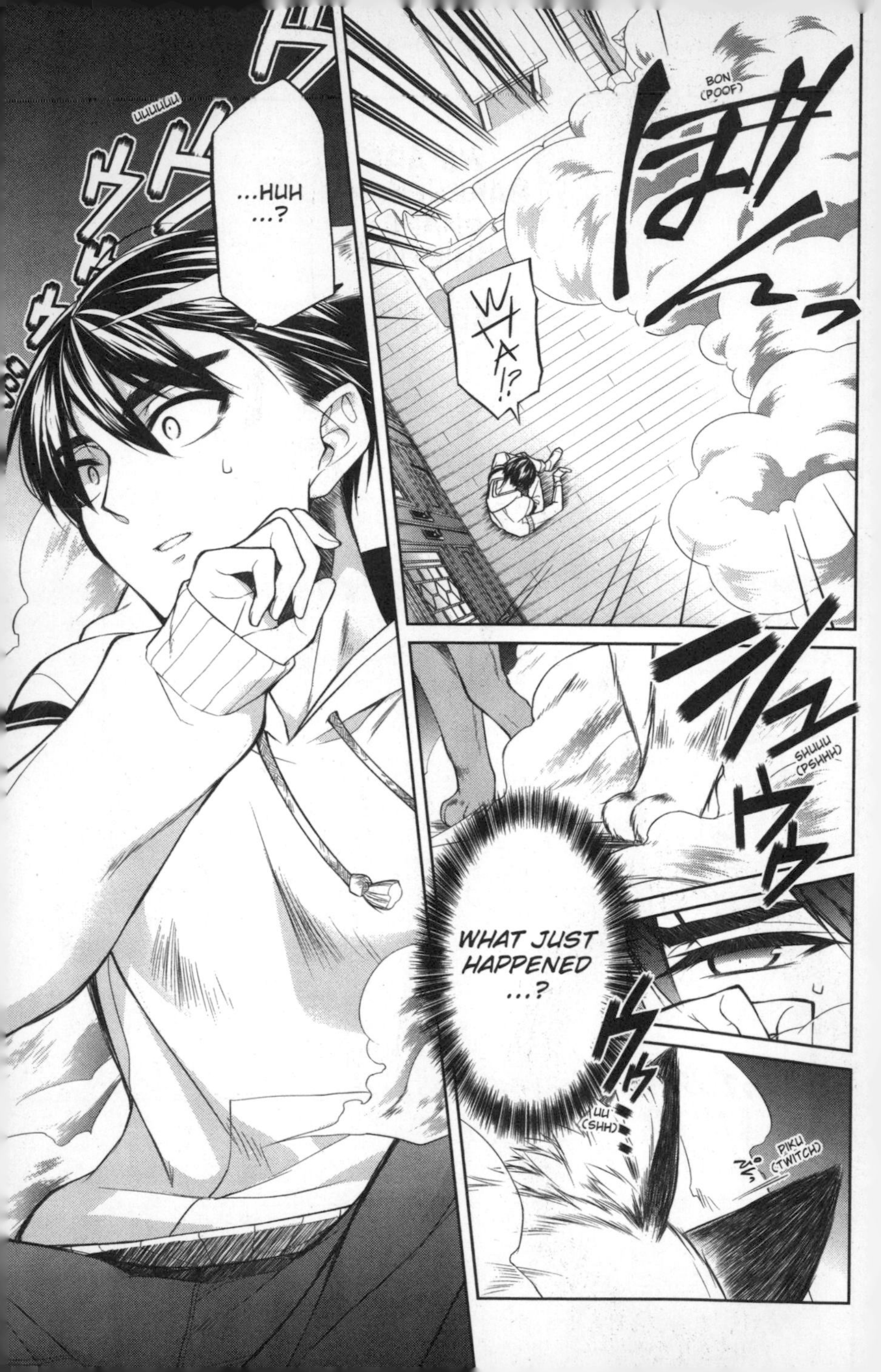
BON (POOF)
WHA!?
SHUUU (PSHHH)
WHAT JUST HAPPENED ...?
UU (SHH)
PIKU (TWITCH)
VOO
UUUUUU
...HUH ...?

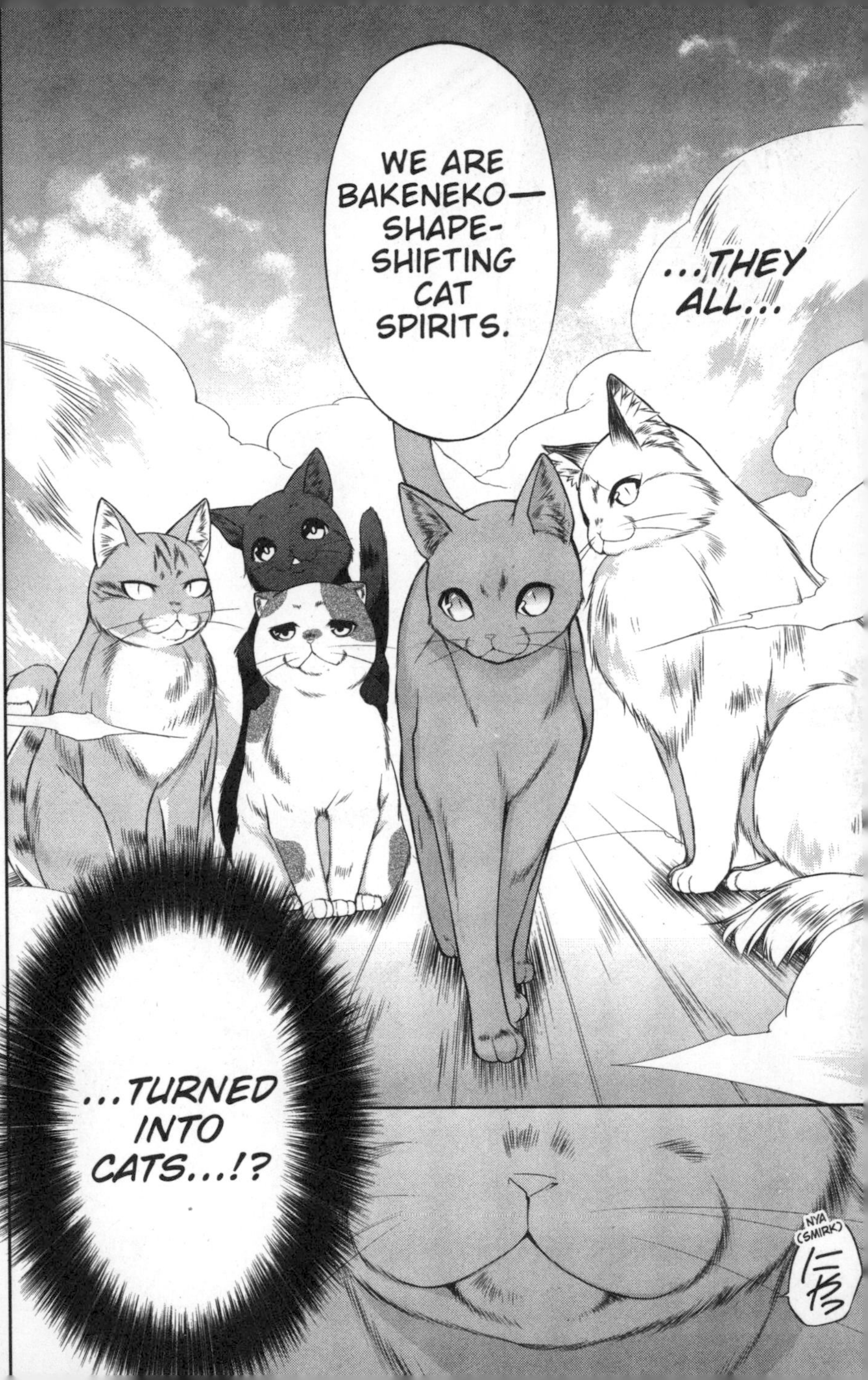
WE ARE BAKENEKO—SHAPE-SHIFTING CAT SPIRITS.
...THEY ALL...
...TURNED INTO CATS...!?
NYA (SMIRK)
にやっ

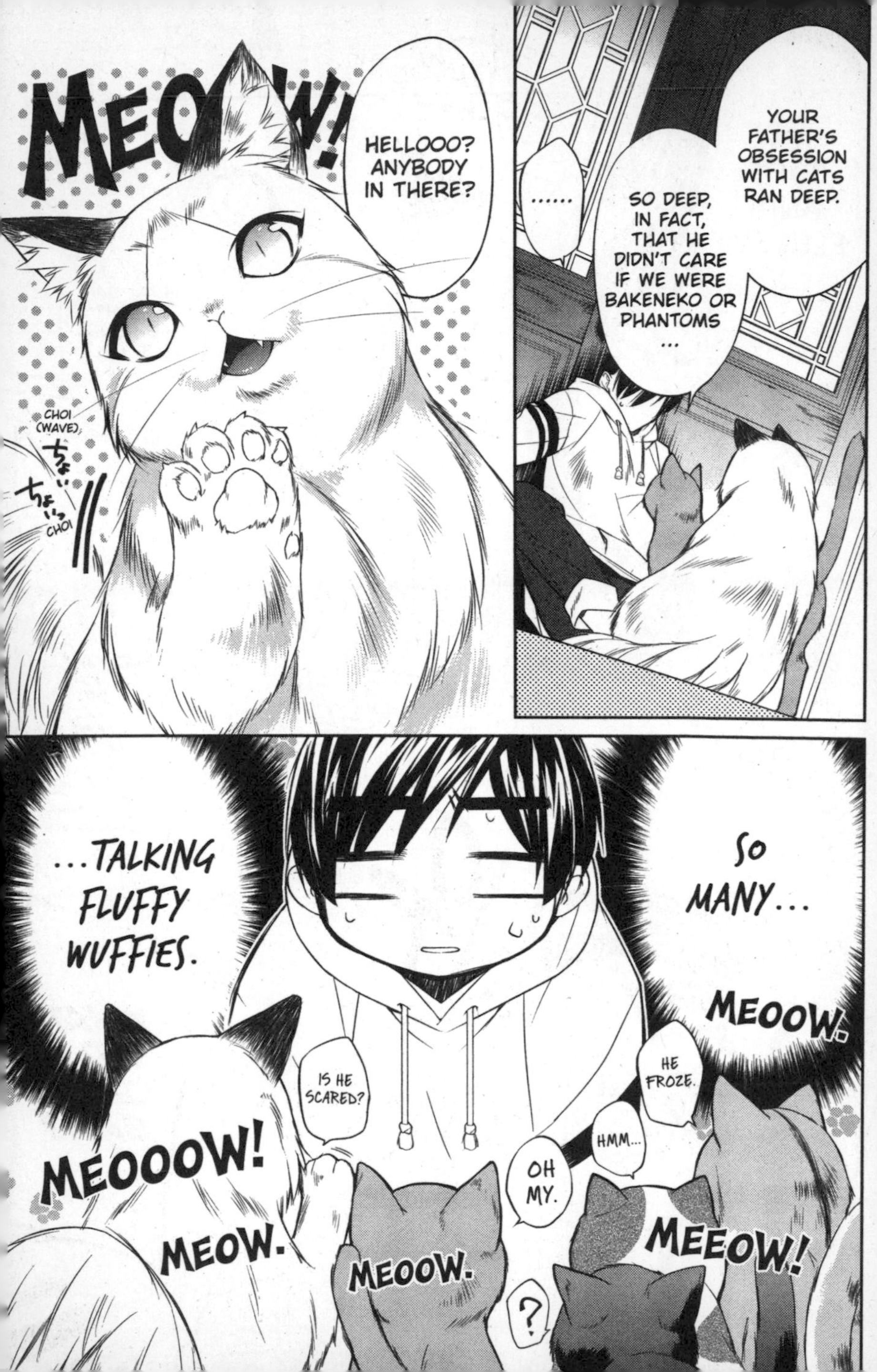
YOUR FATHER'S OBSESSION WITH CATS RAN DEEP.
SO DEEP, IN FACT, THAT HE DIDN'T CARE IF WE WERE BAKENEKO OR PHANTOMS ...
......
HELLOOO? ANYBODY IN THERE?
MEOOW!
CHOI (WAVE)
ちょい
ちょいっ
CHOI
SO MANY...
...TALKING FLUFFY WUFFIES.
MEOOW.
HE FROZE.
HMM...
OH MY.
IS HE SCARED?
MEEOW!
MEOOOW!
?
MEOOW.
MEOW.

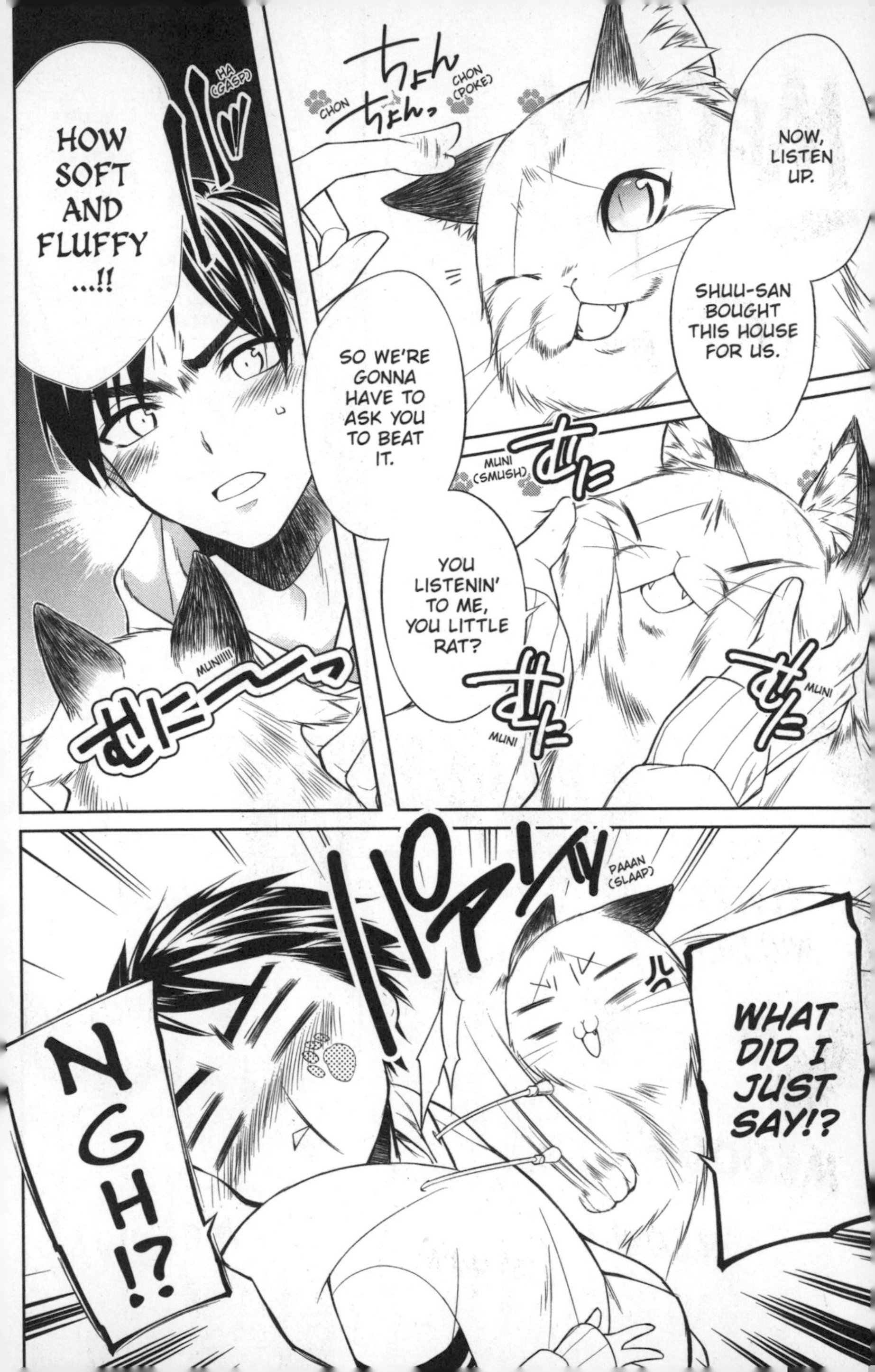
ちょん ちょんっ
CHON
CHON (POKE)
NOW, LISTEN UP.
SHUU-SAN BOUGHT THIS HOUSE FOR US.
SO WE'RE GONNA HAVE TO ASK YOU TO BEAT IT.
MUNI (SMUSH)
YOU LISTENIN' TO ME, YOU LITTLE RAT?
MUNI
MUNI
HA (GASP)
HOW SOFT AND FLUFFY ...!!
MUNIIII
PAAAN (SLAAP)
WHAT DID I JUST SAY!?
NGH!?

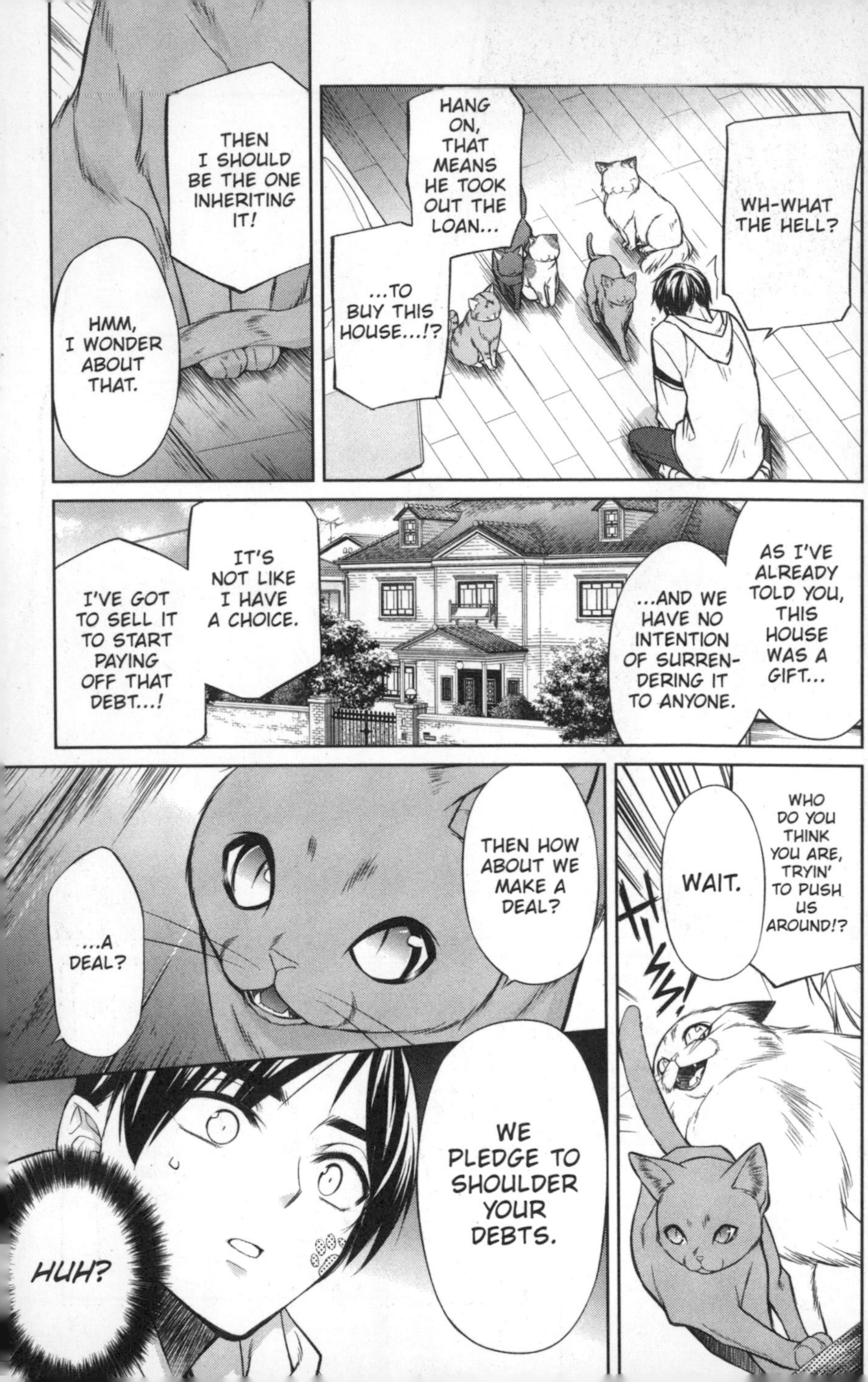
WH-WHAT THE HELL?
HANG ON, THAT MEANS HE TOOK OUT THE LOAN...
...TO BUY THIS HOUSE...!?
THEN I SHOULD BE THE ONE INHERITING IT!
HMM, I WONDER ABOUT THAT.
AS I'VE ALREADY TOLD YOU, THIS HOUSE WAS A GIFT...
...AND WE HAVE NO INTENTION OF SURREN-DERING IT TO ANYONE.
IT'S NOT LIKE I HAVE A CHOICE.
I'VE GOT TO SELL IT TO START PAYING OFF THAT DEBT...!
WHO DO YOU THINK YOU ARE, TRYIN' TO PUSH US AROUND!?
WAIT.
THEN HOW ABOUT WE MAKE A DEAL?
...A DEAL?
WE PLEDGE TO SHOULDER YOUR DEBTS.
HUH?

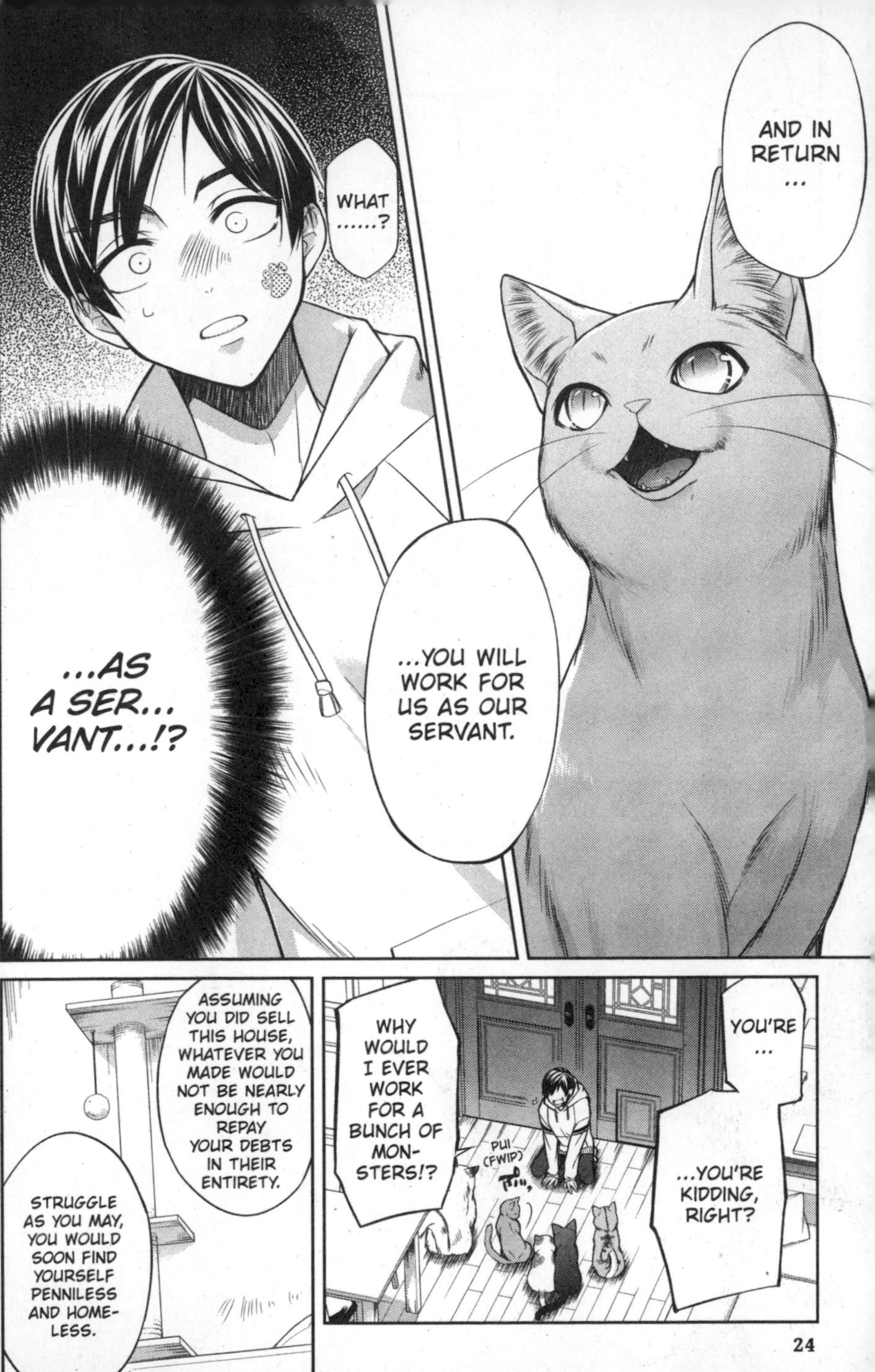
AND IN RETURN ...
...YOU WILL WORK FOR US AS OUR SERVANT.
WHAT ......?
...AS A SER... VANT...!?
YOU'RE ...
...YOU'RE KIDDING, RIGHT?
WHY WOULD I EVER WORK FOR A BUNCH OF MON-STERS!?
PUI (FWIP)
ASSUMING YOU DID SELL THIS HOUSE, WHATEVER YOU MADE WOULD NOT BE NEARLY ENOUGH TO REPAY YOUR DEBTS IN THEIR ENTIRETY.
STRUGGLE AS YOU MAY, YOU WOULD SOON FIND YOURSELF PENNILESS AND HOME-LESS.

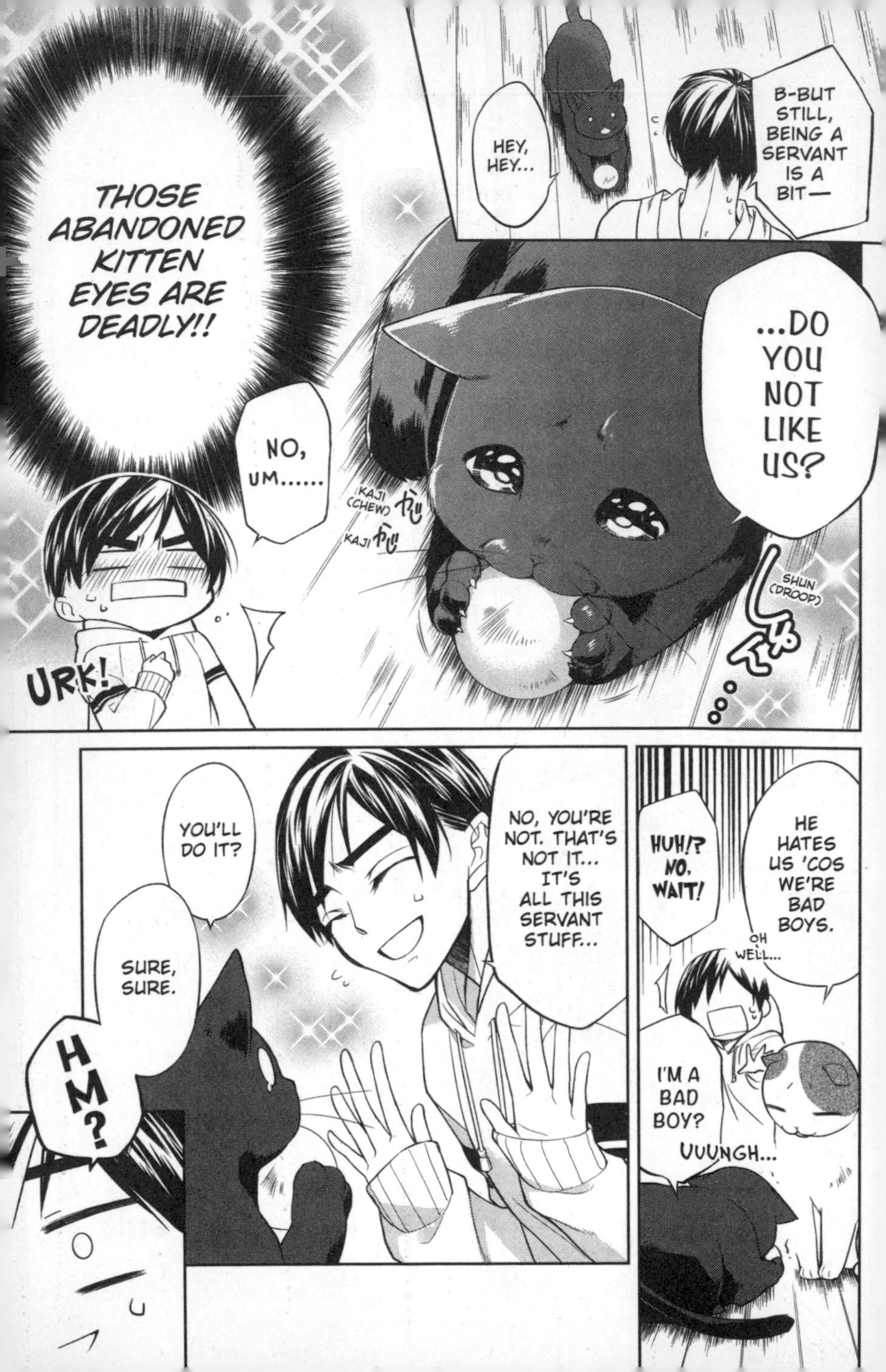
B-BUT STILL, BEING A SERVANT IS A BIT—
HEY, HEY...
...DO YOU NOT LIKE US?
SHUN (DROOP)
KAJI (CHEW)
KAJI
NO, UM......
THOSE ABANDONED KITTEN EYES ARE DEADLY!!
URK!
HE HATES US 'COS WE'RE BAD BOYS.
HUH!? NO. WAIT!
OH WELL...
I'M A BAD BOY?
UUUNGH...
NO, YOU'RE NOT. THAT'S NOT IT... IT'S ALL THIS SERVANT STUFF...
YOU'LL DO IT?
SURE, SURE.
HM?

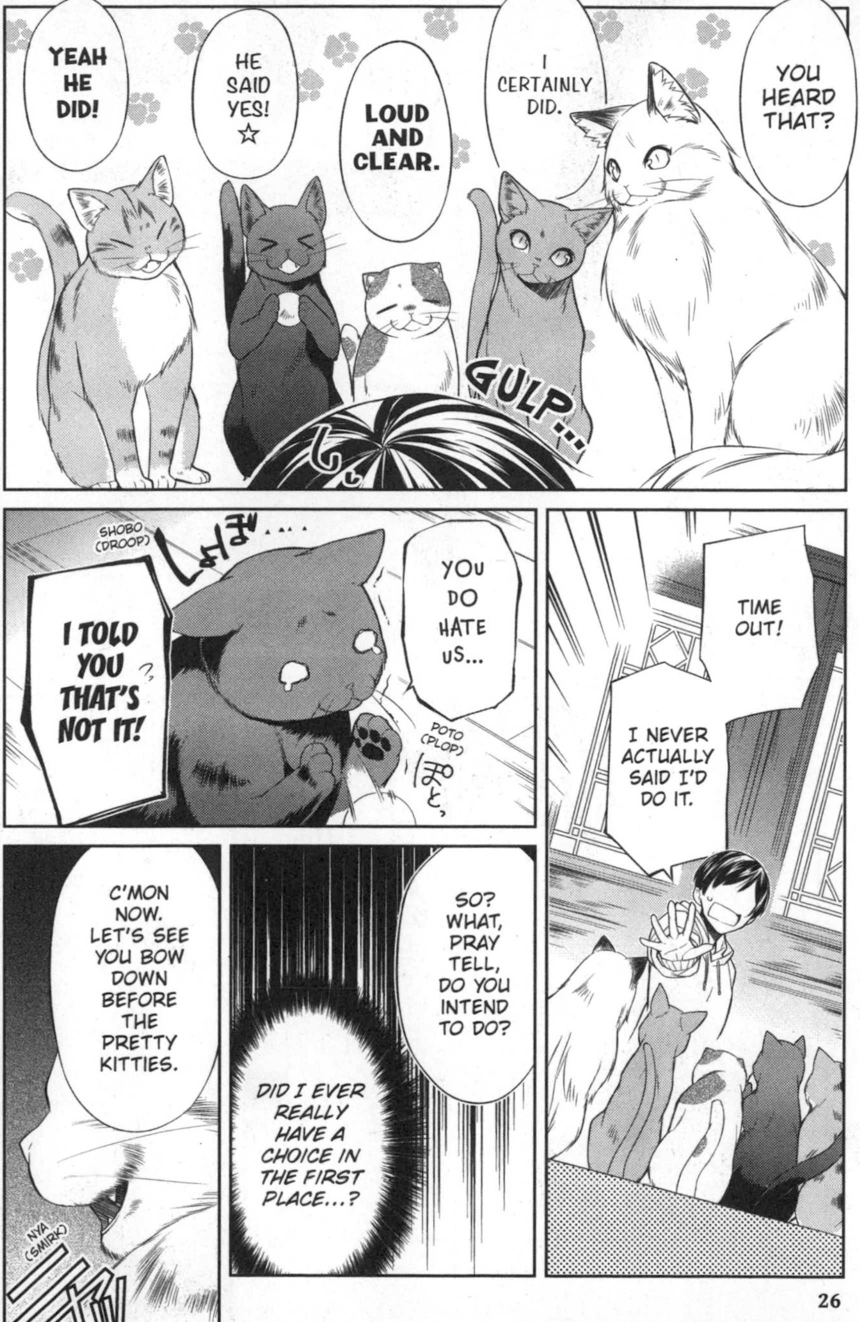
YOU HEARD THAT?
I CERTAINLY DID.
LOUD AND CLEAR.
HE SAID YES! ☆
YEAH HE DID!
GULP...
TIME OUT!
I NEVER ACTUALLY SAID I'D DO IT.
YOU DO HATE US...
POTO (PLOP)
SHOBO (DROOP)
I TOLD YOU THAT'S NOT IT!
SO? WHAT, PRAY TELL, DO YOU INTEND TO DO?
DID I EVER REALLY HAVE A CHOICE IN THE FIRST PLACE...?
C'MON NOW. LET'S SEE YOU BOW DOWN BEFORE THE PRETTY KITTIES.
NYA (SMIRK)

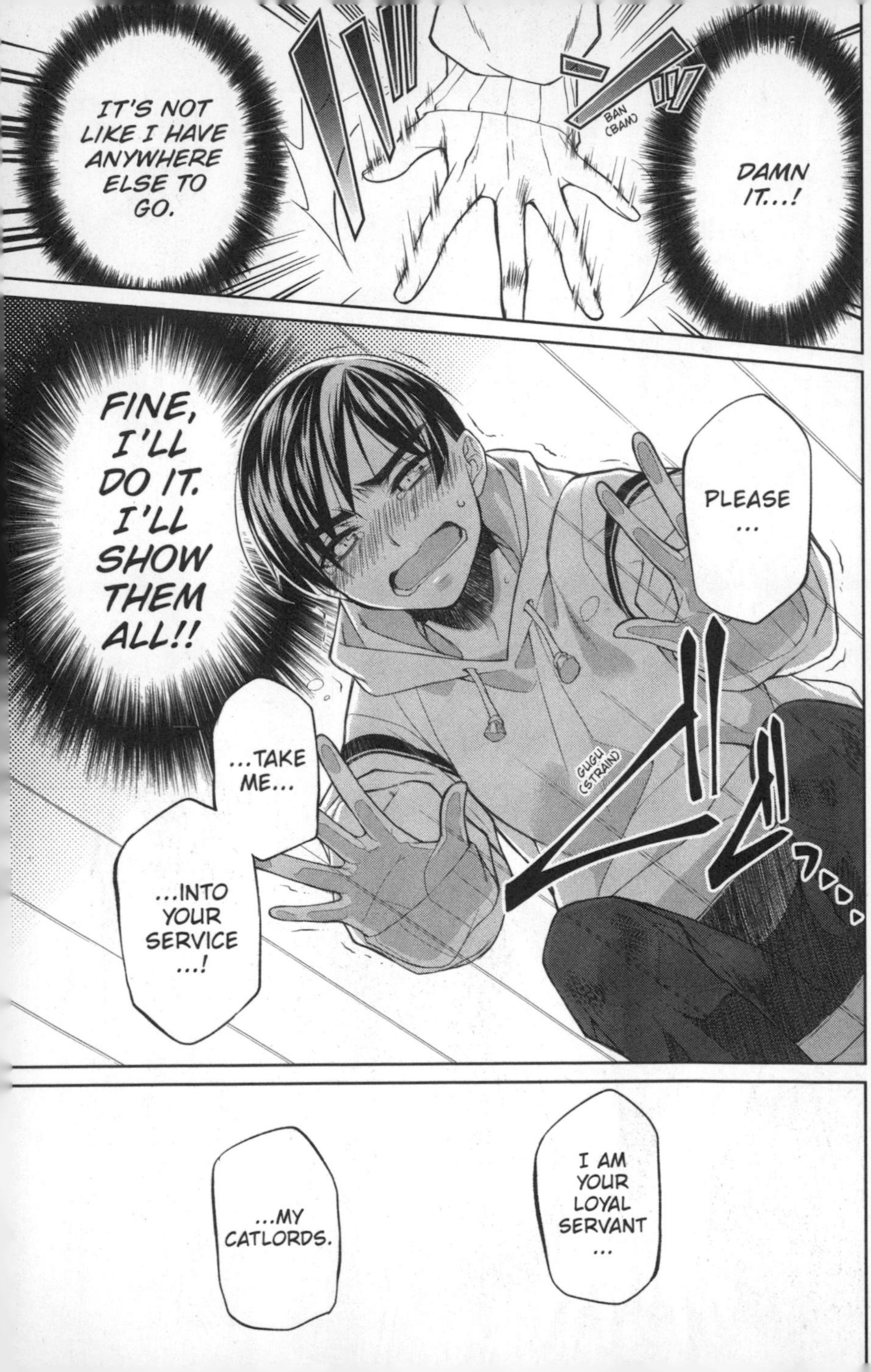
BAN (BAM)
DAMN IT...!
IT'S NOT LIKE I HAVE ANYWHERE ELSE TO GO.
PLEASE...
FINE, I'LL DO IT. I'LL SHOW THEM ALL!!
GUGU (STRAIN)
...TAKE ME...
...INTO YOUR SERVICE...!
I AM YOUR LOYAL SERVANT...
...MY CATLORDS.

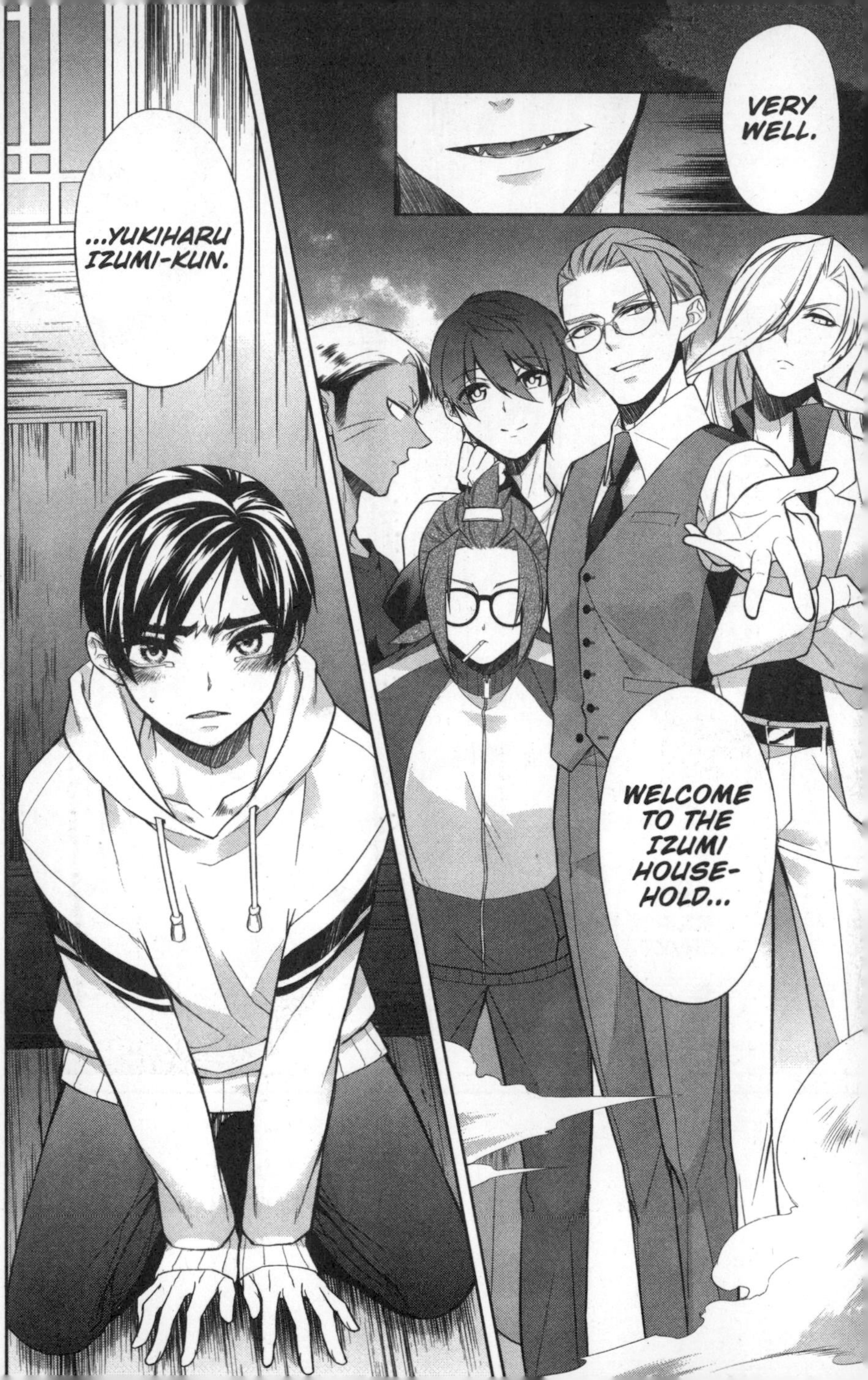
VERY WELL.
WELCOME TO THE IZUMI HOUSE-HOLD...
...YUKIHARU IZUMI-KUN.

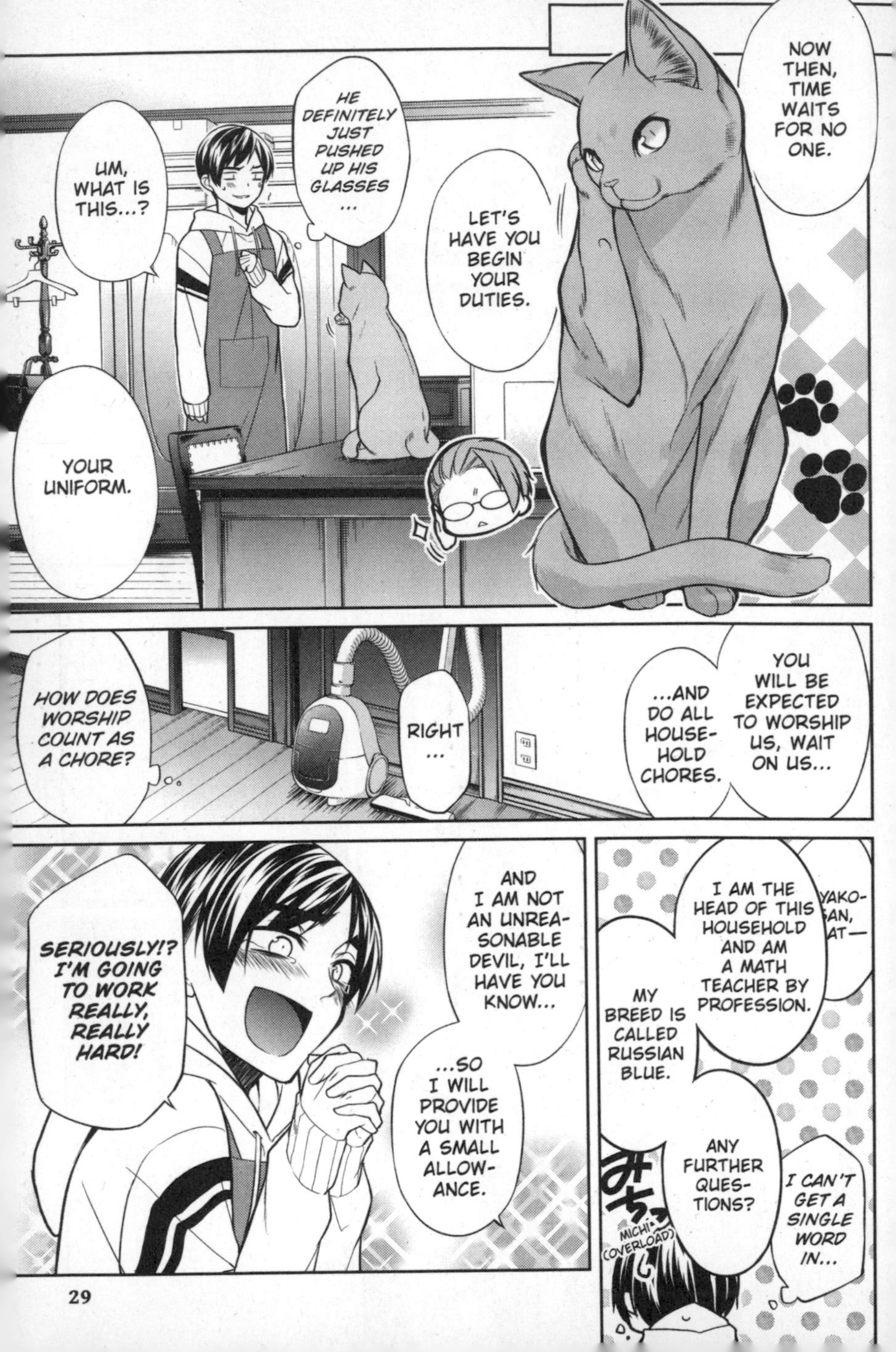
NOW THEN, TIME WAITS FOR NO ONE.
LET'S HAVE YOU BEGIN YOUR DUTIES.
HE DEFINITELY JUST PUSHED UP HIS GLASSES...
UM, WHAT IS THIS...?
YOUR UNIFORM.
YOU WILL BE EXPECTED TO WORSHIP US, WAIT ON US...
...AND DO ALL HOUSE-HOLD CHORES.
RIGHT...
HOW DOES WORSHIP COUNT AS A CHORE?
YAKO-SAN, AT—
I AM THE HEAD OF THIS HOUSEHOLD AND AM A MATH TEACHER BY PROFESSION.
MY BREED IS CALLED RUSSIAN BLUE.
I CAN'T GET A SINGLE WORD IN...
ANY FURTHER QUES-TIONS?
みちっ
MICHI (OVERLOAD)
AND I AM NOT AN UNREA-SONABLE DEVIL, I'LL HAVE YOU KNOW...
...SO I WILL PROVIDE YOU WITH A SMALL ALLOW-ANCE.
SERIOUSLY!? I'M GOING TO WORK REALLY, REALLY HARD!

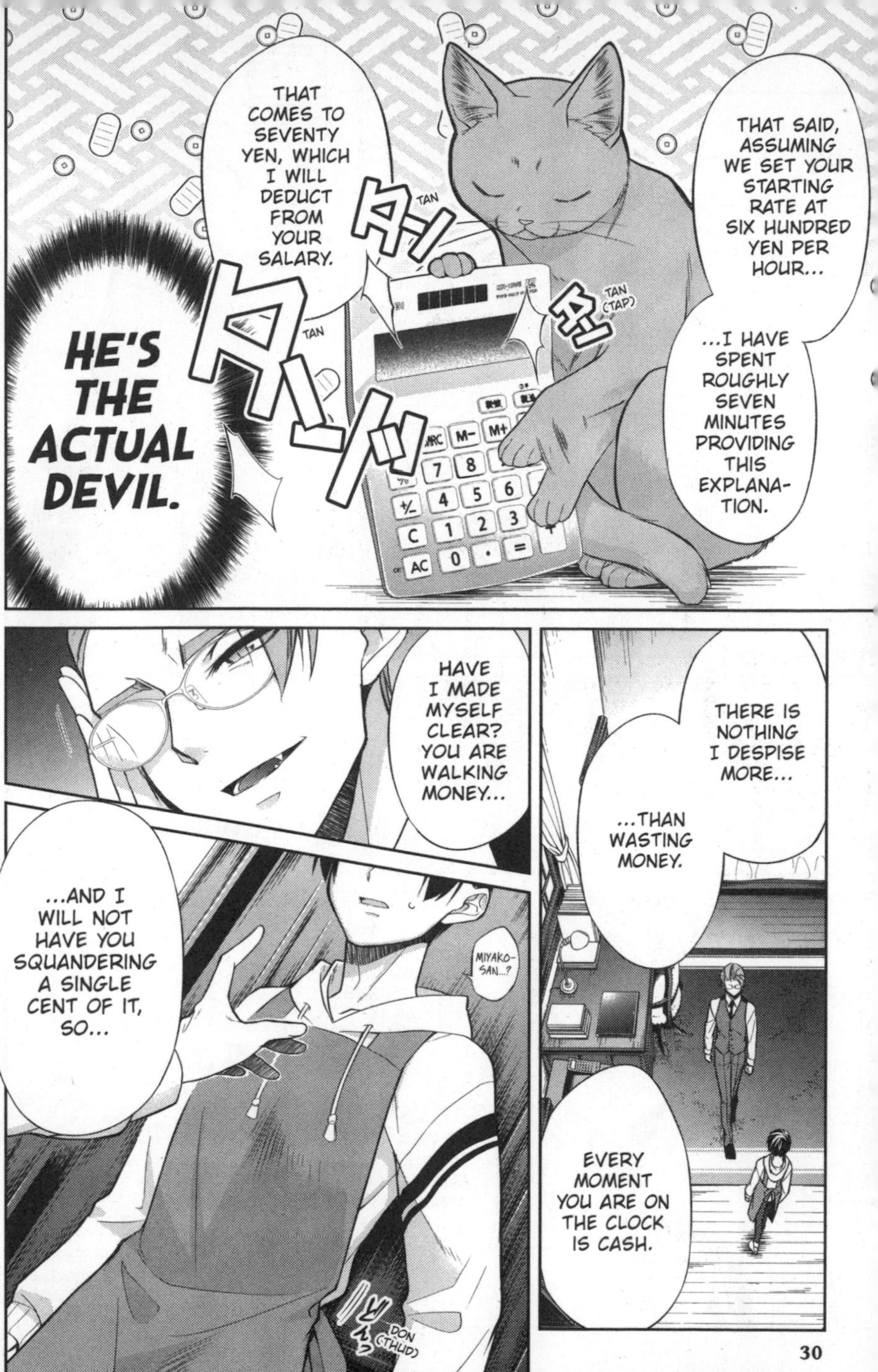
THAT SAID, ASSUMING WE SET YOUR STARTING RATE AT SIX HUNDRED YEN PER HOUR...
...I HAVE SPENT ROUGHLY SEVEN MINUTES PROVIDING THIS EXPLANA-TION.
TAN (TAP)
TAN
TAN
THAT COMES TO SEVENTY YEN, WHICH I WILL DEDUCT FROM YOUR SALARY.
HE'S THE ACTUAL DEVIL.
THERE IS NOTHING I DESPISE MORE...
...THAN WASTING MONEY.
EVERY MOMENT YOU ARE ON THE CLOCK IS CASH.
HAVE I MADE MYSELF CLEAR? YOU ARE WALKING MONEY...
MIYAKO-SAN...?
...AND I WILL NOT HAVE YOU SQUANDERING A SINGLE CENT OF IT, SO...
DON (THUD)

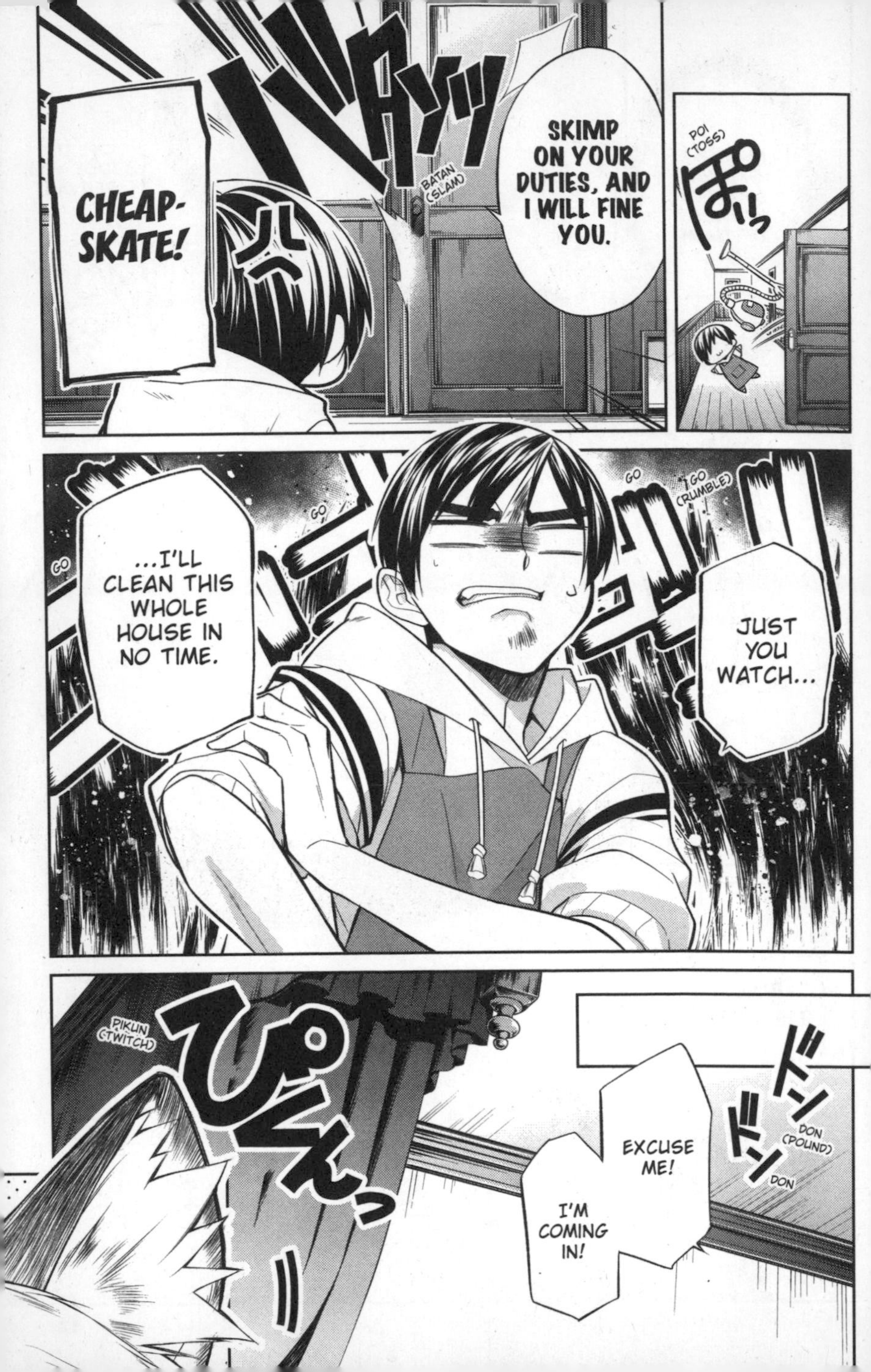
POI (TOSS)
ぽいっ
SKIMP ON YOUR DUTIES, AND I WILL FINE YOU.
BATAN (SLAM)
CHEAP-SKATE!
JUST YOU WATCH...
GO
GO (RUMBLE)
GO
GO
...I'LL CLEAN THIS WHOLE HOUSE IN NO TIME.
ドン
DON (POUND)
ドン
DON
EXCUSE ME!
I'M COMING IN!
PIKUN (TWITCH)
ぴくんっ

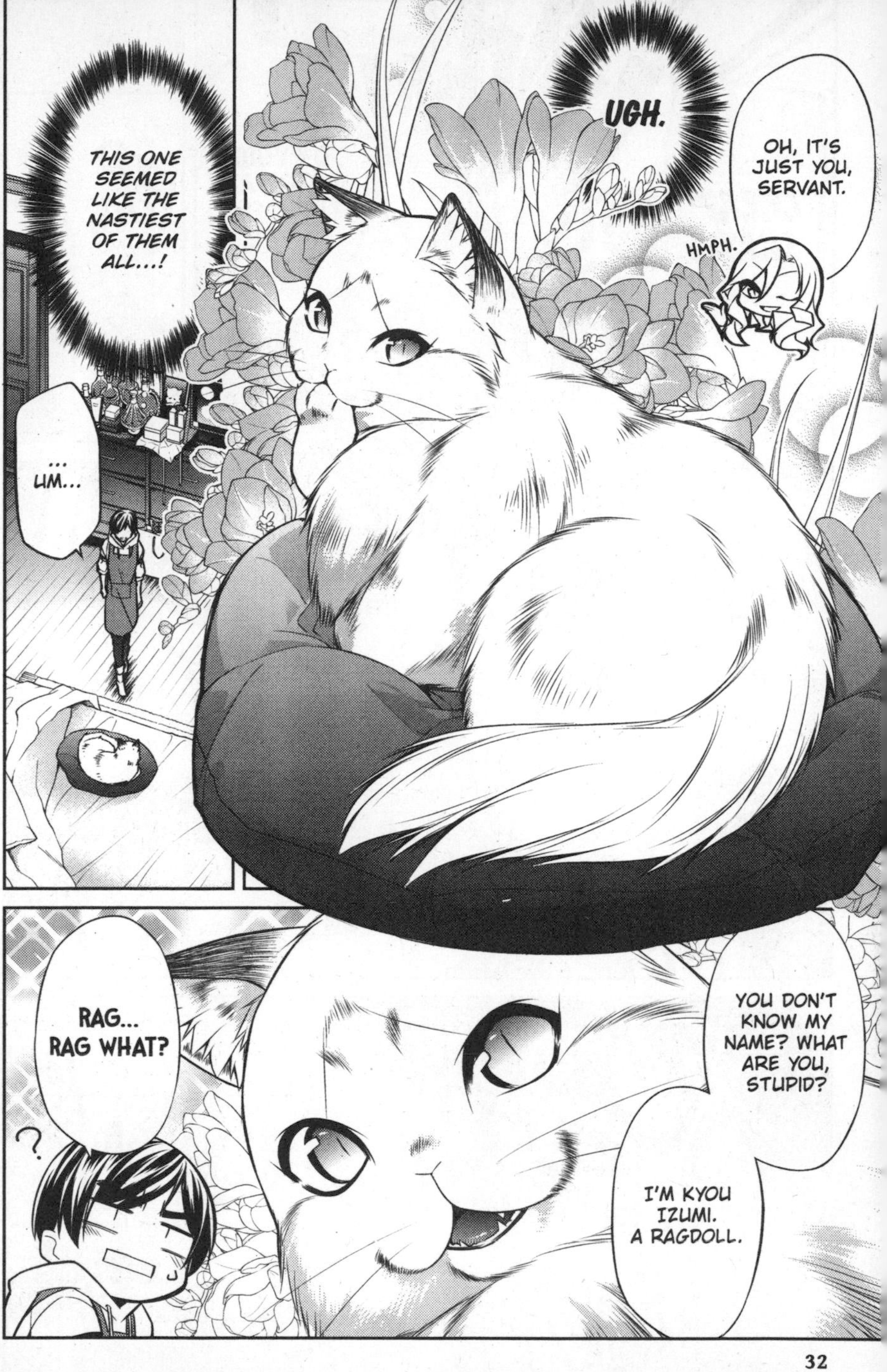
OH, IT'S JUST YOU, SERVANT.
UGH.
HMPH.
THIS ONE SEEMED LIKE THE NASTIEST OF THEM ALL...!
... UM...
YOU DON'T KNOW MY NAME? WHAT ARE YOU, STUPID?
I'M KYOU IZUMI. A RAGDOLL.
RAG... RAG WHAT?

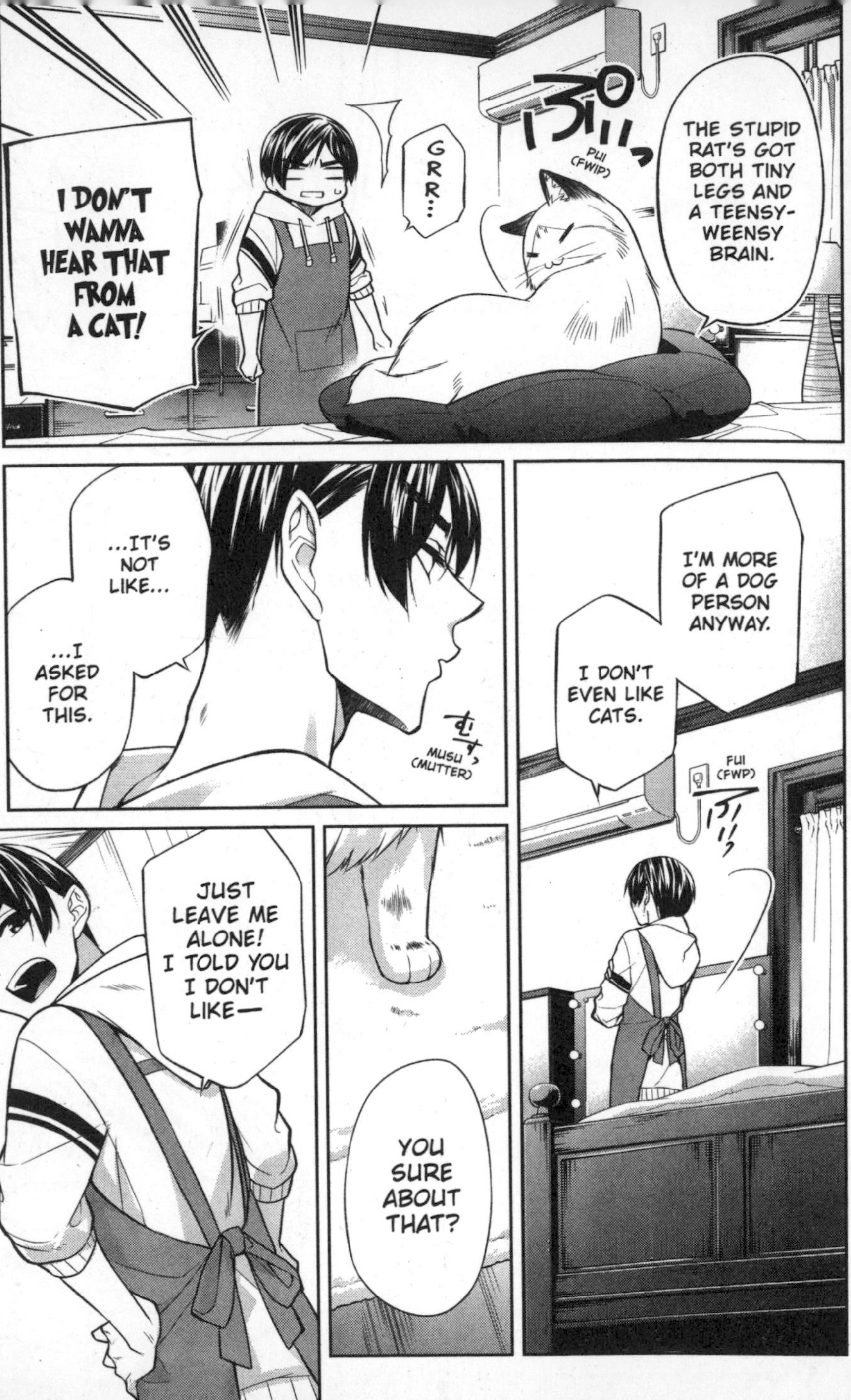
THE STUPID RAT'S GOT BOTH TINY LEGS AND A TEENSY-WEENSY BRAIN.
ぷい
PUI (FWIP)
GRR...
I DON'T WANNA HEAR THAT FROM A CAT!
I'M MORE OF A DOG PERSON ANYWAY.
I DON'T EVEN LIKE CATS.
FUI (FWP)
...IT'S NOT LIKE...
...I ASKED FOR THIS.
MUSU (MUTTER)
JUST LEAVE ME ALONE! I TOLD YOU I DON'T LIKE—
YOU SURE ABOUT THAT?

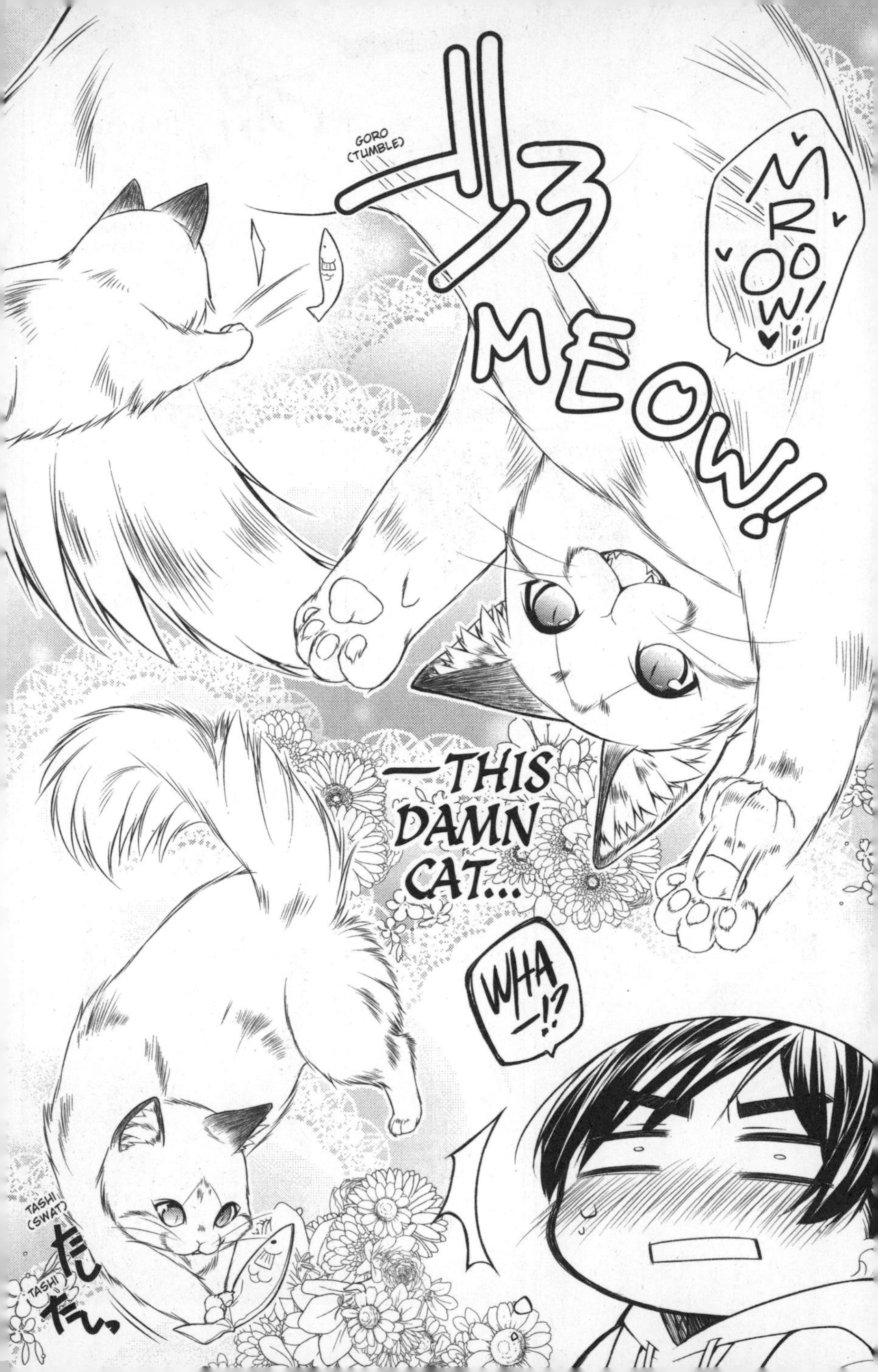
MROOW!
GORO (TUMBLE)
MEOW!
—THIS DAMN CAT...
WHA—!?
TASHI (SWAT)
TASHI

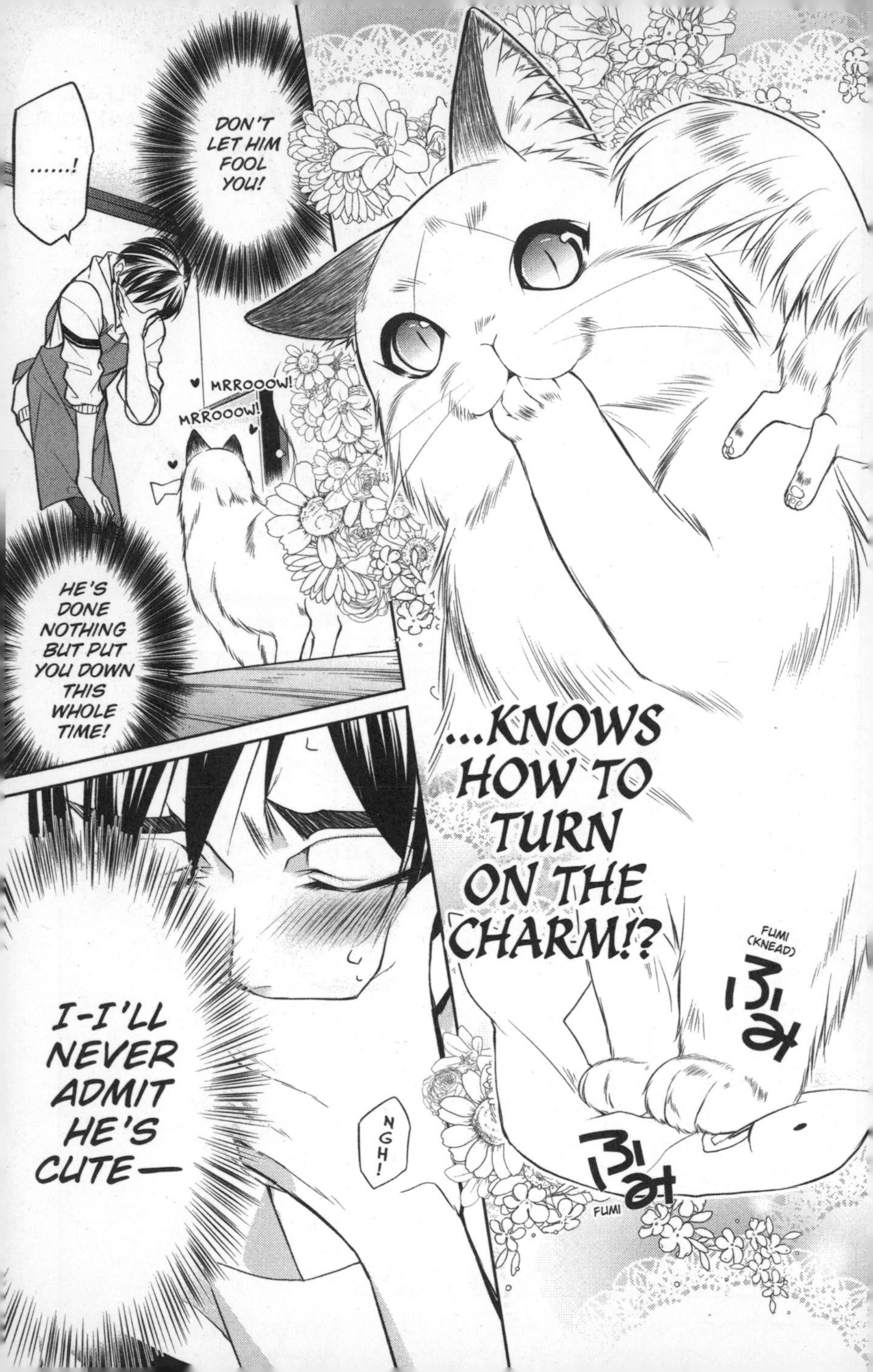

...KNOWS HOW TO TURN ON THE CHARM!?
FUMI (KNEAD)
ふみ
ふみ
FUMI
DON'T LET HIM FOOL YOU!
......!
MRROOOW!
MRROOOW!
HE'S DONE NOTHING BUT PUT YOU DOWN THIS WHOLE TIME!
NGH!
I-I'LL NEVER ADMIT HE'S CUTE—

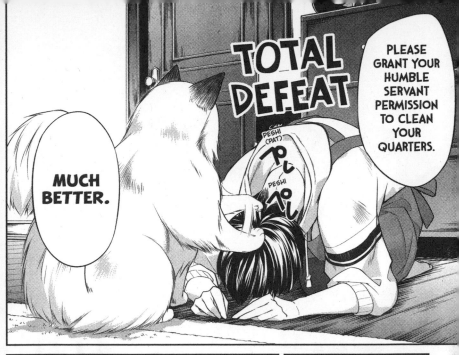

PLEASE GRANT YOUR HUMBLE SERVANT PERMISSION TO CLEAN YOUR QUARTERS.
TOTAL DEFEAT
PESHI (PAT)
PESHI
MUCH BETTER.
WAIT, THIS ISN'T ME!!
WHY AM I...?
THEN HURRY UP AND GET IT DONE, SERVANT.
HEY! YOU DID SOMETHING TO ME, DIDN'T YOU?
HUH?
I MEAN...
...I'VE NEVER FELT ANYTHING LIKE THAT BEFORE...

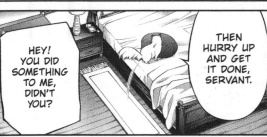

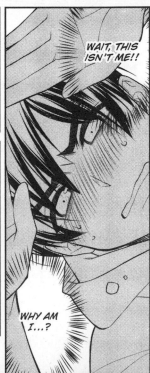

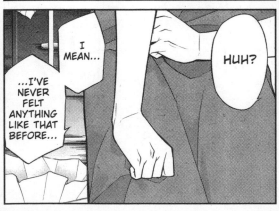

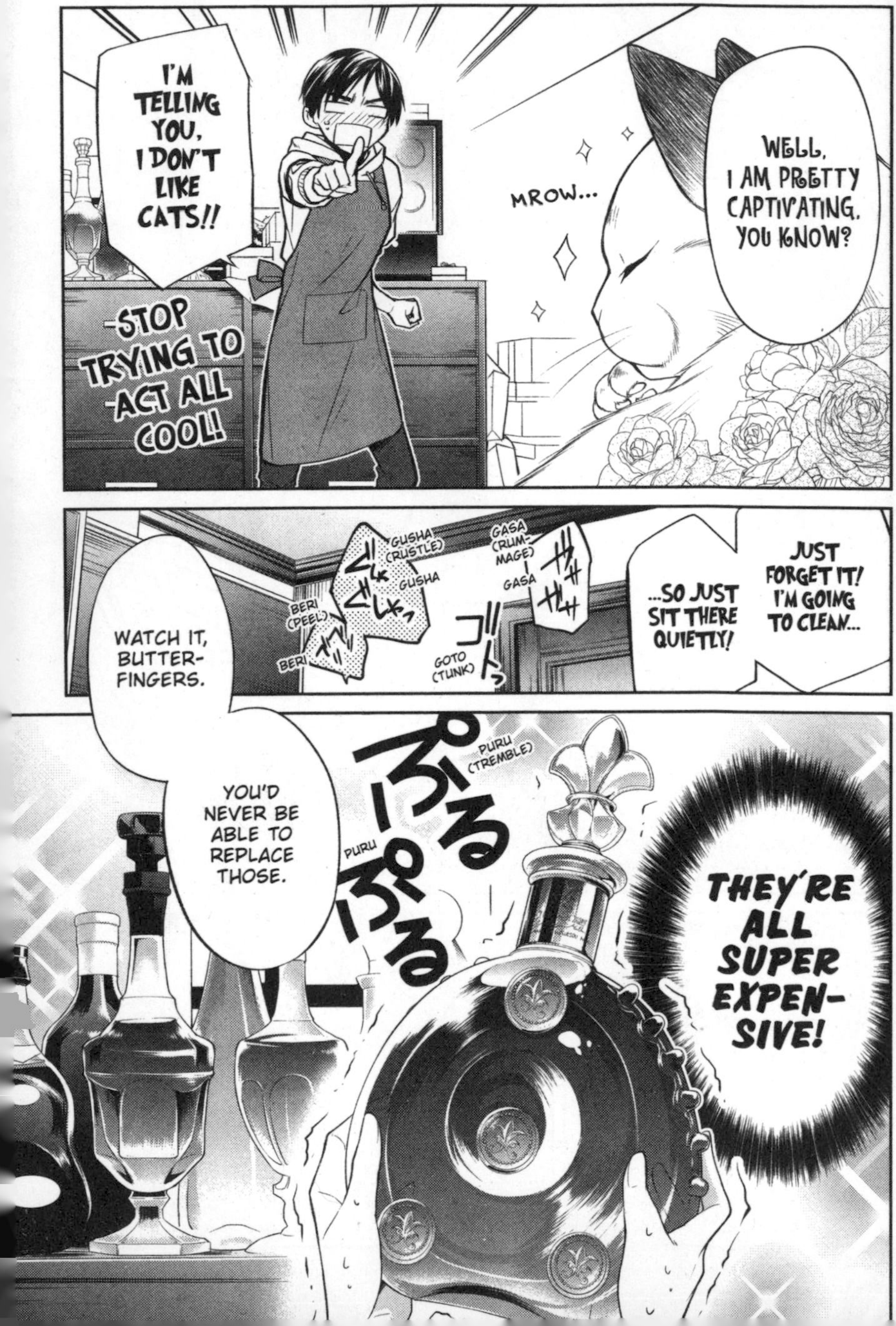

WELL, I AM PRETTY CAPTIVATING, YOU KNOW?
MROW...
I'M TELLING YOU, I DON'T LIKE CATS!!
-STOP TRYING TO -ACT ALL COOL!
JUST FORGET IT! I'M GOING TO CLEAN...
...SO JUST SIT THERE QUIETLY!
GASA (RUMMAGE) GASA
GOTO (TUNK)
GUSHA (RUSTLE) GUSHA
BERI (PEEL) BERI
WATCH IT, BUTTER-FINGERS.
THEY'RE ALL SUPER EXPENSIVE!
PURU (TREMBLE) PURU
YOU'D NEVER BE ABLE TO REPLACE THOSE.

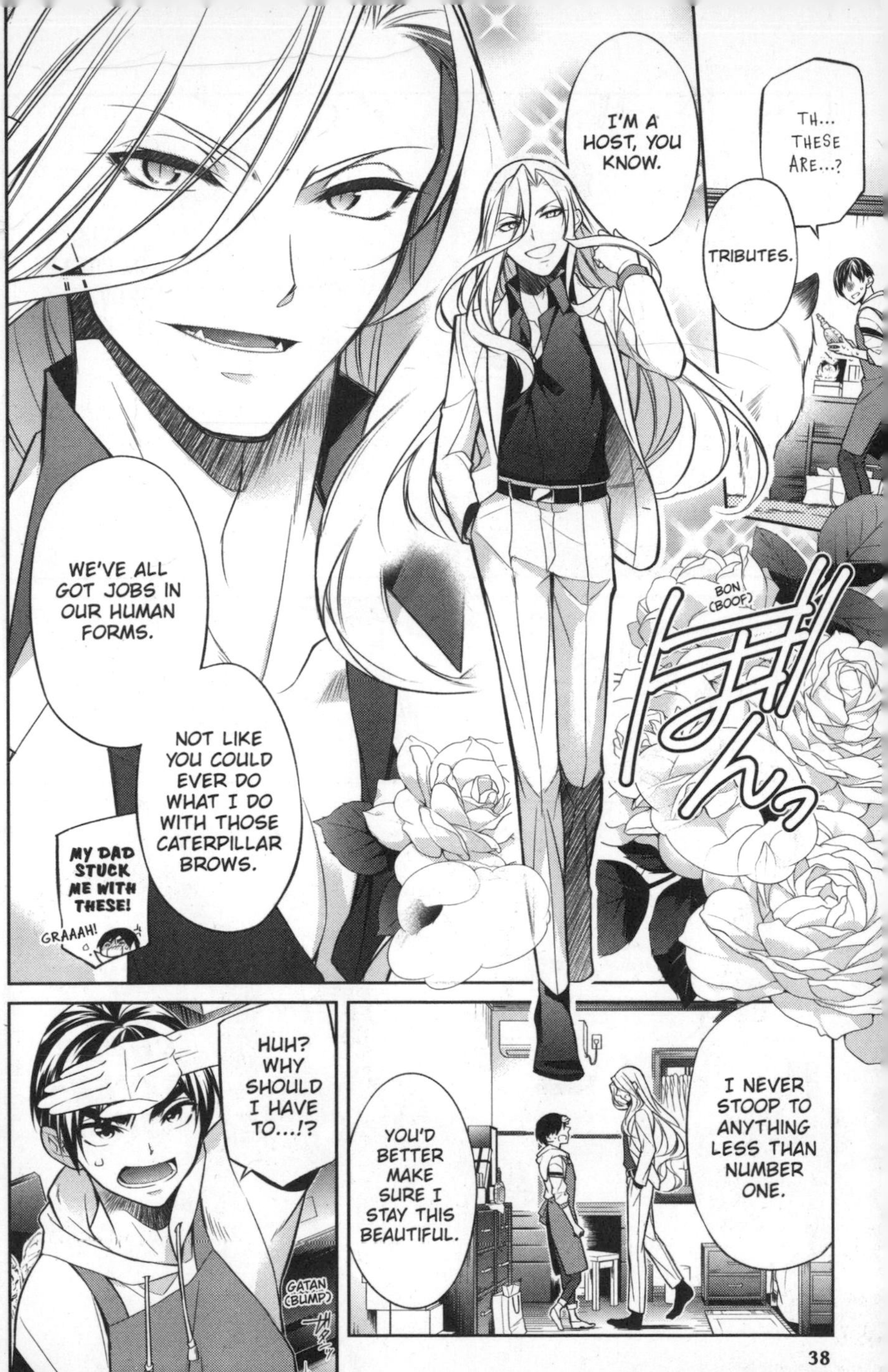
TH... THESE ARE...?
TRIBUTES.
I'M A HOST, YOU KNOW.
BON (BOOF)
WE'VE ALL GOT JOBS IN OUR HUMAN FORMS.
NOT LIKE YOU COULD EVER DO WHAT I DO WITH THOSE CATERPILLAR BROWS.
MY DAD STUCK ME WITH THESE!
GRAAAH!
I NEVER STOOP TO ANYTHING LESS THAN NUMBER ONE.
YOU'D BETTER MAKE SURE I STAY THIS BEAUTIFUL.
HUH? WHY SHOULD I HAVE TO...!?
GATAN (BUMP)

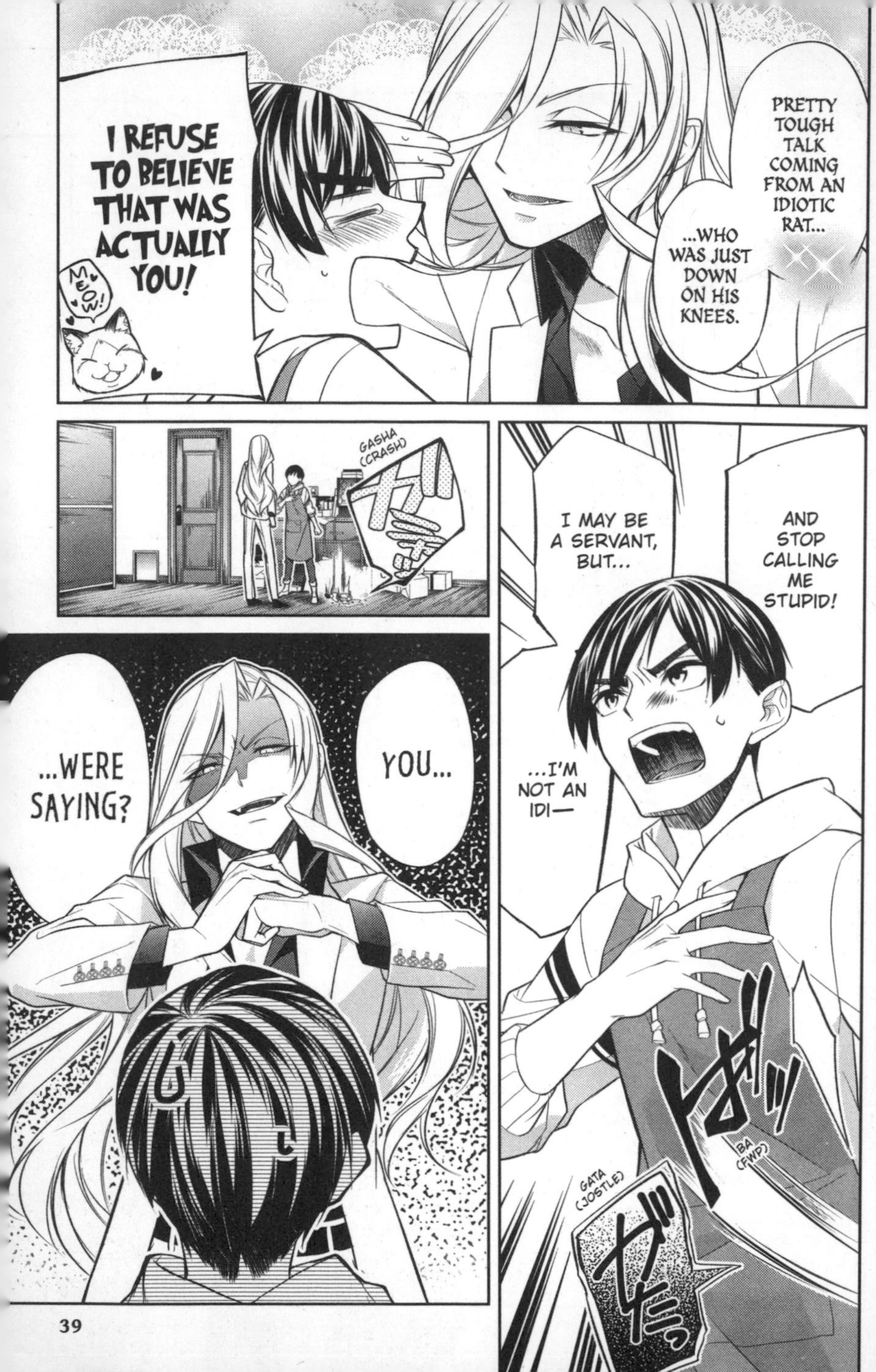
PRETTY TOUGH TALK COMING FROM AN IDIOTIC RAT...
...WHO WAS JUST DOWN ON HIS KNEES.
I REFUSE TO BELIEVE THAT WAS ACTUALLY YOU!
MEOW!
AND STOP CALLING ME STUPID!
I MAY BE A SERVANT, BUT...
...I'M NOT AN IDI—
BA (FWP)
GATA (JOSTLE)
GASHA (CRASH)
YOU...
...WERE SAYING?

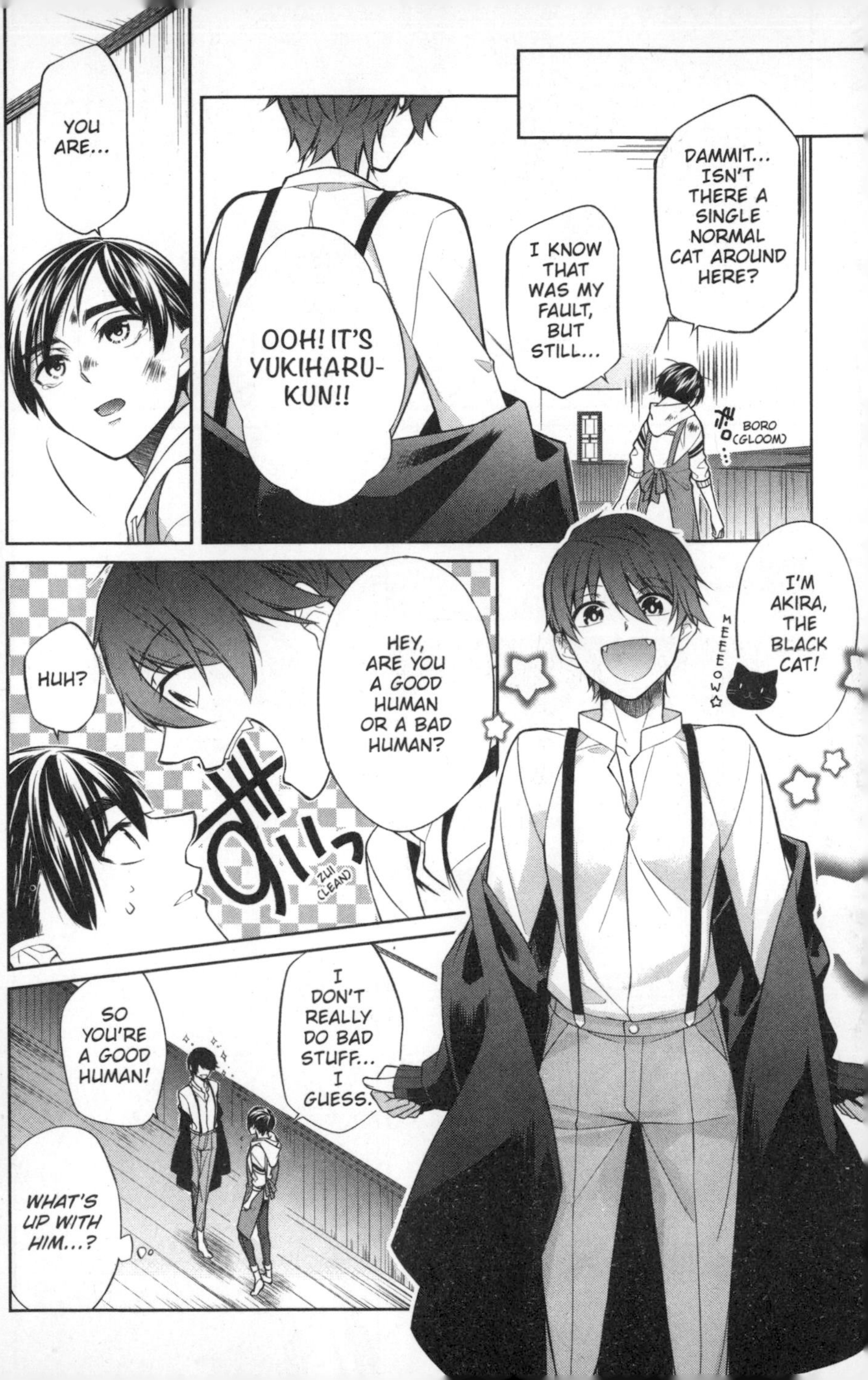
DAMMIT... ISN'T THERE A SINGLE NORMAL CAT AROUND HERE?
I KNOW THAT WAS MY FAULT, BUT STILL...
BORO (GLOOM)
OOH! IT'S YUKIHARU-KUN!!
YOU ARE...
I'M AKIRA, THE BLACK CAT!
MEEEOW☆
HEY, ARE YOU A GOOD HUMAN OR A BAD HUMAN?
HUH?
ZUI (LEAN)
I DON'T REALLY DO BAD STUFF... I GUESS.
SO YOU'RE A GOOD HUMAN!
WHAT'S UP WITH HIM...?

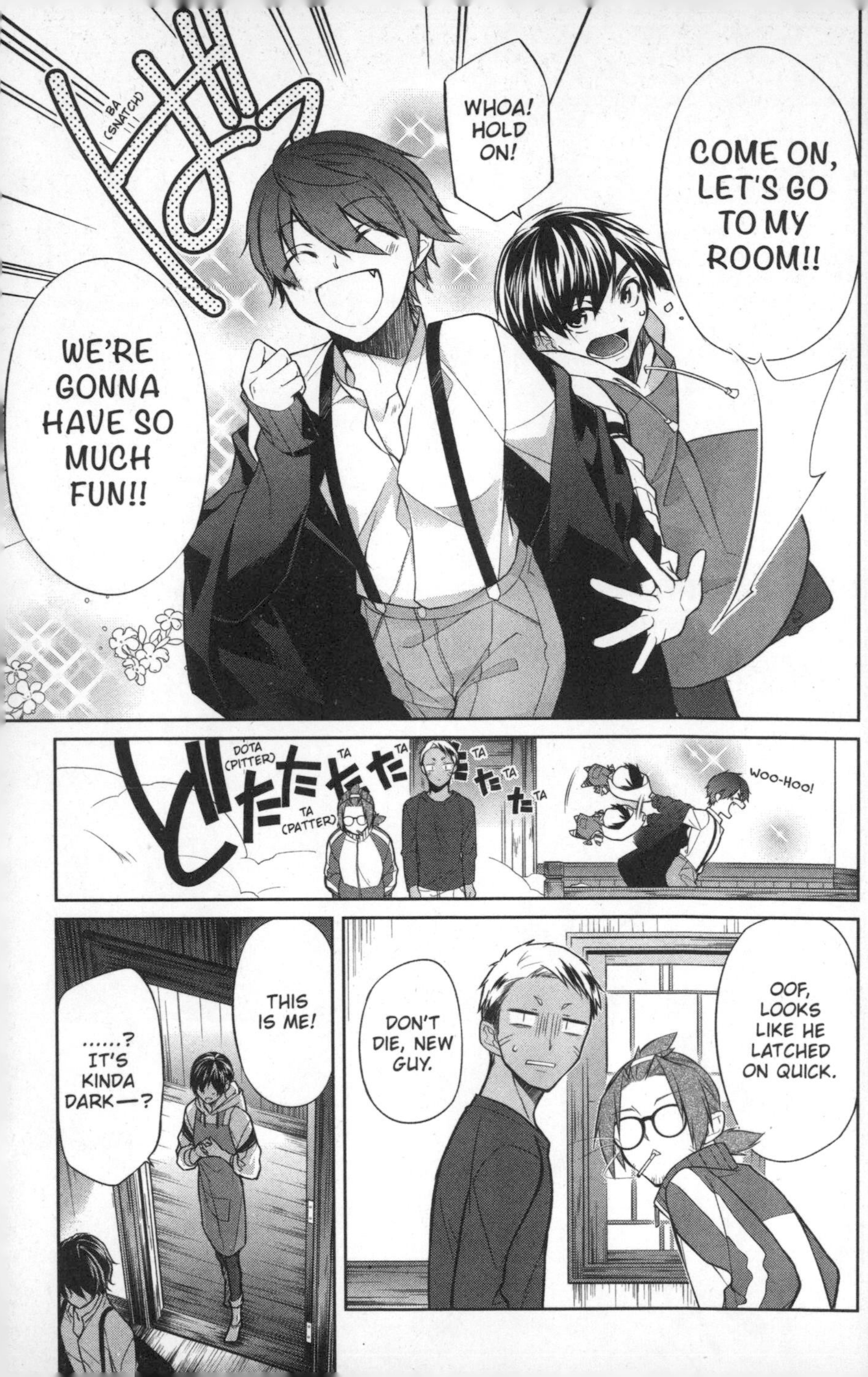
COME ON, LET'S GO TO MY ROOM!!
WHOA! HOLD ON!
BA (SNATCH)
WE'RE GONNA HAVE SO MUCH FUN!!
WOO-HOO!
DOTA (PITTER)
TA TA TA TA TA TA TA
TA (PATTER)
OOF, LOOKS LIKE HE LATCHED ON QUICK.
DON'T DIE, NEW GUY.
THIS IS ME!
......? IT'S KINDA DARK—?

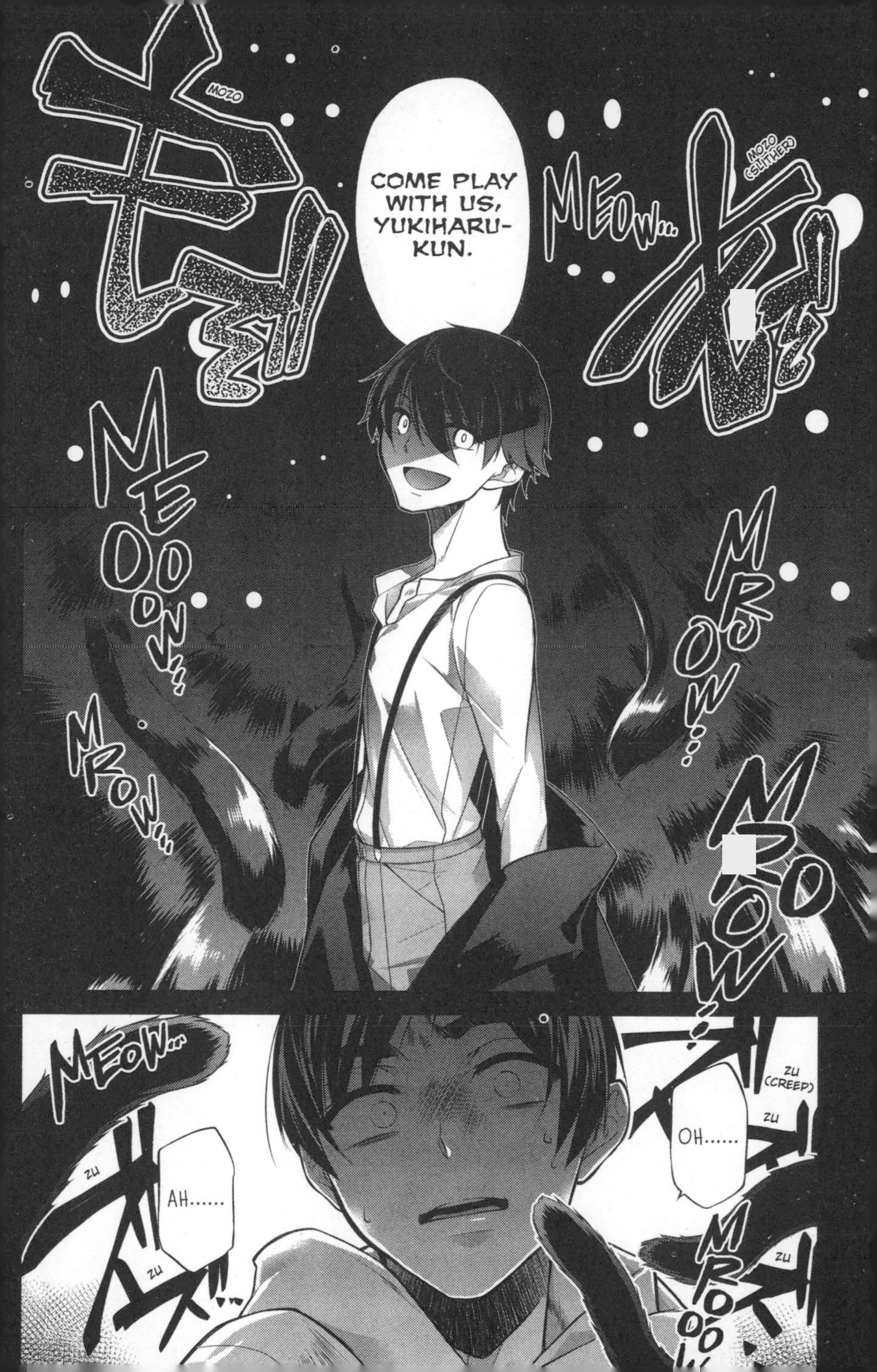
MOZO (SLITHER)
MEOW...
COME PLAY WITH US, YUKIHARU-KUN.
MOZO
MROOOW...!
MROOOW...!
MEOOOW...!
MROW...
ZU (CREEP)
ZU
OH......
ZU
MEOW...
ZU
AH......
ZU

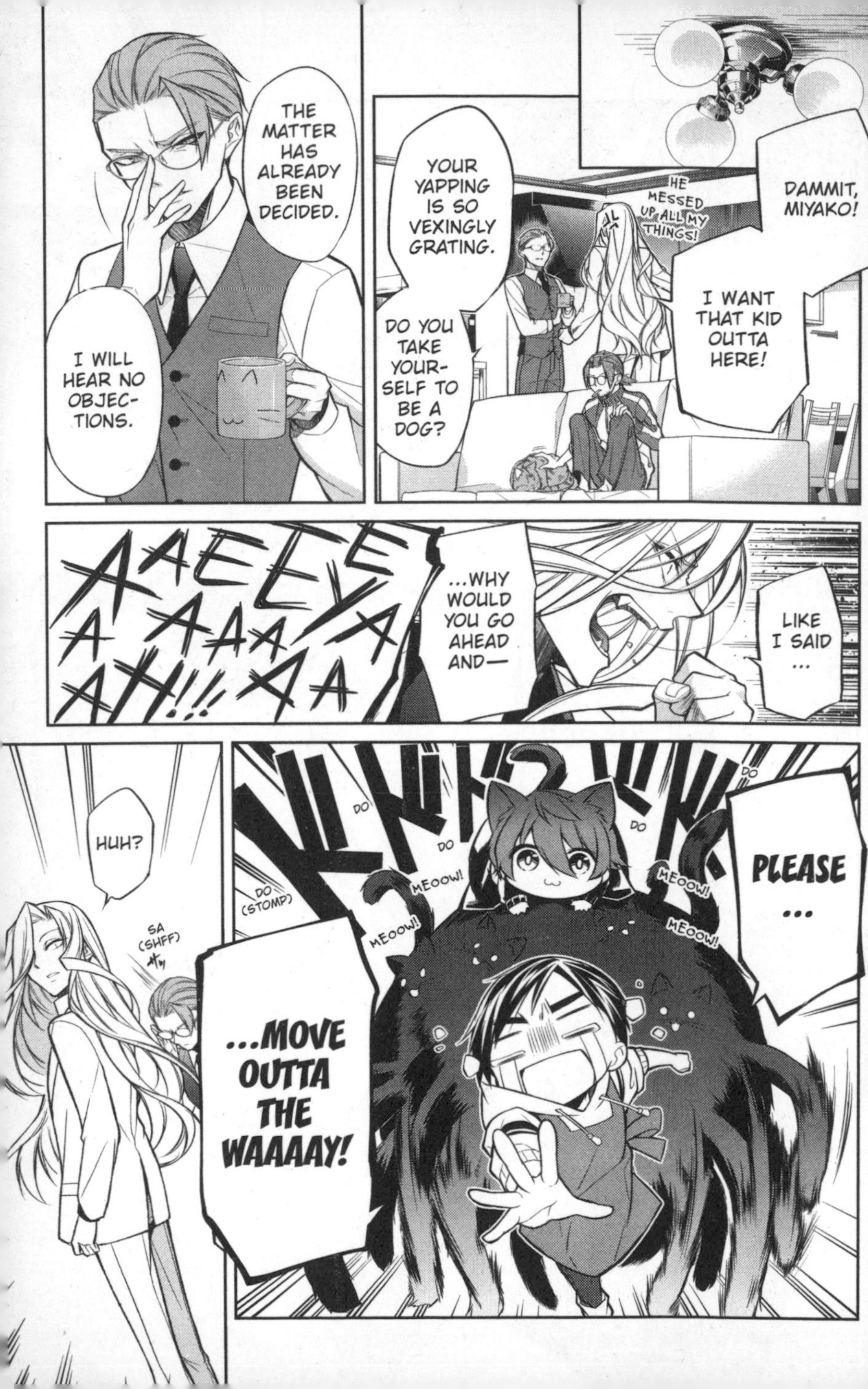
DAMMIT, MIYAKO!
I WANT THAT KID OUTTA HERE!
HE MESSED UP ALL MY THINGS!
YOUR YAPPING IS SO VEXINGLY GRATING.
DO YOU TAKE YOURSELF TO BE A DOG?
THE MATTER HAS ALREADY BEEN DECIDED.
I WILL HEAR NO OBJECTIONS.
LIKE I SAID ...
...WHY WOULD YOU GO AHEAD AND—
AAEEYAAAAAAAAH!!!
DO DO DO DO
PLEASE ...
MEOOW! MEOOW! MEOOW! MEOOW!
DO (STOMP)
...MOVE OUTTA THE WAAAAY!
HUH?
SA (SHFF)

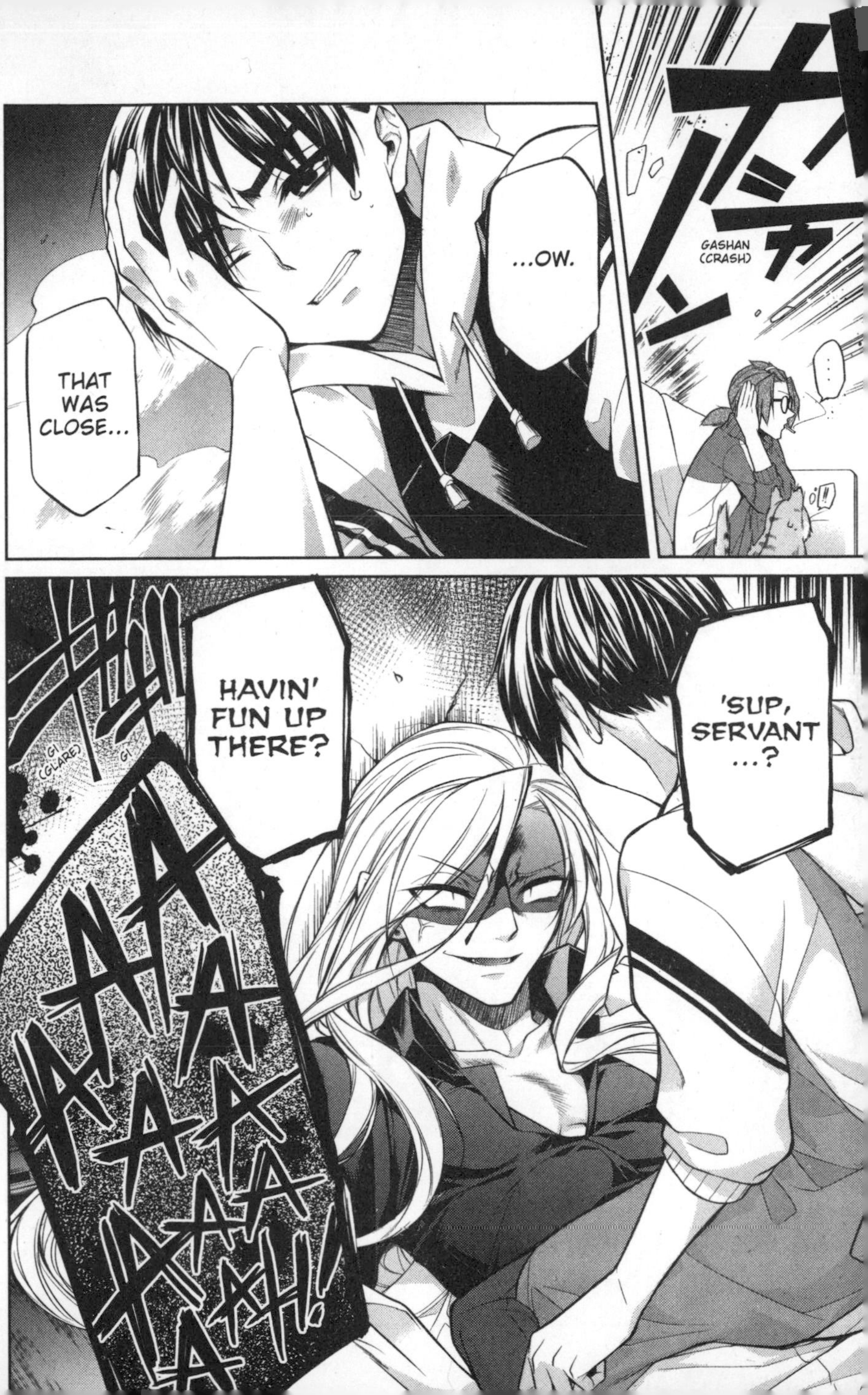
GASHAN (CRASH)
...
!!
...OW.
THAT WAS CLOSE...
'SUP, SERVANT...?
HAVIN' FUN UP THERE?
GI (GLARE) GI
AAAAAAAAAAAAAH!

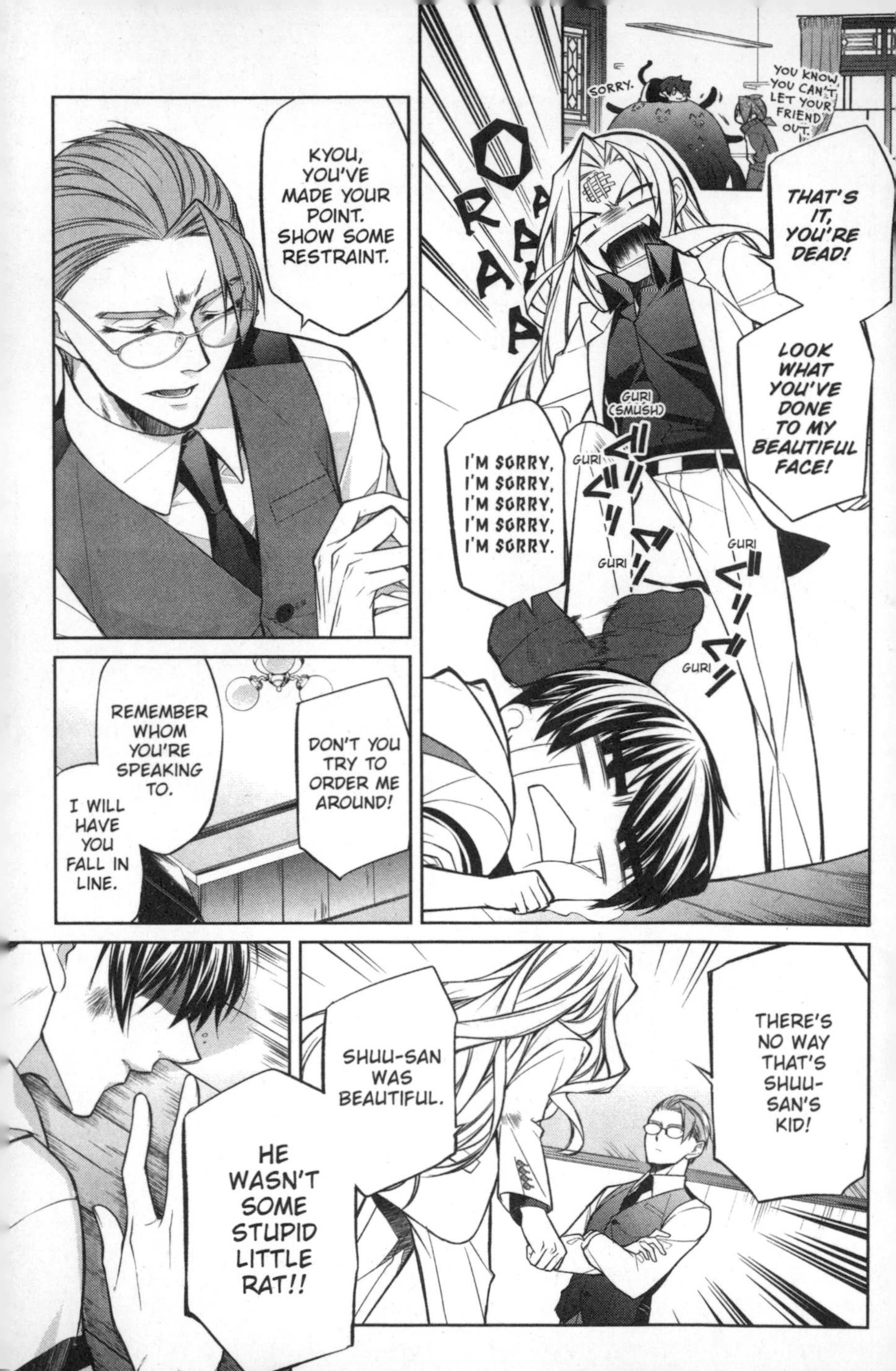
YOU KNOW, YOU CAN'T LET YOUR FRIEND OUT.
SORRY.
THAT'S IT, YOU'RE DEAD!
ORAAAAA
LOOK WHAT YOU'VE DONE TO MY BEAUTIFUL FACE!
GURI (SMUSH)
GURI
GURI
GURI
GURI
I'M SORRY, I'M SORRY, I'M SORRY, I'M SORRY, I'M SORRY.
KYOU, YOU'VE MADE YOUR POINT. SHOW SOME RESTRAINT.
DON'T YOU TRY TO ORDER ME AROUND!
REMEMBER WHOM YOU'RE SPEAKING TO.
I WILL HAVE YOU FALL IN LINE.
THERE'S NO WAY THAT'S SHUU-SAN'S KID!
SHUU-SAN WAS BEAUTIFUL.
HE WASN'T SOME STUPID LITTLE RAT!!

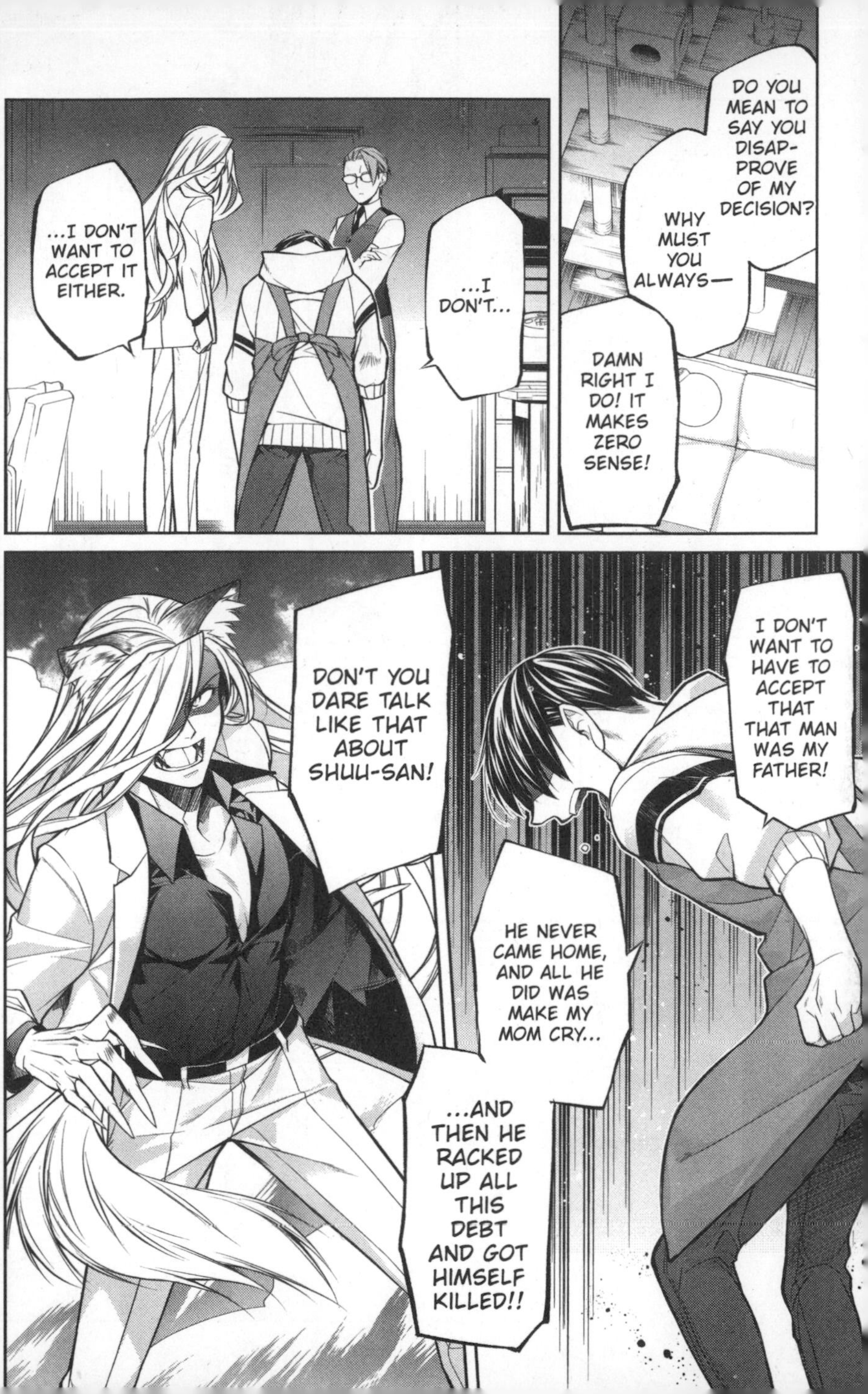
DO YOU MEAN TO SAY YOU DISAPPROVE OF MY DECISION?
WHY MUST YOU ALWAYS—
DAMN RIGHT I DO! IT MAKES ZERO SENSE!
...I DON'T...
...I DON'T WANT TO ACCEPT IT EITHER.
I DON'T WANT TO HAVE TO ACCEPT THAT THAT MAN WAS MY FATHER!
HE NEVER CAME HOME, AND ALL HE DID WAS MAKE MY MOM CRY...
...AND THEN HE RACKED UP ALL THIS DEBT AND GOT HIMSELF KILLED!!
DON'T YOU DARE TALK LIKE THAT ABOUT SHUU-SAN!

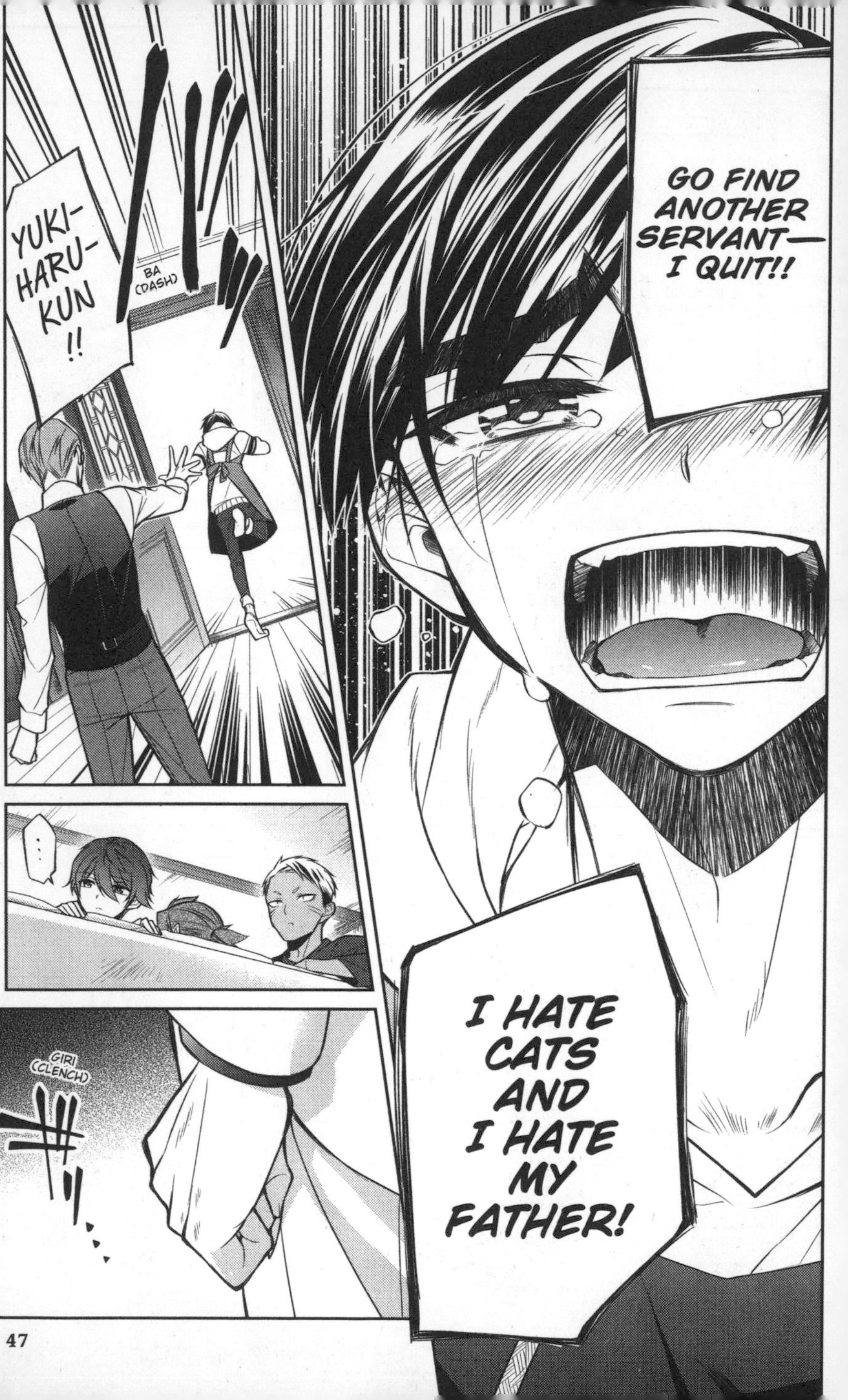
GO FIND ANOTHER SERVANT— I QUIT!!
I HATE CATS AND I HATE MY FATHER!
BA (DASH)
YUKI-HARU-KUN!!
...
GIRI (CLENCH)
...

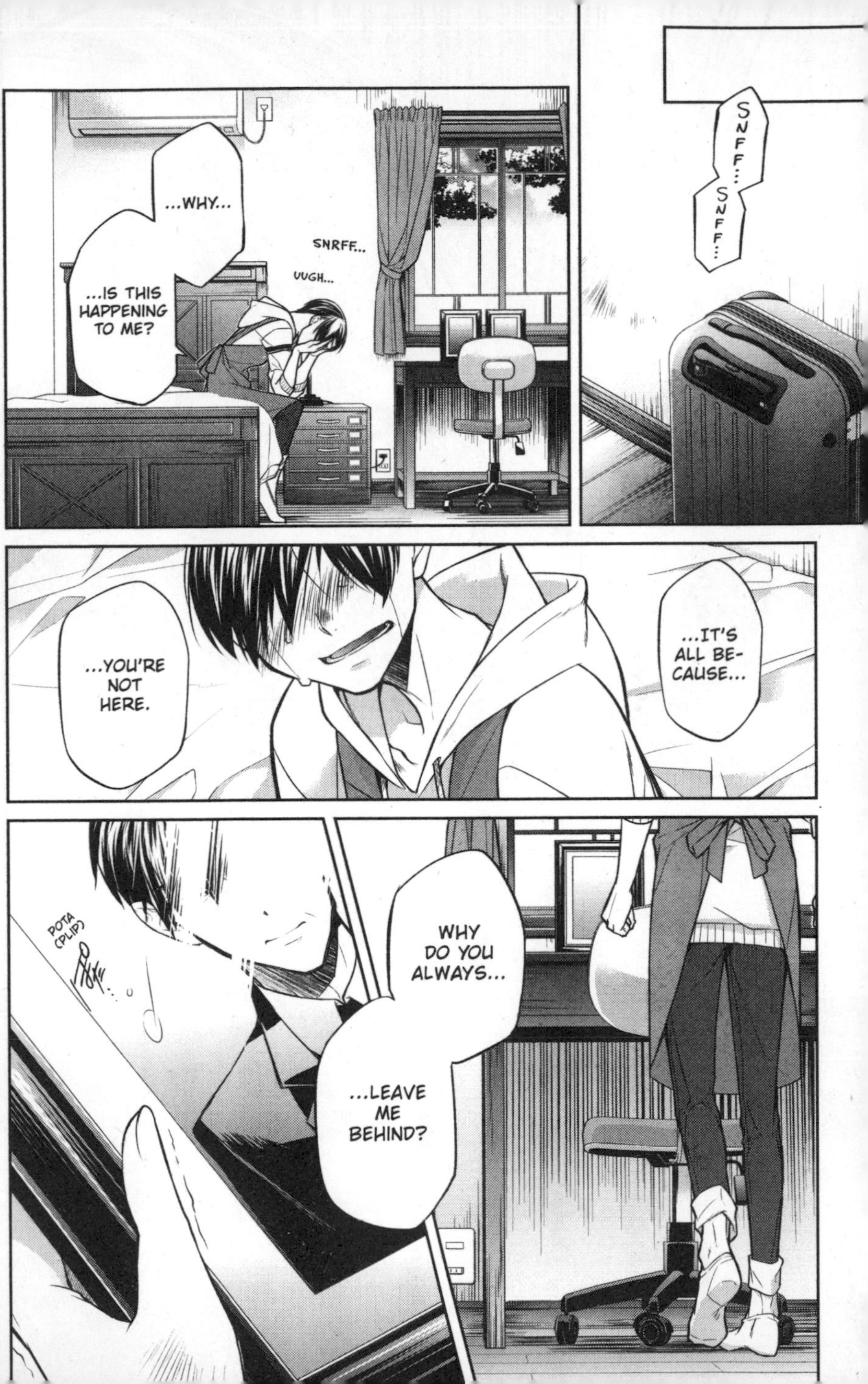
SNFF... SNFF...
...WHY...
...IS THIS HAPPENING TO ME?
SNRFF...
UUGH...
...IT'S ALL BE-CAUSE...
...YOU'RE NOT HERE.
WHY DO YOU ALWAYS...
...LEAVE ME BEHIND?
POTA (PLIP)

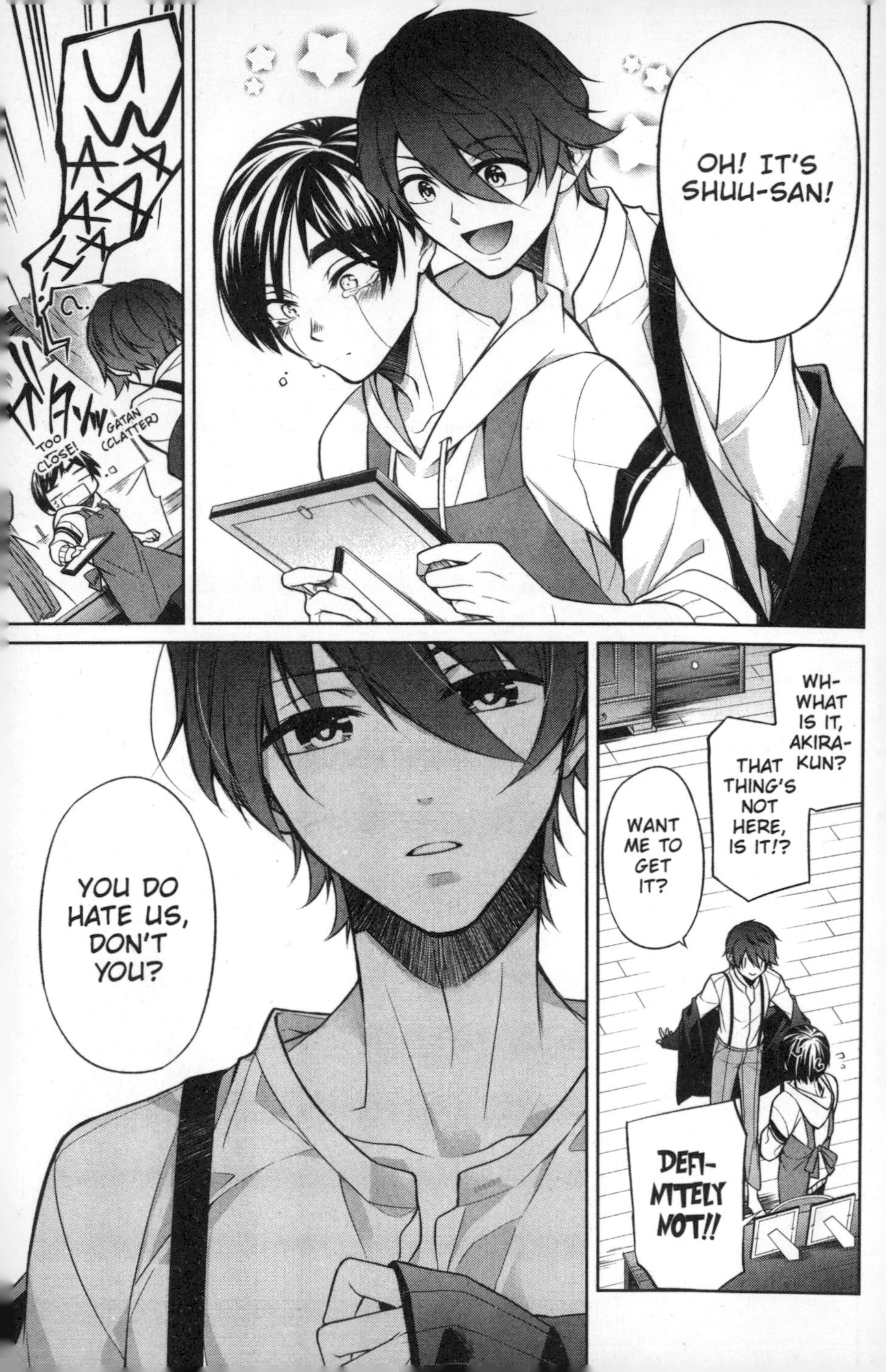
OH! IT'S SHUU-SAN!
UWAAAAA!
GATAN (CLATTER)
TOO CLOSE!
WH-WHAT IS IT, AKIRA-KUN? THAT THING'S NOT HERE, IS IT!?
WANT ME TO GET IT?
DEFI-NITELY NOT!!
YOU DO HATE US, DON'T YOU?

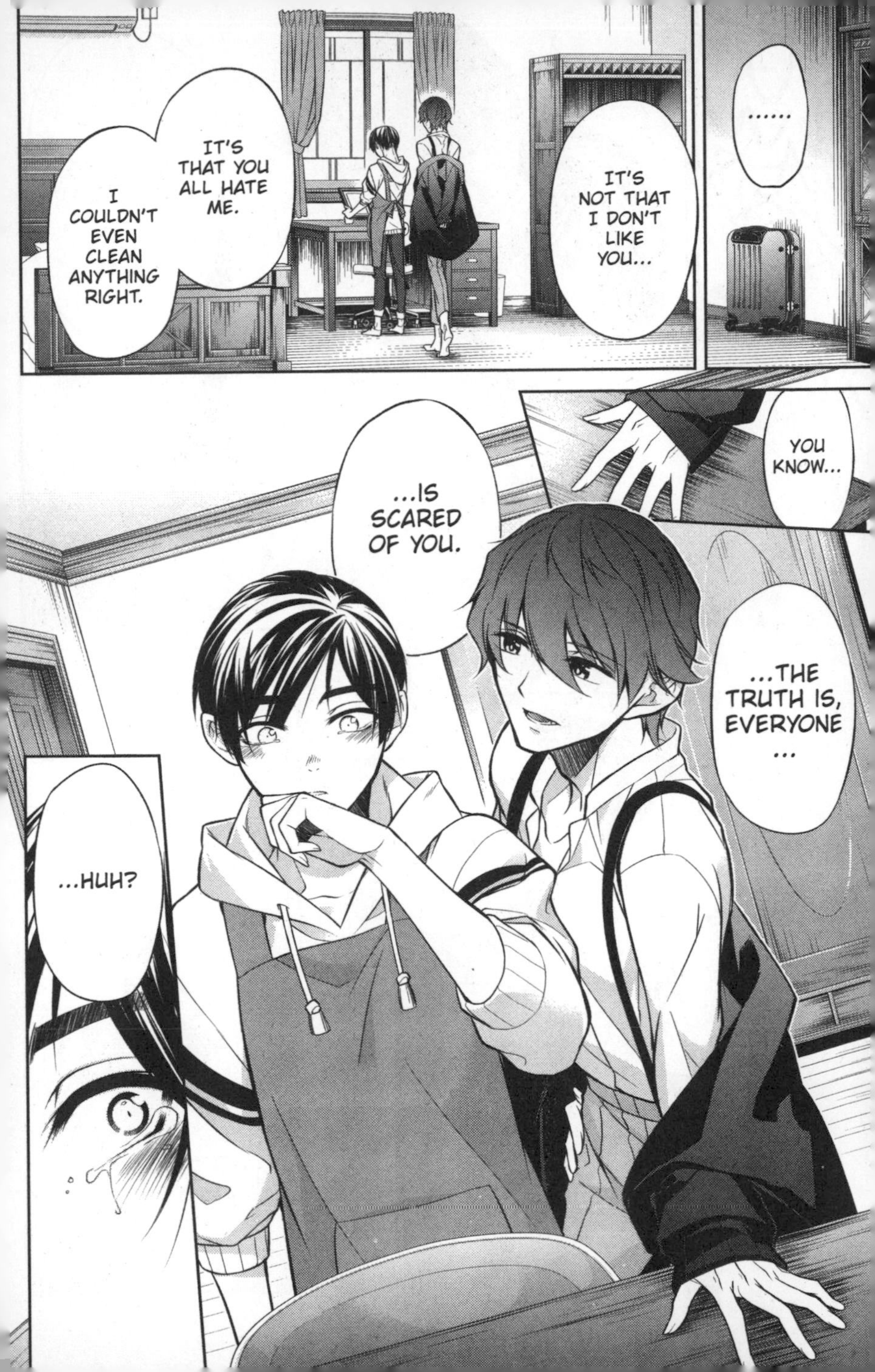
......
IT'S NOT THAT I DON'T LIKE YOU...
IT'S THAT YOU ALL HATE ME.
I COULDN'T EVEN CLEAN ANYTHING RIGHT.
YOU KNOW...
...THE TRUTH IS, EVERYONE ...
...IS SCARED OF YOU.
...HUH?

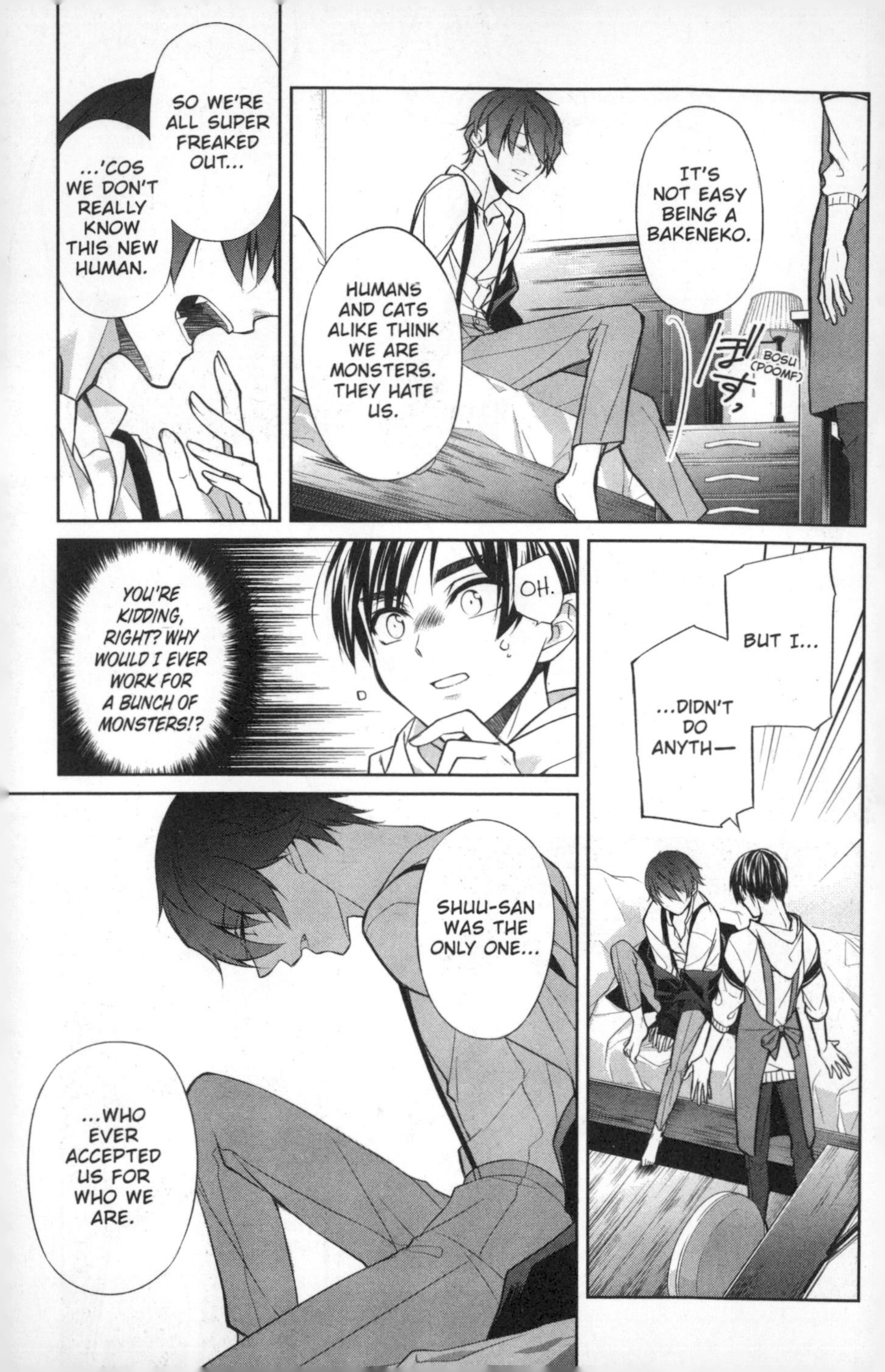
IT'S NOT EASY BEING A BAKENEKO.
BOSU (POOMF)
HUMANS AND CATS ALIKE THINK WE ARE MONSTERS. THEY HATE US.
SO WE'RE ALL SUPER FREAKED OUT...
...'COS WE DON'T REALLY KNOW THIS NEW HUMAN.
BUT I...
...DIDN'T DO ANYTH—
OH.
YOU'RE KIDDING, RIGHT? WHY WOULD I EVER WORK FOR A BUNCH OF MONSTERS!?
SHUU-SAN WAS THE ONLY ONE...
...WHO EVER ACCEPTED US FOR WHO WE ARE.

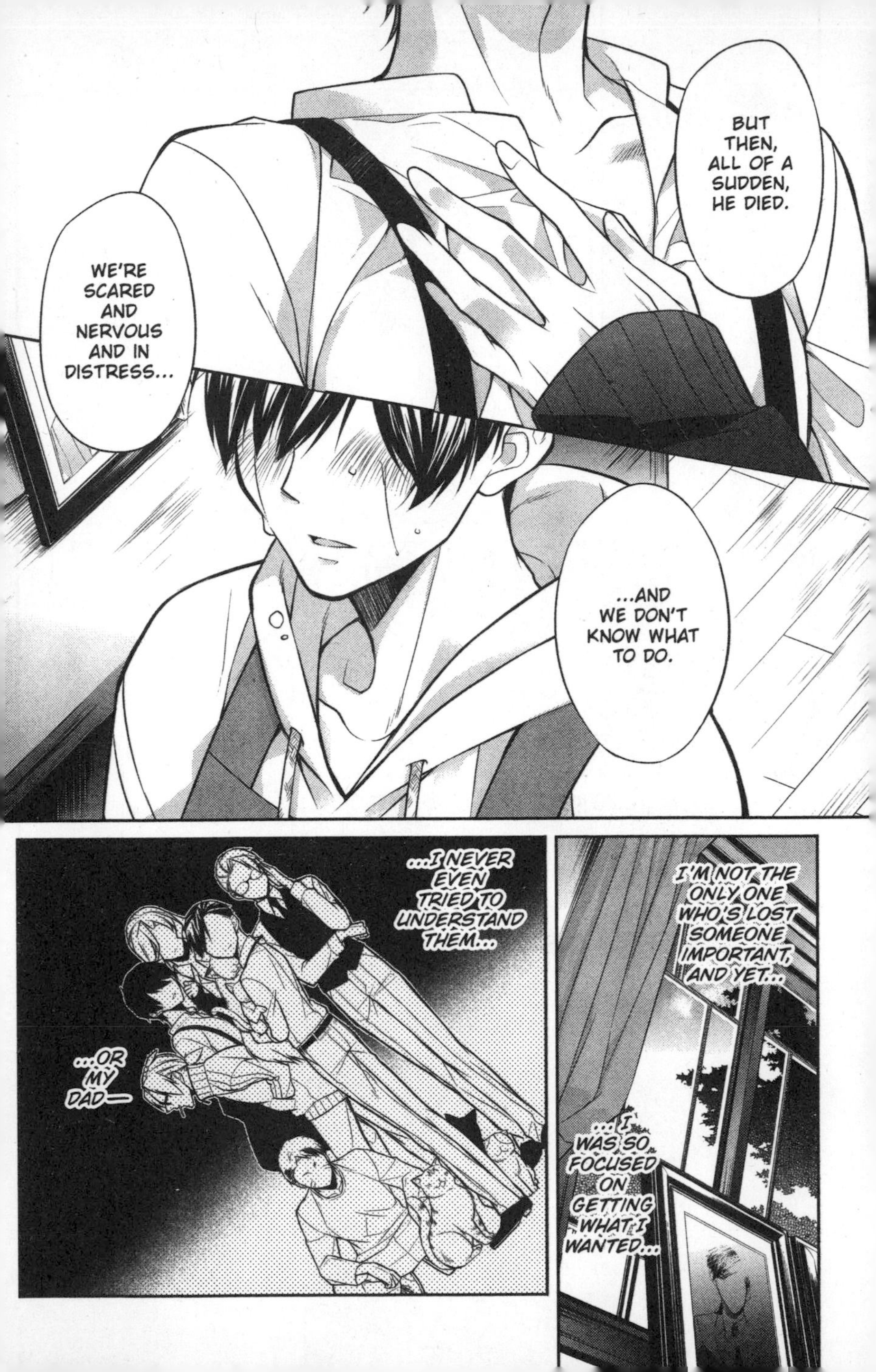
BUT THEN, ALL OF A SUDDEN, HE DIED.
WE'RE SCARED AND NERVOUS AND IN DISTRESS...
...AND WE DON'T KNOW WHAT TO DO.
I'M NOT THE ONLY ONE WHO'S LOST SOMEONE IMPORTANT, AND YET...
...I WAS SO FOCUSED ON GETTING WHAT I WANTED...
...I NEVER EVEN TRIED TO UNDERSTAND THEM...
...OR MY DAD—

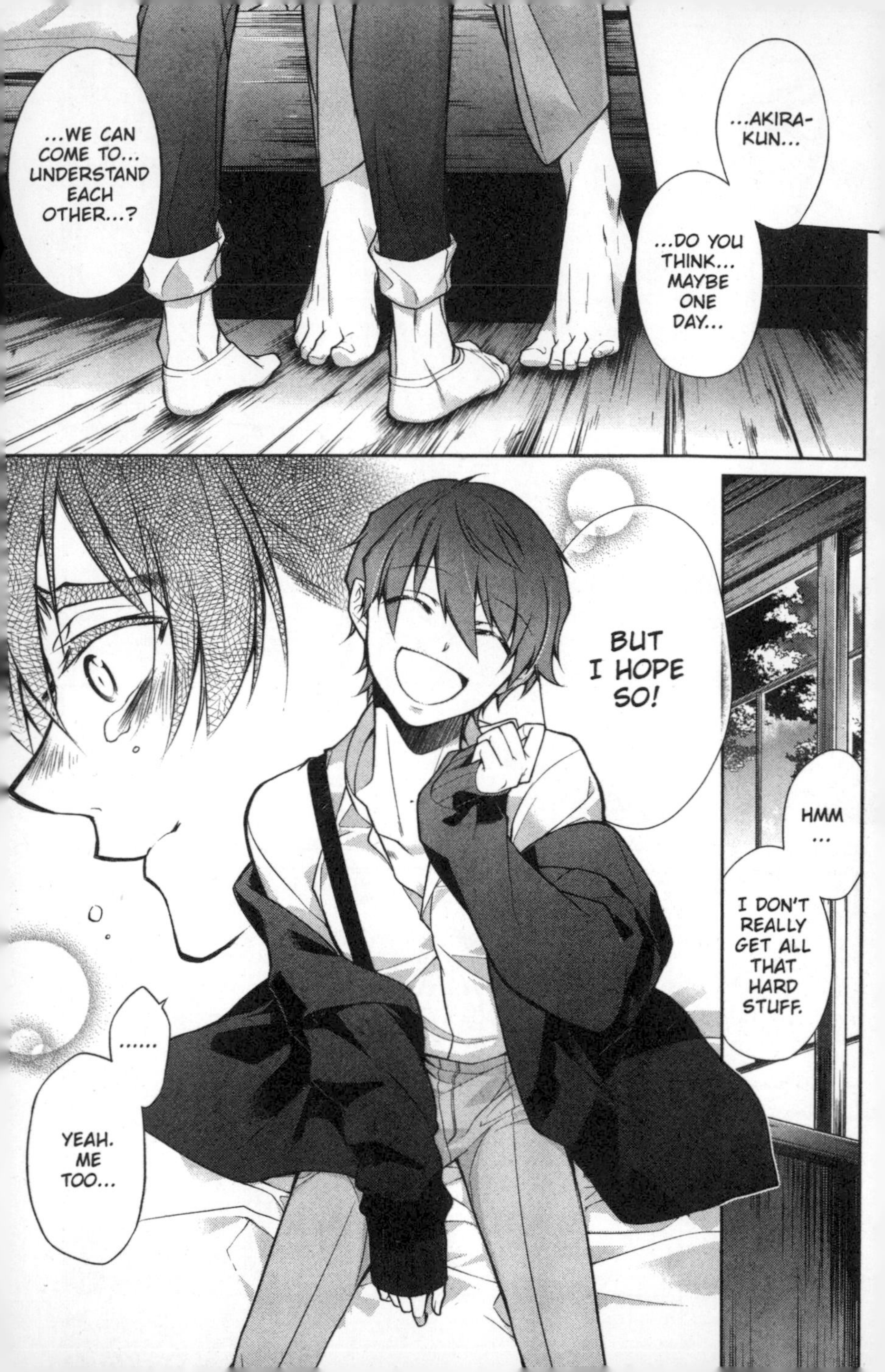
...AKIRA-KUN...
...DO YOU THINK... MAYBE ONE DAY...
...WE CAN COME TO... UNDERSTAND EACH OTHER...?
HMM...
I DON'T REALLY GET ALL THAT HARD STUFF.
BUT I HOPE SO!
......
YEAH. ME TOO...

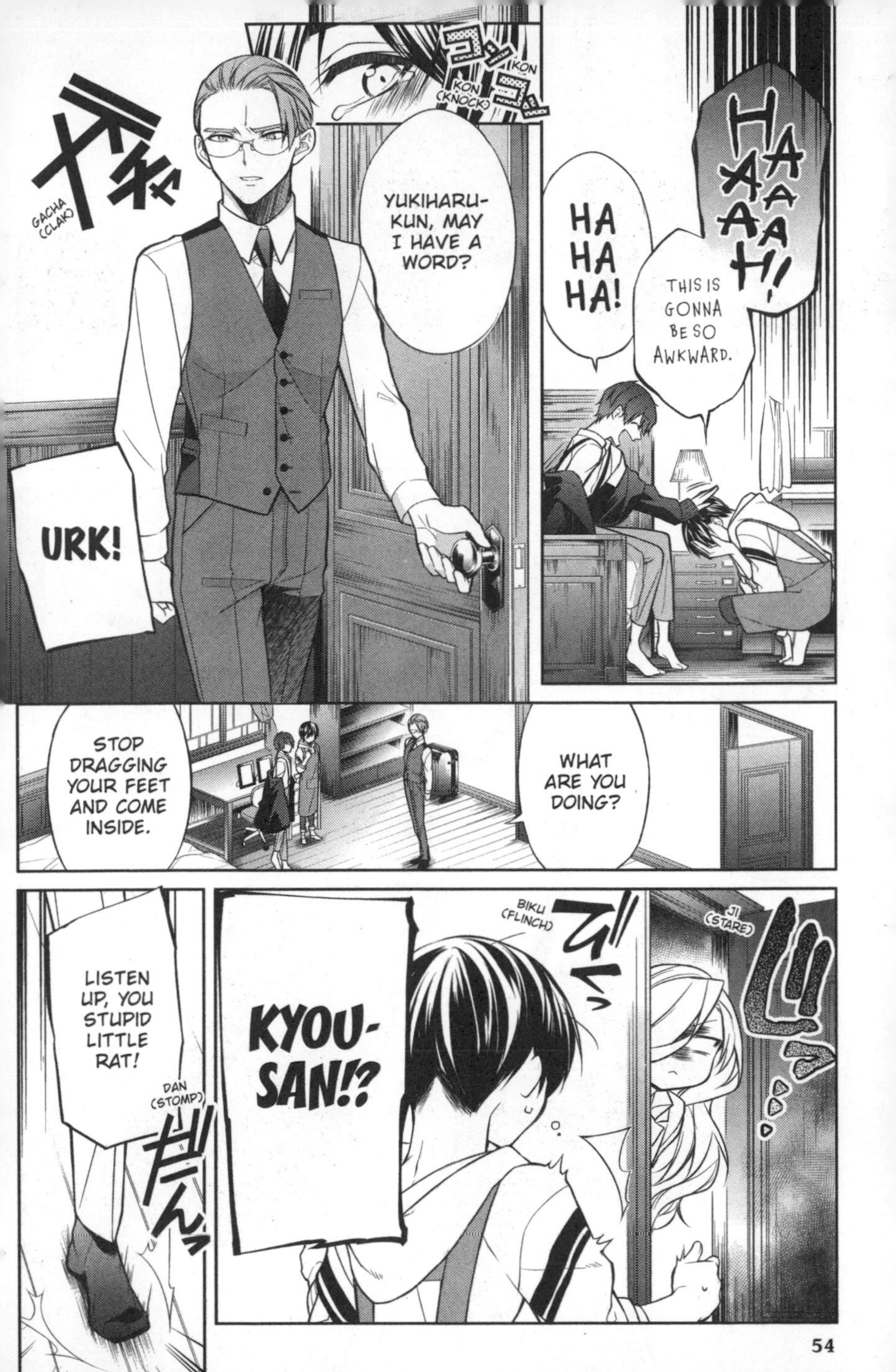
HAAAAAH!!
THIS IS GONNA BE SO AWKWARD.
HA HA HA!
KON KON (KNOCK)
YUKIHARU-KUN, MAY I HAVE A WORD?
GACHA (CLAK)
URK!
WHAT ARE YOU DOING?
STOP DRAGGING YOUR FEET AND COME INSIDE.
JI (STARE)
BIKU (FLINCH)
KYOU-SAN!?
LISTEN UP, YOU STUPID LITTLE RAT!
DAN (STOMP)

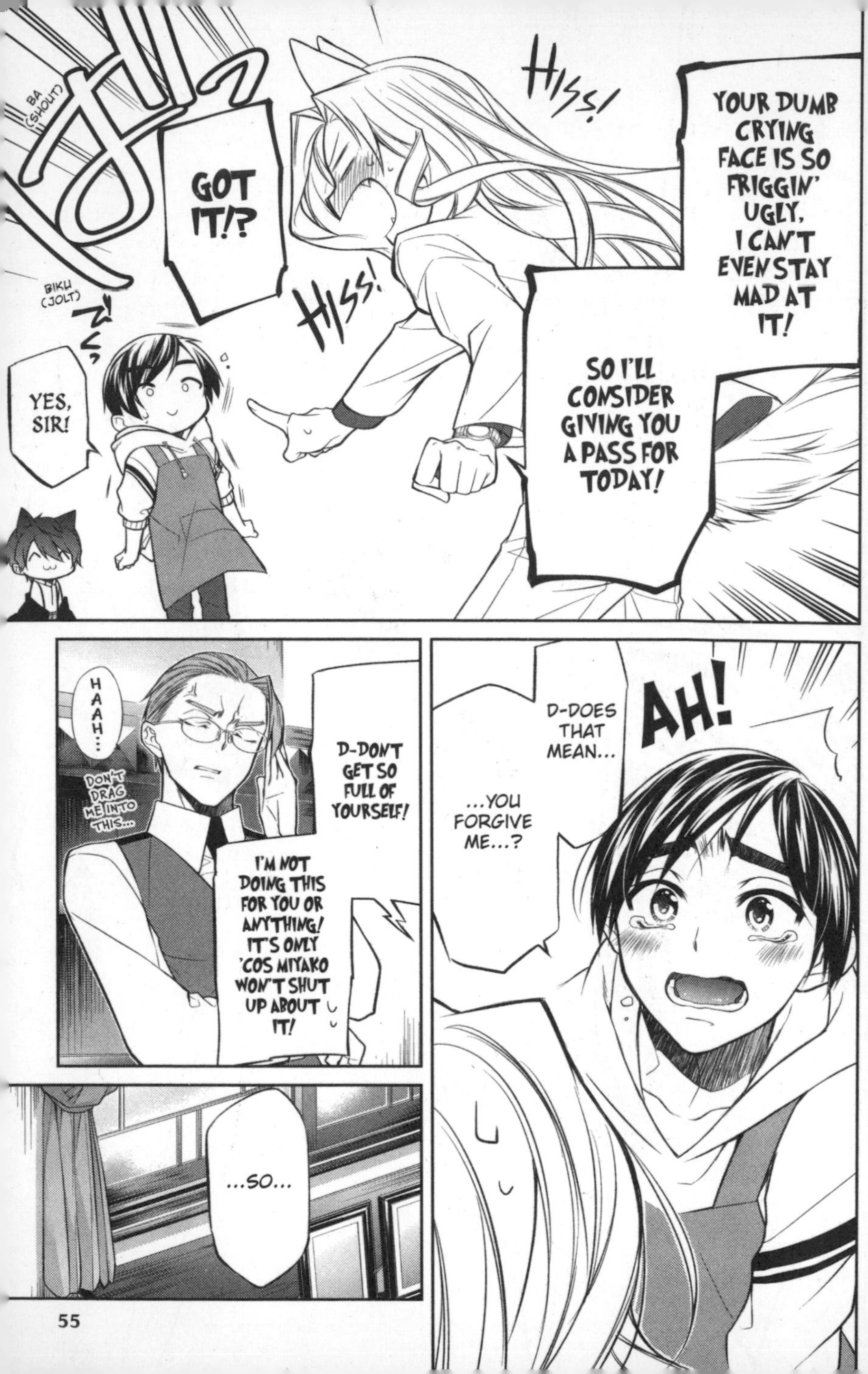
YOUR DUMB CRYING FACE IS SO FRIGGIN' UGLY, I CAN'T EVEN STAY MAD AT IT!
HISS!
SO I'LL CONSIDER GIVING YOU A PASS FOR TODAY!
HISS!
GOT IT!?
BA (SHOUT)
BIKU (JOLT)
YES, SIR!
AH!
D-DOES THAT MEAN...
...YOU FORGIVE ME...?
D-DON'T GET SO FULL OF YOURSELF!
I'M NOT DOING THIS FOR YOU OR ANYTHING! IT'S ONLY 'COS MIYAKO WON'T SHUT UP ABOUT IT!
HAAAH...
DON'T DRAG ME INTO THIS...
...SO...

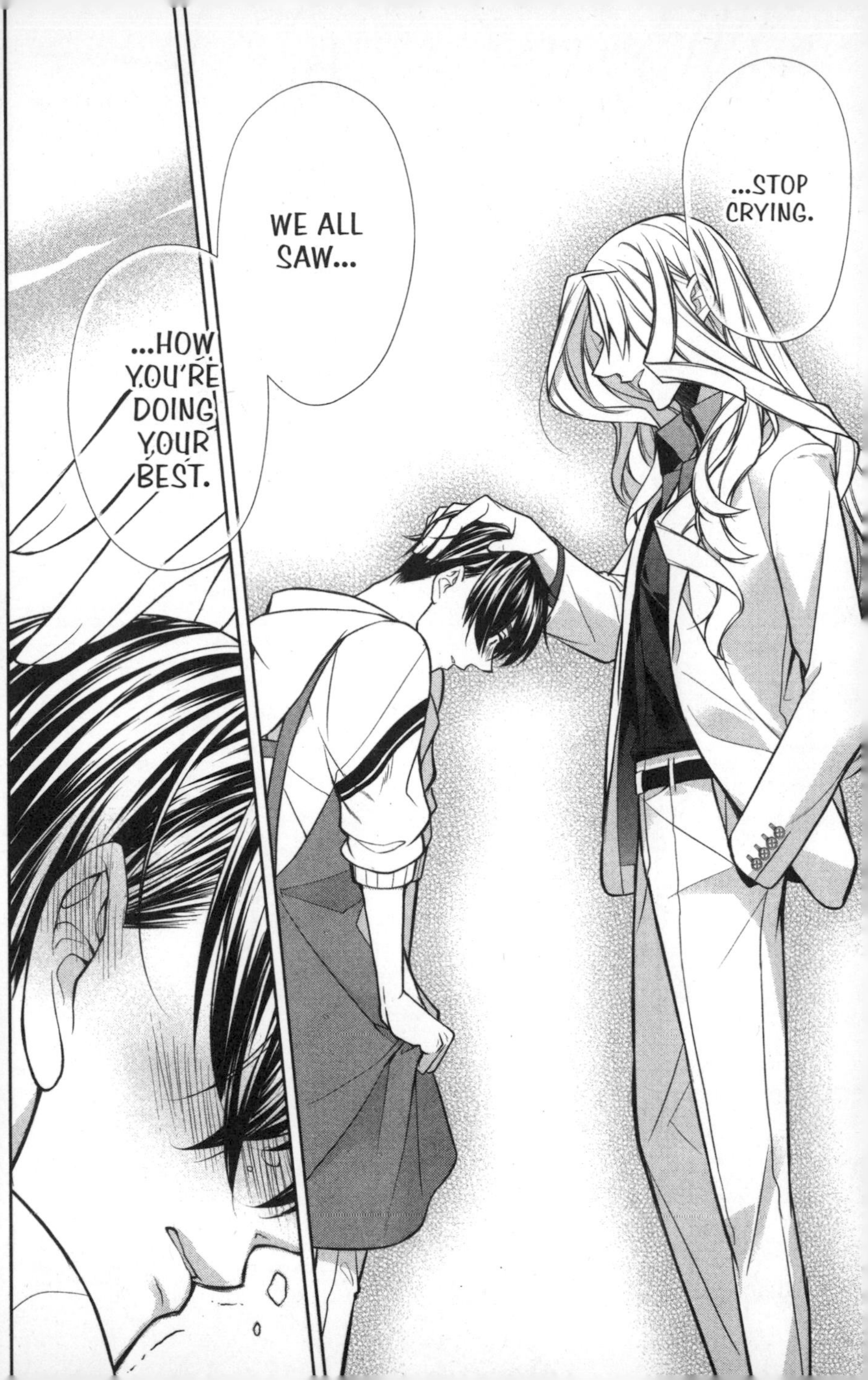
...STOP CRYING.
WE ALL SAW...
...HOW YOU'RE DOING YOUR BEST.

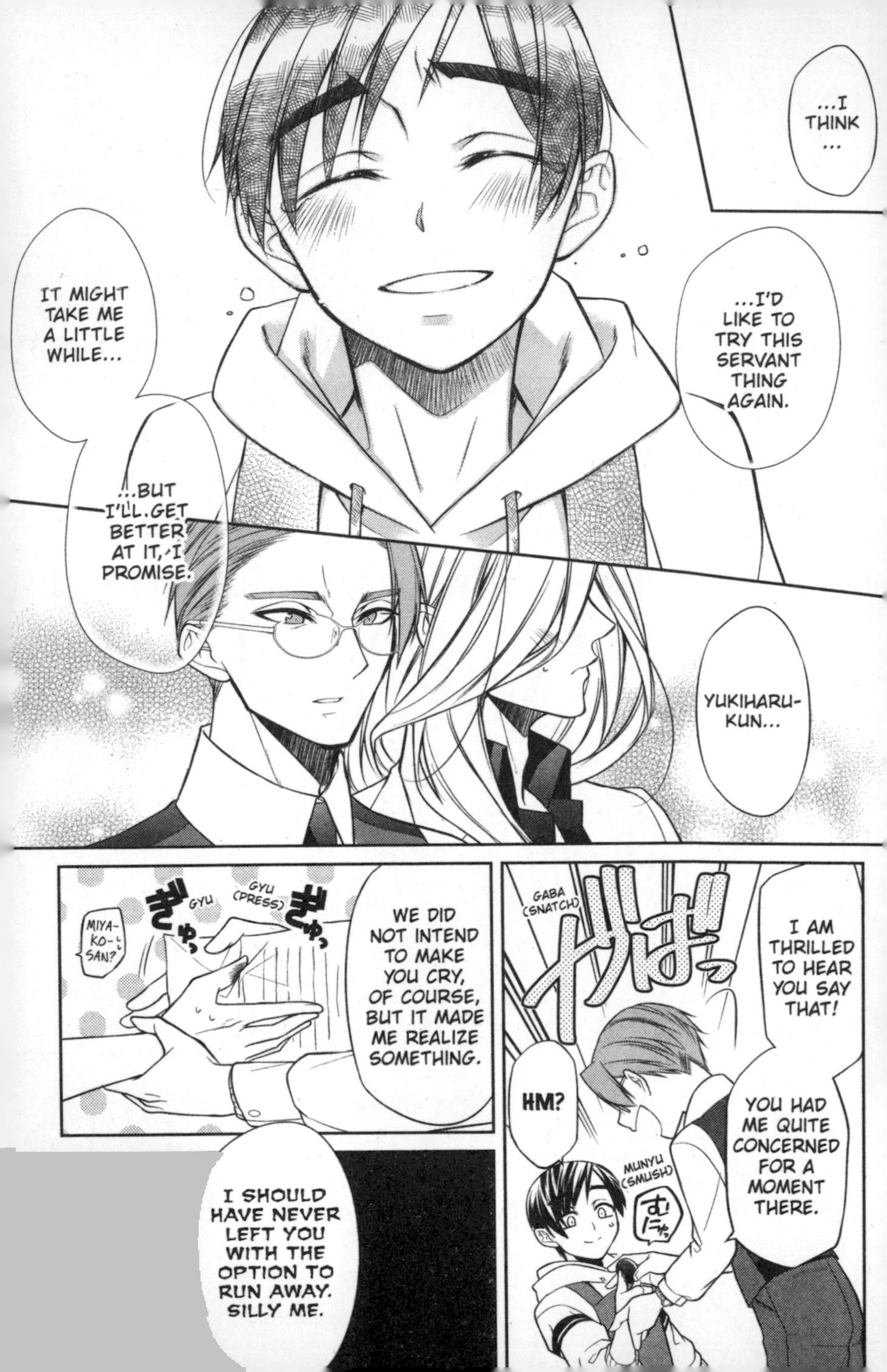
...I THINK...
...I'D LIKE TO TRY THIS SERVANT THING AGAIN.
IT MIGHT TAKE ME A LITTLE WHILE...
...BUT I'LL GET BETTER AT IT, I PROMISE.
YUKIHARU-KUN...
GABA (SNATCH)
I AM THRILLED TO HEAR YOU SAY THAT!
HM?
YOU HAD ME QUITE CONCERNED FOR A MOMENT THERE.
MUNYU (SMUSH)
WE DID NOT INTEND TO MAKE YOU CRY, OF COURSE, BUT IT MADE ME REALIZE SOMETHING.
GYU (PRESS)
GYU
MIYAKO-SAN?
I SHOULD HAVE NEVER LEFT YOU WITH THE OPTION TO RUN AWAY. SILLY ME.

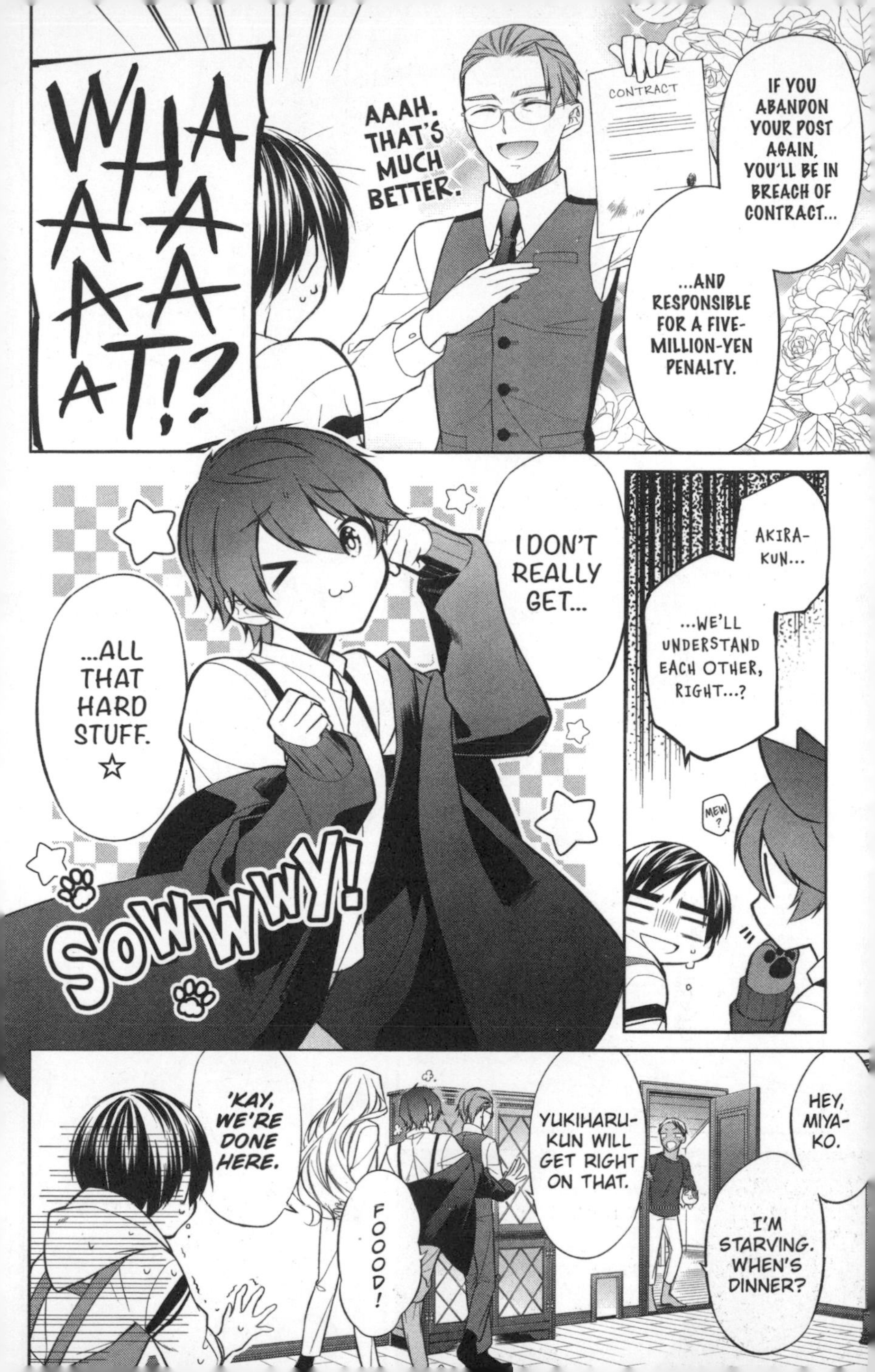
CONTRACT
IF YOU ABANDON YOUR POST AGAIN, YOU'LL BE IN BREACH OF CONTRACT...
...AND RESPONSIBLE FOR A FIVE-MILLION-YEN PENALTY.
AAAH. THAT'S MUCH BETTER.
WHAAAAAAT!?
AKIRA-KUN...
...WE'LL UNDERSTAND EACH OTHER, RIGHT...?
MEW?
I DON'T REALLY GET...
...ALL THAT HARD STUFF. ☆
SOWWWY!
HEY, MIYA-KO.
I'M STARVING. WHEN'S DINNER?
YUKIHARU-KUN WILL GET RIGHT ON THAT.
FOOOOD!
'KAY, WE'RE DONE HERE.

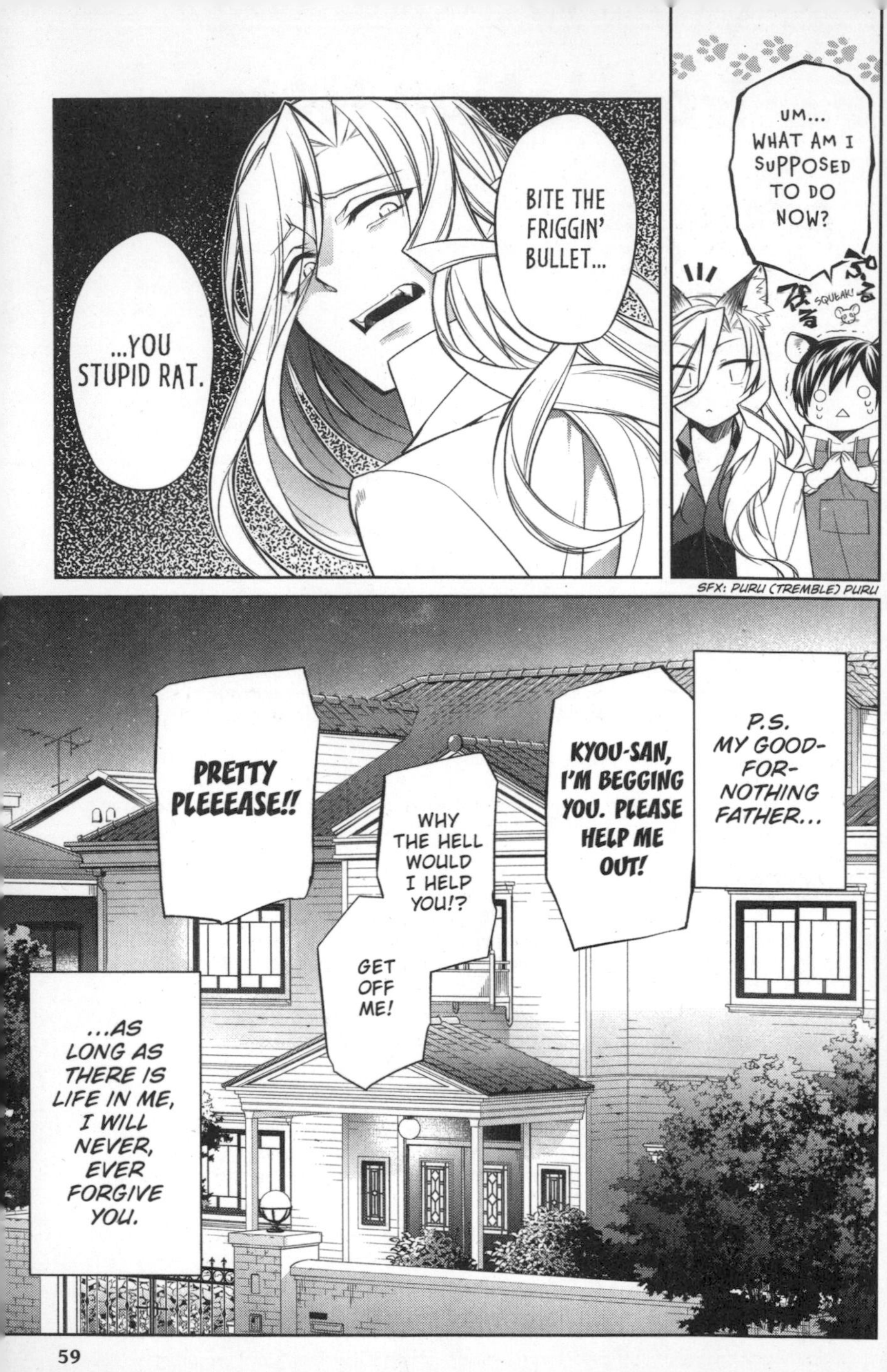
UM... WHAT AM I SUPPOSED TO DO NOW?
SQUEAK!
SFX: PURU (TREMBLE) PURU
BITE THE FRIGGIN' BULLET...
...YOU STUPID RAT.
P.S. MY GOOD-FOR-NOTHING FATHER...
KYOU-SAN, I'M BEGGING YOU. PLEASE HELP ME OUT!
WHY THE HELL WOULD I HELP YOU!?
PRETTY PLEEEASE!!
GET OFF ME!
...AS LONG AS THERE IS LIFE IN ME, I WILL NEVER, EVER FORGIVE YOU.

Translation Notes

Common Honorifics

no honorific: Indicates familiarity or closeness; if used without permission or reason, addressing someone in this manner would constitute an insult.

-san: The Japanese equivalent of Mr./Mrs./Miss. If a situation calls for politeness, this is the fail-safe honorific.

-kun: Used most often when referring to boys, this indicates affection or familiarity. Occasionally used by older men among their peers, but it may also be used by anyone referring to a person of lower standing.

-chan: An affectionate honorific indicating familiarity used mostly in reference to girls; also used in reference to cute persons or animals regardless of gender.

-sensei: A respectful term for teachers, artists, or high-level professionals.

General

Bakeneko are a type of Japanese supernatural being, translated roughly as "shapeshifting cats." There are various beliefs regarding their origins and abilities, but it is said that once a cat reaches a certain age, it becomes a *bakeneko* and gains the power to speak to humans.

Page 9

Japanese names ending with *-ko* often imply a name is feminine, which is why Yukiharu imagines "Miyako" to be a cute girl.

Page 38

Hosts refers to people who work in host clubs. They usually have an all-male staff and cater predominantly to women. Hosts with the highest number of customers and the most sales are considered to the "number one."

Repeat customers often have a favorite host who they will gift with various presents, including expensive accessories and liquor.

Page 133

Daifuku are Japanese sweets made from *mochi*, or glutinous rice cakes, with some kind of filling. Sweet red bean is a popular filling for *daifuku*. Generally, the *mochi* exterior is white and shaped in small, round, bite-size pieces.

Page 167

Salt is considered a way to purify oneself or an area from evil spirits in both Buddhism and Shinto, the two main religions of Japan.

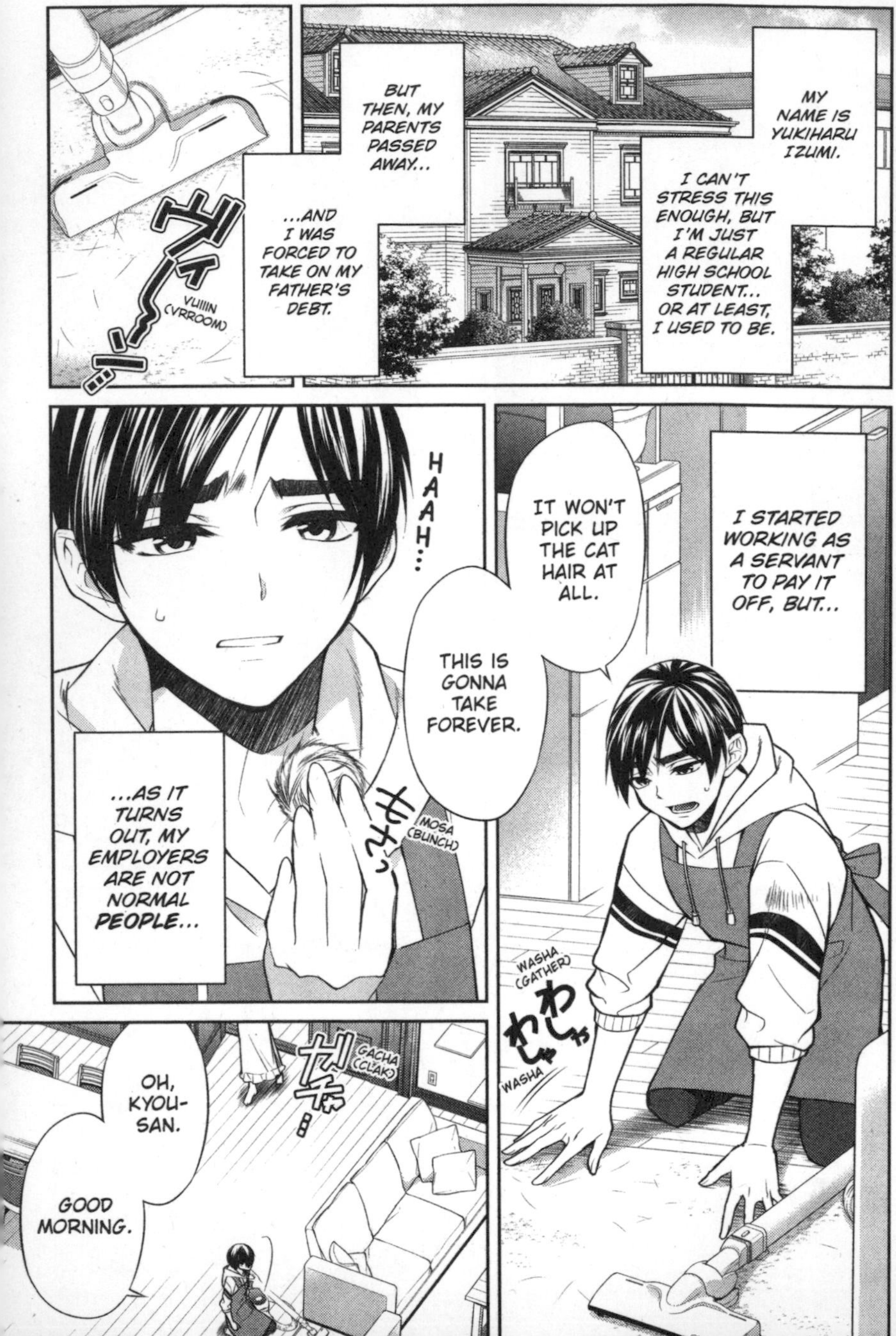

MY NAME IS YUKIHARU IZUMI.
I CAN'T STRESS THIS ENOUGH, BUT I'M JUST A REGULAR HIGH SCHOOL STUDENT... OR AT LEAST, I USED TO BE.
BUT THEN, MY PARENTS PASSED AWAY...
...AND I WAS FORCED TO TAKE ON MY FATHER'S DEBT.
VUIIIN (VRROOM)
I STARTED WORKING AS A SERVANT TO PAY IT OFF, BUT...
IT WON'T PICK UP THE CAT HAIR AT ALL.
THIS IS GONNA TAKE FOREVER.
WASHA (GATHER)
WASHA
HAAAH...
MOSA (BUNCH)
...AS IT TURNS OUT, MY EMPLOYERS ARE NOT NORMAL PEOPLE...
GACHA (CLAK)
OH, KYOU-SAN.
GOOD MORNING.

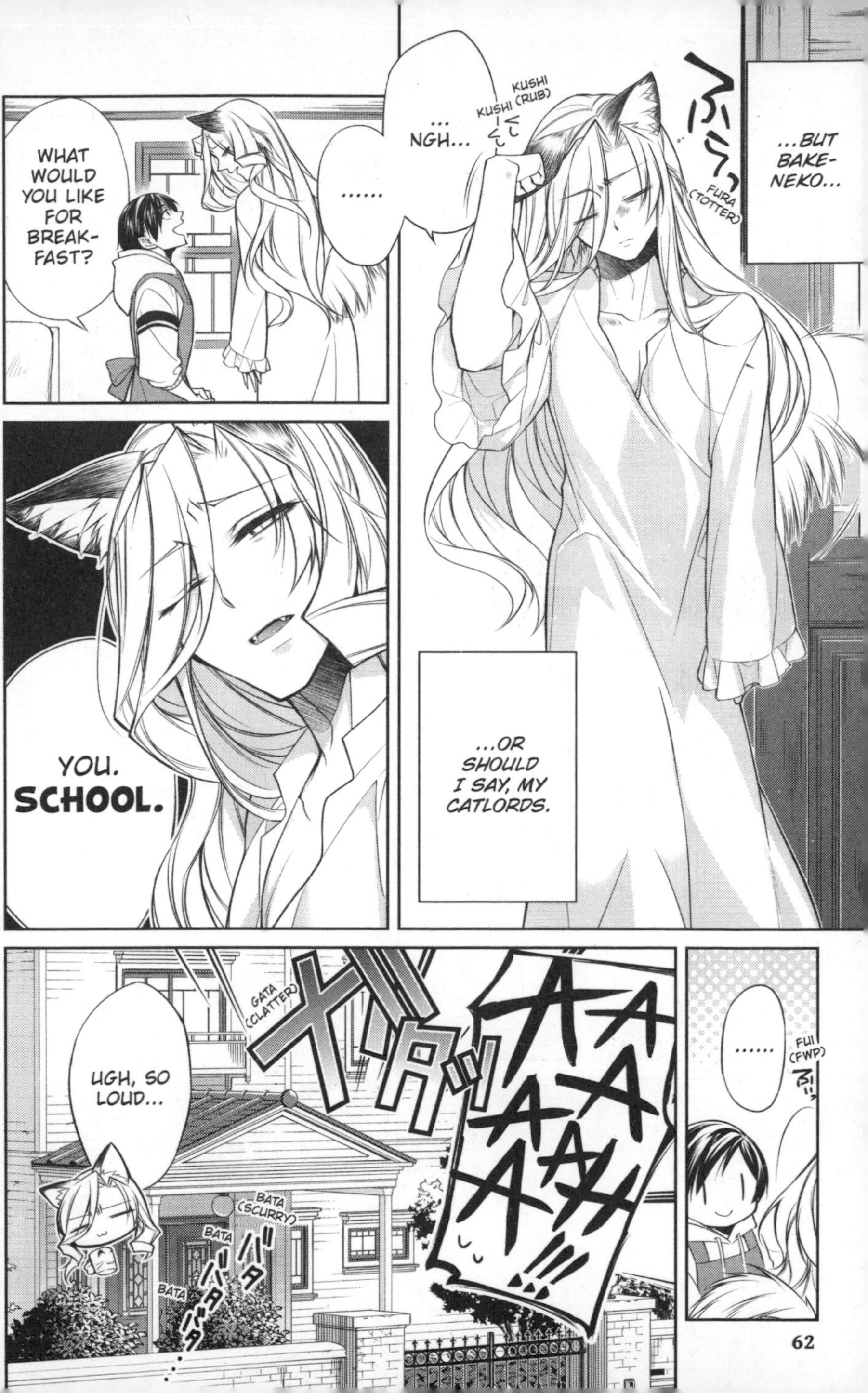

...BUT BAKE-NEKO...
FURA (TOTTER)
KUSHI KUSHI (RUB)
... NGH...
......
...OR SHOULD I SAY, MY CATLORDS.
WHAT WOULD YOU LIKE FOR BREAKFAST?
YOU. SCHOOL.
......
FUI (FWP)
AAAAAAAA!!!
GATA (CLATTER)
UGH, SO LOUD...
BATA BATA BATA (SCURRY)

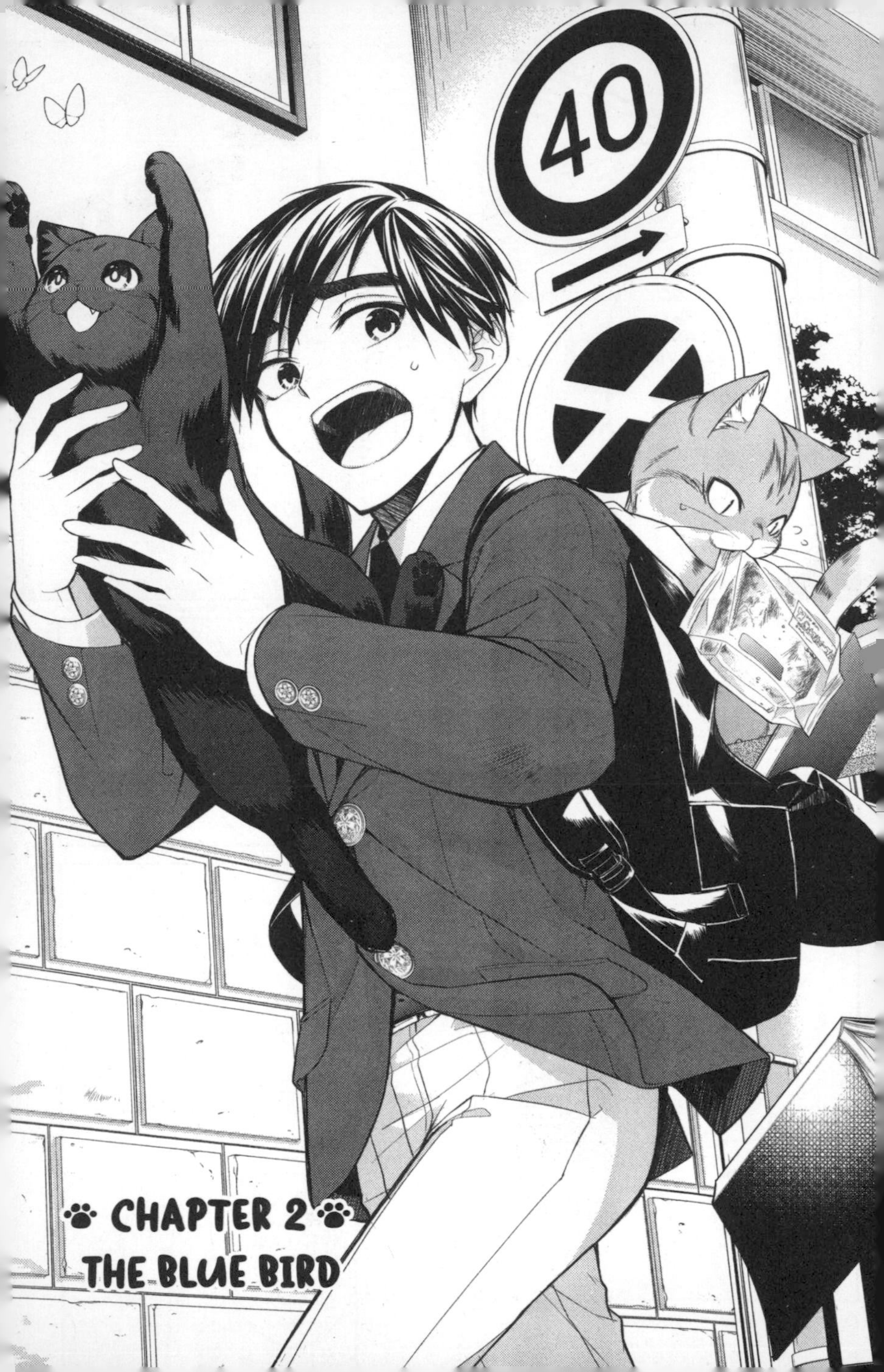
40

CHAPTER 2
THE BLUE BIRD

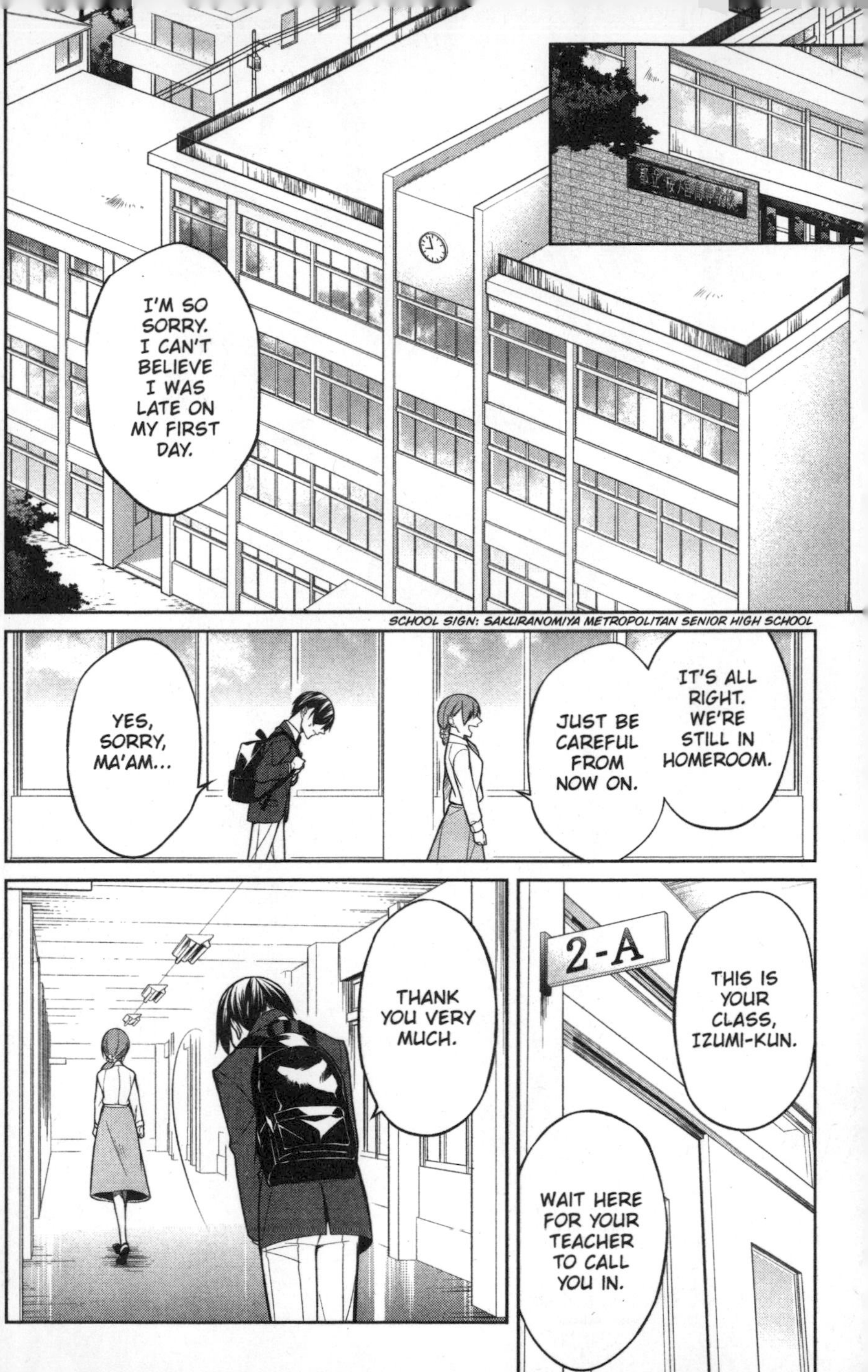
I'M SO SORRY. I CAN'T BELIEVE I WAS LATE ON MY FIRST DAY.
SCHOOL SIGN: SAKURANOMIYA METROPOLITAN SENIOR HIGH SCHOOL
IT'S ALL RIGHT. WE'RE STILL IN HOMEROOM.
JUST BE CAREFUL FROM NOW ON.
YES, SORRY, MA'AM...
2-A
THIS IS YOUR CLASS, IZUMI-KUN.
WAIT HERE FOR YOUR TEACHER TO CALL YOU IN.
THANK YOU VERY MUCH.

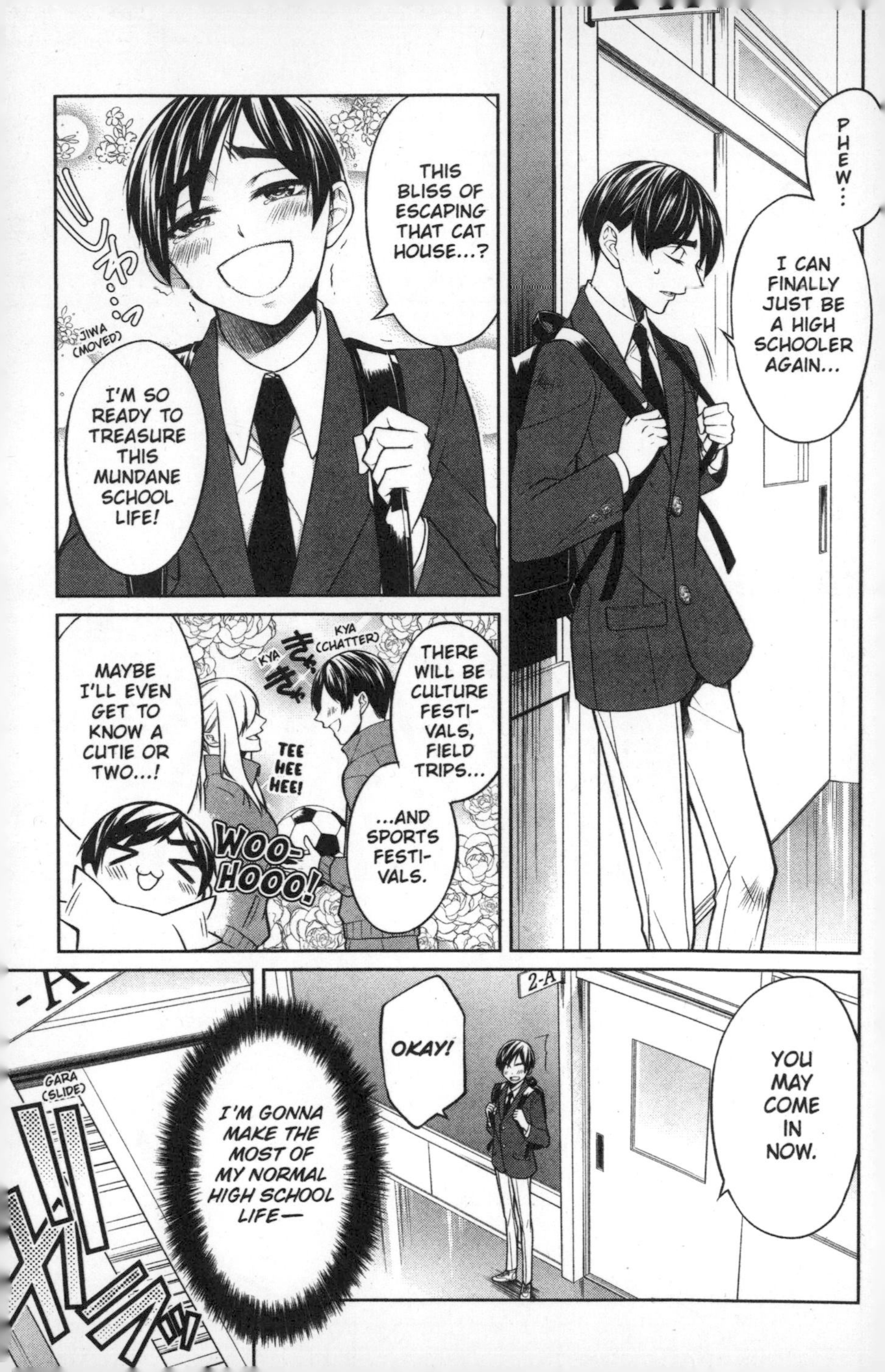
PHEW...
I CAN FINALLY JUST BE A HIGH SCHOOLER AGAIN...
THIS BLISS OF ESCAPING THAT CAT HOUSE...?
JIWA (MOVED)
I'M SO READY TO TREASURE THIS MUNDANE SCHOOL LIFE!
THERE WILL BE CULTURE FESTI-VALS, FIELD TRIPS...
KYA KYA (CHATTER)
MAYBE I'LL EVEN GET TO KNOW A CUTIE OR TWO...!
TEE HEE HEE!
...AND SPORTS FESTI-VALS.
WOO-HOOO!
2-A
YOU MAY COME IN NOW.
OKAY!
I'M GONNA MAKE THE MOST OF MY NORMAL HIGH SCHOOL LIFE—
GARA (SLIDE)

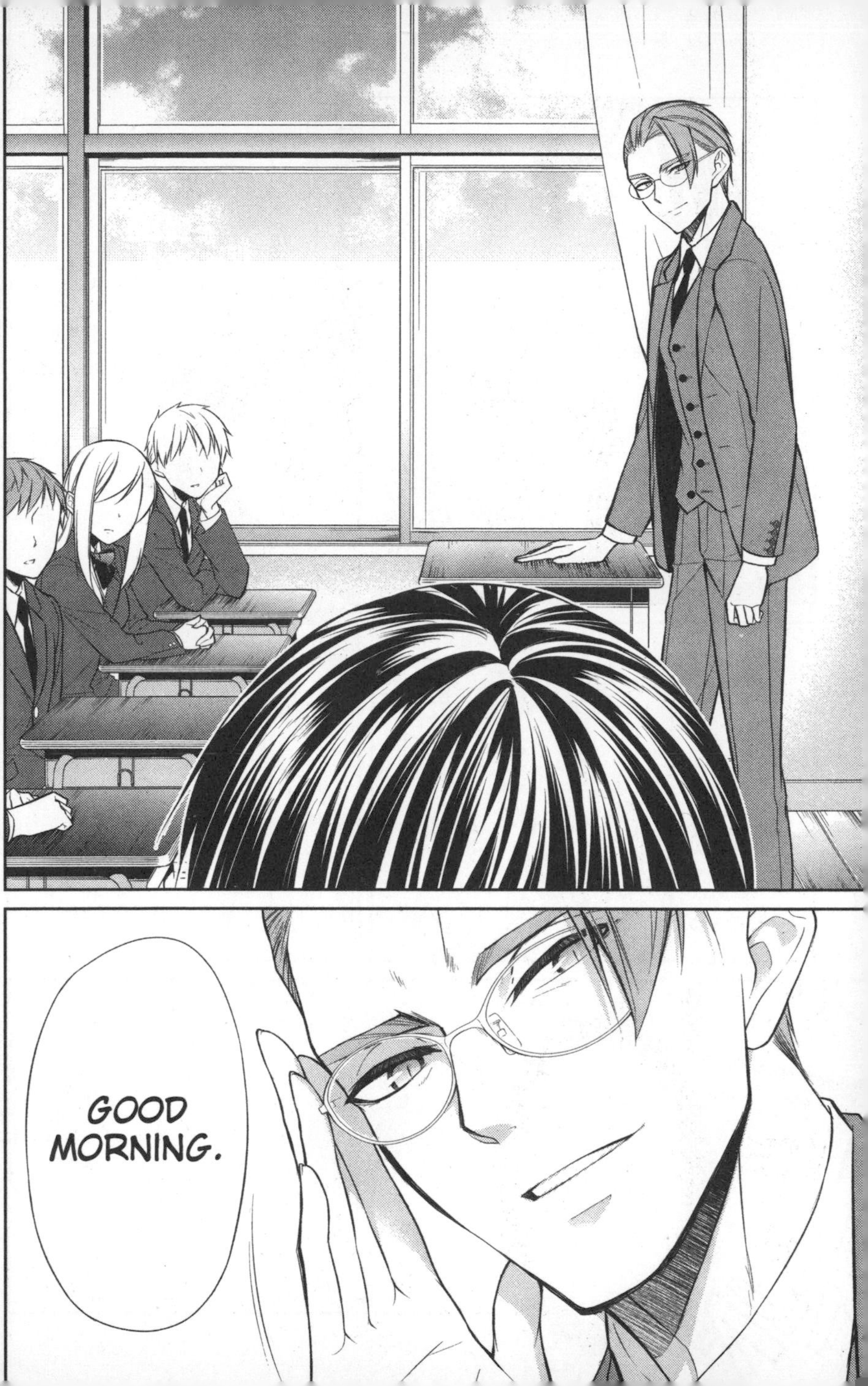
GOOD MORNING.

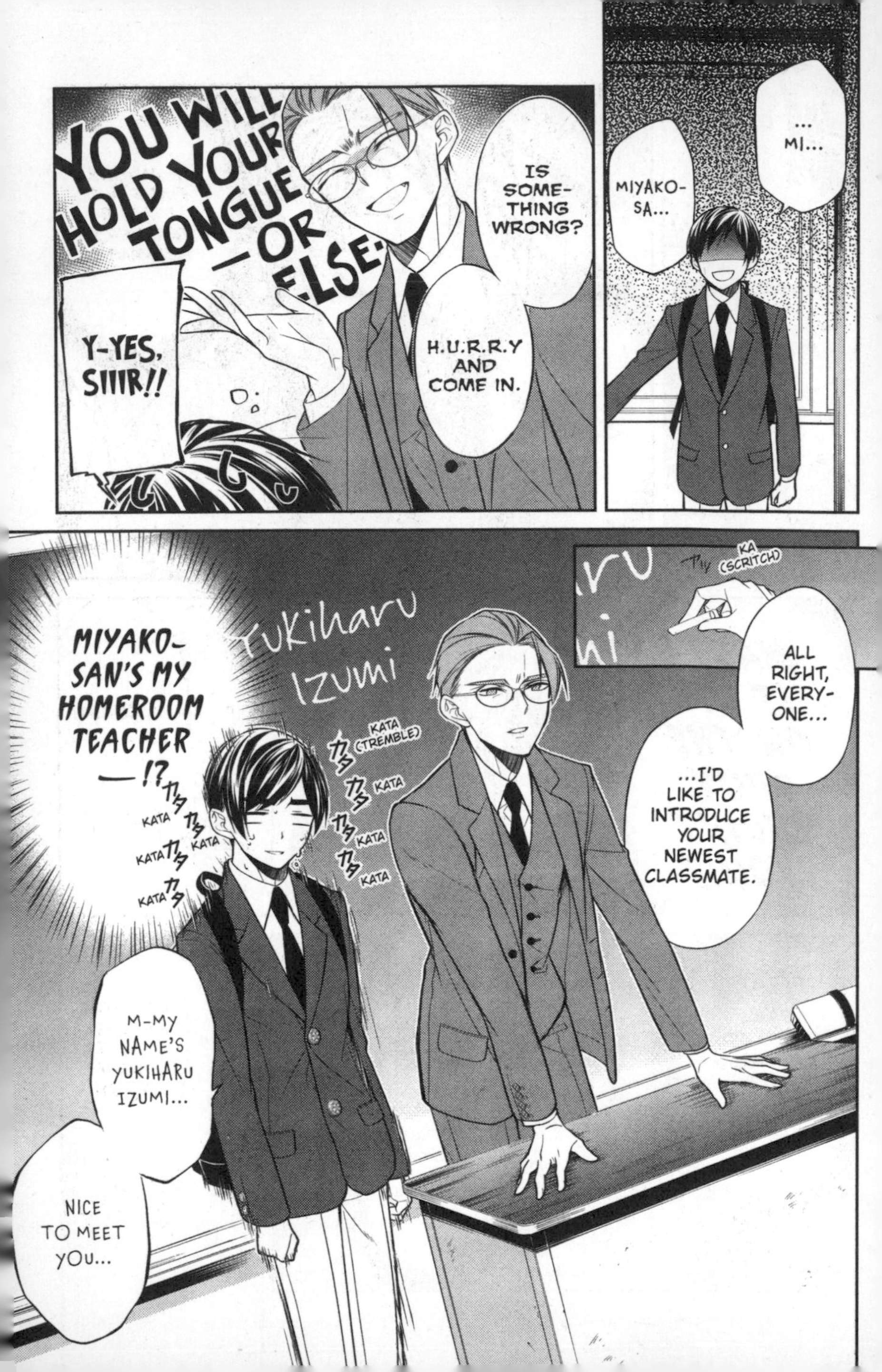
... MI...
MIYAKO-SA...
IS SOME-THING WRONG?
H.U.R.R.Y AND COME IN.
YOU WILL HOLD YOUR TONGUE —OR ELSE.
Y-YES, SIIIR!!
カッ KA (SCRITCH)
ALL RIGHT, EVERY-ONE...
...I'D LIKE TO INTRODUCE YOUR NEWEST CLASSMATE.
YUKIHARU IZUMI
カタ KATA (TREMBLE) カタ KATA カタ KATA カタ KATA
MIYAKO-SAN'S MY HOMEROOM TEACHER—!?
カタ KATA カタ KATA カタ KATA カタ KATA
M-MY NAME'S YUKIHARU IZUMI...
NICE TO MEET YOU...

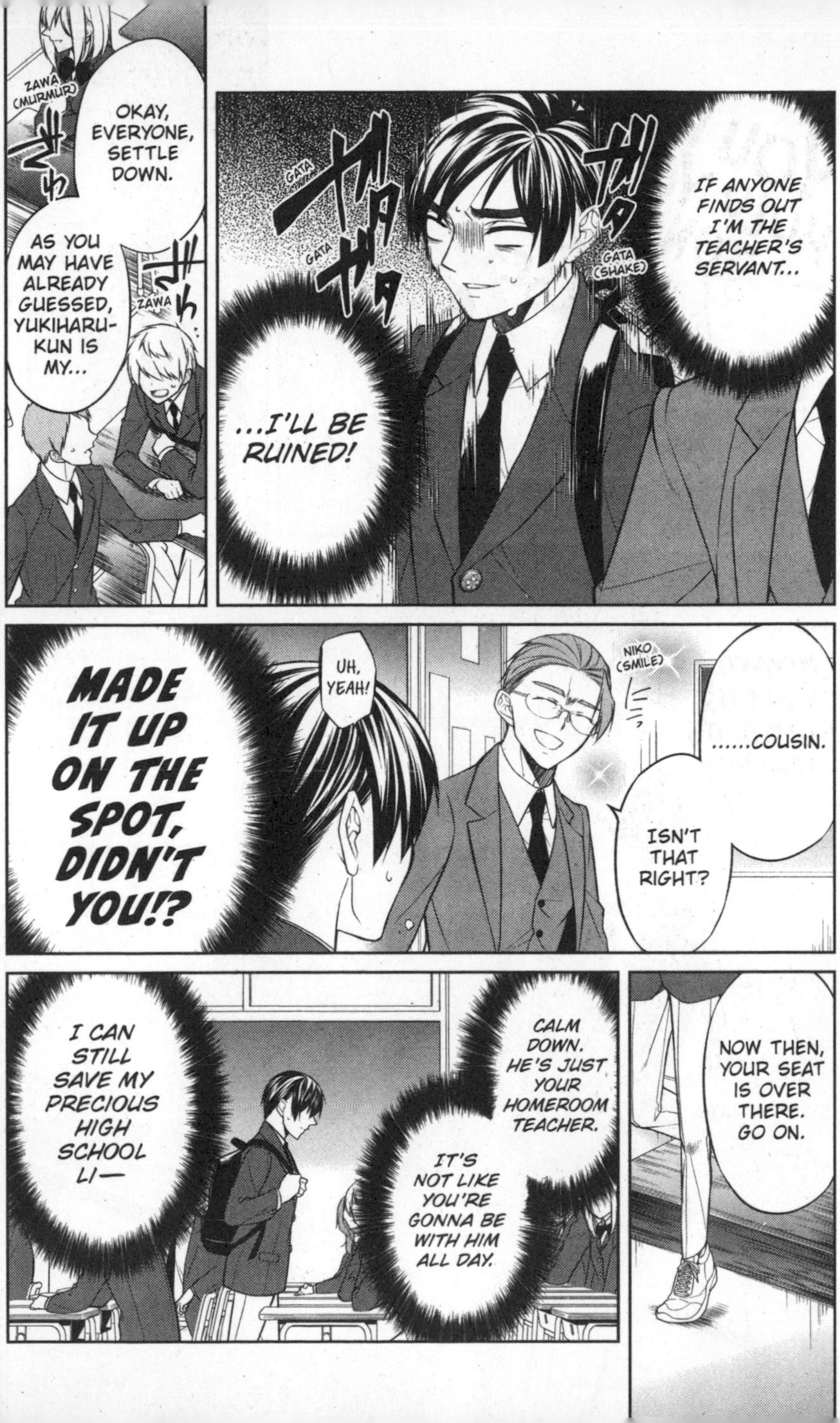
IF ANYONE FINDS OUT I'M THE TEACHER'S SERVANT...
GATA (SHAKE)
GATA
GATA
...I'LL BE RUINED!
ZAWA (MURMUR)
OKAY, EVERYONE, SETTLE DOWN.
AS YOU MAY HAVE ALREADY GUESSED, YUKIHARU-KUN IS MY...
ZAWA
NIKO (SMILE)
......COUSIN.
ISN'T THAT RIGHT?
UH, YEAH!
MADE IT UP ON THE SPOT, DIDN'T YOU!?
NOW THEN, YOUR SEAT IS OVER THERE. GO ON.
CALM DOWN. HE'S JUST YOUR HOMEROOM TEACHER.
IT'S NOT LIKE YOU'RE GONNA BE WITH HIM ALL DAY.
I CAN STILL SAVE MY PRECIOUS HIGH SCHOOL LI—

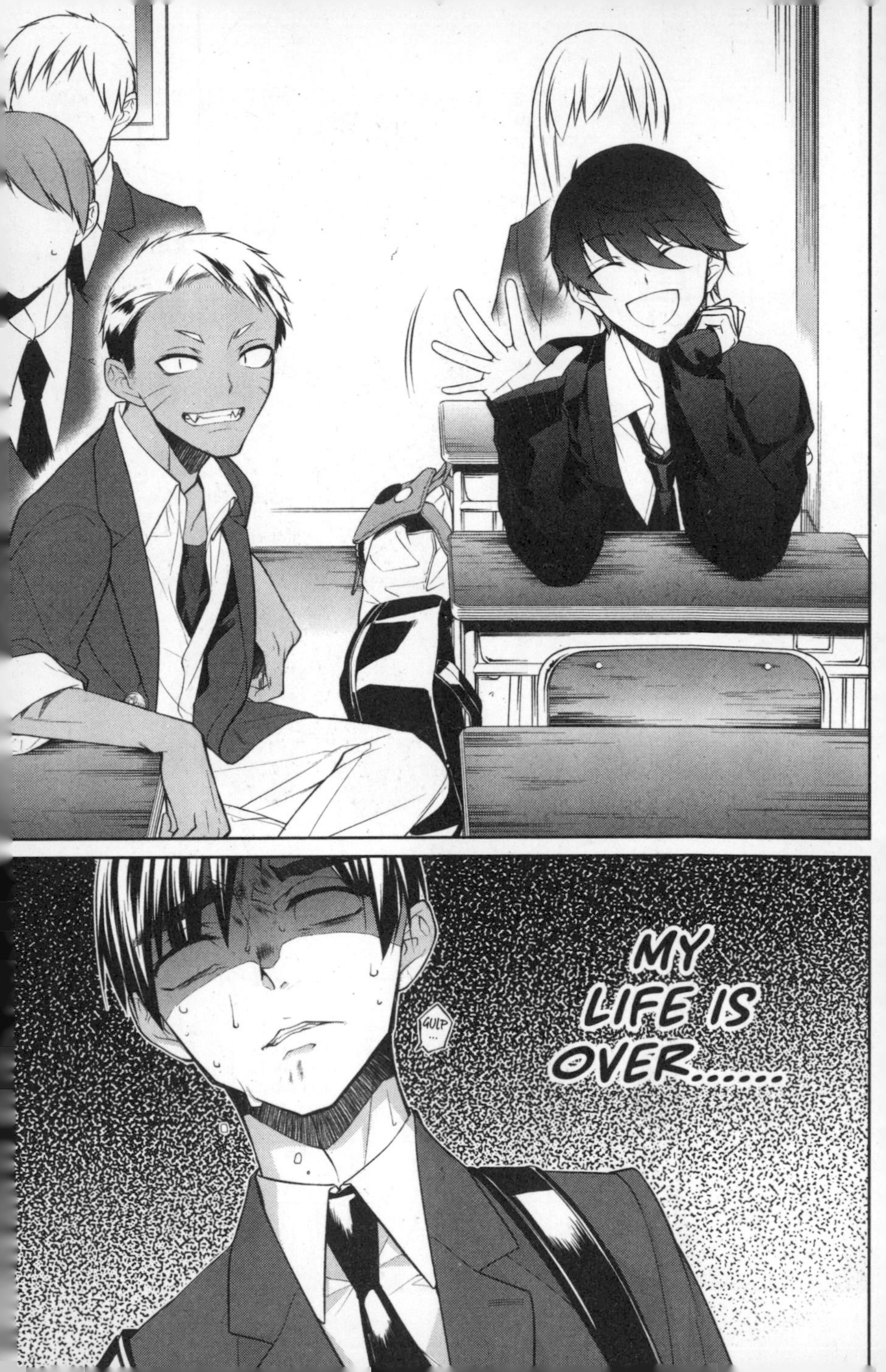
GULP
...
MY LIFE IS OVER......

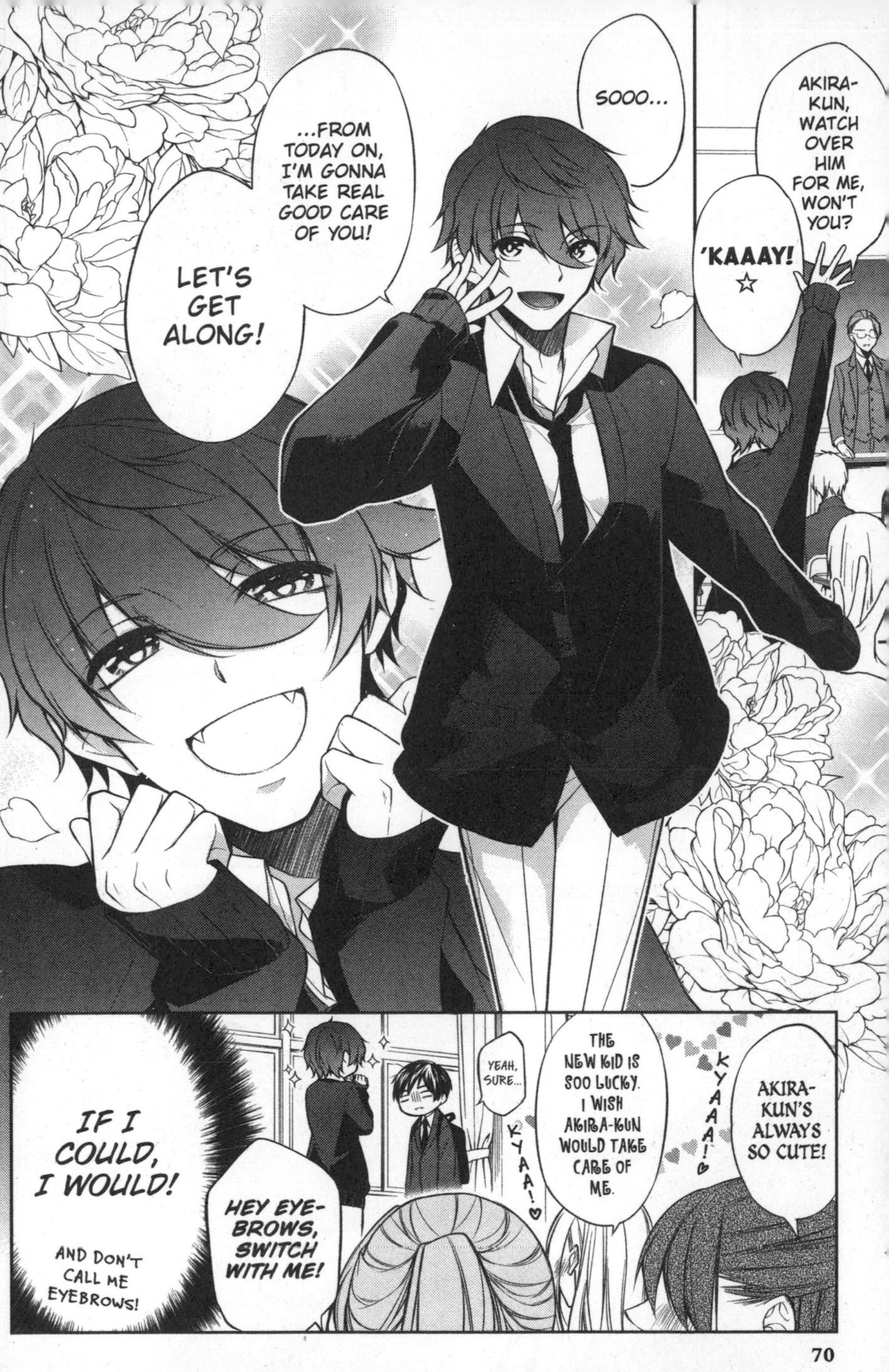
AKIRA-KUN, WATCH OVER HIM FOR ME, WON'T YOU?
'KAAAY! ☆
SOOO...
...FROM TODAY ON, I'M GONNA TAKE REAL GOOD CARE OF YOU!
LET'S GET ALONG!
AKIRA-KUN'S ALWAYS SO CUTE!
KYAAA!♡
THE NEW KID IS SOO LUCKY. I WISH AKIRA-KUN WOULD TAKE CARE OF ME.
KYAA!♡
YEAH, SURE...
HEY EYE-BROWS, SWITCH WITH ME!
IF I COULD, I WOULD!
AND DON'T CALL ME EYEBROWS!

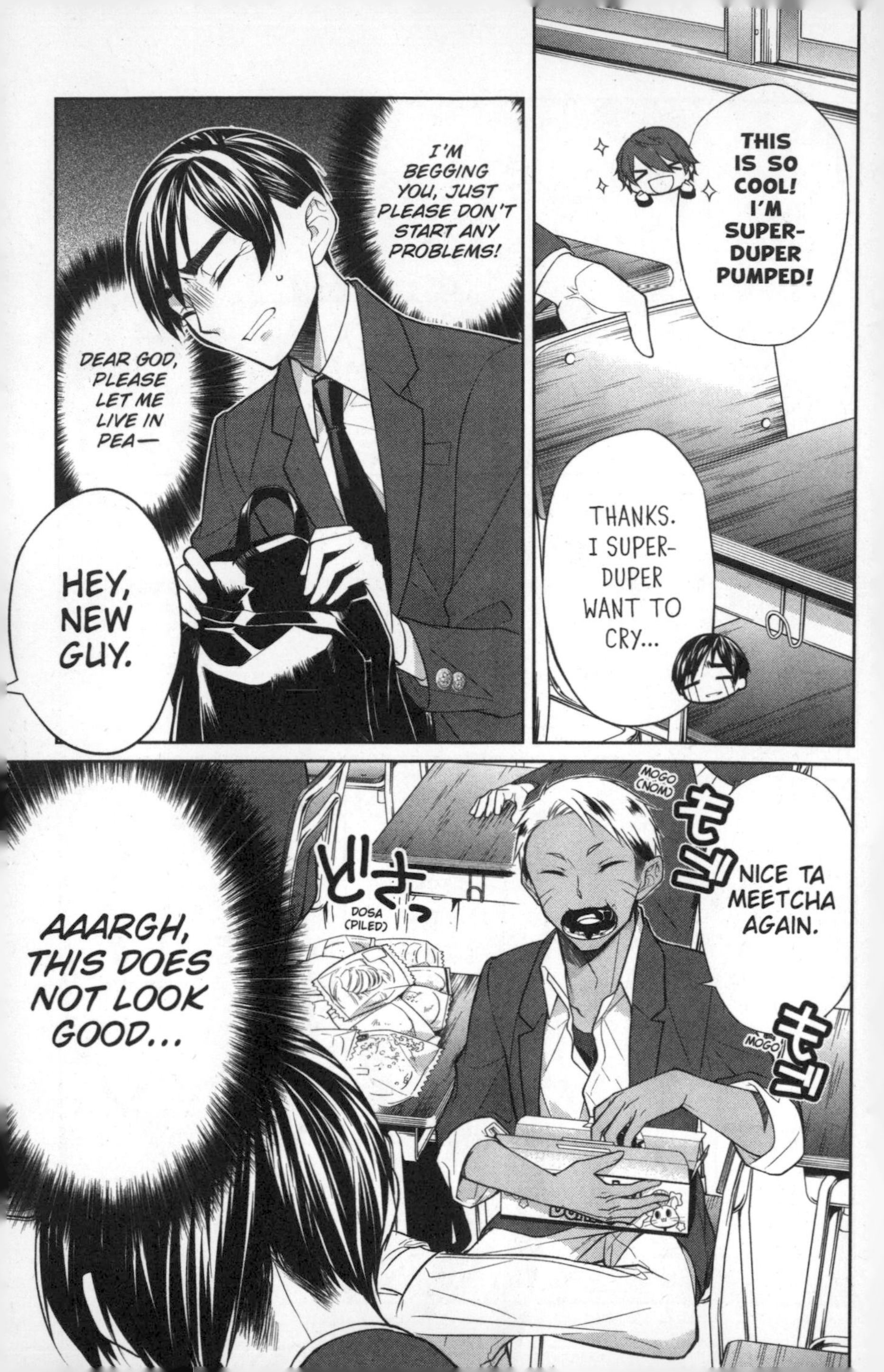
THIS IS SO COOL! I'M SUPER-DUPER PUMPED!
THANKS. I SUPER-DUPER WANT TO CRY...
I'M BEGGING YOU, JUST PLEASE DON'T START ANY PROBLEMS!
DEAR GOD, PLEASE LET ME LIVE IN PEA—
HEY, NEW GUY.
MOGO (NOM)
NICE TA MEETCHA AGAIN.
MOGO
DOSA (PILED)
AAARGH, THIS DOES NOT LOOK GOOD...

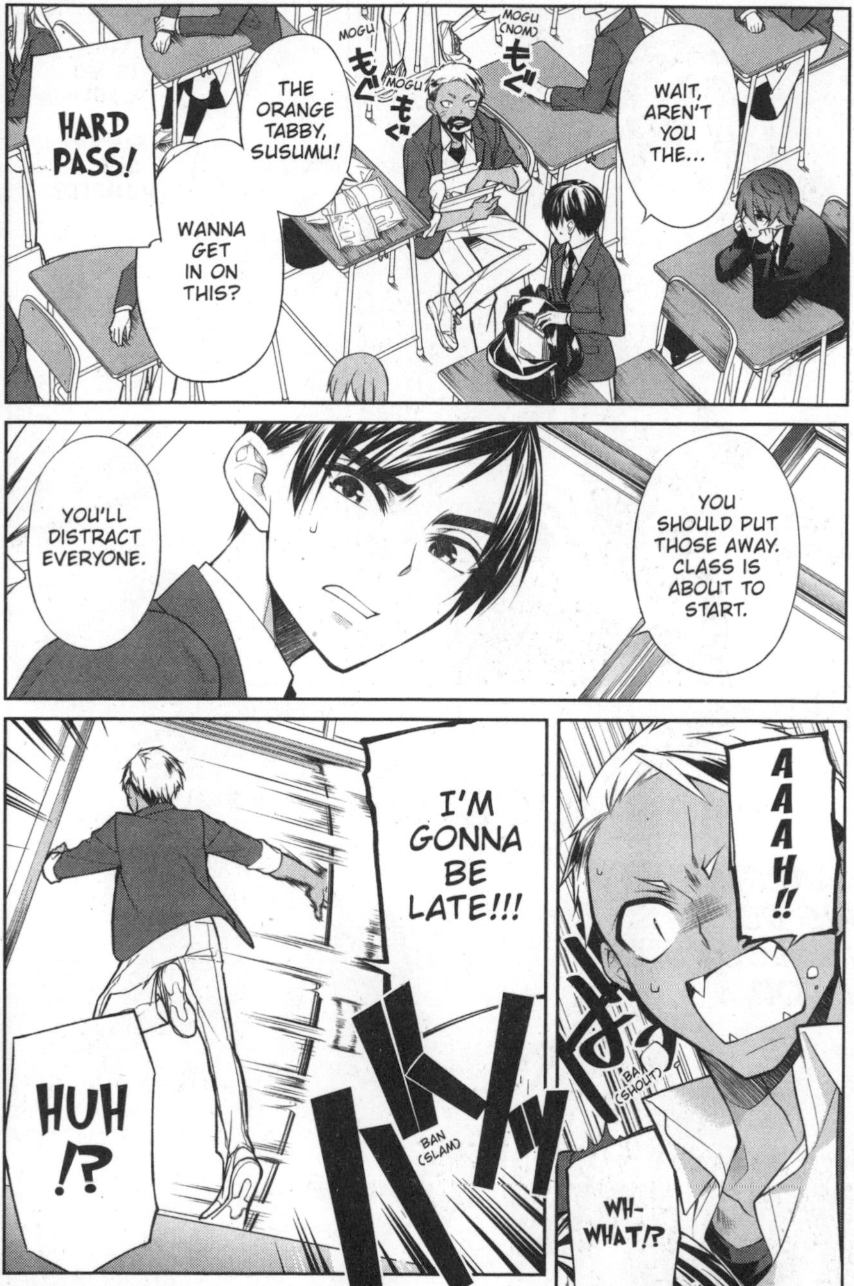
WAIT, AREN'T YOU THE...
MOGU (NOM)
もぐ
THE ORANGE TABBY, SUSUMU!
MOGU
もぐ
MOGU
もぐ
HARD PASS!
WANNA GET IN ON THIS?
YOU SHOULD PUT THOSE AWAY. CLASS IS ABOUT TO START.
YOU'LL DISTRACT EVERYONE.
AAAAH!!
ばっ
BA (SHOUT)
WH-WHAT!?
I'M GONNA BE LATE!!!
バンッ
BAN (SLAM)
HUH!?

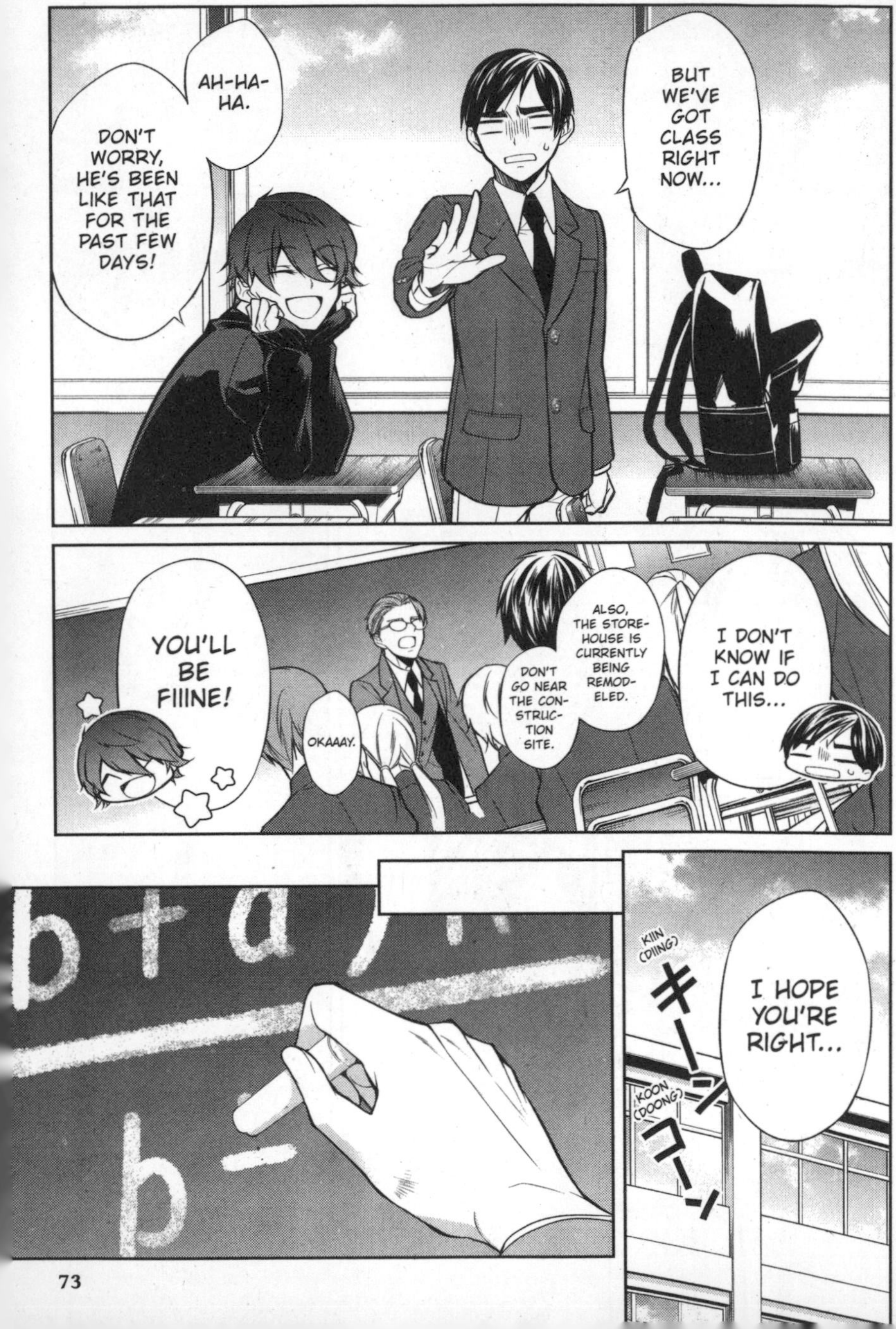
BUT WE'VE GOT CLASS RIGHT NOW...
AH-HA-HA.
DON'T WORRY, HE'S BEEN LIKE THAT FOR THE PAST FEW DAYS!
I DON'T KNOW IF I CAN DO THIS...
ALSO, THE STORE-HOUSE IS CURRENTLY BEING REMOD-ELED.
DON'T GO NEAR THE CON-STRUC-TION SITE.
OKAAAY.
YOU'LL BE FIIINE!
KIIN (DIIING)
I HOPE YOU'RE RIGHT...
KOON (DOONG)

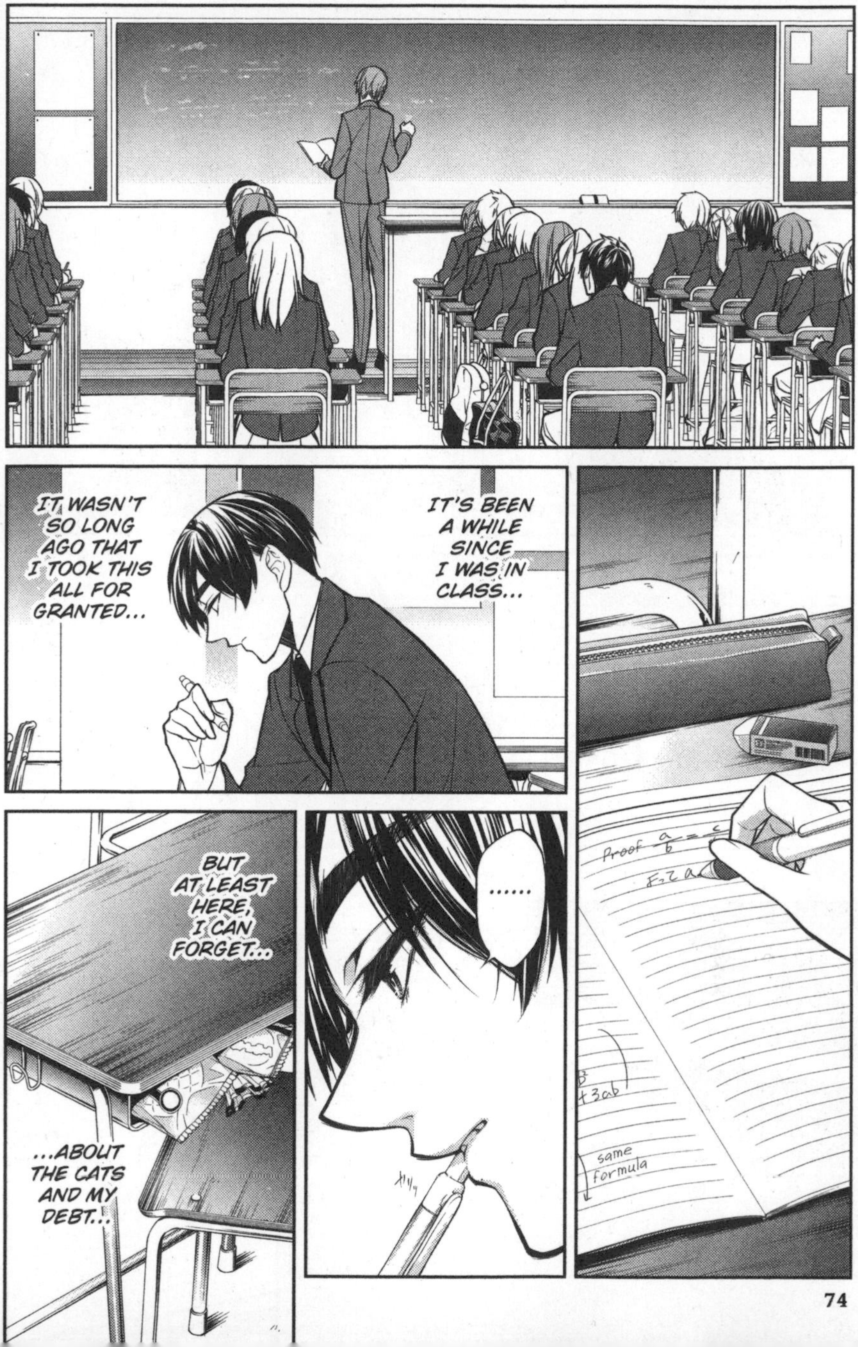
Proof
same formula
IT'S BEEN A WHILE SINCE I WAS IN CLASS...
IT WASN'T SO LONG AGO THAT I TOOK THIS ALL FOR GRANTED...
......
BUT AT LEAST HERE, I CAN FORGET...
...ABOUT THE CATS AND MY DEBT...

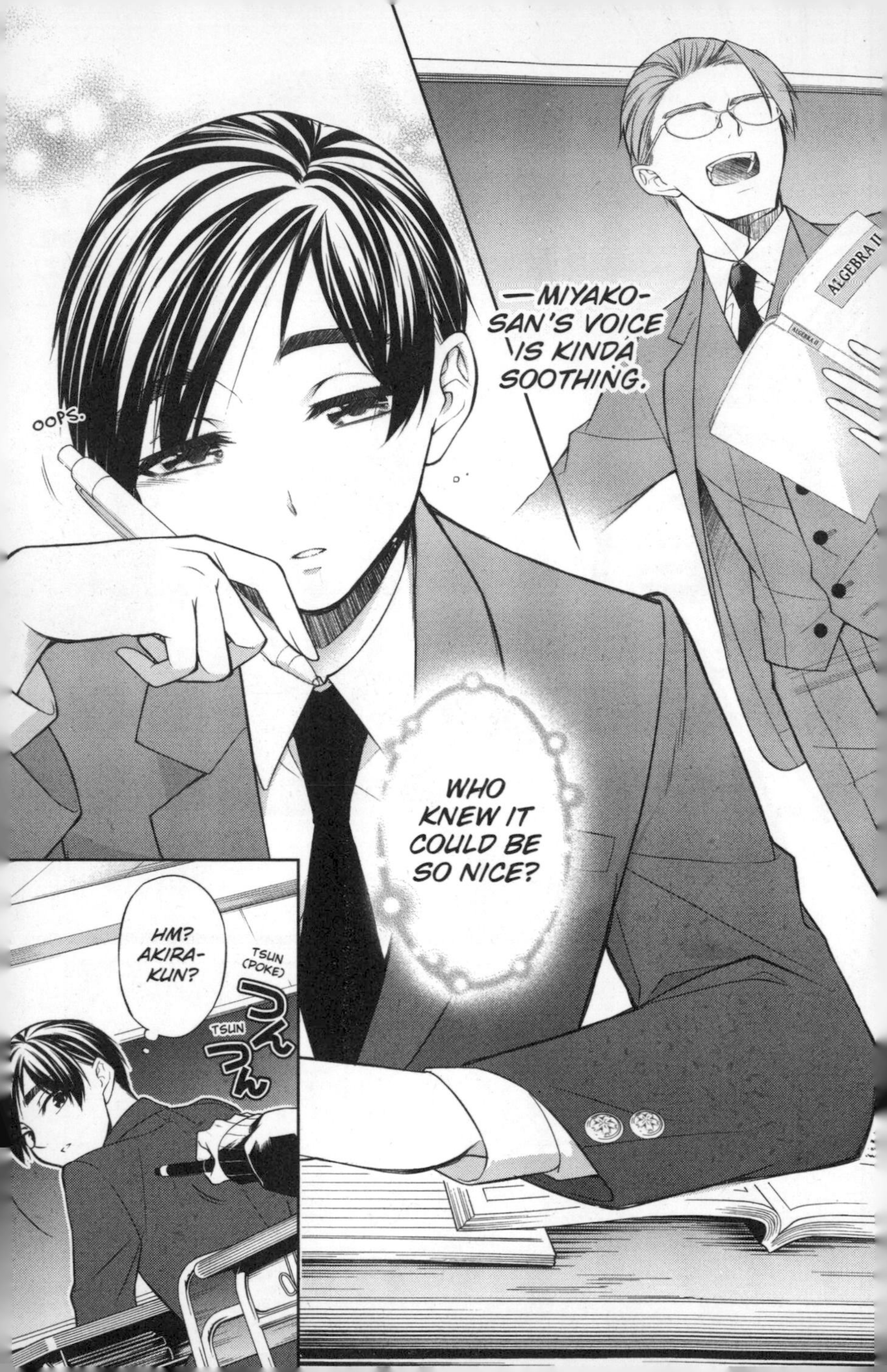

—MIYAKO-SAN'S VOICE IS KINDA SOOTHING.
WHO KNEW IT COULD BE SO NICE?
OOPS.
TSUN (POKE)
TSUN
HM? AKIRA-KUN?

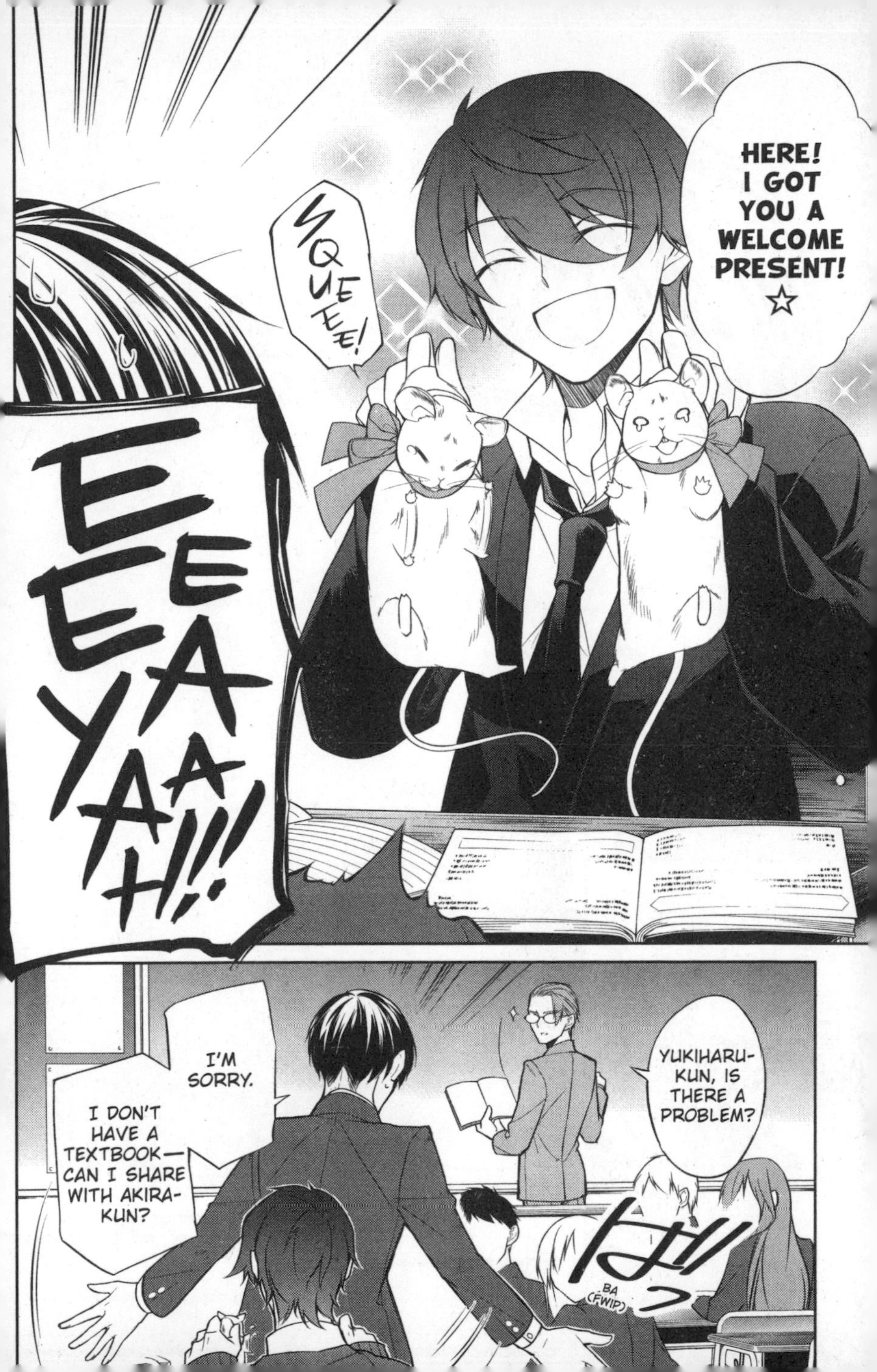
HERE! I GOT YOU A WELCOME PRESENT! ☆
SQUEEE!
EEEYAAAH!!!
YUKIHARU-KUN, IS THERE A PROBLEM?
はっ
BA (FWIP)
I'M SORRY.
I DON'T HAVE A TEXTBOOK— CAN I SHARE WITH AKIRA-KUN?

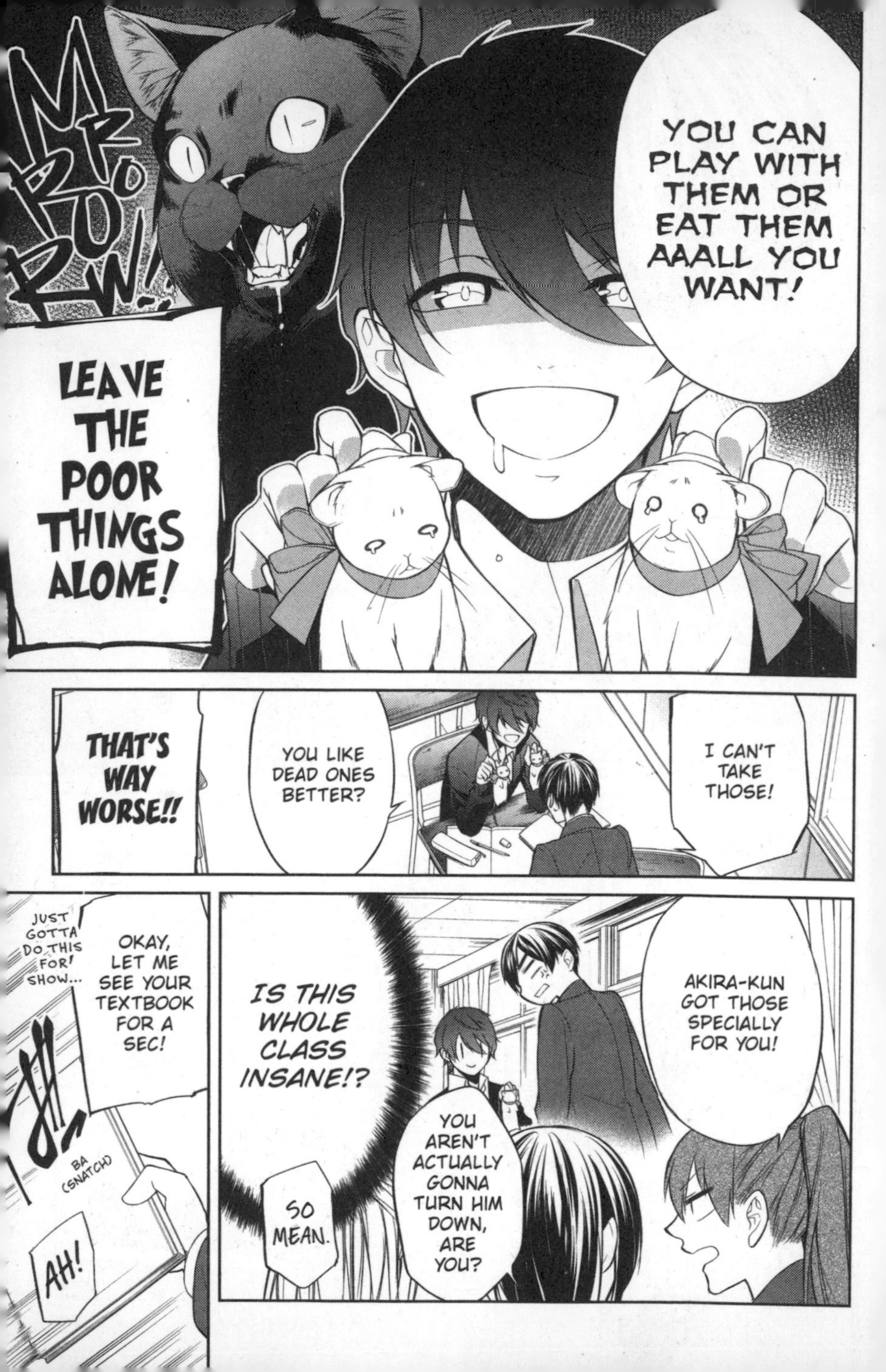
YOU CAN PLAY WITH THEM OR EAT THEM AAALL YOU WANT!
LEAVE THE POOR THINGS ALONE!
I CAN'T TAKE THOSE!
YOU LIKE DEAD ONES BETTER?
THAT'S WAY WORSE!!
AKIRA-KUN GOT THOSE SPECIALLY FOR YOU!
YOU AREN'T ACTUALLY GONNA TURN HIM DOWN, ARE YOU?
IS THIS WHOLE CLASS INSANE!?
SO MEAN.
OKAY, LET ME SEE YOUR TEXTBOOK FOR A SEC!
JUST GOTTA DO THIS FOR SHOW...
BA (SNATCH)
AH!

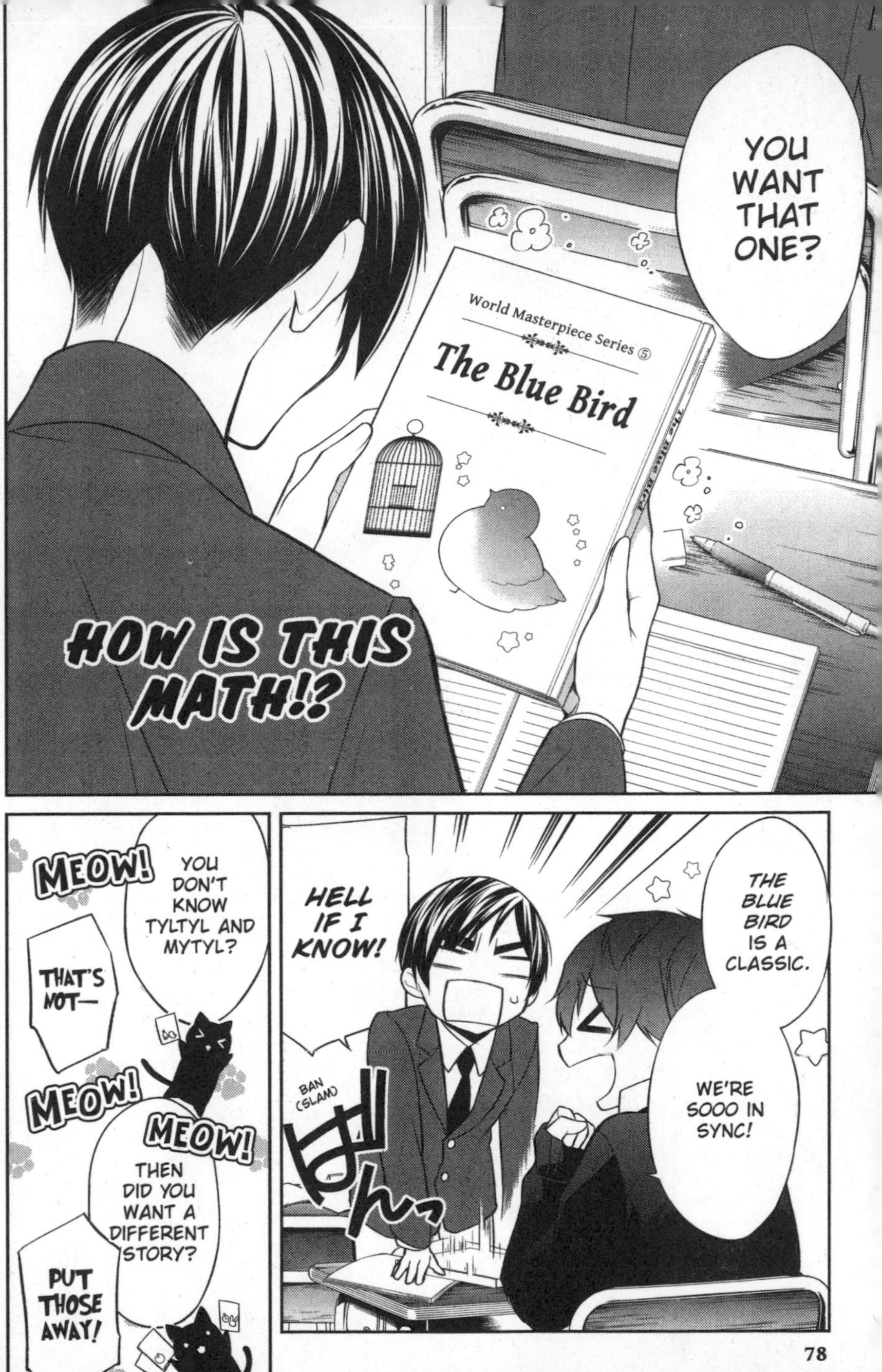
YOU WANT THAT ONE?
World Masterpiece Series ⑤
The Blue Bird
The Blue Bird
HOW IS THIS MATH!?
THE BLUE BIRD IS A CLASSIC.
WE'RE SOOO IN SYNC!
HELL IF I KNOW!
BAN (SLAM)
YOU DON'T KNOW TYLTYL AND MYTYL?
MEOW!
THAT'S NOT—
MEOW!
MEOW!
THEN DID YOU WANT A DIFFERENT STORY?
PUT THOSE AWAY!

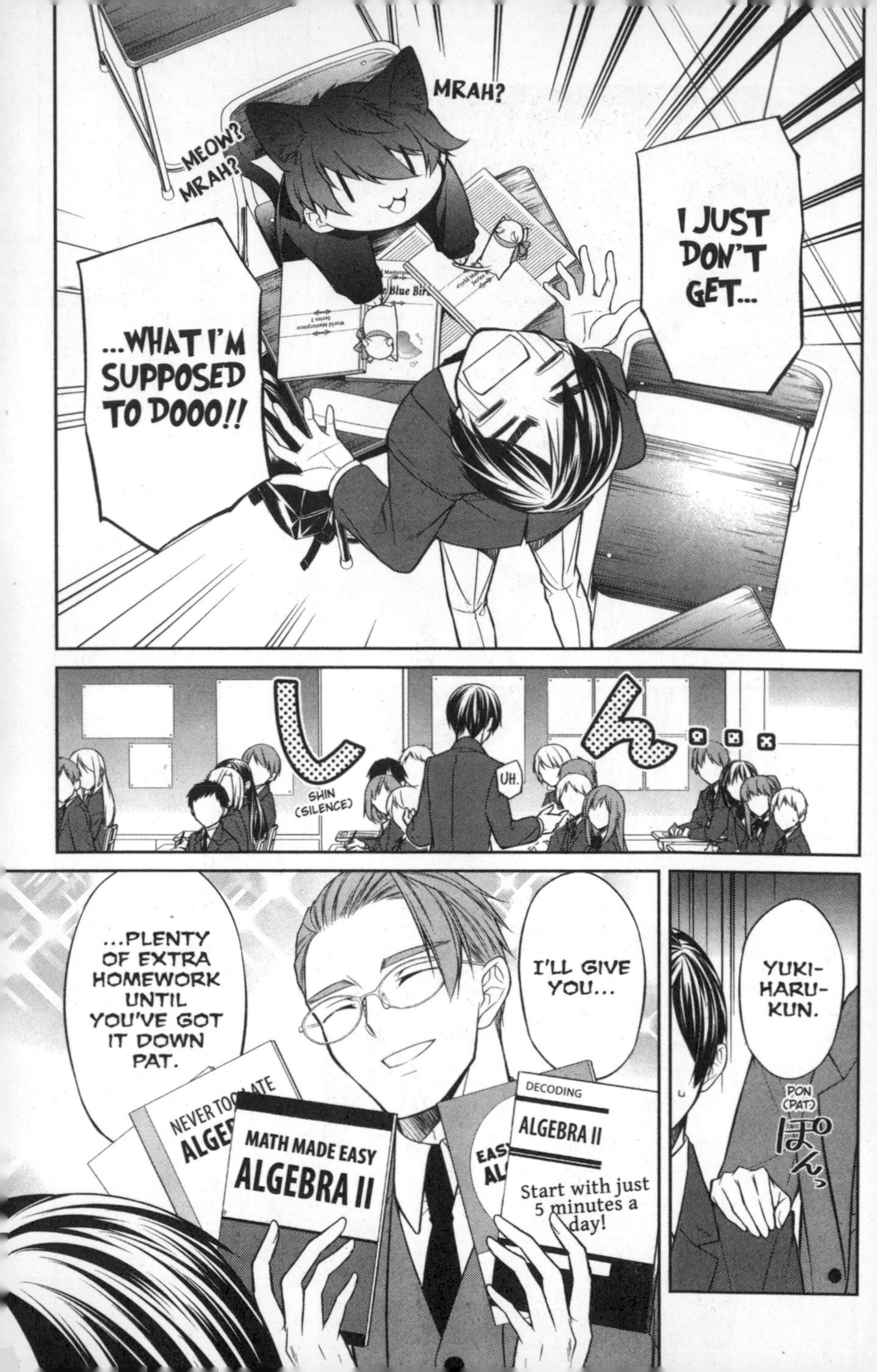
I JUST DON'T GET...
MRAH?
MEOW? MRAH?
...WHAT I'M SUPPOSED TO DOOO!!
しん...
SHIN (SILENCE)
UH.
YUKI-HARU-KUN.
PON (PAT)
ぽんっ
I'LL GIVE YOU...
...PLENTY OF EXTRA HOMEWORK UNTIL YOU'VE GOT IT DOWN PAT.
DECODING
ALGEBRA II
Start with just 5 minutes a day!
MATH MADE EASY
ALGEBRA II

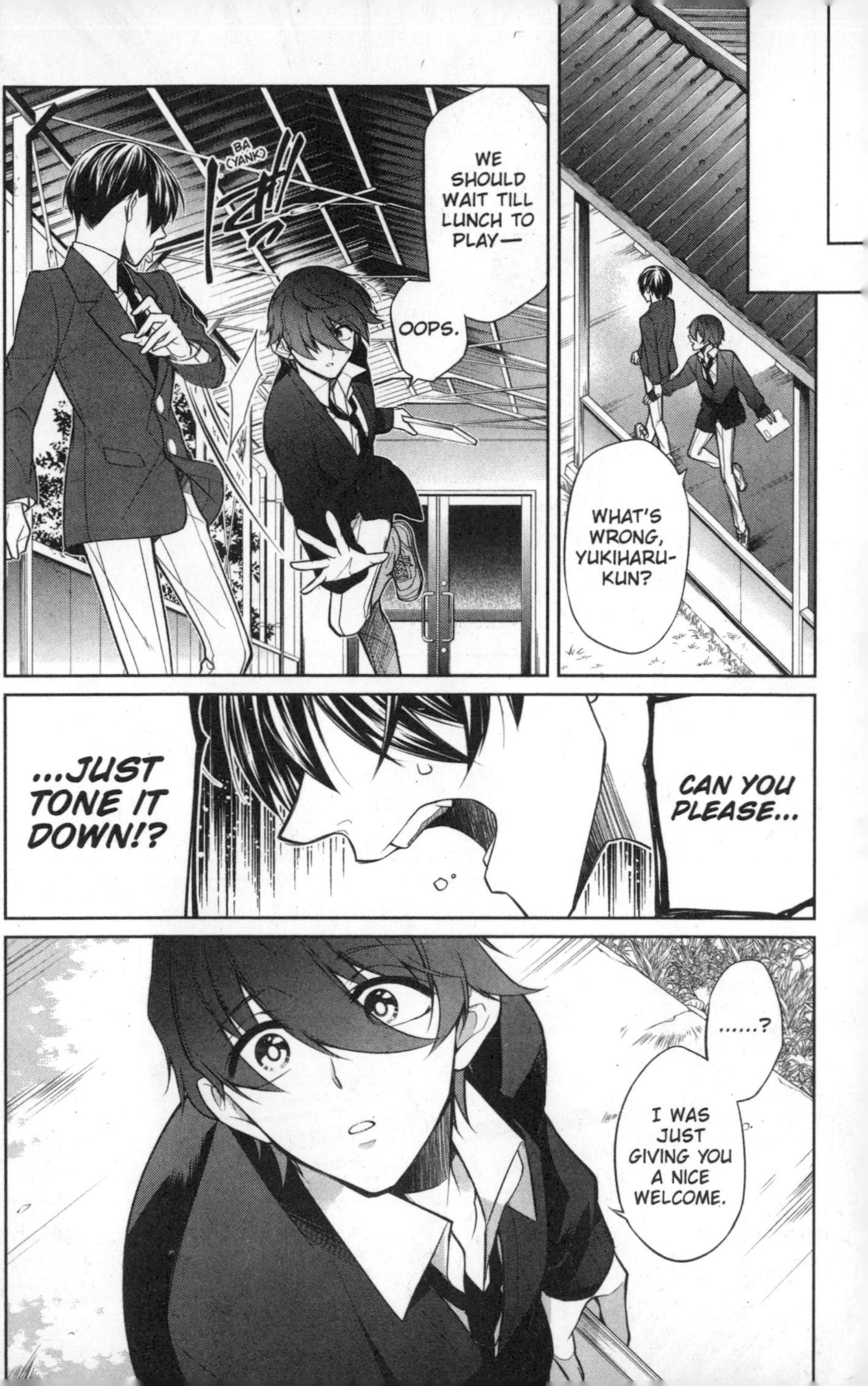
WHAT'S WRONG, YUKIHARU-KUN?
WE SHOULD WAIT TILL LUNCH TO PLAY—
BA (YANK)
OOPS.
CAN YOU PLEASE...
...JUST TONE IT DOWN!?
......?
I WAS JUST GIVING YOU A NICE WELCOME.

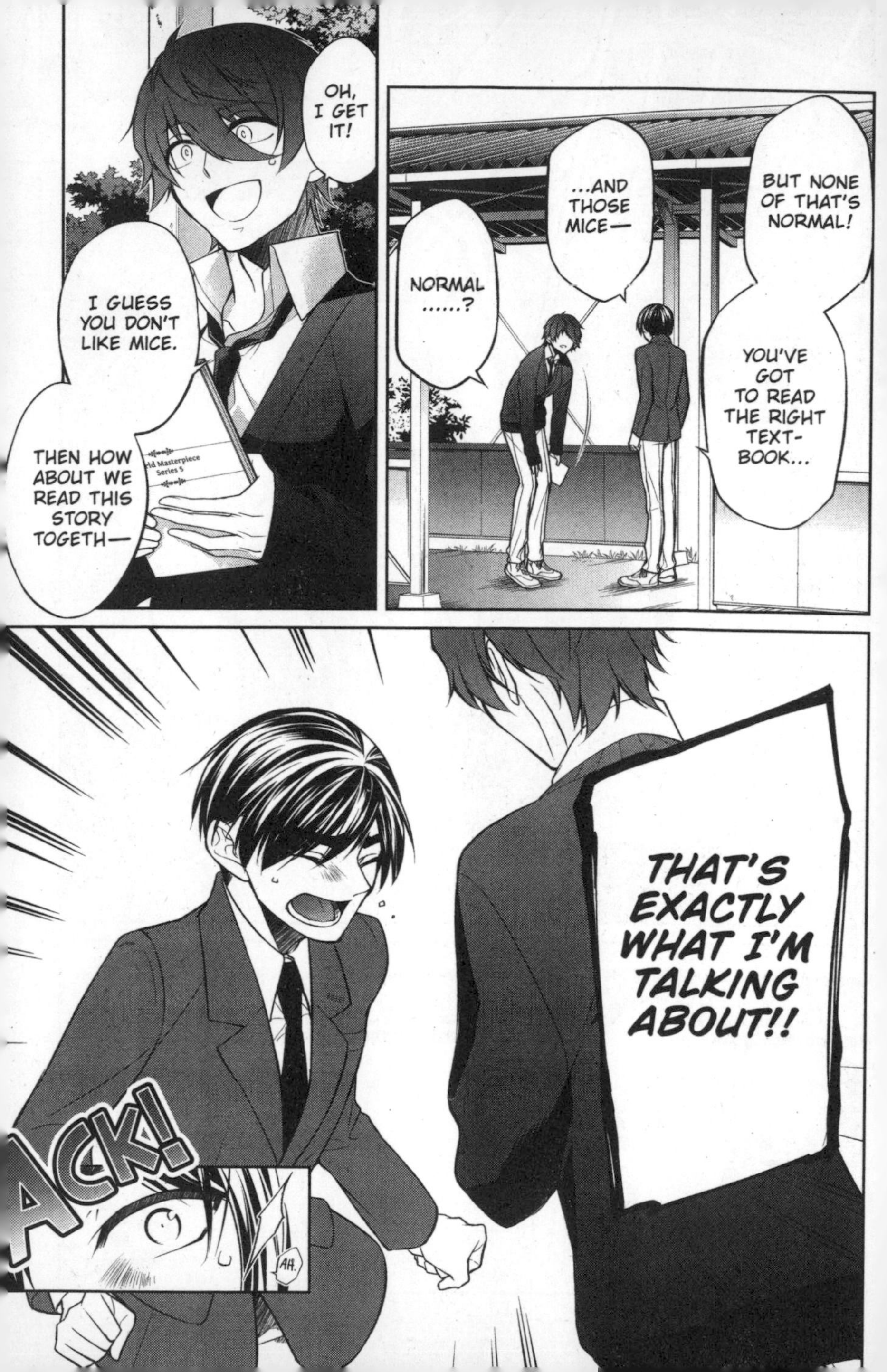
BUT NONE OF THAT'S NORMAL!
YOU'VE GOT TO READ THE RIGHT TEXT-BOOK...
...AND THOSE MICE—
NORMAL......?
OH, I GET IT!
I GUESS YOU DON'T LIKE MICE.
THEN HOW ABOUT WE READ THIS STORY TOGETH—
THAT'S EXACTLY WHAT I'M TALKING ABOUT!!
ACK!
AH.

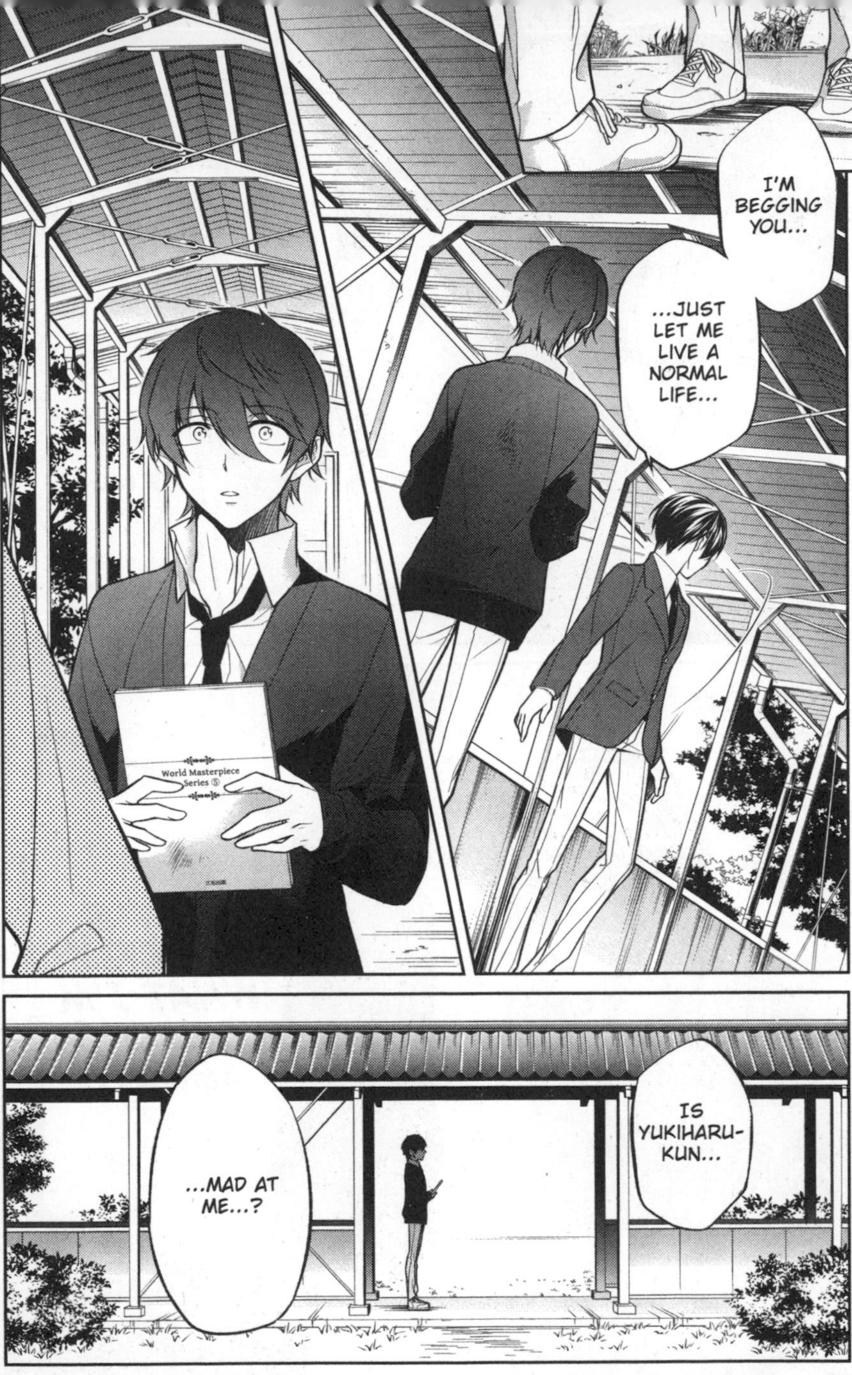
I'M BEGGING YOU...
...JUST LET ME LIVE A NORMAL LIFE...
World Masterpiece Series ⑤
IS YUKIHARU-KUN...
...MAD AT ME...?

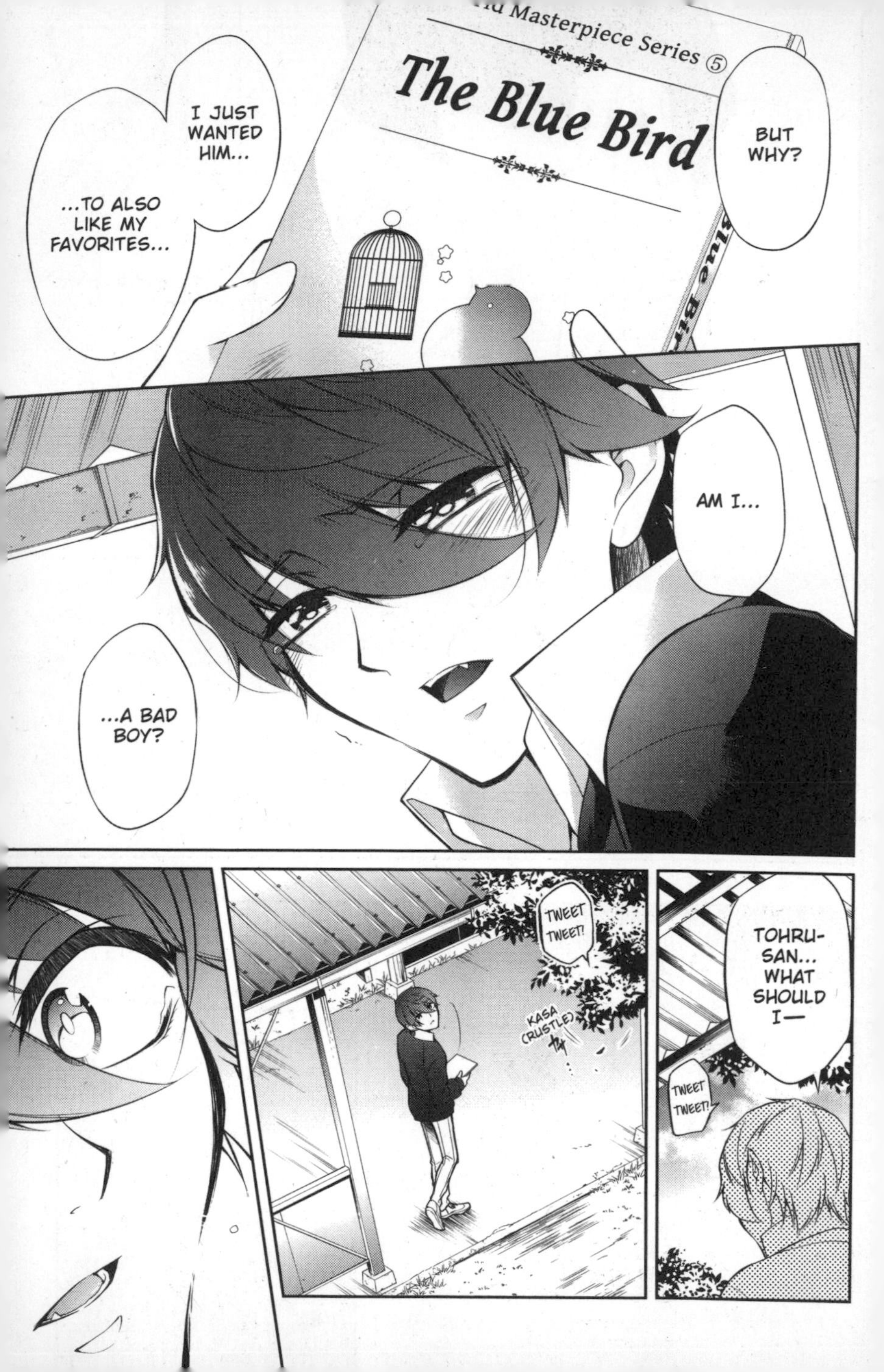Masterpiece Series ⑤
The Blue Bird
BUT WHY?
I JUST WANTED HIM...
...TO ALSO LIKE MY FAVORITES...
AM I...
...A BAD BOY?
TOHRU-SAN... WHAT SHOULD I—
TWEET TWEET!
TWEET TWEET!
KASA (RUSTLE)

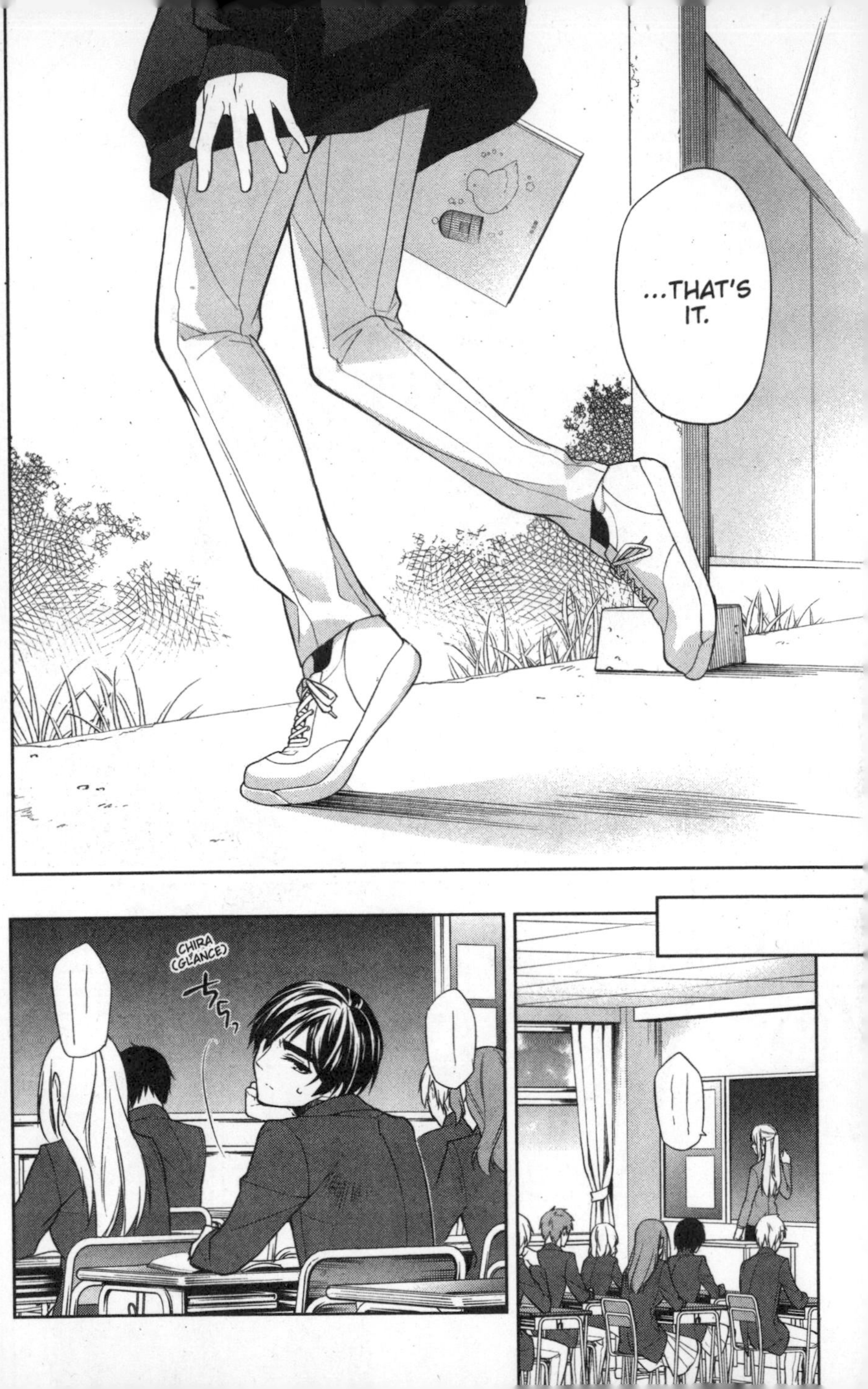
...THAT'S IT.
CHIRA (GLANCE)

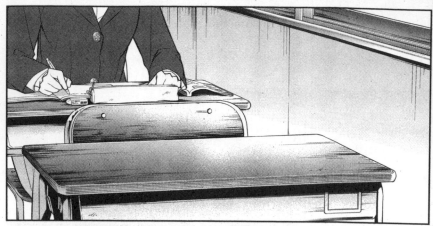

AKIRA-KUN...

...NEVER CAME BACK...

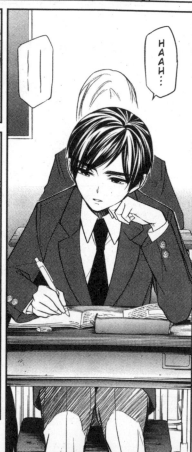

HAAH...

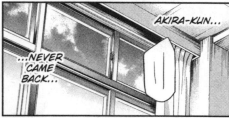

THIS IS SO FUN!

I'M SUPER-DUPER PUMPED!

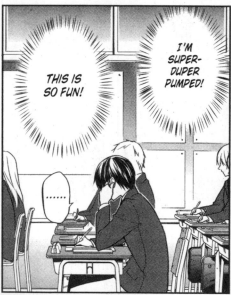

......

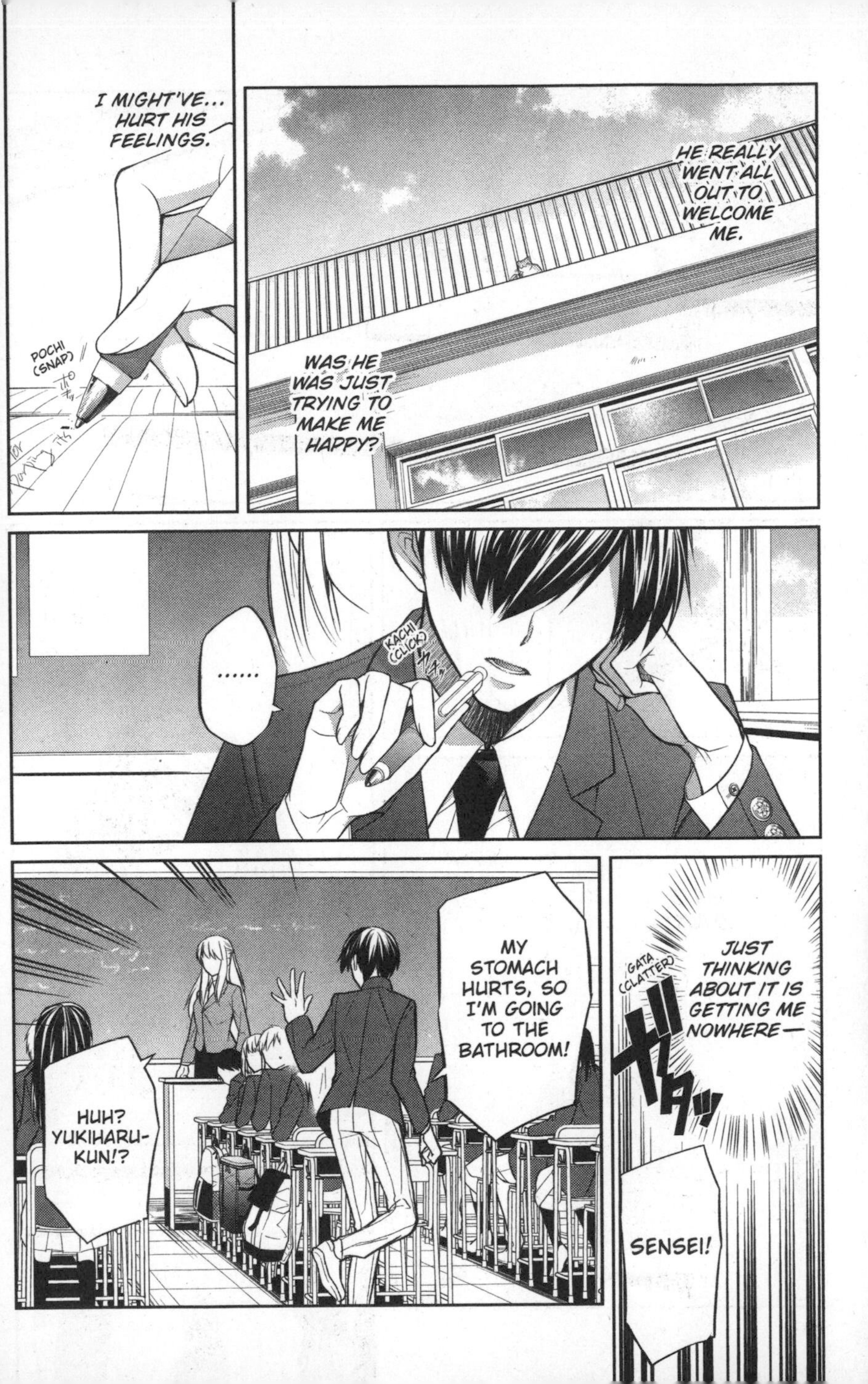
HE REALLY WENT ALL OUT TO WELCOME ME.
WAS HE WAS JUST TRYING TO MAKE ME HAPPY?
I MIGHT'VE... HURT HIS FEELINGS.
POCHI (SNAP)
KACHI (CLICK)
......
JUST THINKING ABOUT IT IS GETTING ME NOWHERE—
GATA (CLATTER)
SENSEI!
MY STOMACH HURTS, SO I'M GOING TO THE BATHROOM!
HUH? YUKIHARU-KUN!?

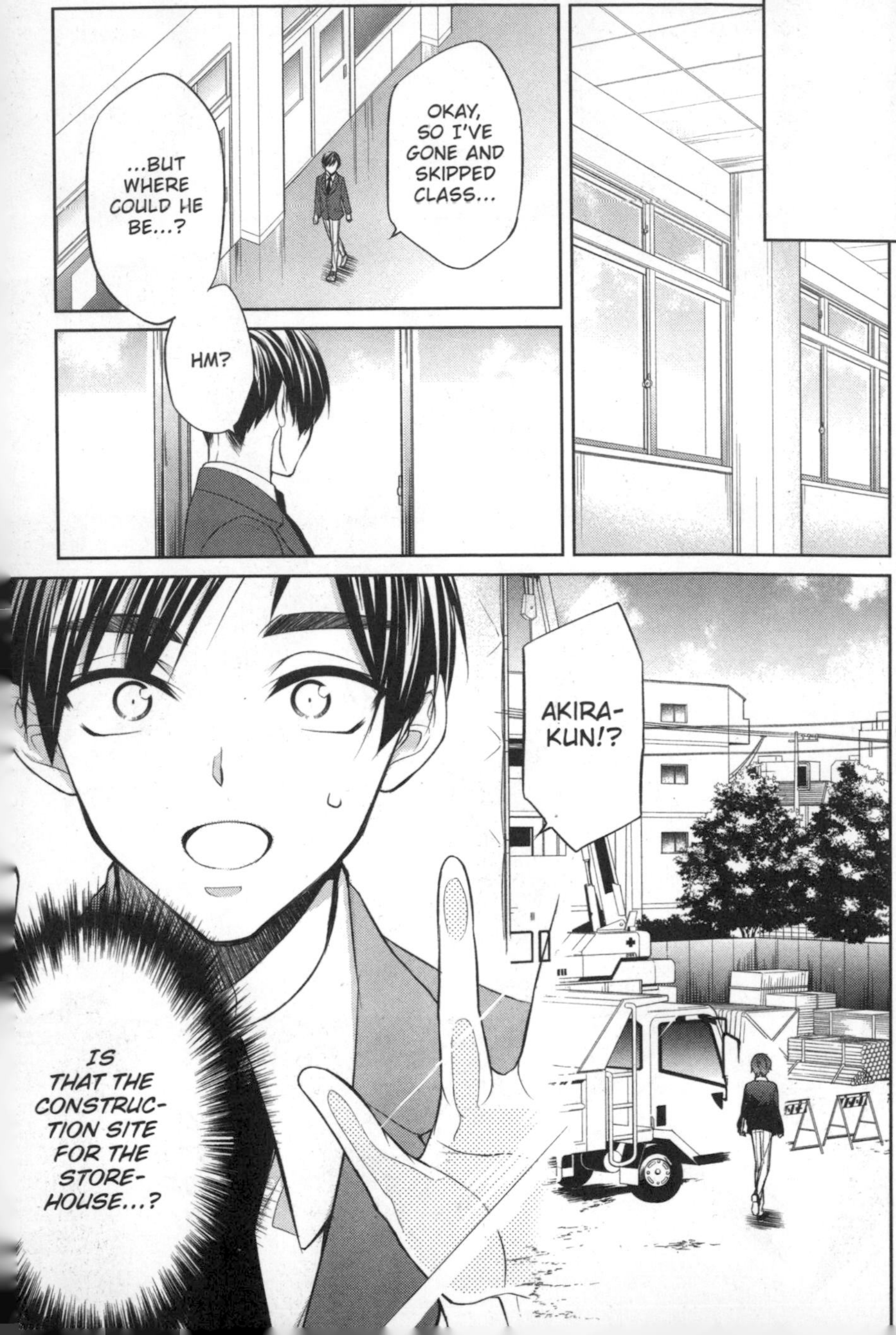
OKAY, SO I'VE GONE AND SKIPPED CLASS...
...BUT WHERE COULD HE BE...?
HM?
AKIRA-KUN!?
IS THAT THE CONSTRUCTION SITE FOR THE STOREHOUSE...?

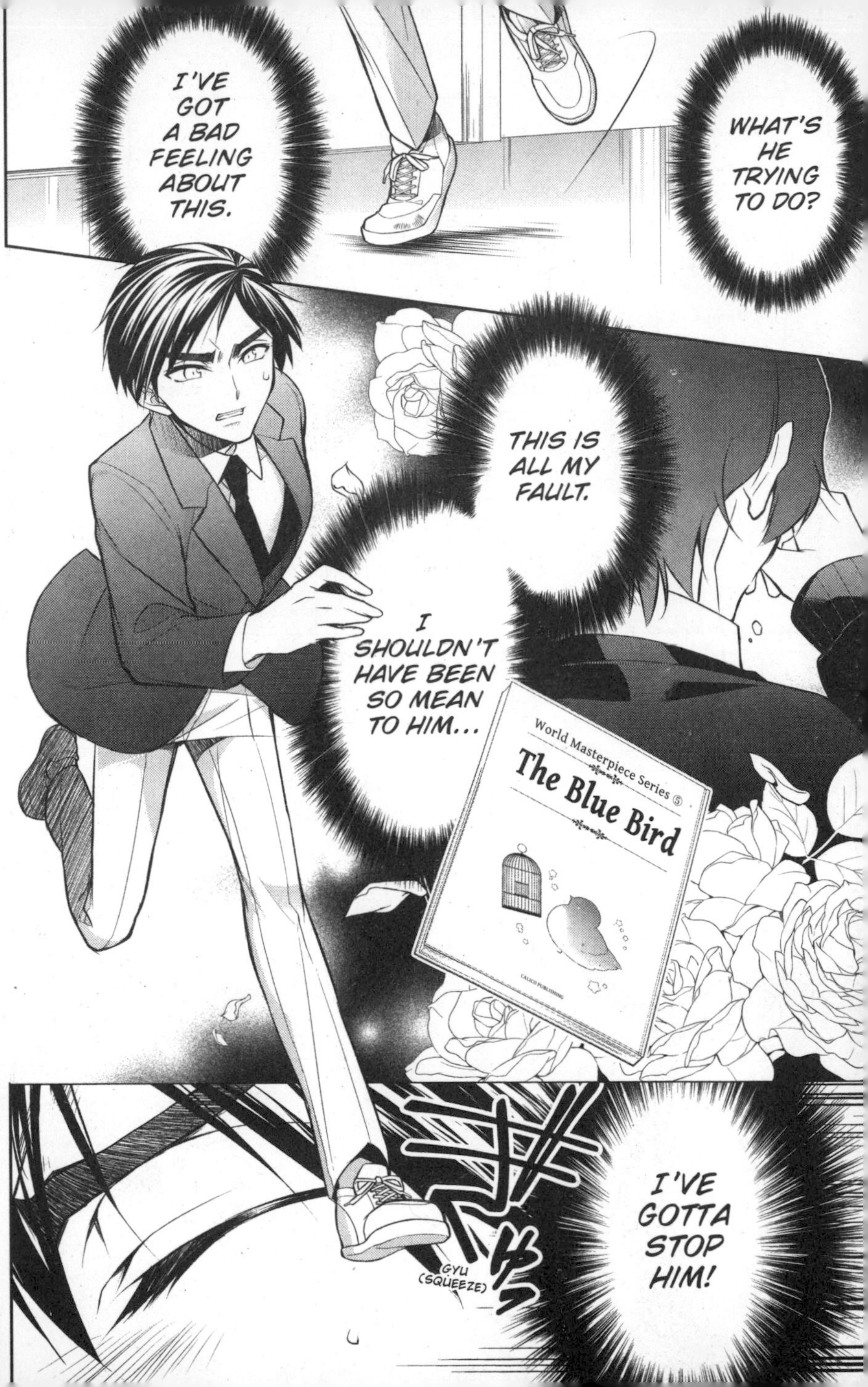
WHAT'S HE TRYING TO DO?
I'VE GOT A BAD FEELING ABOUT THIS.
THIS IS ALL MY FAULT.
I SHOULDN'T HAVE BEEN SO MEAN TO HIM...
World Masterpiece Series 5
The Blue Bird
CALICO PUBLISHING
I'VE GOTTA STOP HIM!
GYU (SQUEEZE)

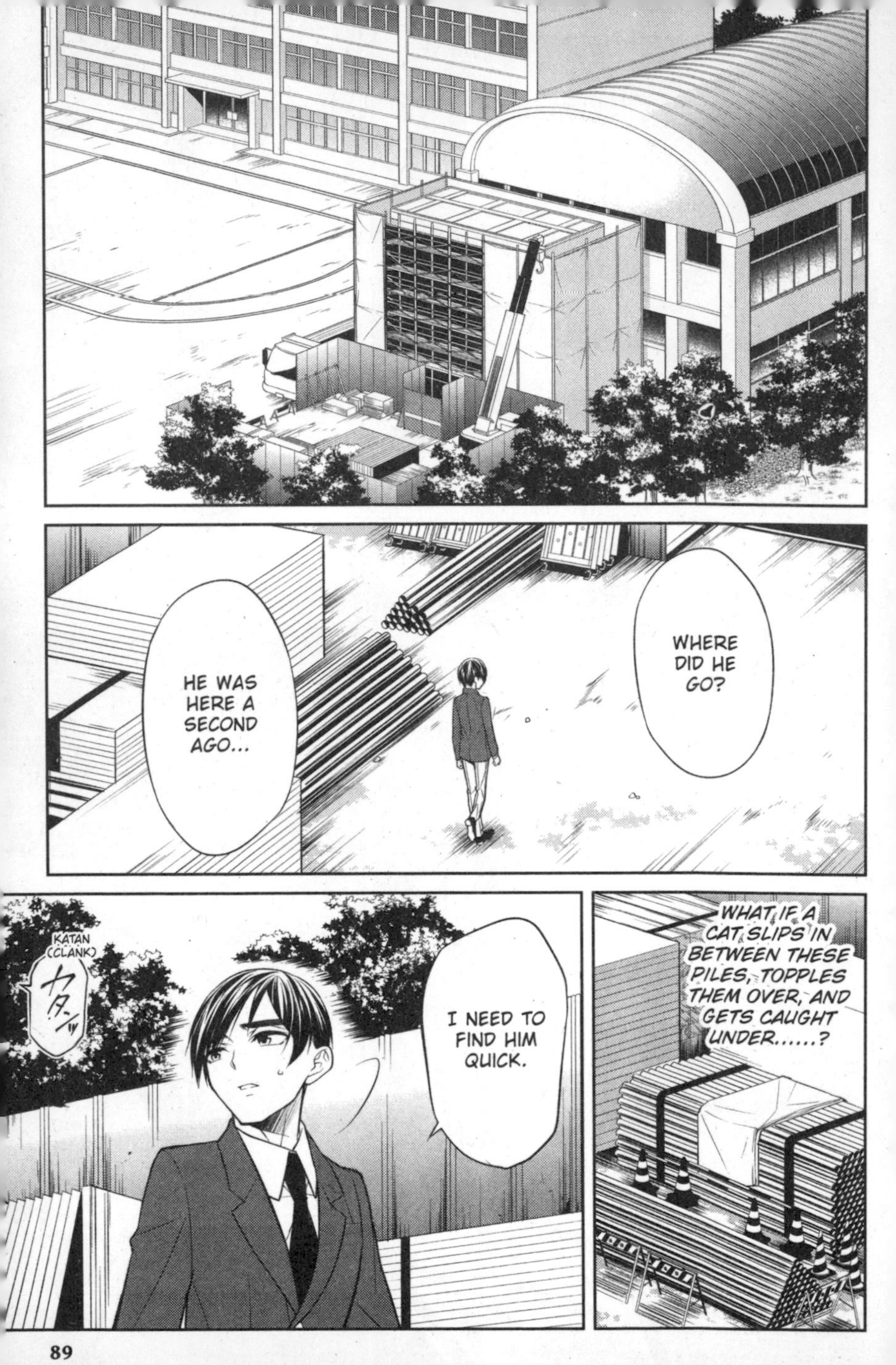
WHERE DID HE GO?
HE WAS HERE A SECOND AGO...
WHAT IF A CAT SLIPS IN BETWEEN THESE PILES, TOPPLES THEM OVER, AND GETS CAUGHT UNDER......?
I NEED TO FIND HIM QUICK.
KATAN (CLANK)

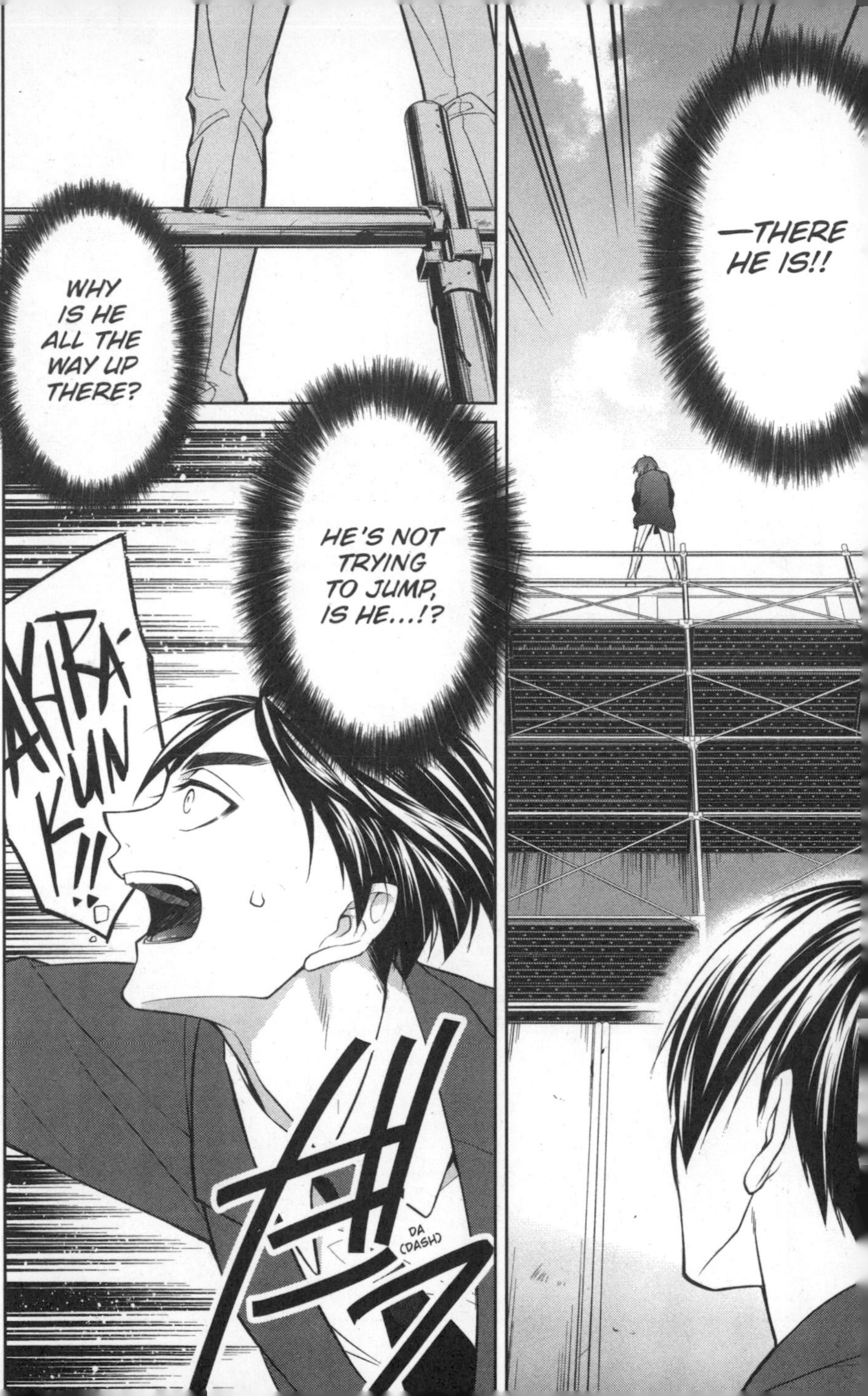
—THERE HE IS!!
WHY IS HE ALL THE WAY UP THERE?
HE'S NOT TRYING TO JUMP, IS HE...!?
AKIRA-KUN!!
DA (DASH)

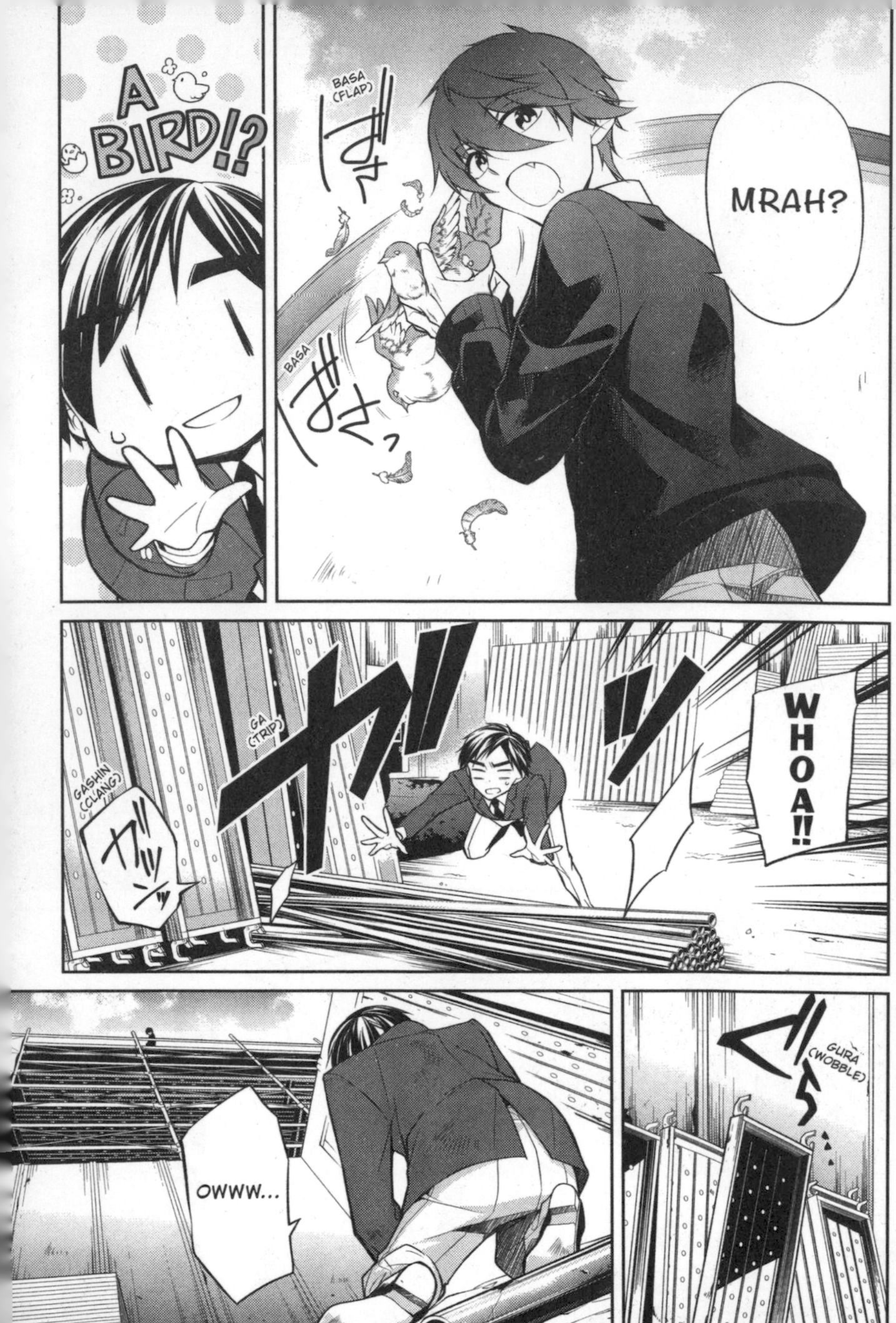
MRAH?
BASA (FLAP)
BASA
A BIRD!?
WHOA!!
GA (TRIP)
GASHIN (CLANG)
GURA (WOBBLE)
OWWW...

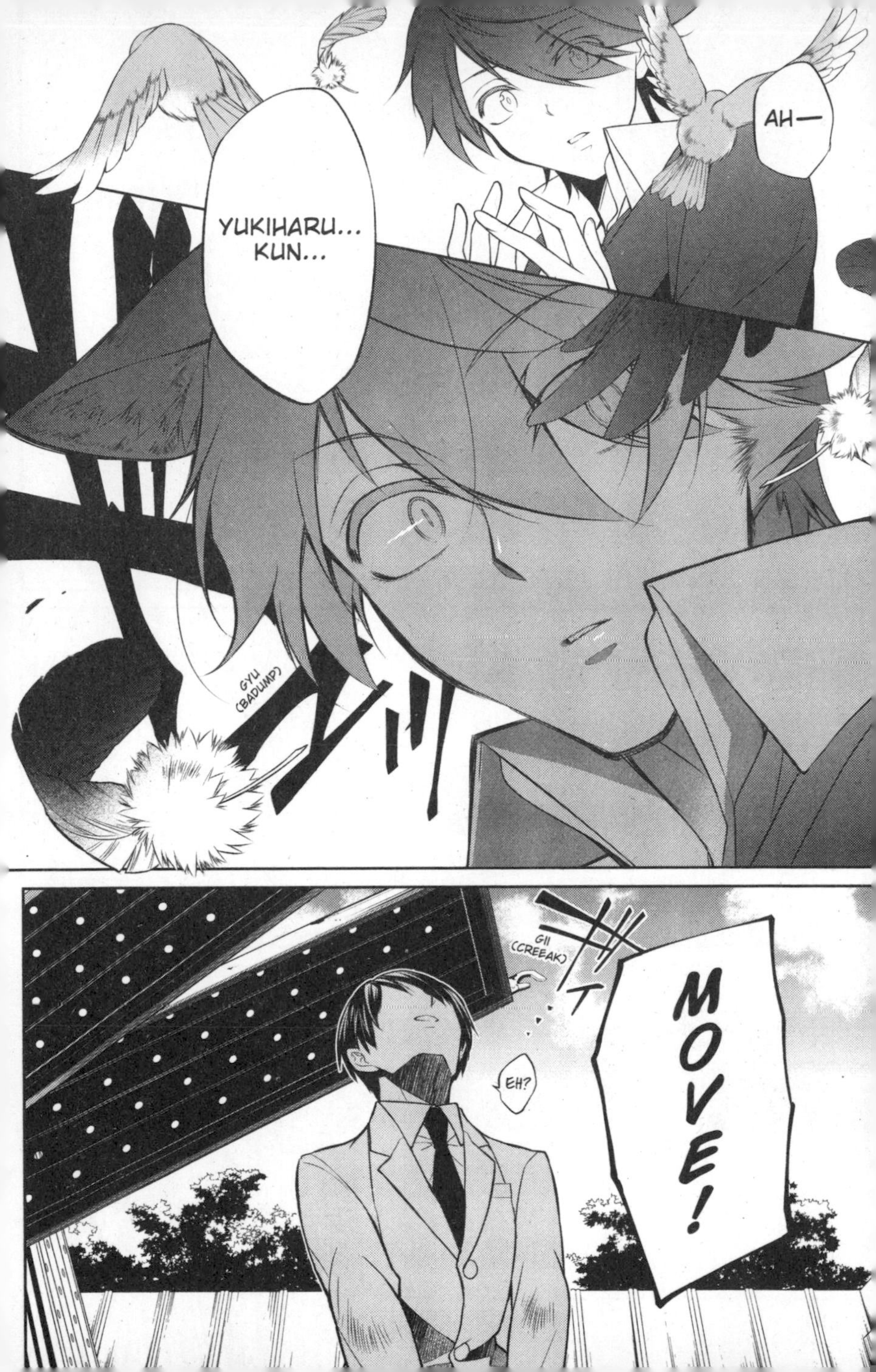
AH—
YUKIHARU... KUN...
GYU (BADUMP)
GII (CREEAK)
MOVE!
EH?

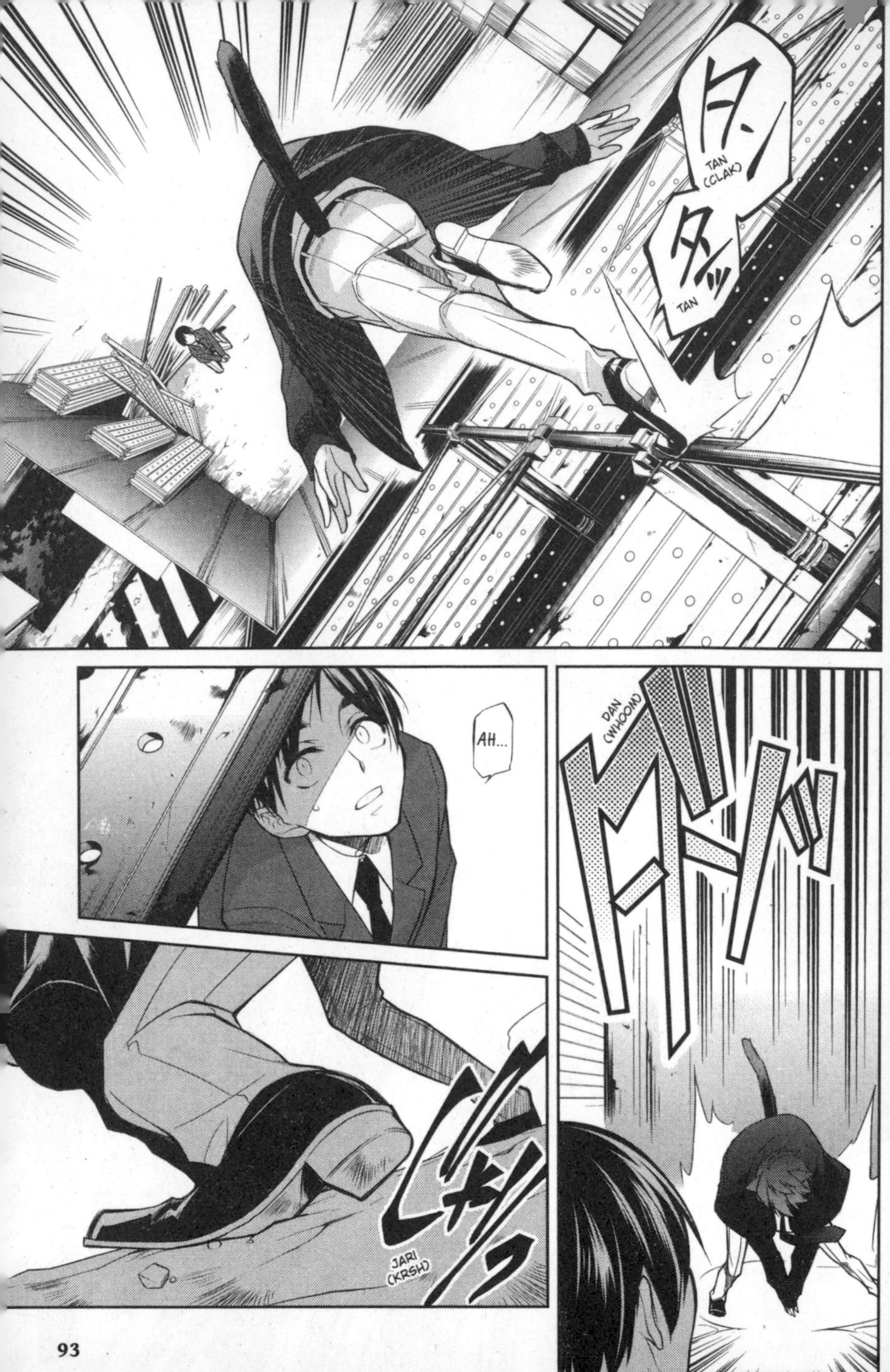
TAN (CLAK)
TAN
DAN (WHOOM)
AH...
JARI (KRSH)

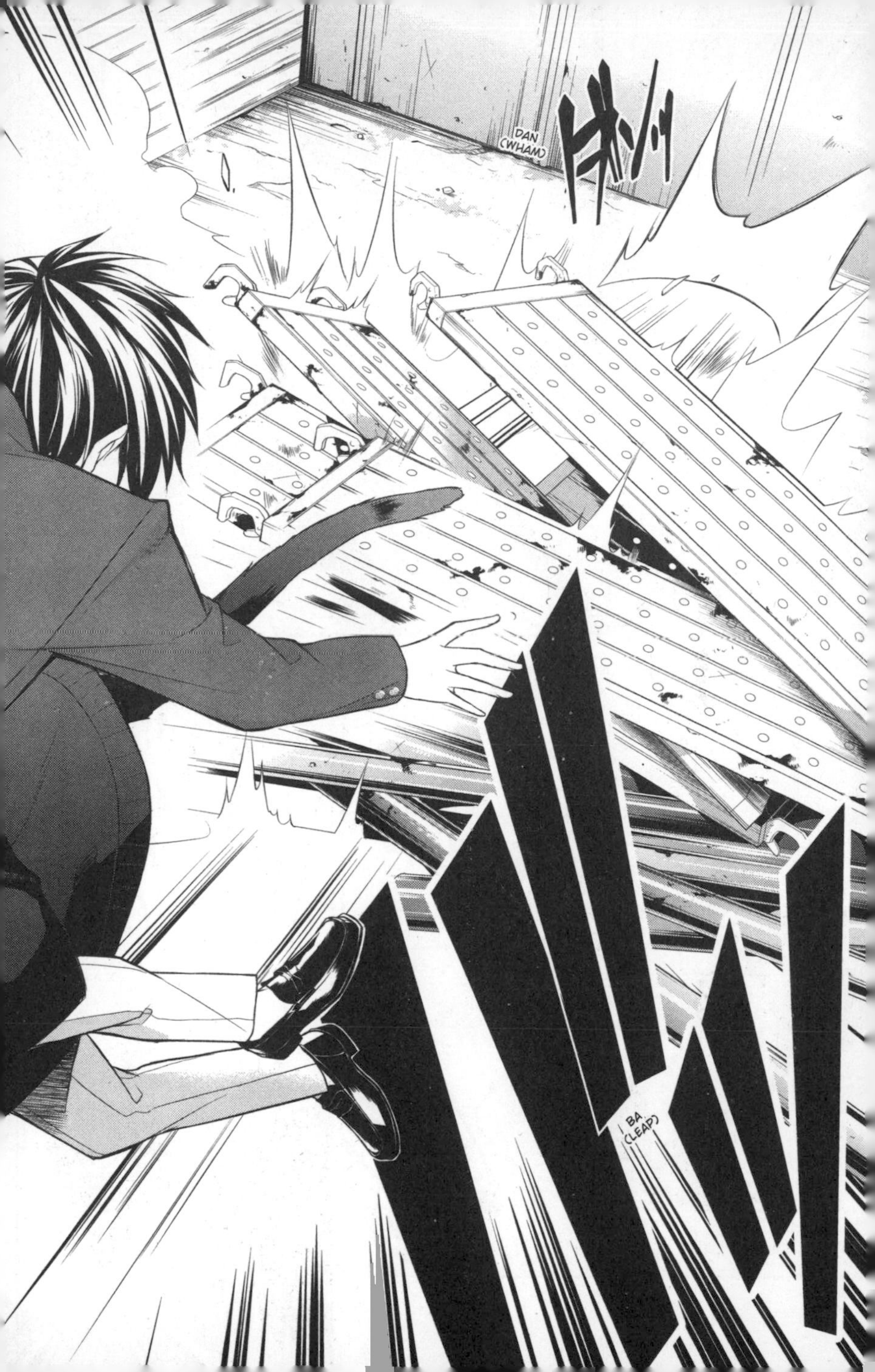
DAN (WHAM)
ドガンッ
BA (LEAP)

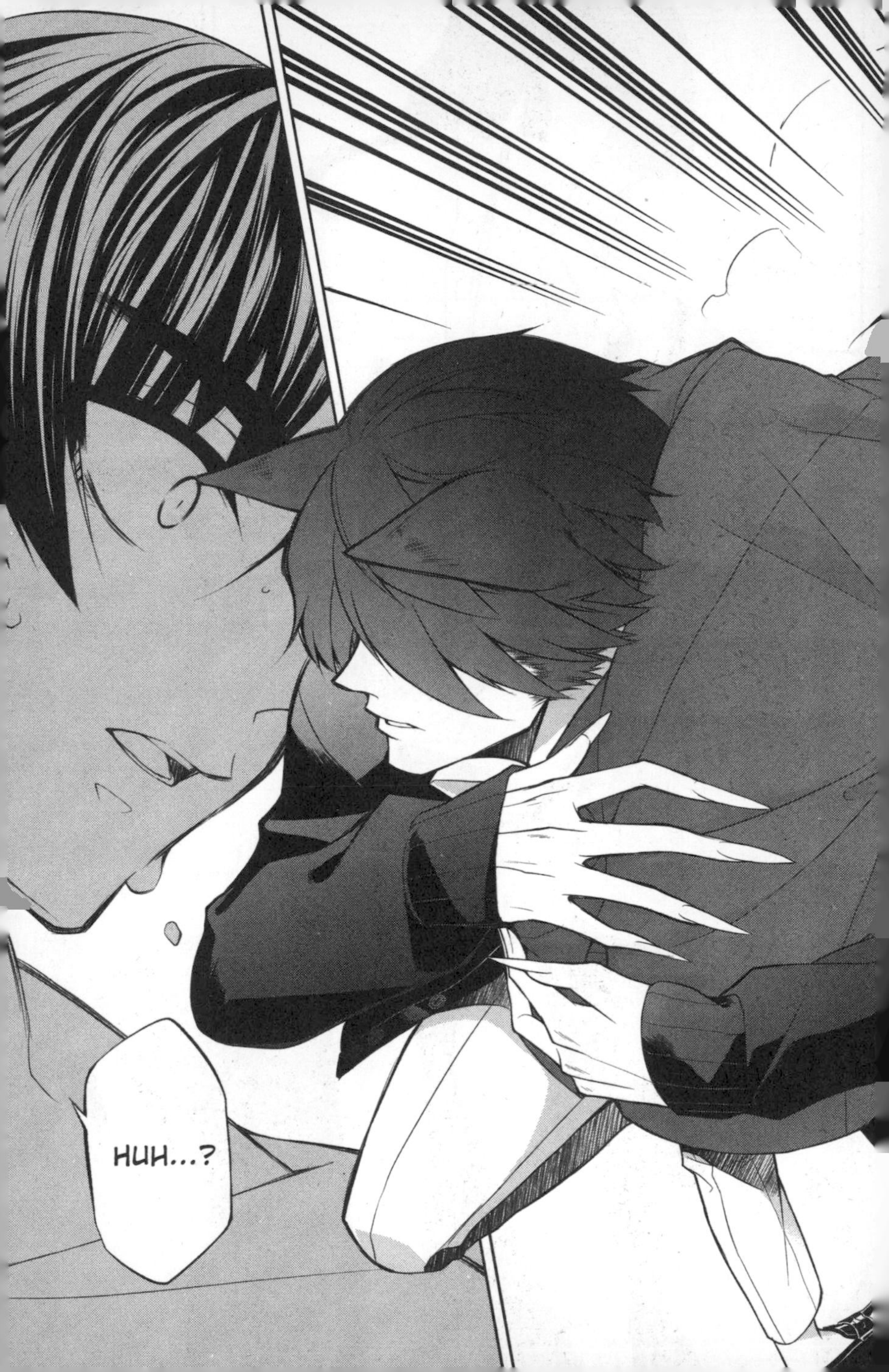
HUH...?

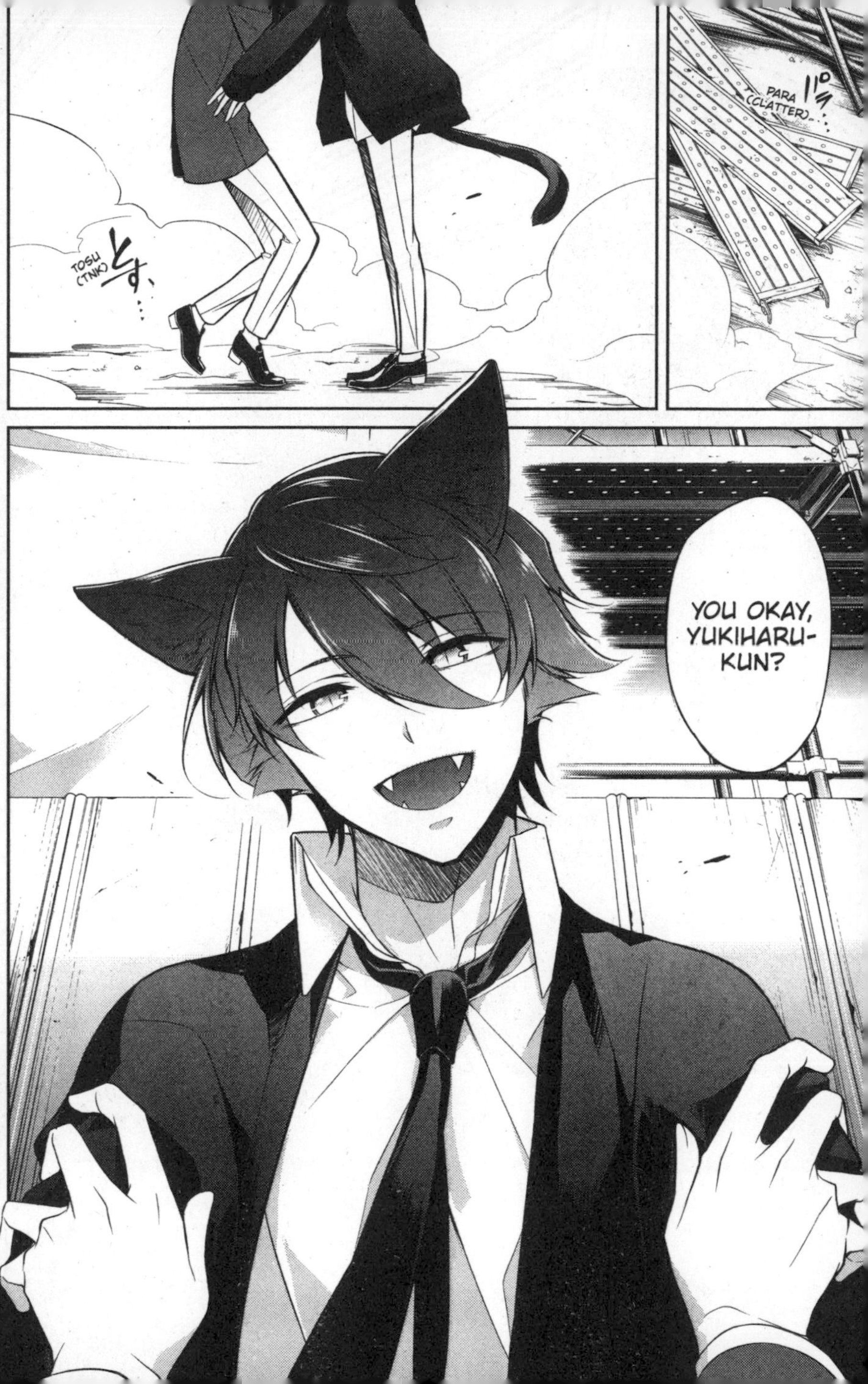
パラ
PARA (CLATTER)...
とす、
TOSU (TNK)
YOU OKAY, YUKIHARU-KUN?

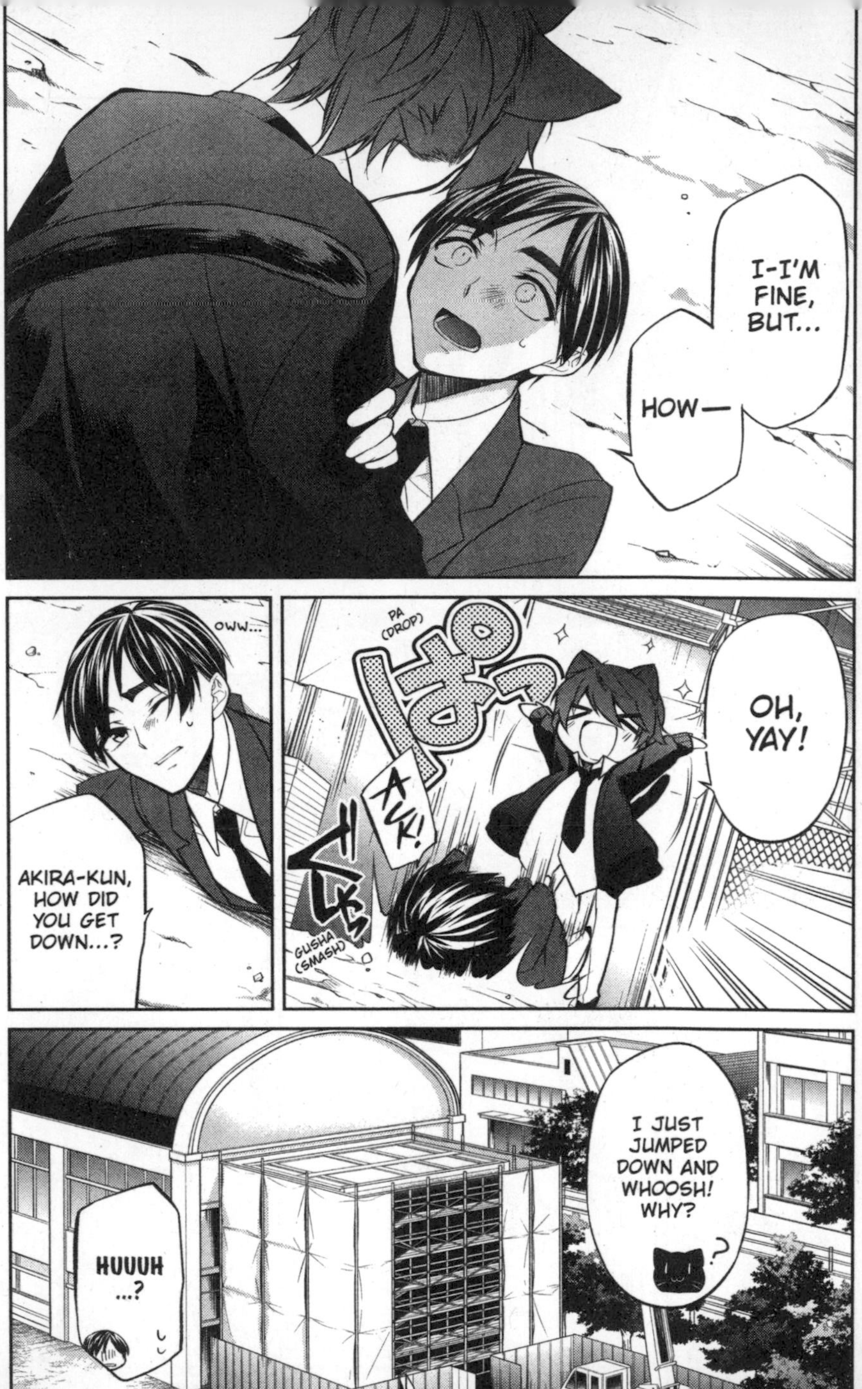
I-I'M FINE, BUT...
HOW—
OH, YAY!
PA (DROP)
ACK!
GUSHA (SMASH)
OWW...
AKIRA-KUN, HOW DID YOU GET DOWN...?
I JUST JUMPED DOWN AND WHOOSH! WHY?
HUUUH ...?

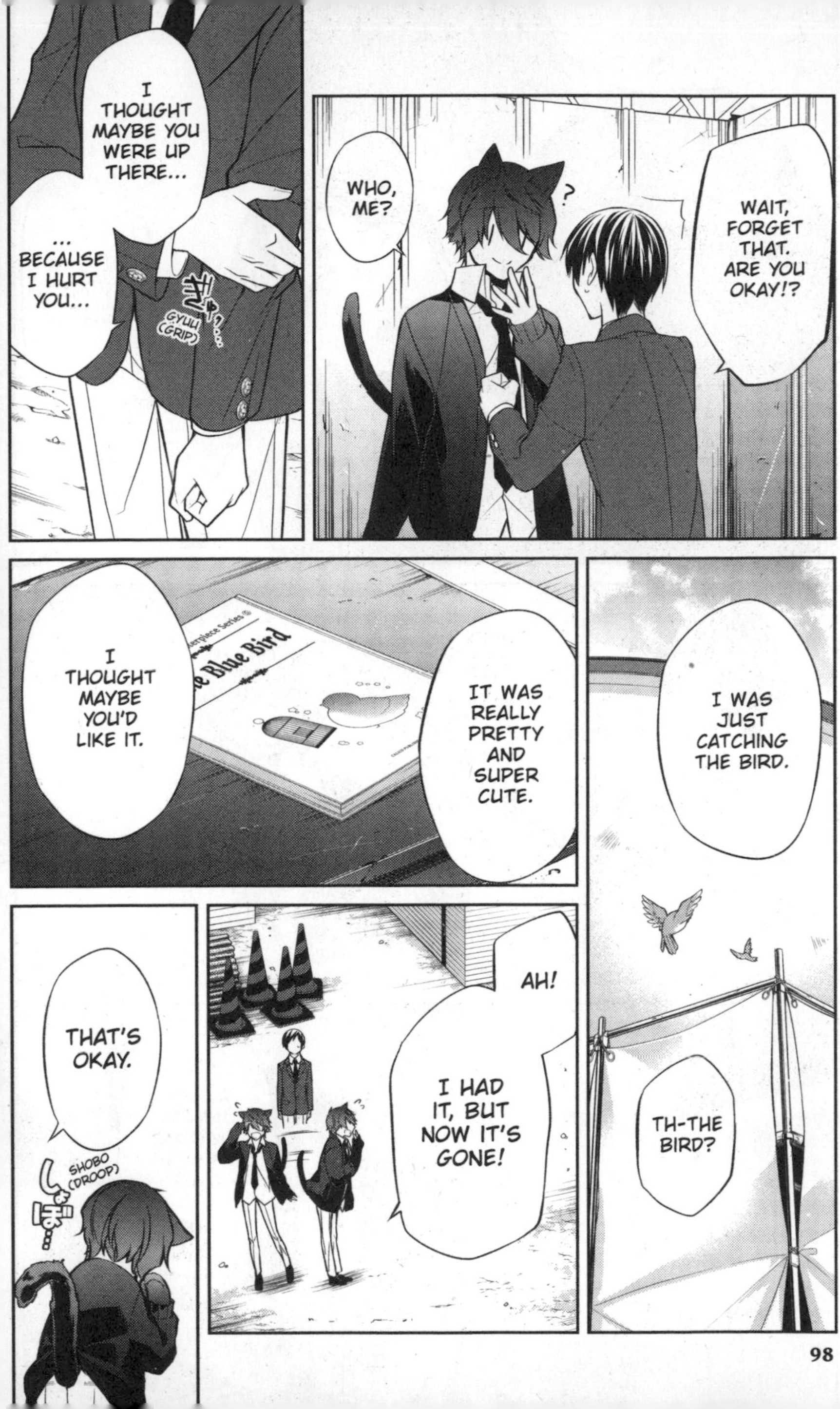
WAIT, FORGET THAT. ARE YOU OKAY!?
WHO, ME?
?
I THOUGHT MAYBE YOU WERE UP THERE...
...BECAUSE I HURT YOU...
GYUU (GRIP)
I WAS JUST CATCHING THE BIRD.
TH-THE BIRD?
The Blue Bird
IT WAS REALLY PRETTY AND SUPER CUTE.
I THOUGHT MAYBE YOU'D LIKE IT.
AH!
I HAD IT, BUT NOW IT'S GONE!
THAT'S OKAY.
SHOBO (DROOP)

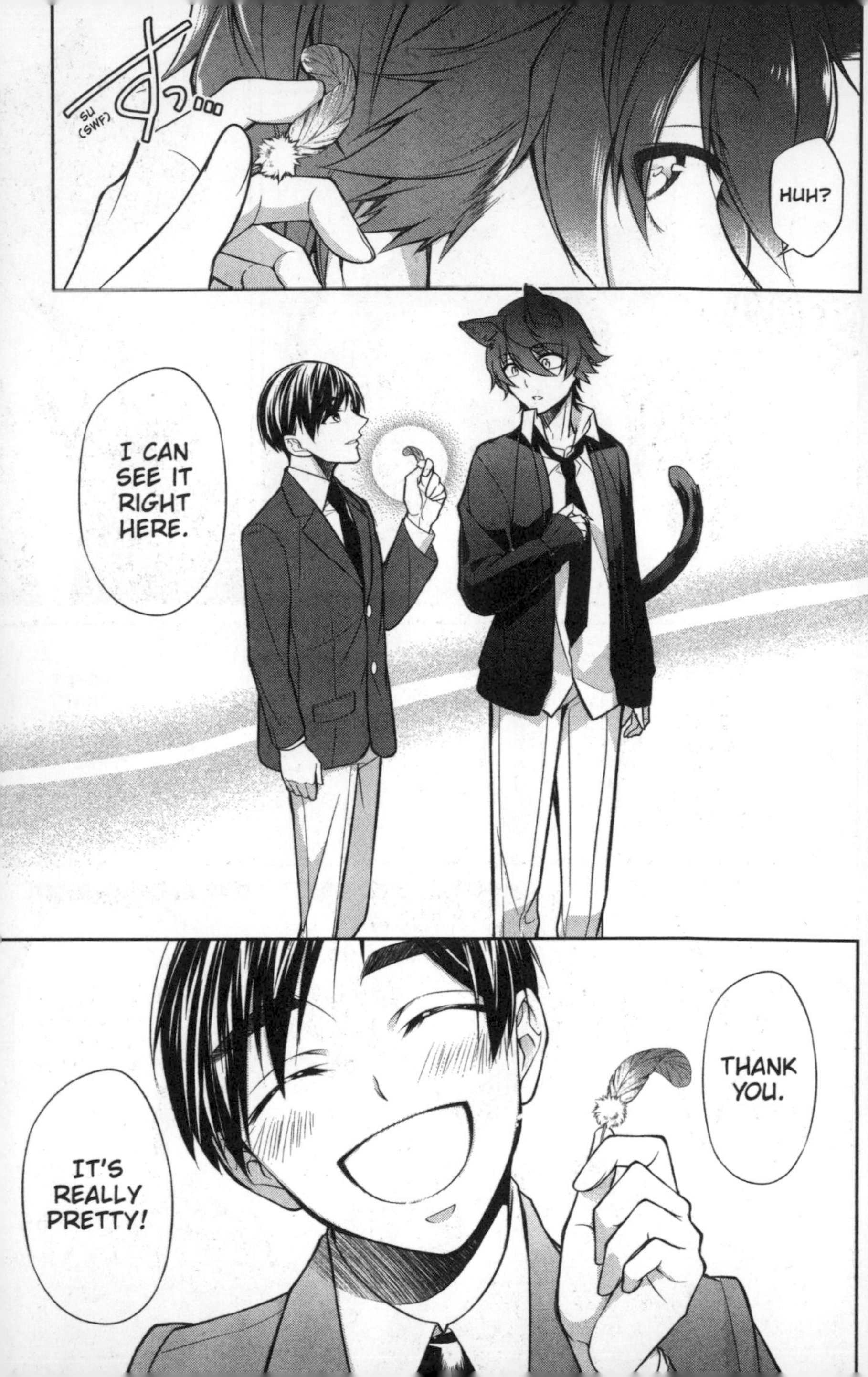
HUH?
すっ…
SU (SWF)
I CAN SEE IT RIGHT HERE.
THANK YOU.
IT'S REALLY PRETTY!

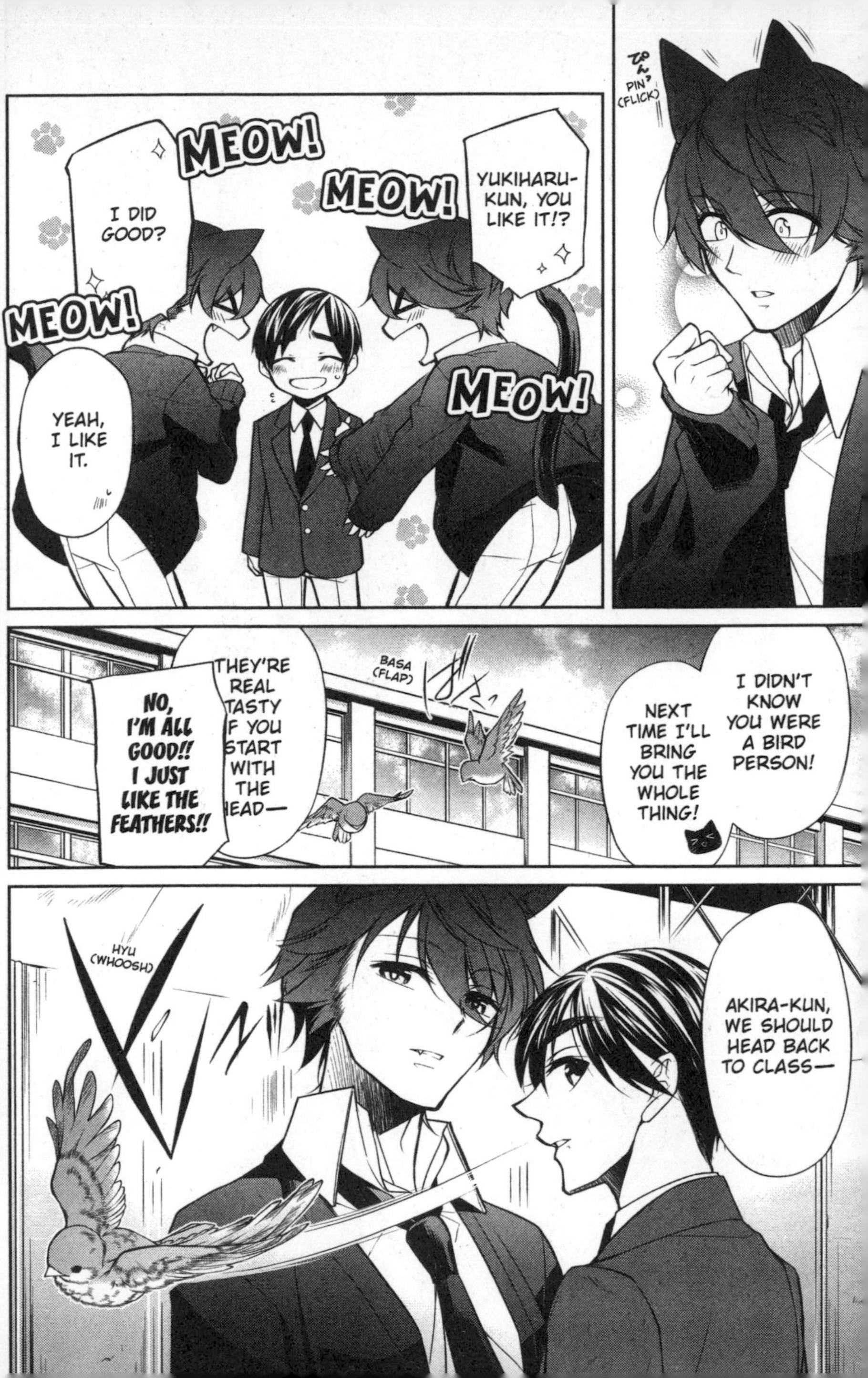

ぴんっ
PIN (FLICK)
MEOW!
YUKIHARU-KUN, YOU LIKE IT!?
MEOW!
I DID GOOD?
MEOW!
MEOW!
YEAH, I LIKE IT.
I DIDN'T KNOW YOU WERE A BIRD PERSON!
NEXT TIME I'LL BRING YOU THE WHOLE THING!
BASA (FLAP)
THEY'RE REAL TASTY F YOU START WITH THE EAD—
NO, I'M ALL GOOD!! I JUST LIKE THE FEATHERS!!
AKIRA-KUN, WE SHOULD HEAD BACK TO CLASS—
HYU (WHOOSH)

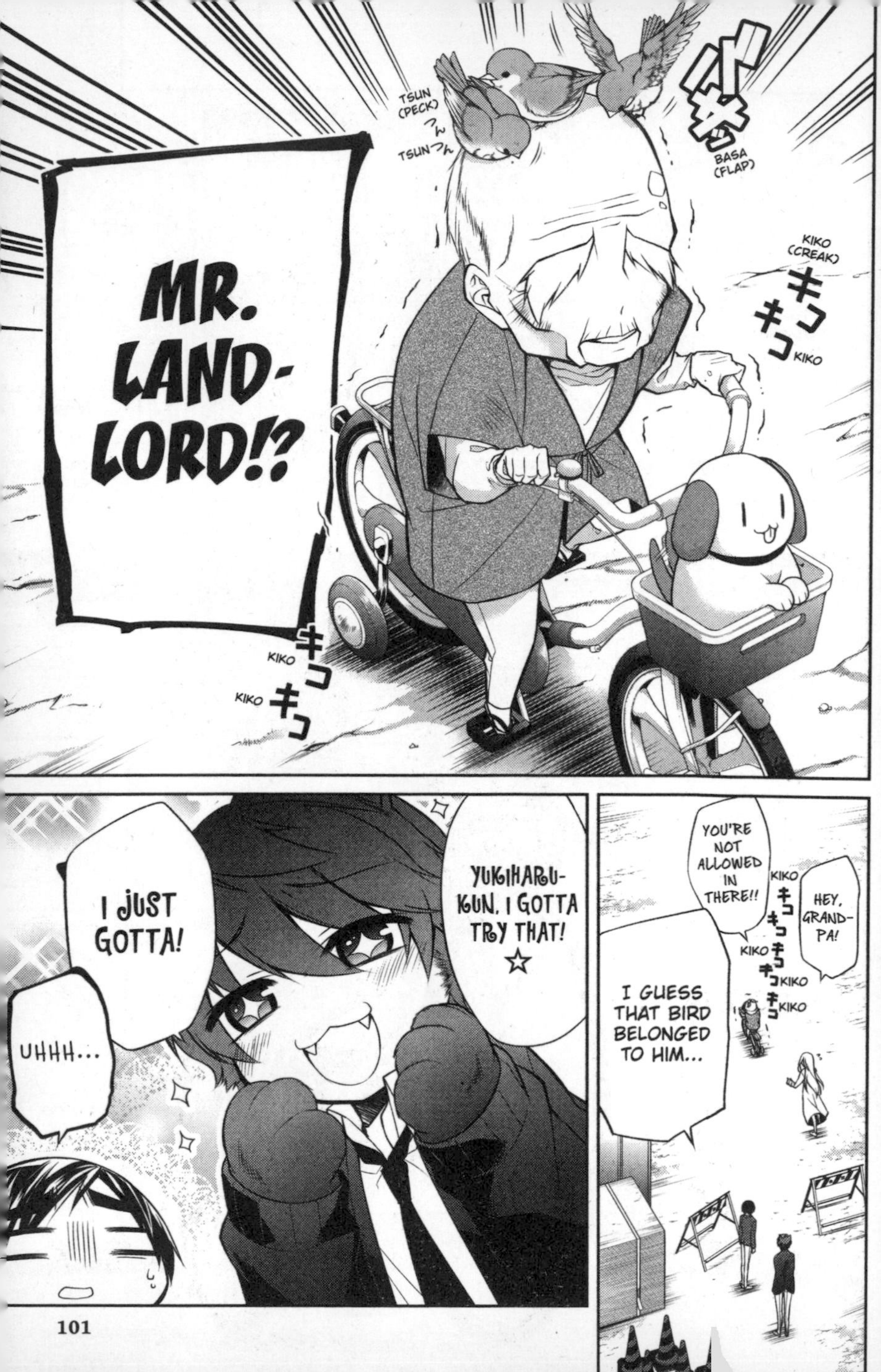

BASA (FLAP)
TSUN (PECK) つん
TSUN つん
KIKO (CREAK) キコ キコ KIKO
MR. LAND-LORD!?
KIKO キコ
KIKO キコ
HEY, GRAND-PA!
YOU'RE NOT ALLOWED IN THERE!!
KIKO キコ キコ
KIKO キコ キコ KIKO キコ KIKO
I GUESS THAT BIRD BELONGED TO HIM...
YUKIHARU-KUN, I GOTTA TRY THAT! ☆
I JUST GOTTA!
UHHH...

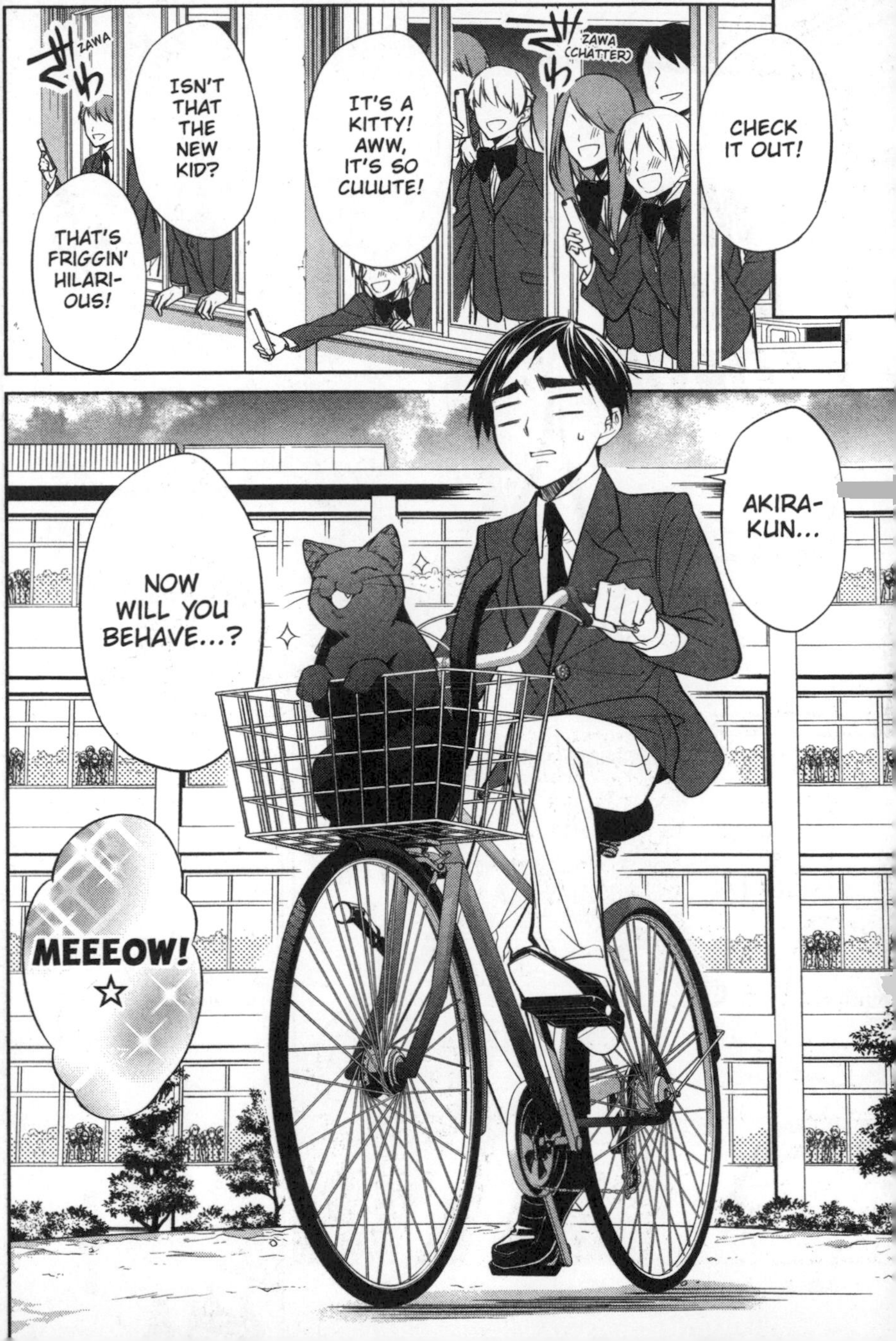
ざわ
ZAWA (CHATTER)
CHECK IT OUT!
IT'S A KITTY! AWW, IT'S SO CUUUTE!
ISN'T THAT THE NEW KID?
ざわ
ZAWA
THAT'S FRIGGIN' HILARIOUS!
AKIRA-KUN...
NOW WILL YOU BEHAVE...?
MEEEOW! ☆

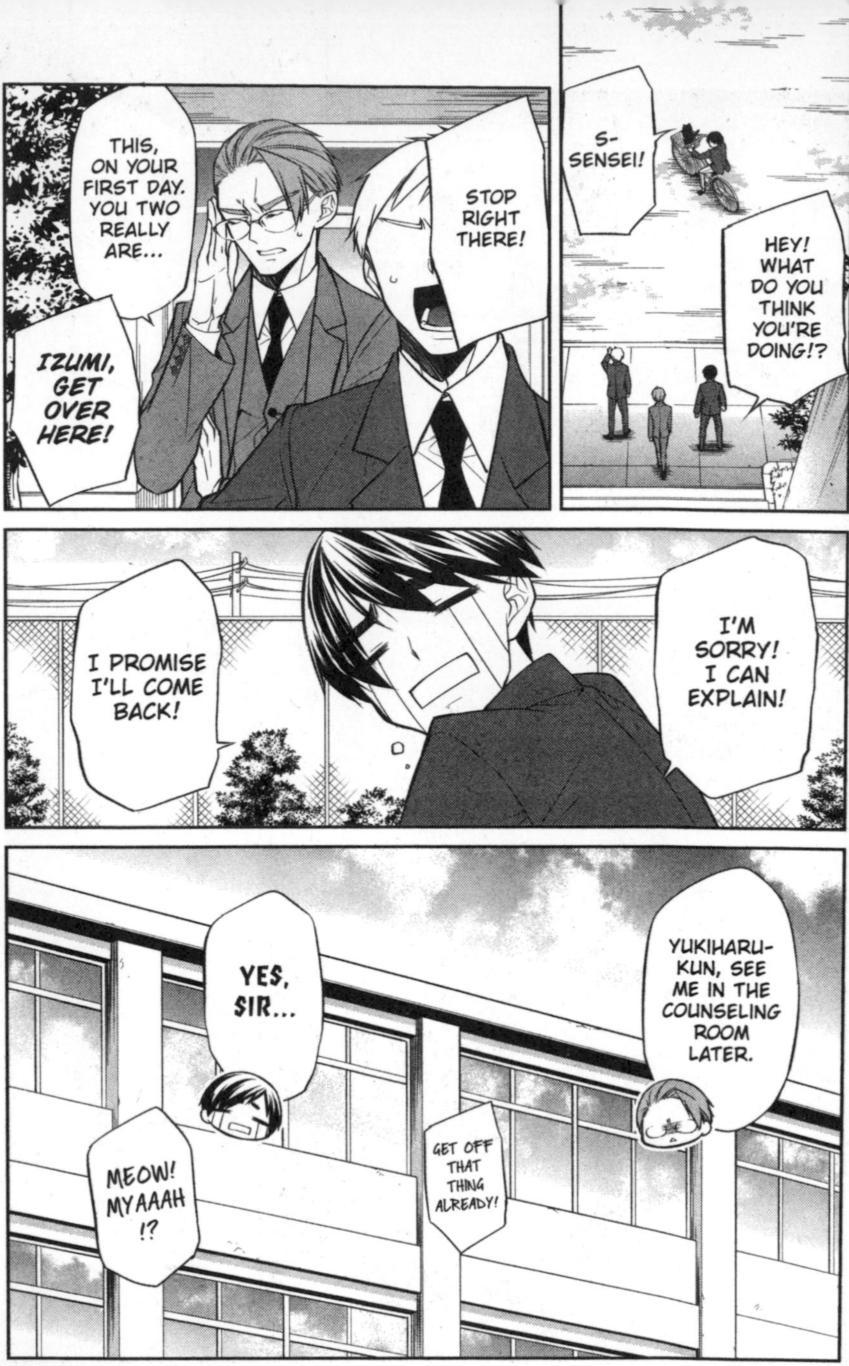
HEY! WHAT DO YOU THINK YOU'RE DOING!?
S-SENSEI!
STOP RIGHT THERE!
THIS, ON YOUR FIRST DAY. YOU TWO REALLY ARE...
IZUMI, GET OVER HERE!
I'M SORRY! I CAN EXPLAIN!
I PROMISE I'LL COME BACK!
YUKIHARU-KUN, SEE ME IN THE COUNSELING ROOM LATER.
YES, SIR...
GET OFF THAT THING ALREADY!
MEOW! MYAAAH !?

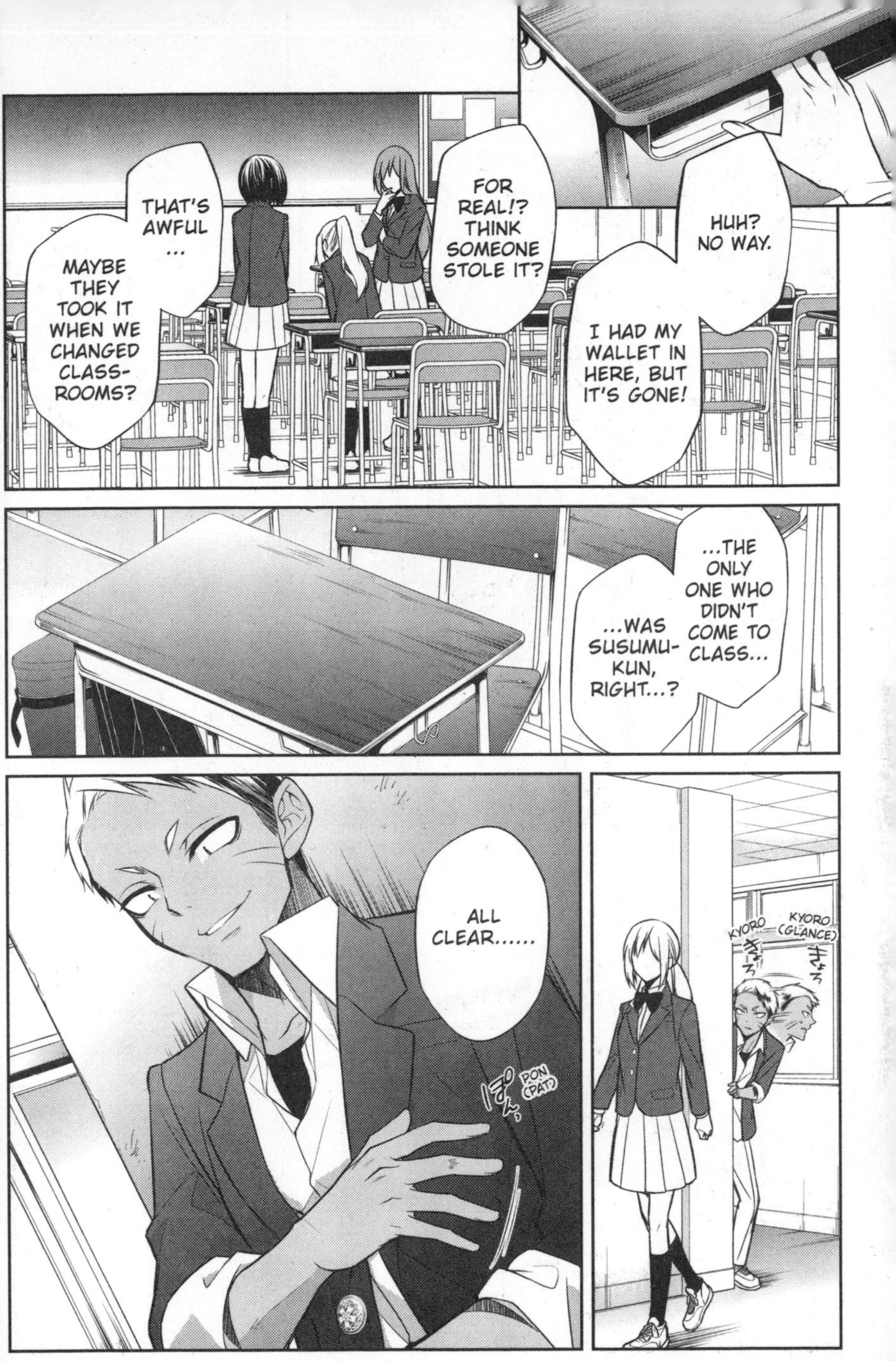
HUH? NO WAY.
I HAD MY WALLET IN HERE, BUT IT'S GONE!
FOR REAL!? THINK SOMEONE STOLE IT?
THAT'S AWFUL...
MAYBE THEY TOOK IT WHEN WE CHANGED CLASS-ROOMS?
...THE ONLY ONE WHO DIDN'T COME TO CLASS...
...WAS SUSUMU-KUN, RIGHT...?
KYORO KYORO (GLANCE)
ALL CLEAR......
PON (PAT)

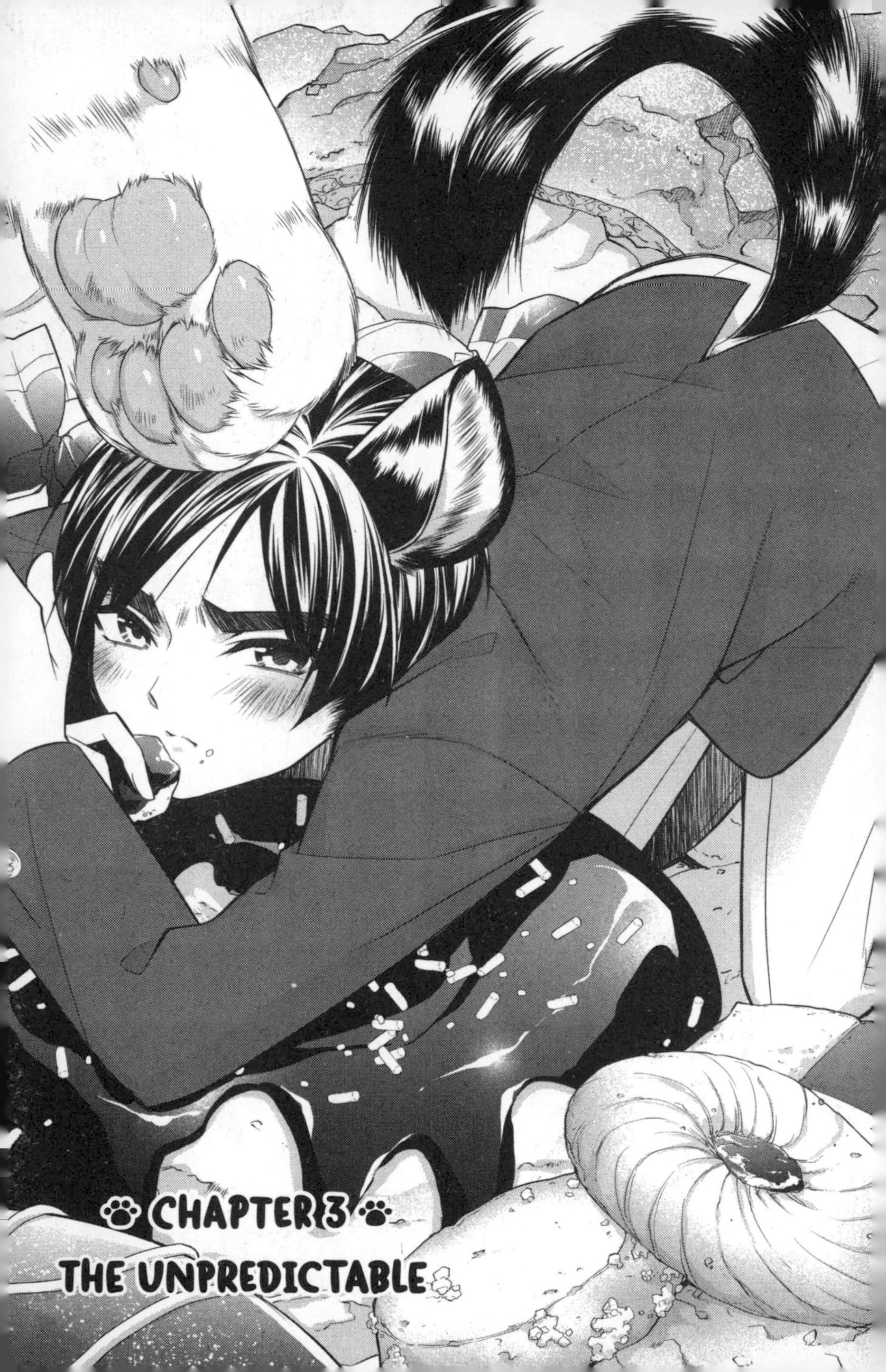
CHAPTER 3
THE UNPREDICTABLE

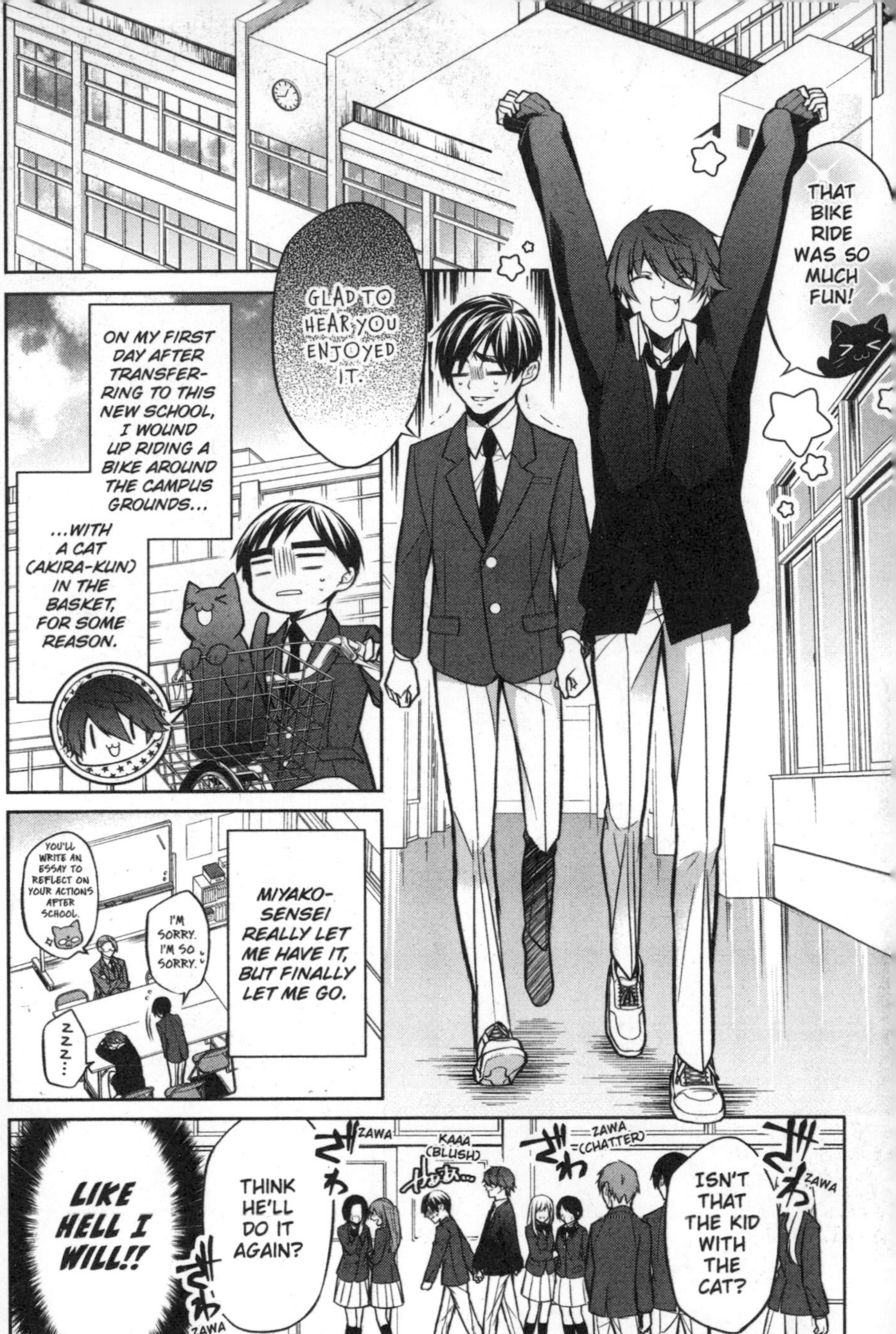
THAT BIKE RIDE WAS SO MUCH FUN!
GLAD TO HEAR YOU ENJOYED IT.
ON MY FIRST DAY AFTER TRANSFERRING TO THIS NEW SCHOOL, I WOUND UP RIDING A BIKE AROUND THE CAMPUS GROUNDS...
...WITH A CAT (AKIRA-KUN) IN THE BASKET, FOR SOME REASON.
MIYAKO-SENSEI REALLY LET ME HAVE IT, BUT FINALLY LET ME GO.
YOU'LL WRITE AN ESSAY TO REFLECT ON YOUR ACTIONS AFTER SCHOOL.
I'M SORRY. I'M SO SORRY.
ZZZ...
ZAWA
ISN'T THAT THE KID WITH THE CAT?
ZAWA (CHATTER)
KAAA (BLUSH)
ZAWA
THINK HE'LL DO IT AGAIN?
ZAWA
LIKE HELL I WILL!!

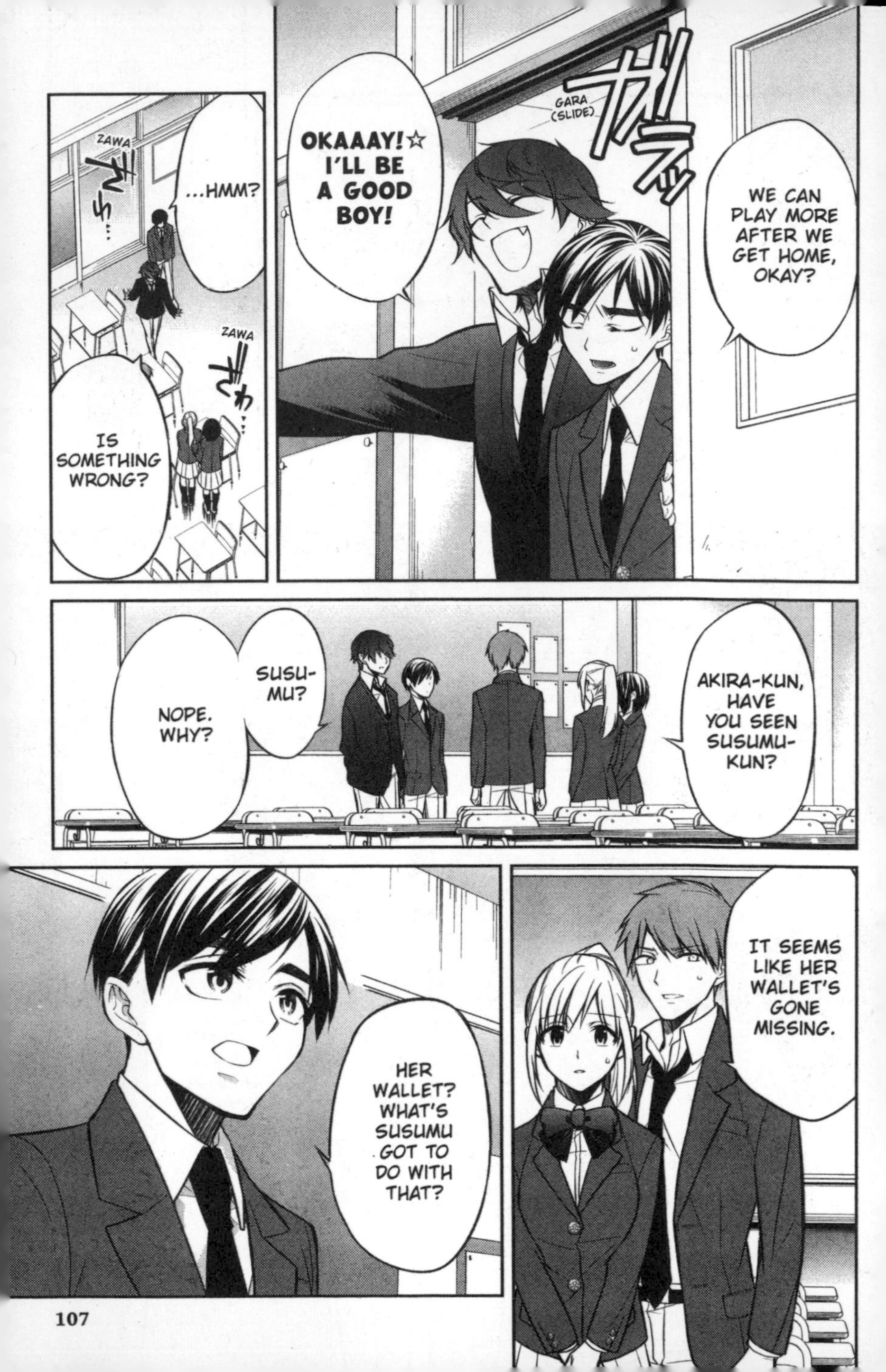
GARA (SLIDE)
WE CAN PLAY MORE AFTER WE GET HOME, OKAY?
OKAAAY!☆ I'LL BE A GOOD BOY!
ZAWA
...HMM?
ZAWA
IS SOMETHING WRONG?
AKIRA-KUN, HAVE YOU SEEN SUSUMU-KUN?
SUSU-MU?
NOPE. WHY?
IT SEEMS LIKE HER WALLET'S GONE MISSING.
HER WALLET? WHAT'S SUSUMU GOT TO DO WITH THAT?

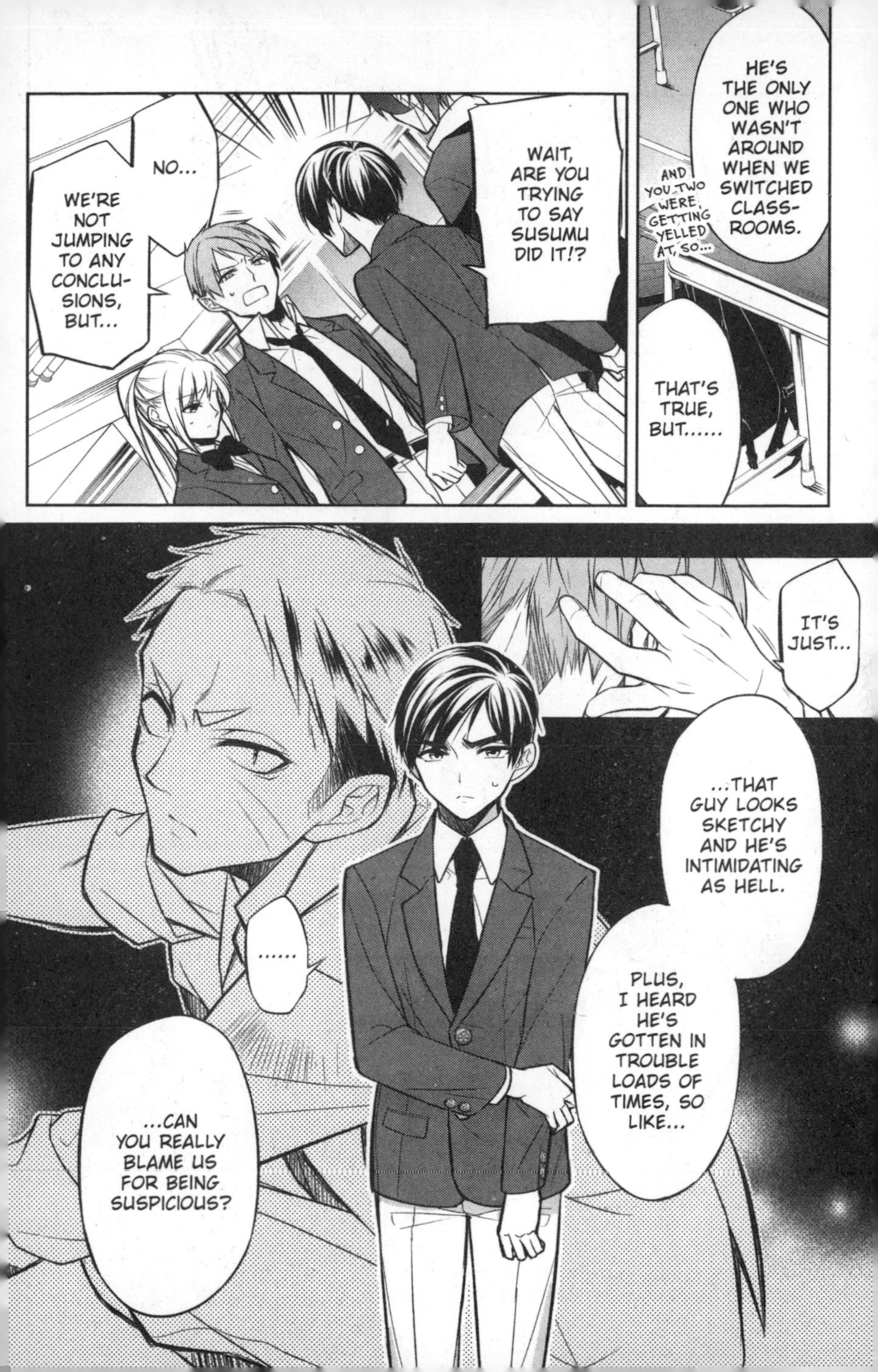
HE'S THE ONLY ONE WHO WASN'T AROUND WHEN WE SWITCHED CLASS-ROOMS.
AND YOU TWO WERE GETTING YELLED AT, SO...
THAT'S TRUE, BUT......
WAIT, ARE YOU TRYING TO SAY SUSUMU DID IT!?
NO...
WE'RE NOT JUMPING TO ANY CONCLU-SIONS, BUT...
IT'S JUST...
...THAT GUY LOOKS SKETCHY AND HE'S INTIMIDATING AS HELL.
PLUS, I HEARD HE'S GOTTEN IN TROUBLE LOADS OF TIMES, SO LIKE...
......
...CAN YOU REALLY BLAME US FOR BEING SUSPICIOUS?

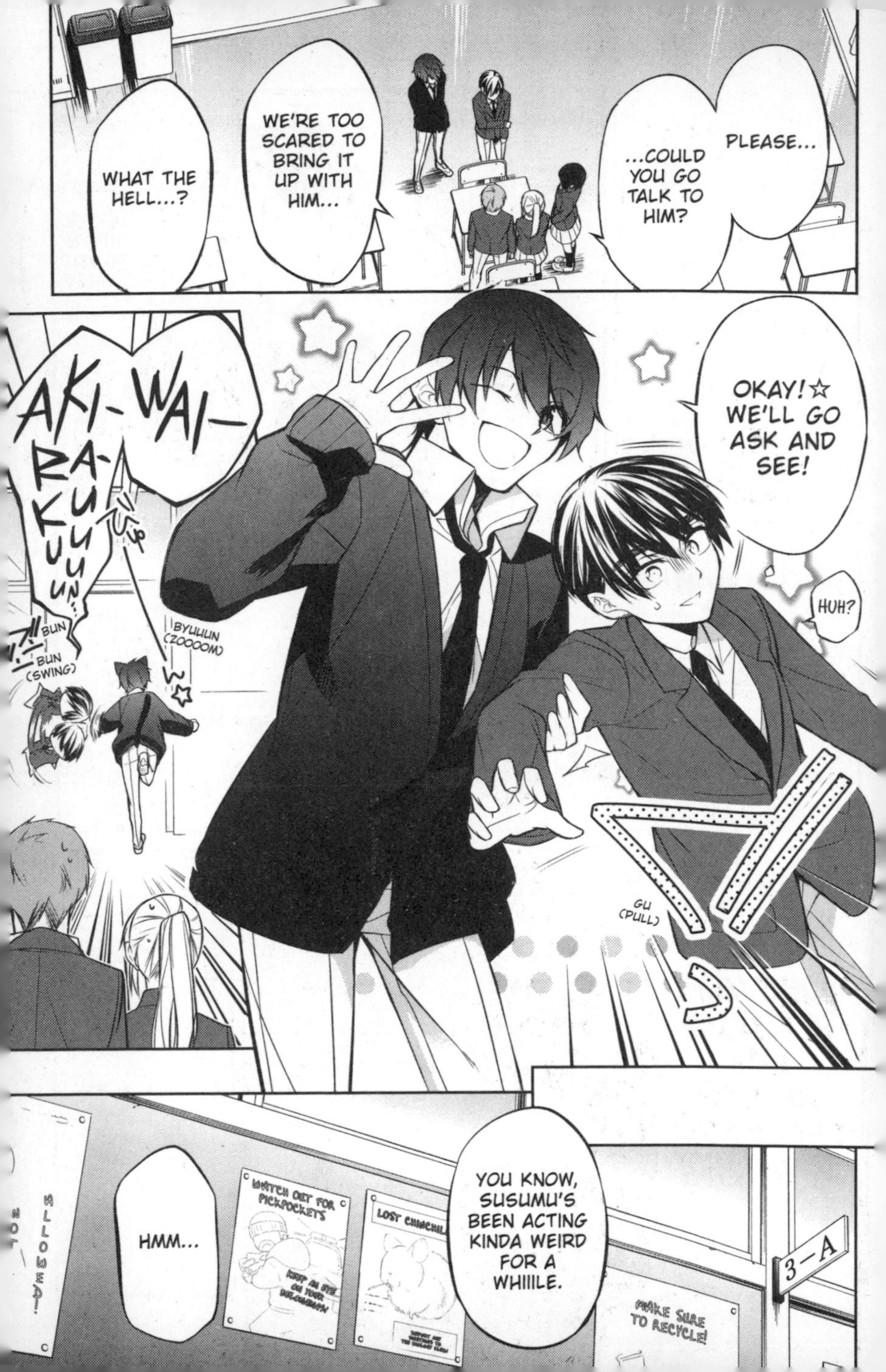
PLEASE...
...COULD YOU GO TALK TO HIM?
WE'RE TOO SCARED TO BRING IT UP WITH HIM...
WHAT THE HELL...?
OKAY!☆ WE'LL GO ASK AND SEE!
HUH?
GU (PULL)
WAI—
AKI-RA-KUUUUUUN...
BYUUUN (ZOOOOM)
BUN BUN (SWING)
3—A
MAKE SURE TO RECYCLE!
YOU KNOW, SUSUMU'S BEEN ACTING KINDA WEIRD FOR A WHIIILE.
LOST CHINCHIL
WATCH OUT FOR PICKPOCKETS
HMM...
NOT ALLOWED!

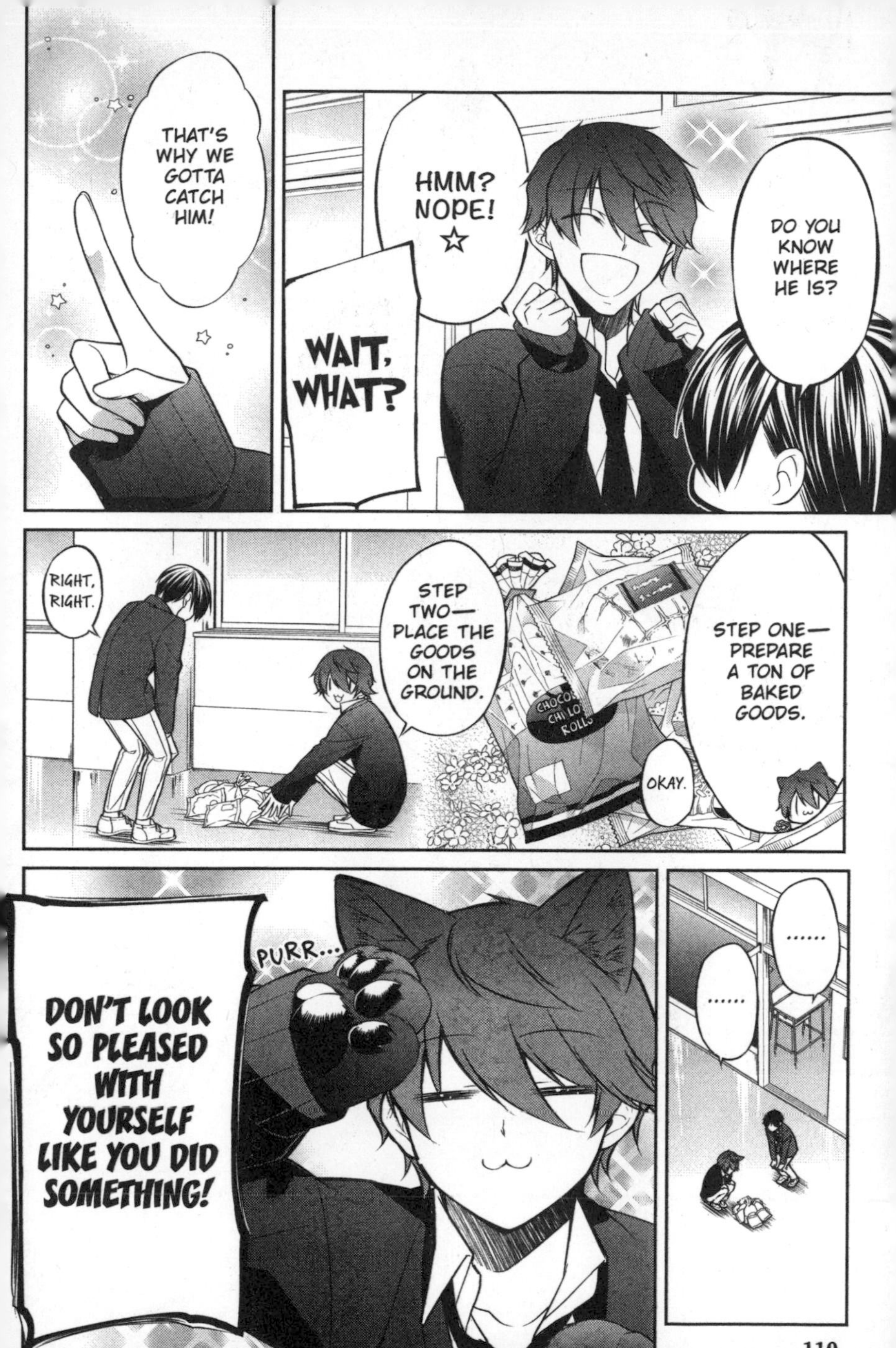
DO YOU KNOW WHERE HE IS?
HMM? NOPE! ☆
WAIT, WHAT?
THAT'S WHY WE GOTTA CATCH HIM!
STEP ONE—PREPARE A TON OF BAKED GOODS.
OKAY.
STEP TWO—PLACE THE GOODS ON THE GROUND.
RIGHT, RIGHT.
......
......
PURR...
DON'T LOOK SO PLEASED WITH YOURSELF LIKE YOU DID SOMETHING!

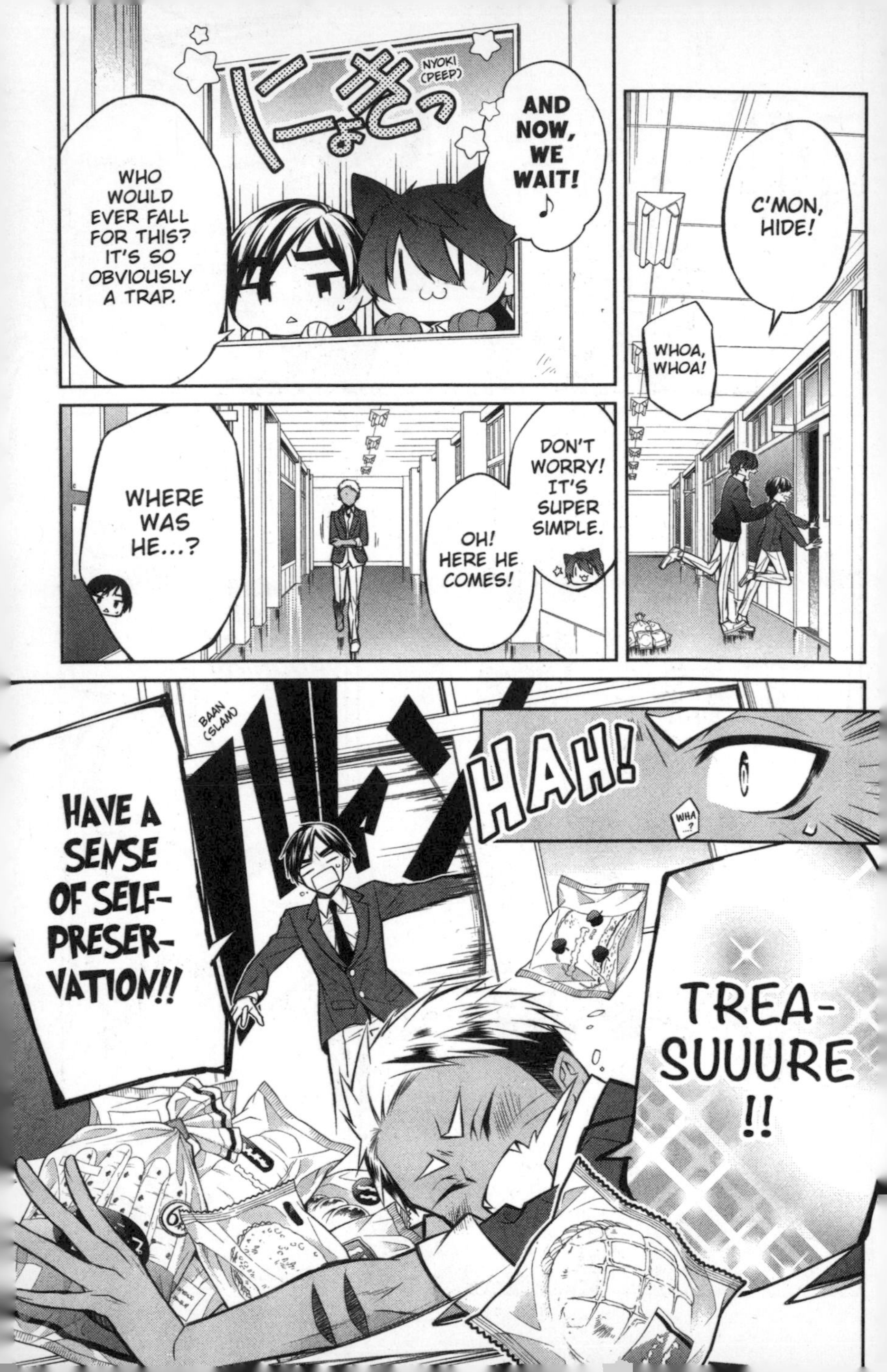
C'MON, HIDE!
WHOA, WHOA!
NYOKI (PEEP)
AND NOW, WE WAIT! ♪
WHO WOULD EVER FALL FOR THIS? IT'S SO OBVIOUSLY A TRAP.
DON'T WORRY! IT'S SUPER SIMPLE.
OH! HERE HE COMES!
WHERE WAS HE...?
HAH!
WHA...?
TREA-SUUURE!!
BAAN (SLAM)
HAVE A SENSE OF SELF-PRESERVATION!!

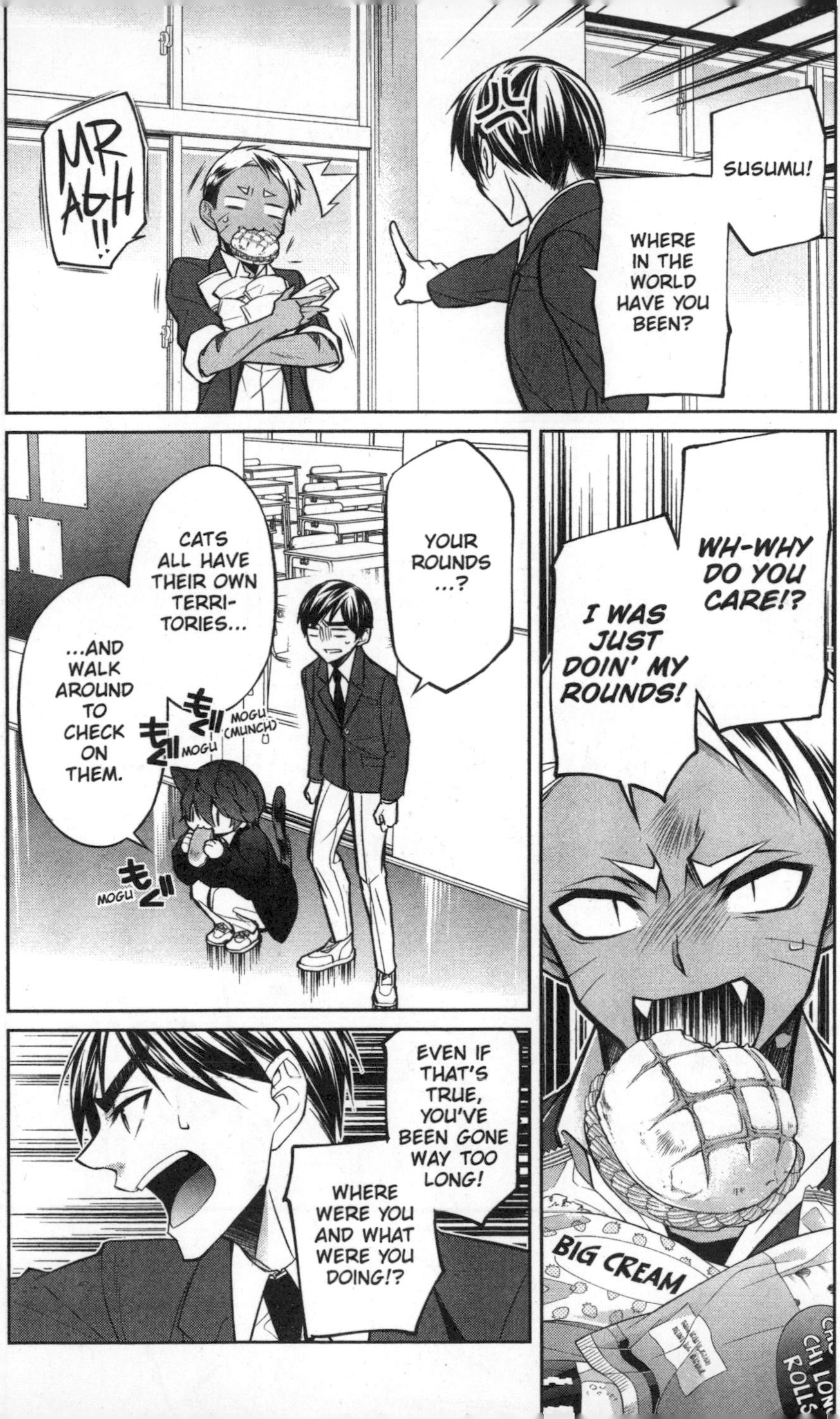
SUSUMU!
WHERE IN THE WORLD HAVE YOU BEEN?
MRAGH!!
WH-WHY DO YOU CARE!?
I WAS JUST DOIN' MY ROUNDS!
BIG CREAM
YOUR ROUNDS...?
CATS ALL HAVE THEIR OWN TERRI-TORIES...
...AND WALK AROUND TO CHECK ON THEM.
もぐ MOGU (MUNCH)
もぐ MOGU
もぐ MOGU
EVEN IF THAT'S TRUE, YOU'VE BEEN GONE WAY TOO LONG!
WHERE WERE YOU AND WHAT WERE YOU DOING!?

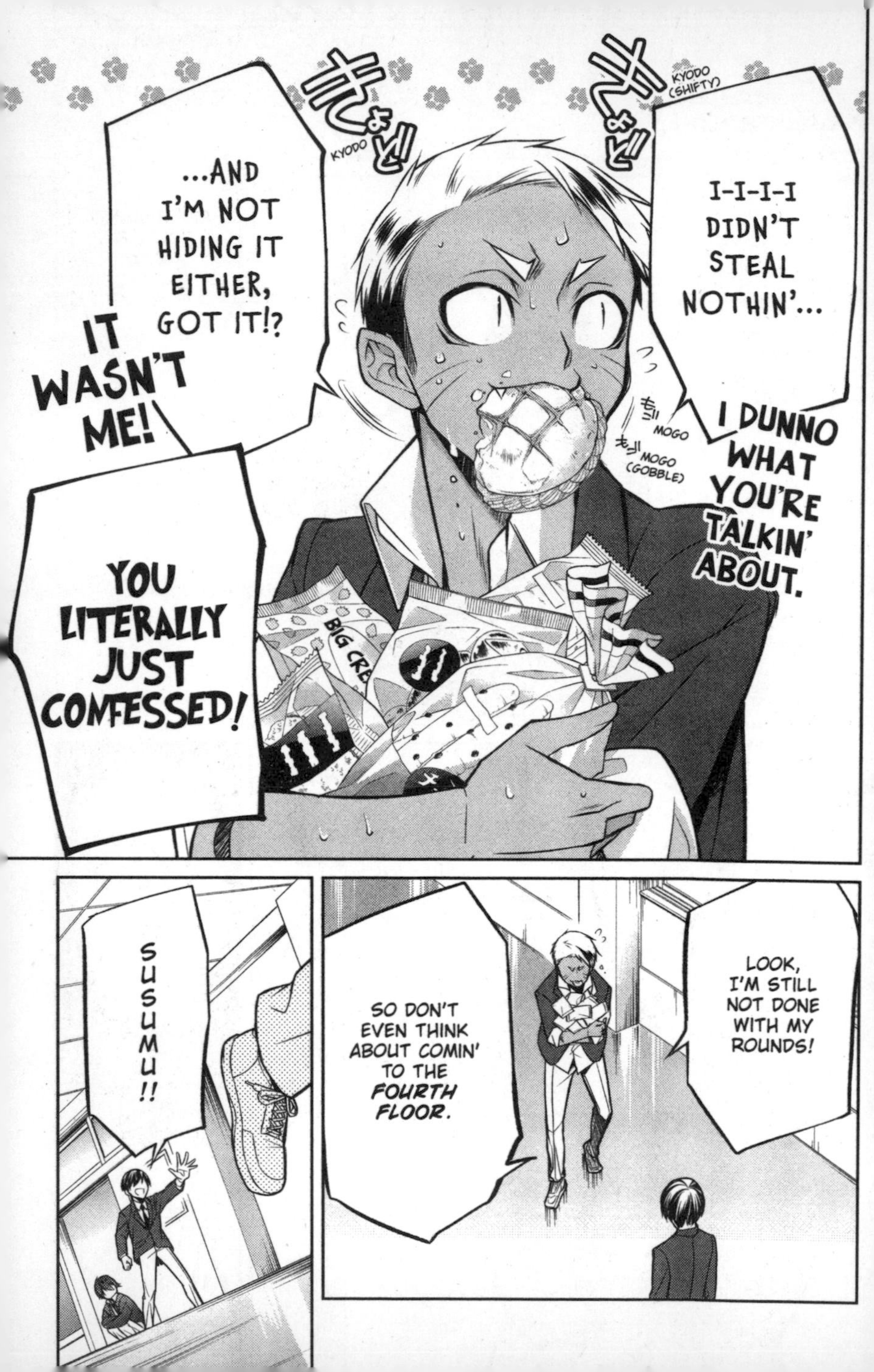
きょど
KYODO (SHIFTY)
I-I-I-I DIDN'T STEAL NOTHIN'...
きょど
KYODO
...AND I'M NOT HIDING IT EITHER, GOT IT!?
IT WASN'T ME!
MOGO
MOGO (GOBBLE)
I DUNNO WHAT YOU'RE TALKIN' ABOUT.
YOU LITERALLY JUST CONFESSED!
LOOK, I'M STILL NOT DONE WITH MY ROUNDS!
SO DON'T EVEN THINK ABOUT COMIN' TO THE *FOURTH FLOOR*.
SUSUMU!!

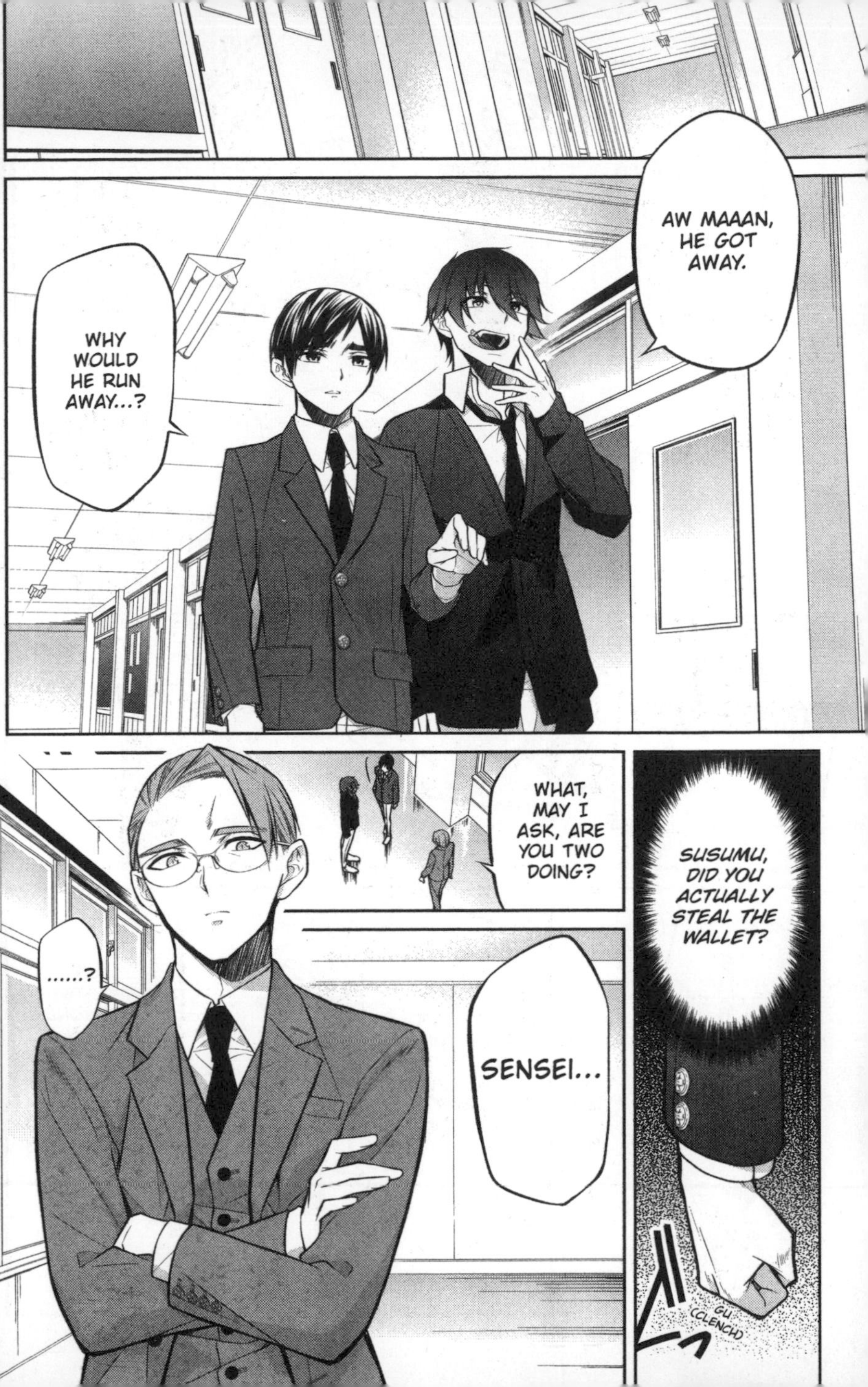
AW MAAAN, HE GOT AWAY.
WHY WOULD HE RUN AWAY...?
SUSUMU, DID YOU ACTUALLY STEAL THE WALLET?
GU (CLENCH)
WHAT, MAY I ASK, ARE YOU TWO DOING?
SENSEI...
......?

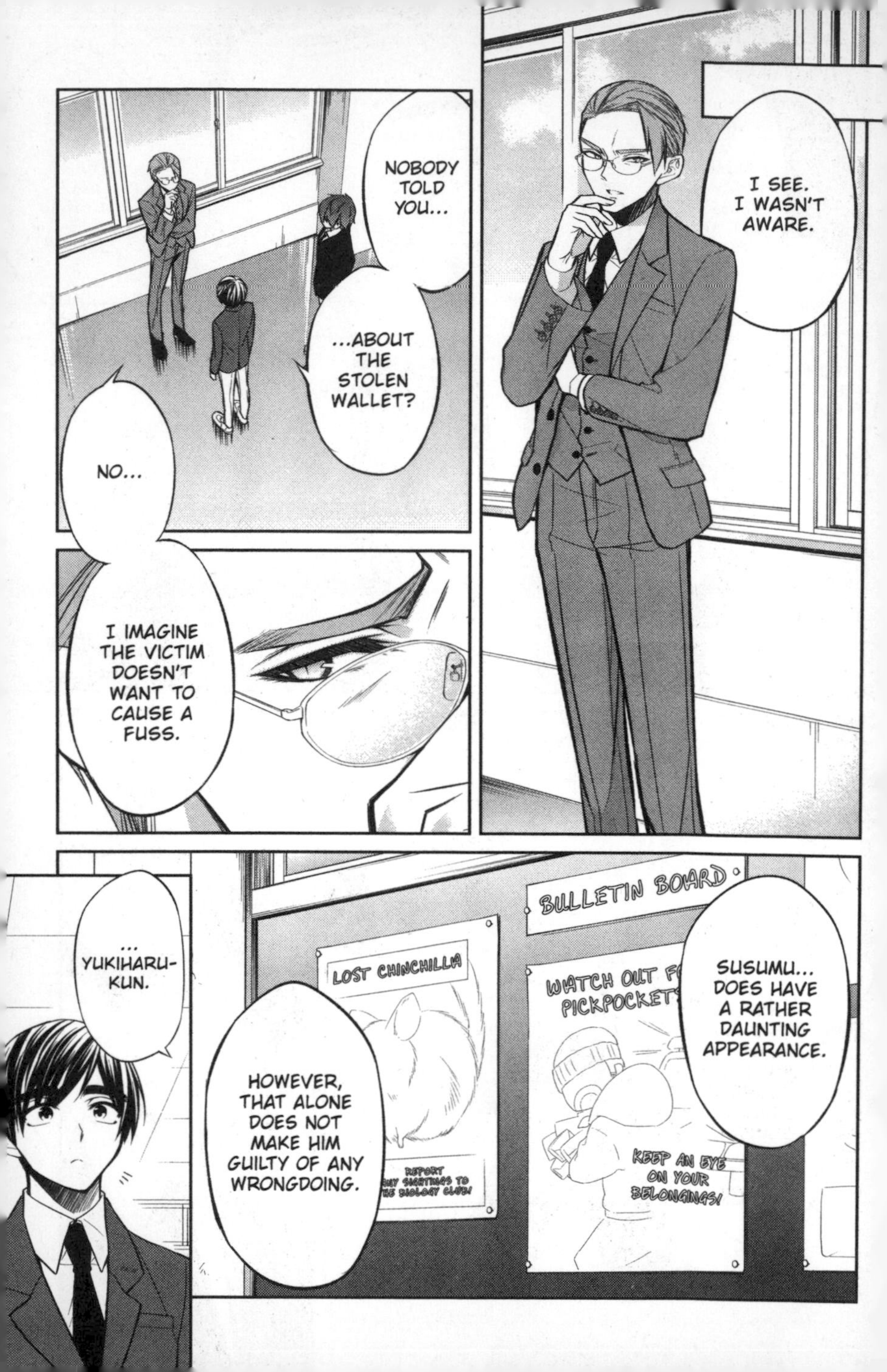
I SEE. I WASN'T AWARE.
NOBODY TOLD YOU...
...ABOUT THE STOLEN WALLET?
NO...
I IMAGINE THE VICTIM DOESN'T WANT TO CAUSE A FUSS.
BULLETIN BOARD
SUSUMU... DOES HAVE A RATHER DAUNTING APPEARANCE.
KEEP AN EYE ON YOUR BELONGINGS!
LOST CHINCHILLA
REPORT
HOWEVER, THAT ALONE DOES NOT MAKE HIM GUILTY OF ANY WRONGDOING.
...YUKIHARU-KUN.

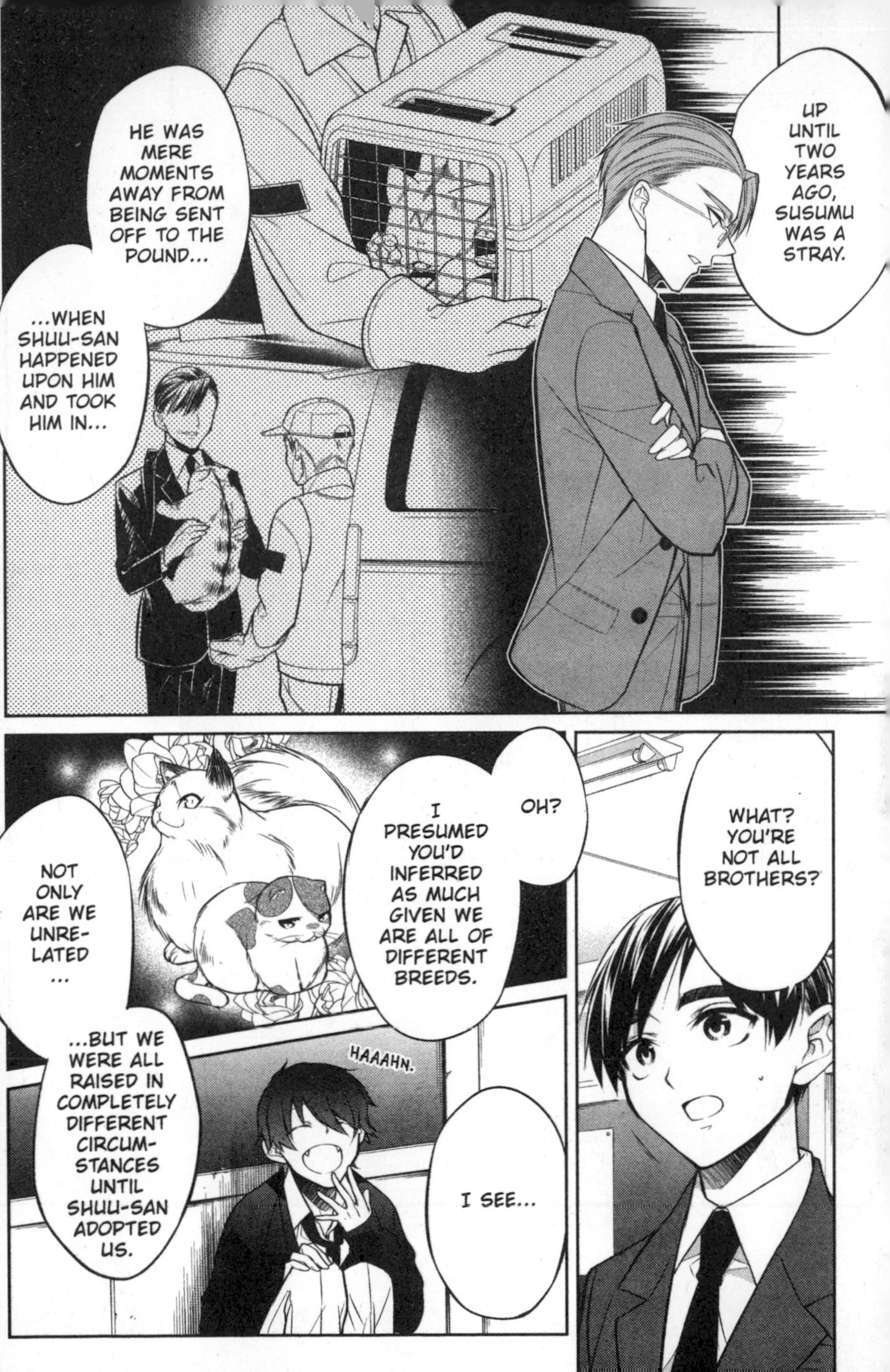
UP UNTIL TWO YEARS AGO, SUSUMU WAS A STRAY.
HE WAS MERE MOMENTS AWAY FROM BEING SENT OFF TO THE POUND...
...WHEN SHUU-SAN HAPPENED UPON HIM AND TOOK HIM IN...
WHAT? YOU'RE NOT ALL BROTHERS?
OH?
I PRESUMED YOU'D INFERRED AS MUCH GIVEN WE ARE ALL OF DIFFERENT BREEDS.
NOT ONLY ARE WE UNRELATED...
...BUT WE WERE ALL RAISED IN COMPLETELY DIFFERENT CIRCUMSTANCES UNTIL SHUU-SAN ADOPTED US.
HAAAAHN.
I SEE...

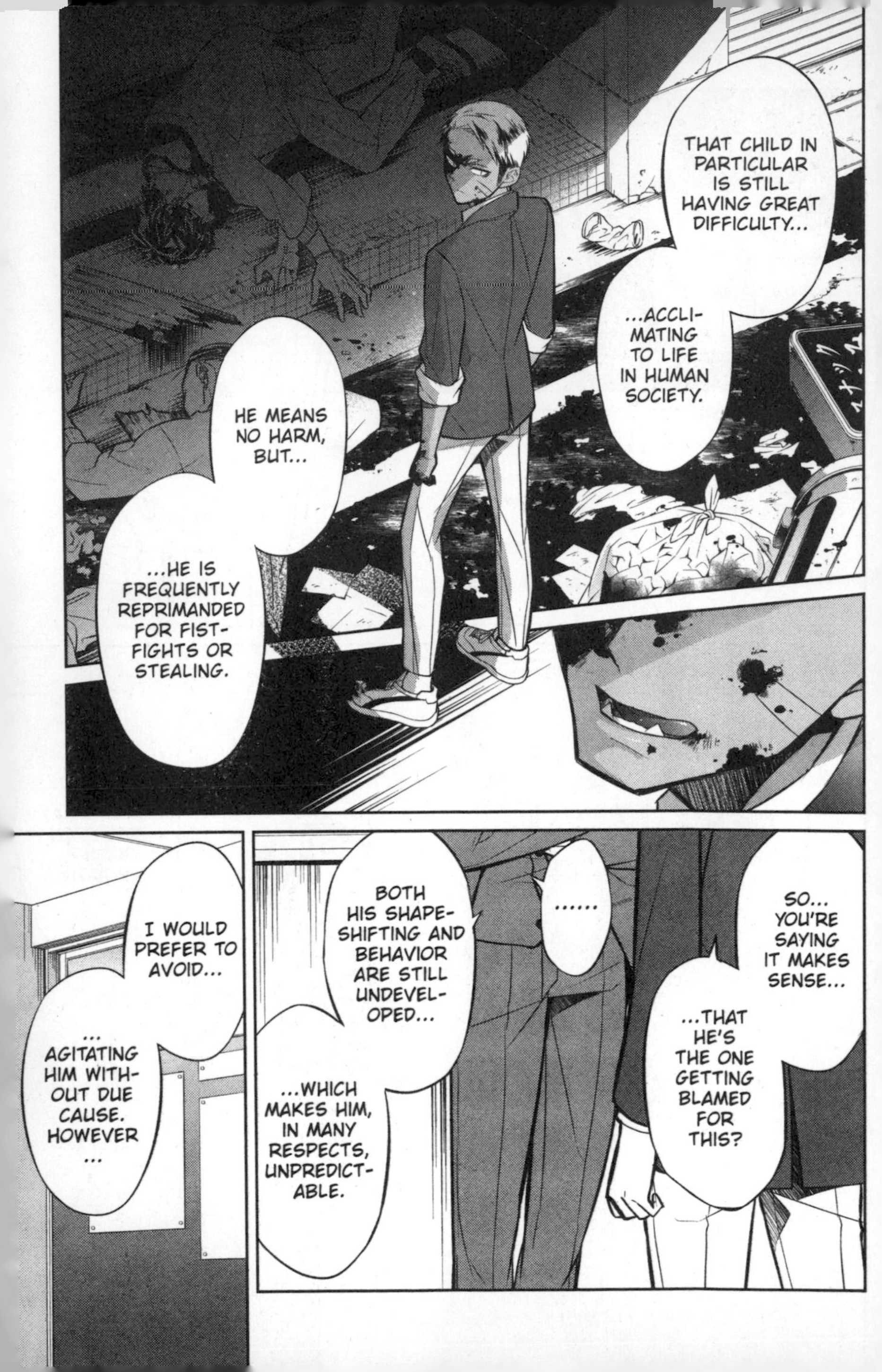
THAT CHILD IN PARTICULAR IS STILL HAVING GREAT DIFFICULTY...
...ACCLIMATING TO LIFE IN HUMAN SOCIETY.
HE MEANS NO HARM, BUT...
...HE IS FREQUENTLY REPRIMANDED FOR FIST-FIGHTS OR STEALING.
SO... YOU'RE SAYING IT MAKES SENSE...
...THAT HE'S THE ONE GETTING BLAMED FOR THIS?
......
BOTH HIS SHAPE-SHIFTING AND BEHAVIOR ARE STILL UNDEVELOPED...
...WHICH MAKES HIM, IN MANY RESPECTS, UNPREDICTABLE.
I WOULD PREFER TO AVOID...
...AGITATING HIM WITHOUT DUE CAUSE. HOWEVER...

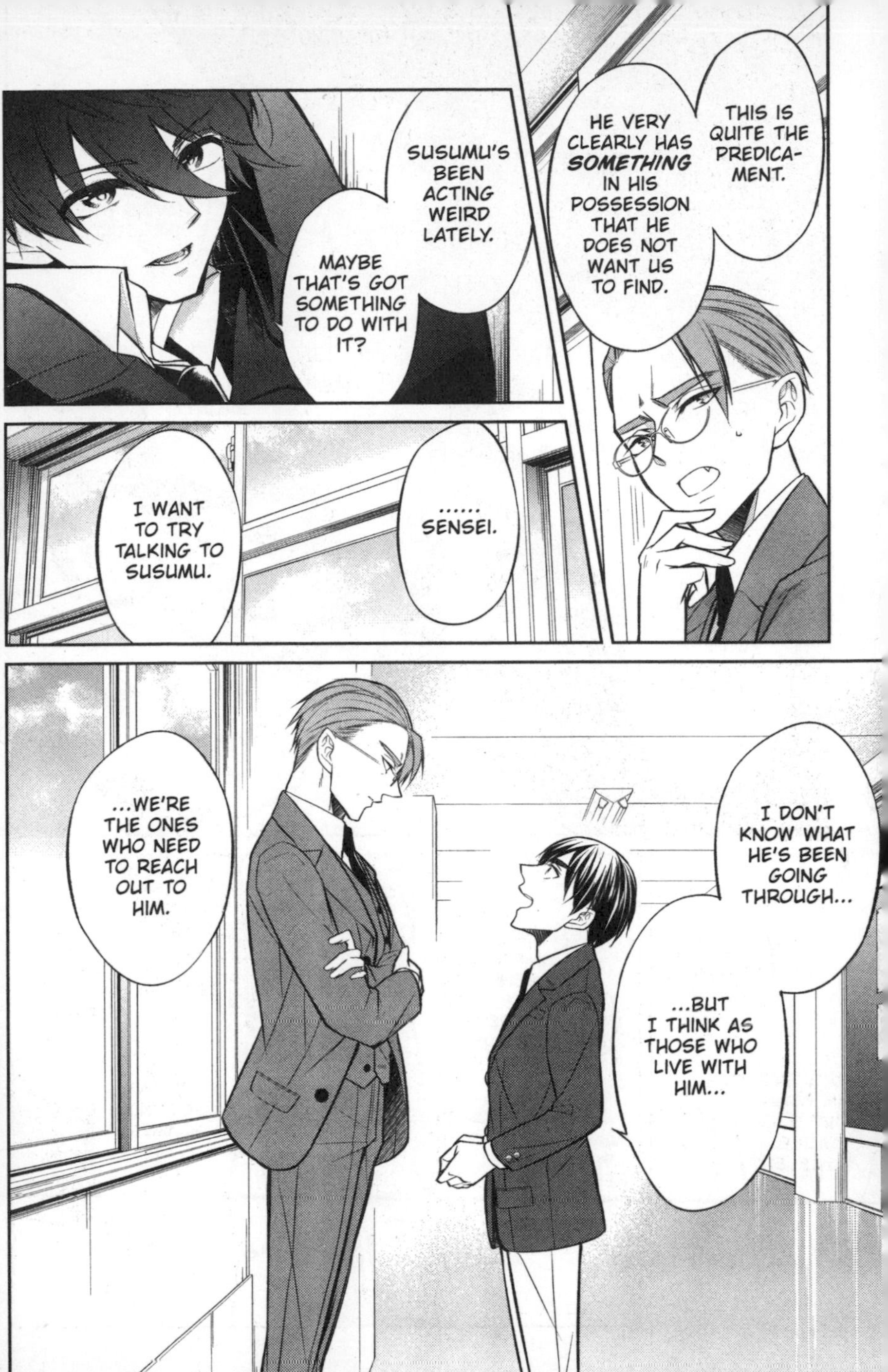
THIS IS QUITE THE PREDICA-MENT.
HE VERY CLEARLY HAS ***SOMETHING*** IN HIS POSSESSION THAT HE DOES NOT WANT US TO FIND.
SUSUMU'S BEEN ACTING WEIRD LATELY.
MAYBE THAT'S GOT SOMETHING TO DO WITH IT?
......SENSEI.
I WANT TO TRY TALKING TO SUSUMU.
I DON'T KNOW WHAT HE'S BEEN GOING THROUGH...
...BUT I THINK AS THOSE WHO LIVE WITH HIM...
...WE'RE THE ONES WHO NEED TO REACH OUT TO HIM.

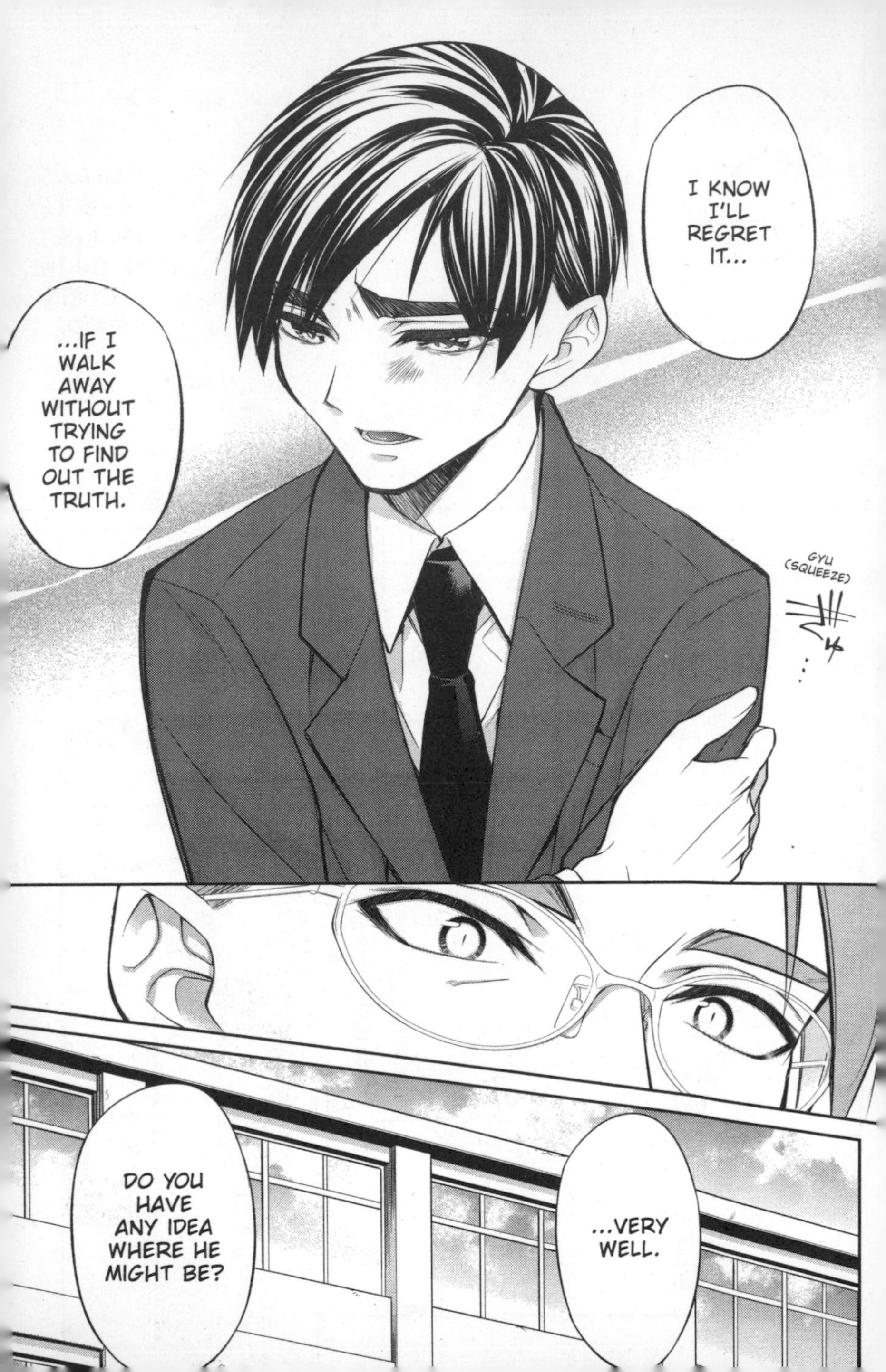
I KNOW I'LL REGRET IT...
...IF I WALK AWAY WITHOUT TRYING TO FIND OUT THE TRUTH.
GYU (SQUEEZE)
...VERY WELL.
DO YOU HAVE ANY IDEA WHERE HE MIGHT BE?

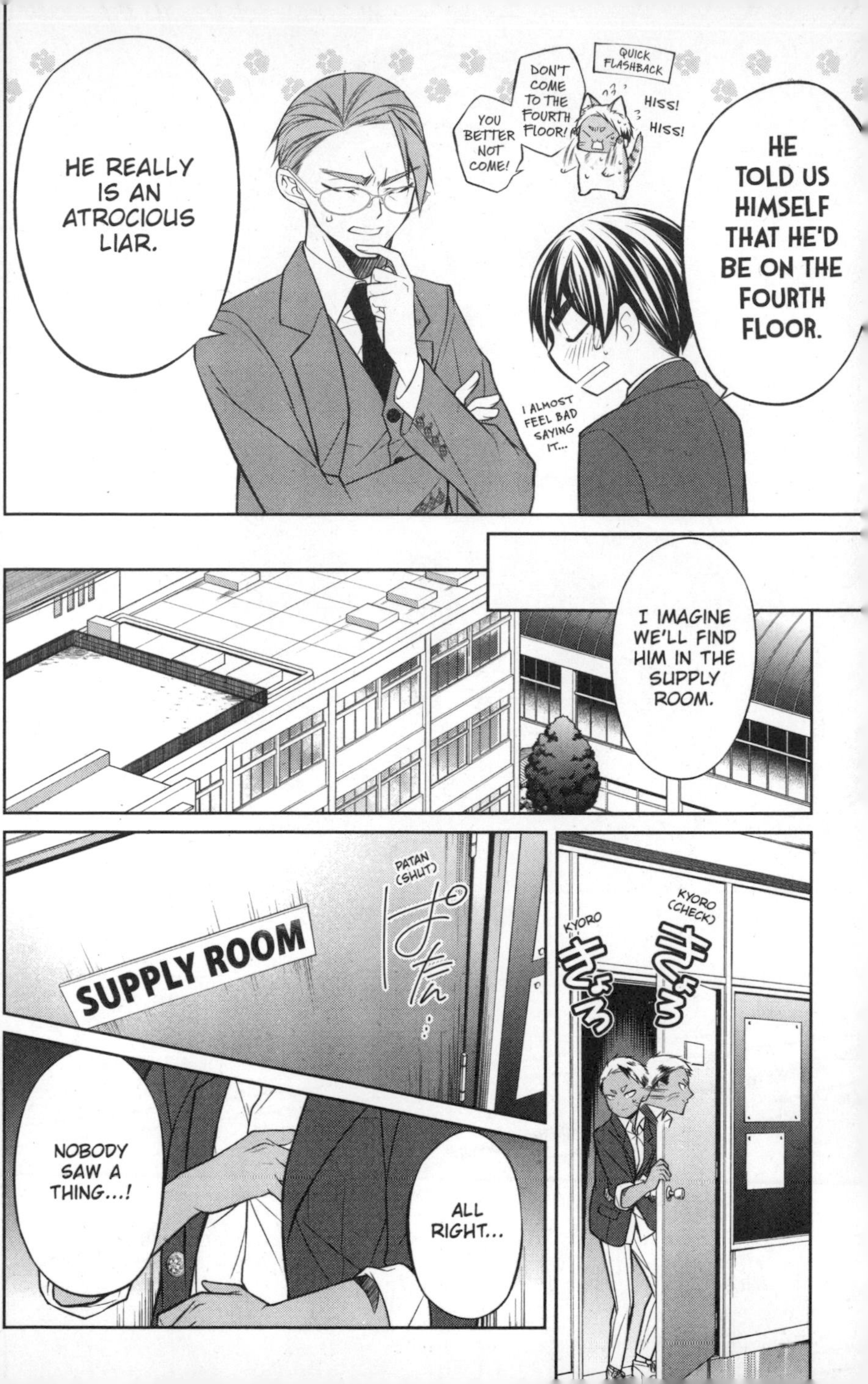
HE TOLD US HIMSELF THAT HE'D BE ON THE FOURTH FLOOR.
I ALMOST FEEL BAD SAYING IT...
QUICK FLASHBACK
DON'T COME TO THE FOURTH FLOOR!
HISS!
HISS!
YOU BETTER NOT COME!
HE REALLY IS AN ATROCIOUS LIAR.
I IMAGINE WE'LL FIND HIM IN THE SUPPLY ROOM.
KYORO (CHECK)
きょろ
KYORO
きょろ
SUPPLY ROOM
PATAN (SHUT)
ぱたん…
ALL RIGHT...
NOBODY SAW A THING...!

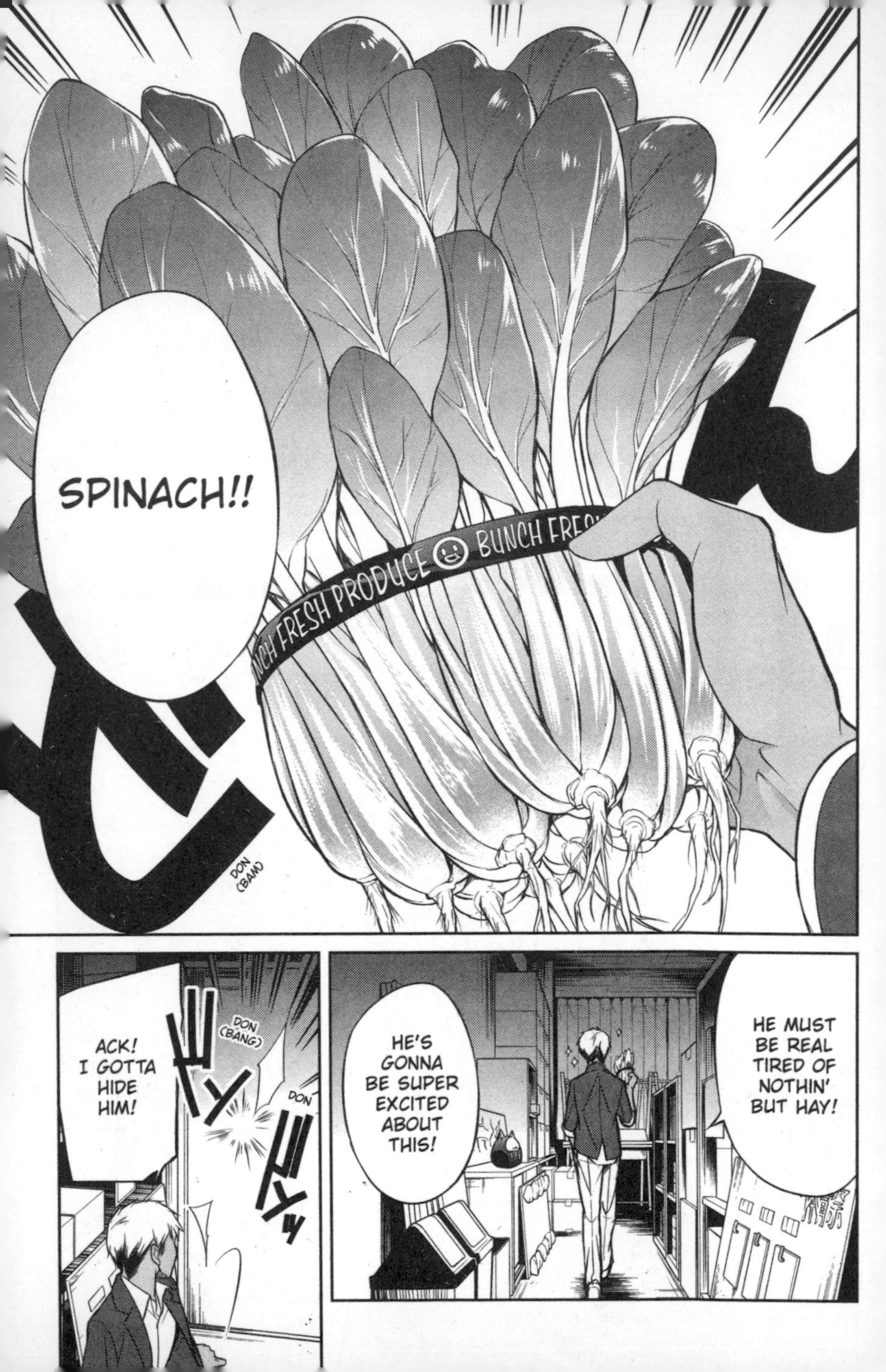
SPINACH!!
FRESH PRODUCE BUNCH
DON (BAM)
HE MUST BE REAL TIRED OF NOTHIN' BUT HAY!
HE'S GONNA BE SUPER EXCITED ABOUT THIS!
DON (BANG)
DON
ACK! I GOTTA HIDE HIM!

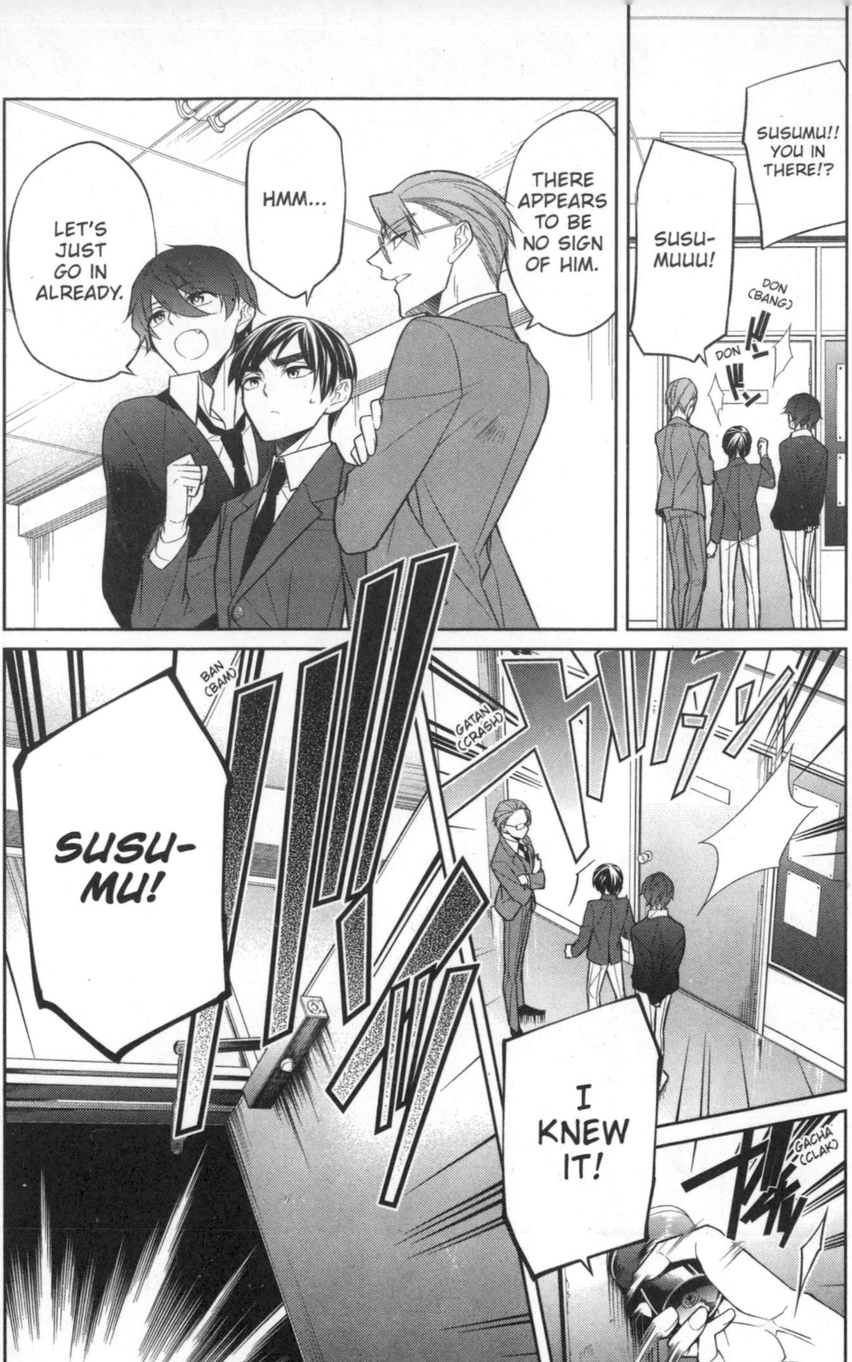
SUSUMU!! YOU IN THERE!?
SUSU-MUUU!
DON (BANG)
DON
THERE APPEARS TO BE NO SIGN OF HIM.
HMM...
LET'S JUST GO IN ALREADY.
GATAN (CRASH)
BAN (BAM)
SUSU-MU!
I KNEW IT!
GACHA (CLAK)

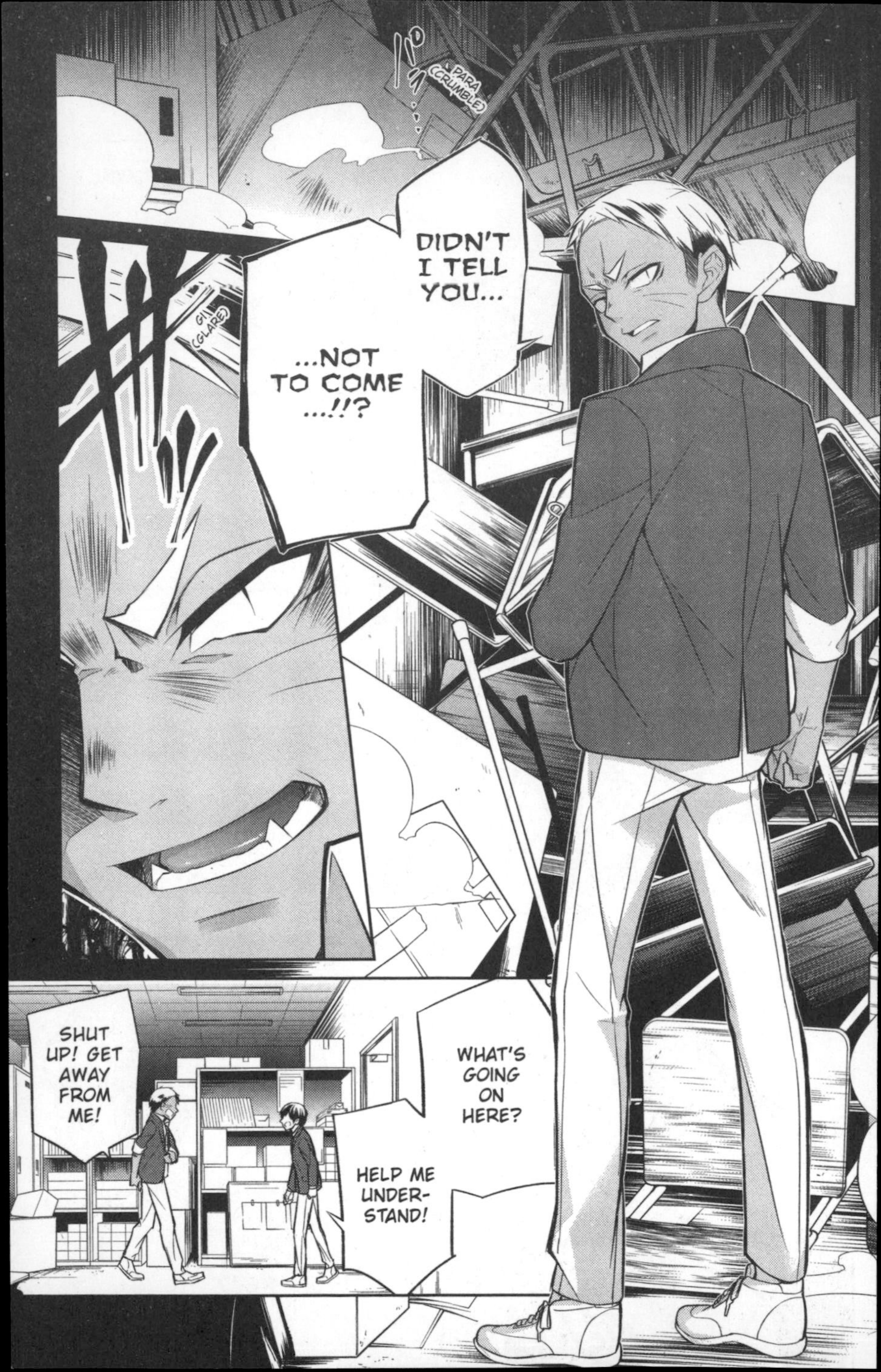
PARA (CRUMBLE)
DIDN'T I TELL YOU...
...NOT TO COME ...!!?
GI! (GLARE)
WHAT'S GOING ON HERE?
HELP ME UNDER-STAND!
SHUT UP! GET AWAY FROM ME!

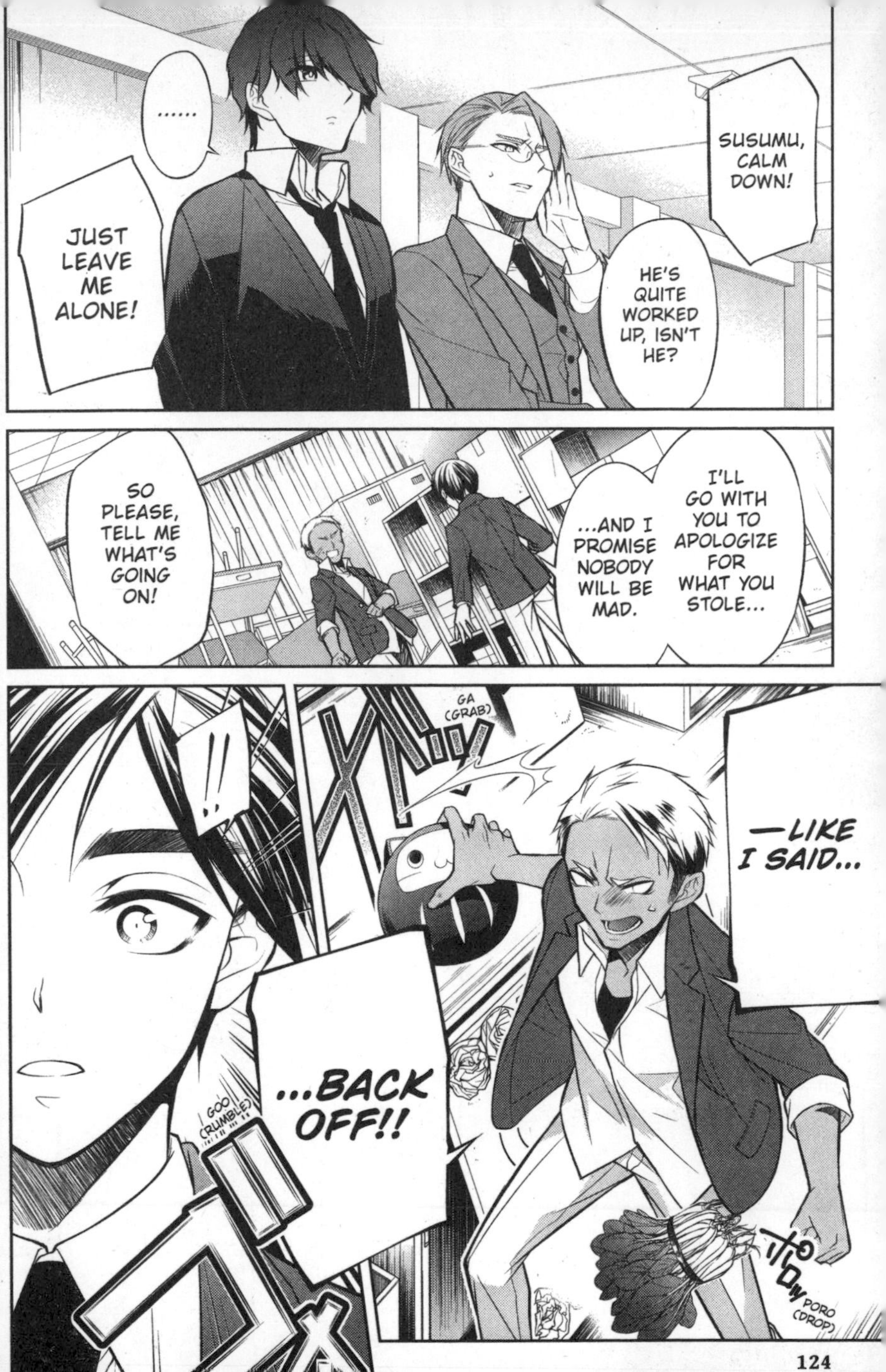
SUSUMU, CALM DOWN!
HE'S QUITE WORKED UP, ISN'T HE?
......
JUST LEAVE ME ALONE!
I'LL GO WITH YOU TO APOLOGIZE FOR WHAT YOU STOLE...
...AND I PROMISE NOBODY WILL BE MAD.
SO PLEASE, TELL ME WHAT'S GOING ON!
—LIKE I SAID...
GA (GRAB)
PORO (DROP)
!!
...BACK OFF!!
GOO (RUMBLE)

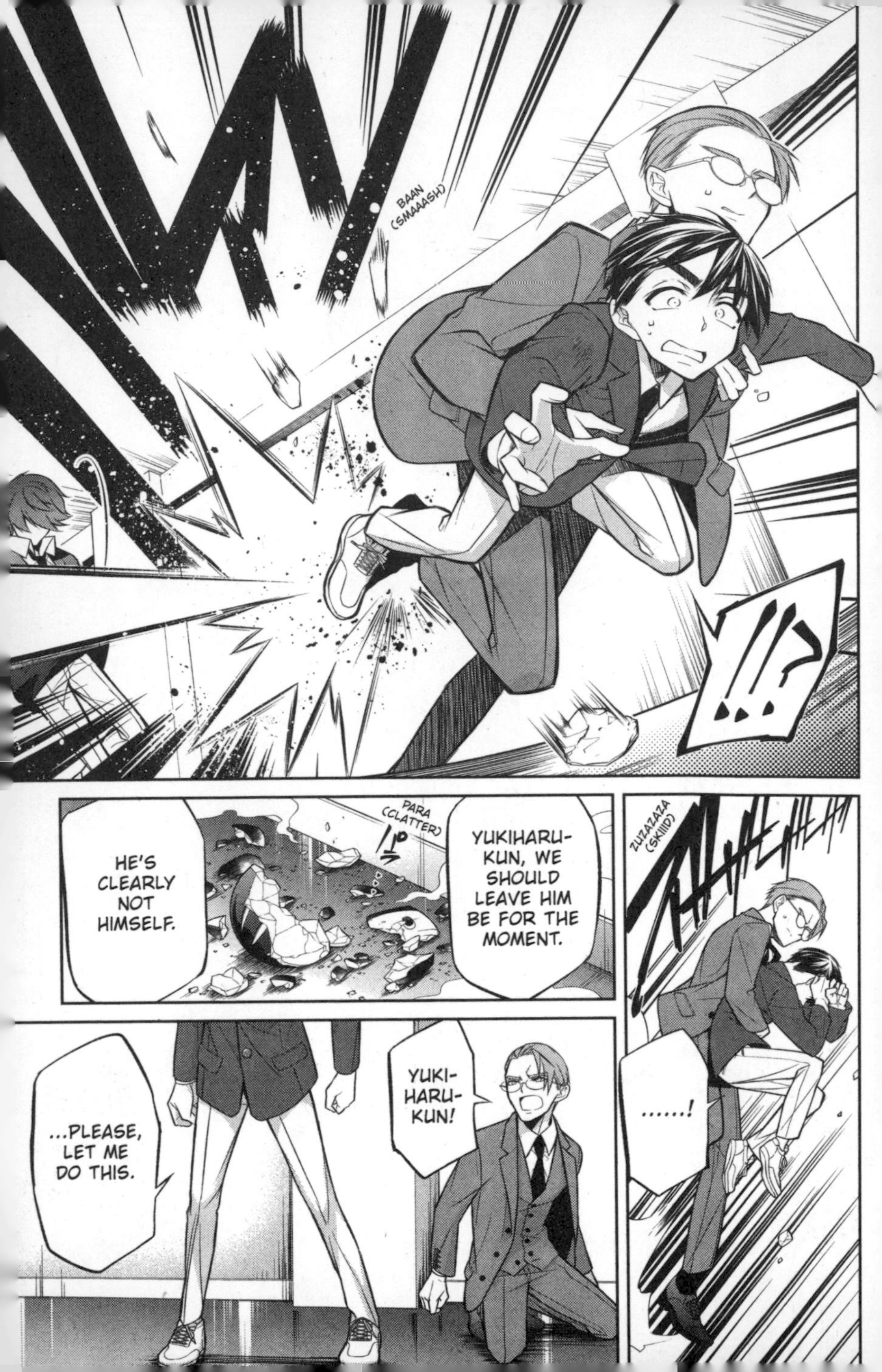
BAAN (SMAAASH)
!!?
ZUZAZAZA (SKIIID)
......!
PARA (CLATTER)
YUKIHARU-KUN, WE SHOULD LEAVE HIM BE FOR THE MOMENT.
HE'S CLEARLY NOT HIMSELF.
YUKI-HARU-KUN!
...PLEASE, LET ME DO THIS.

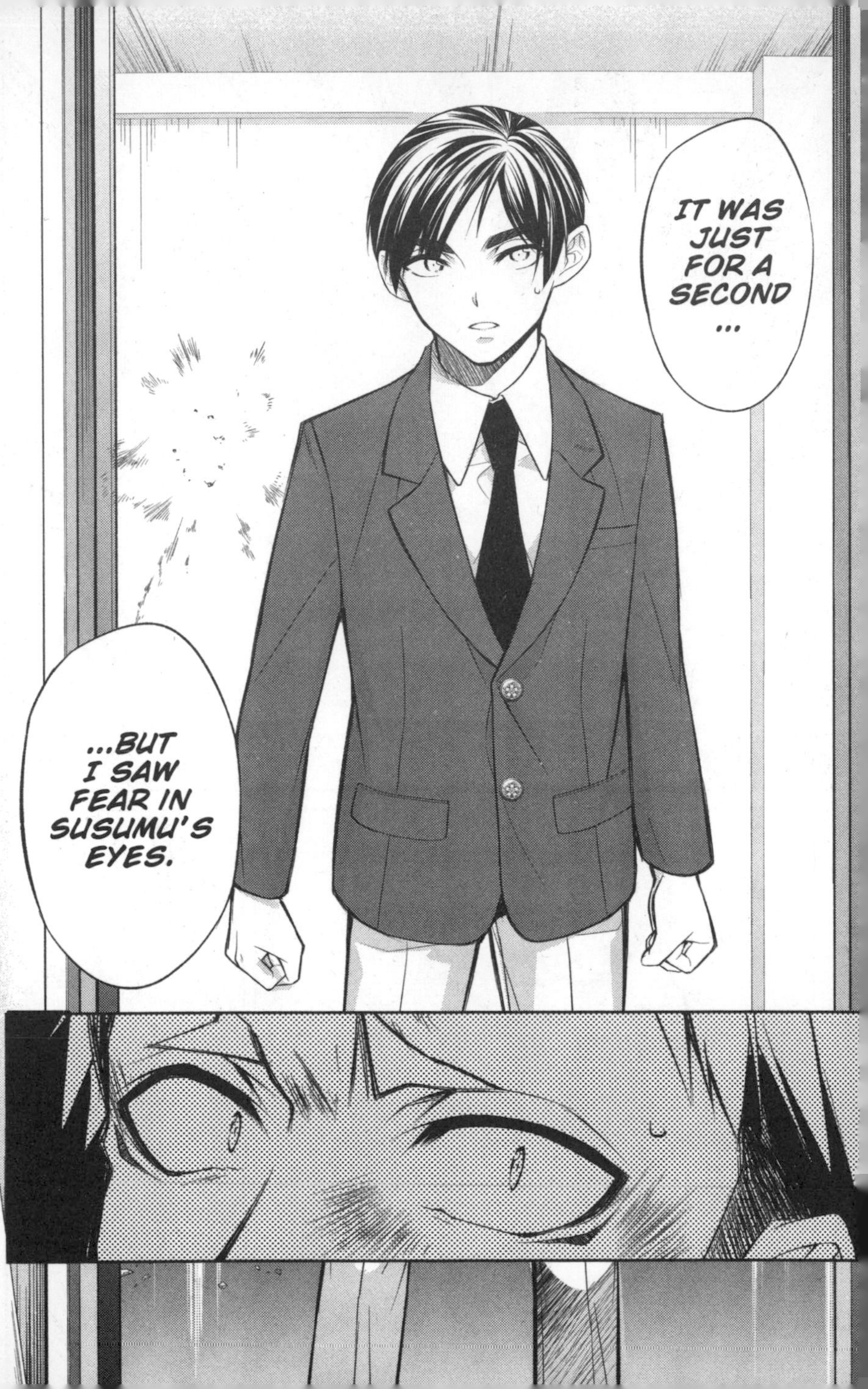
IT WAS JUST FOR A SECOND ...
...BUT I SAW FEAR IN SUSUMU'S EYES.

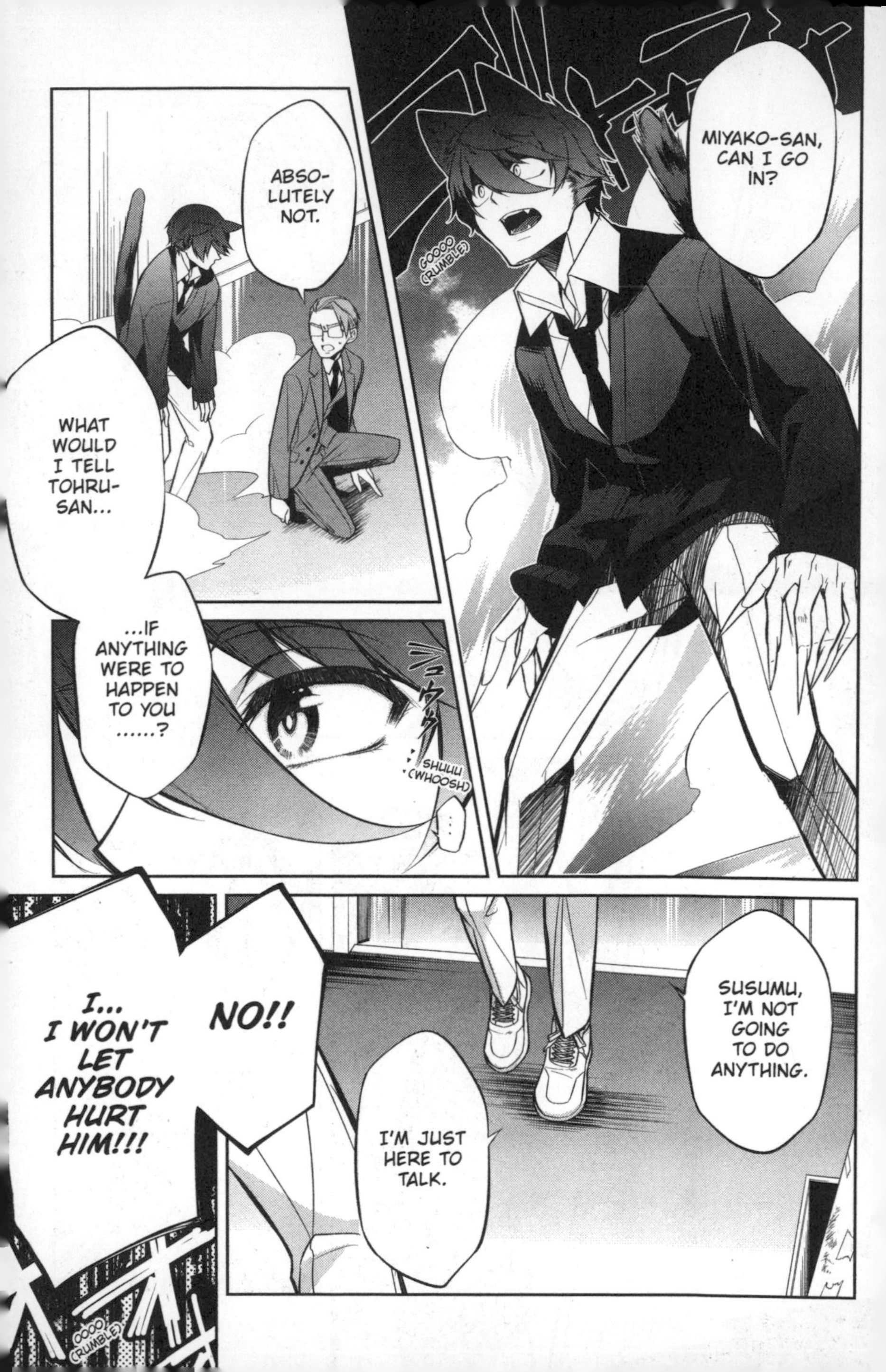
MIYAKO-SAN, CAN I GO IN?
GOOOO (RUMBLE)
ABSO-LUTELY NOT.
WHAT WOULD I TELL TOHRU-SAN...
...IF ANYTHING WERE TO HAPPEN TO YOU ......?
SHUUU (WHOOSH)
...
SUSUMU, I'M NOT GOING TO DO ANYTHING.
I'M JUST HERE TO TALK.
NO!!
I... I WON'T LET ANYBODY HURT HIM!!!
OOOO (RUMBLE)

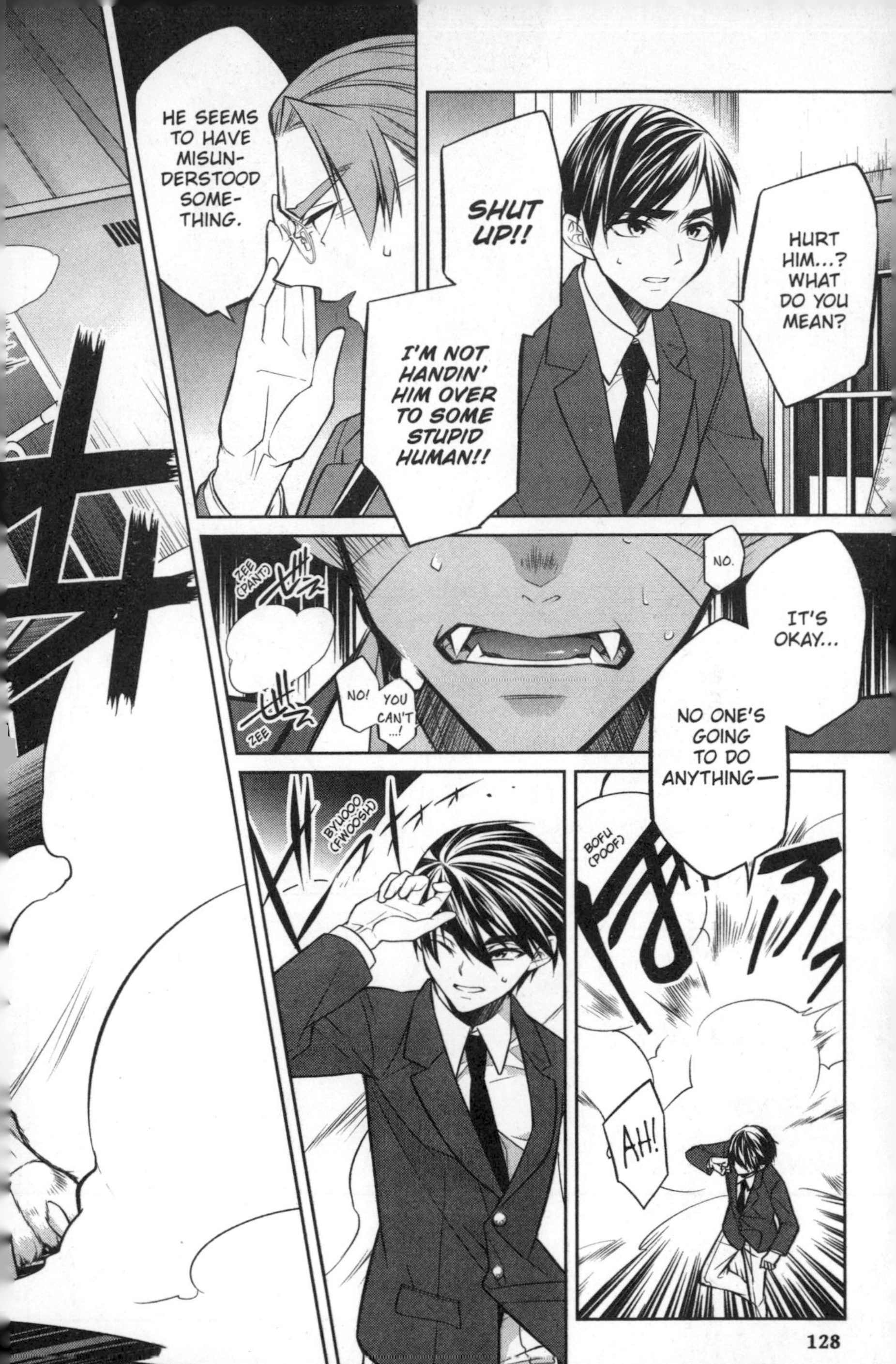
HURT HIM...? WHAT DO YOU MEAN?
SHUT UP!!
I'M NOT HANDIN' HIM OVER TO SOME STUPID HUMAN!!
HE SEEMS TO HAVE MISUN-DERSTOOD SOME-THING.
NO.
IT'S OKAY...
NO ONE'S GOING TO DO ANYTHING—
NO!
YOU CAN'T...!
ZEE (PANT)
ZEE
BOFU (POOF)
AH!
BYUOOO (FWOOSH)

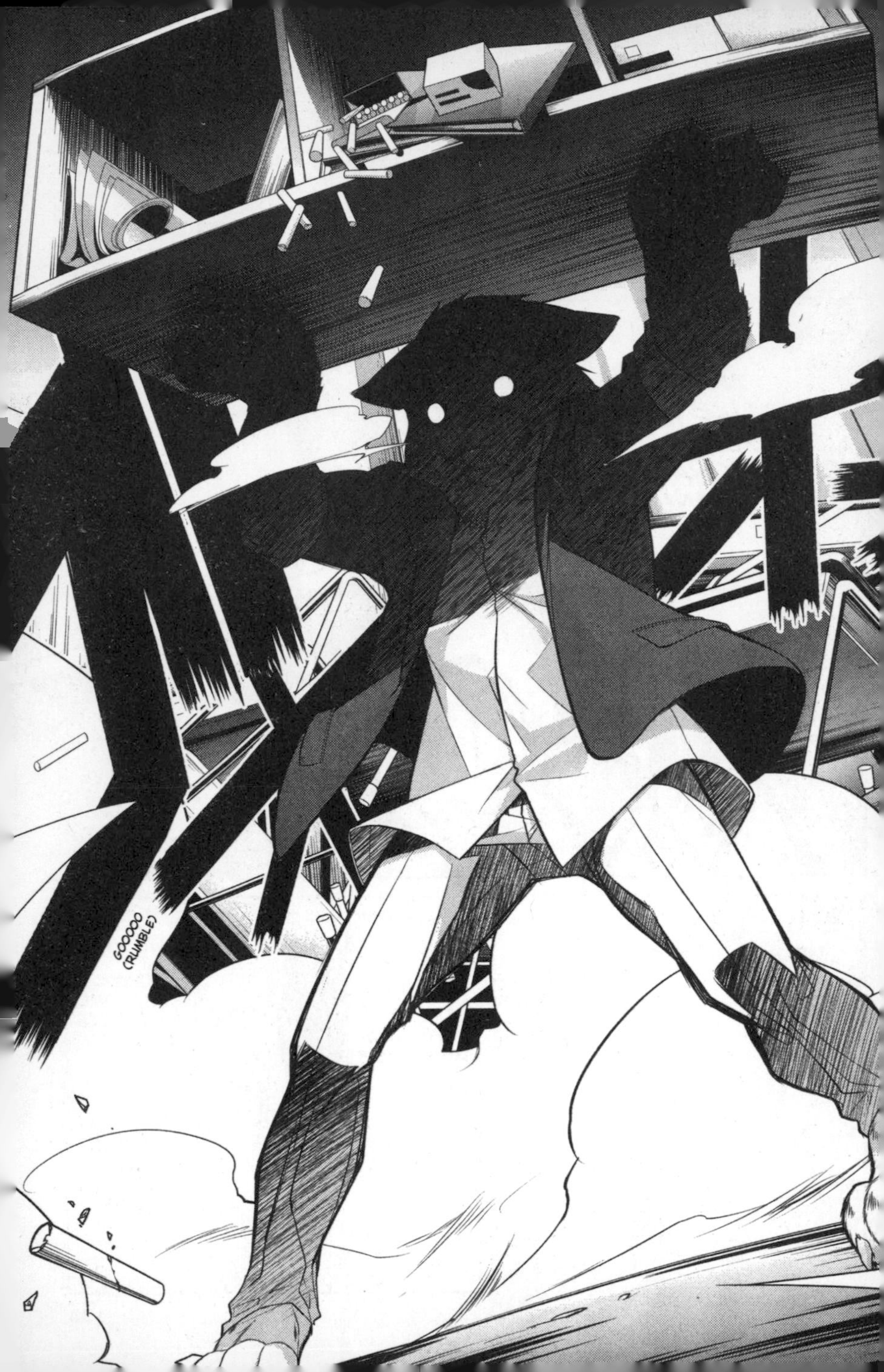
GOOOOO
(RUMBLE)

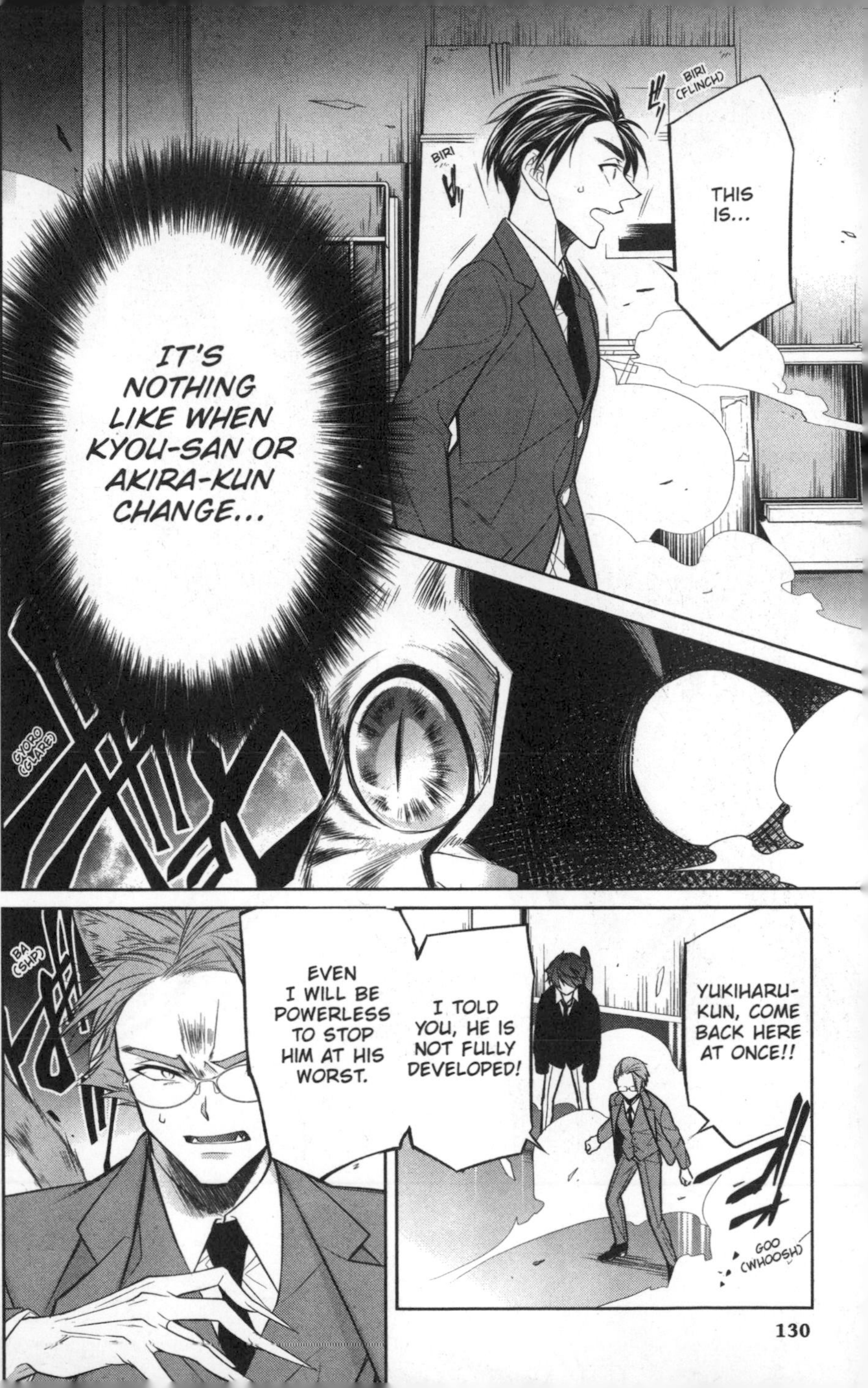
BIRI (FLINCH)
BIRI
THIS IS...
IT'S NOTHING LIKE WHEN KYOU-SAN OR AKIRA-KUN CHANGE...
GYORO (GLARE)
YUKIHARU-KUN, COME BACK HERE AT ONCE!!
GOO (WHOOSH)
I TOLD YOU, HE IS NOT FULLY DEVELOPED!
EVEN I WILL BE POWERLESS TO STOP HIM AT HIS WORST.
BA (SHP)

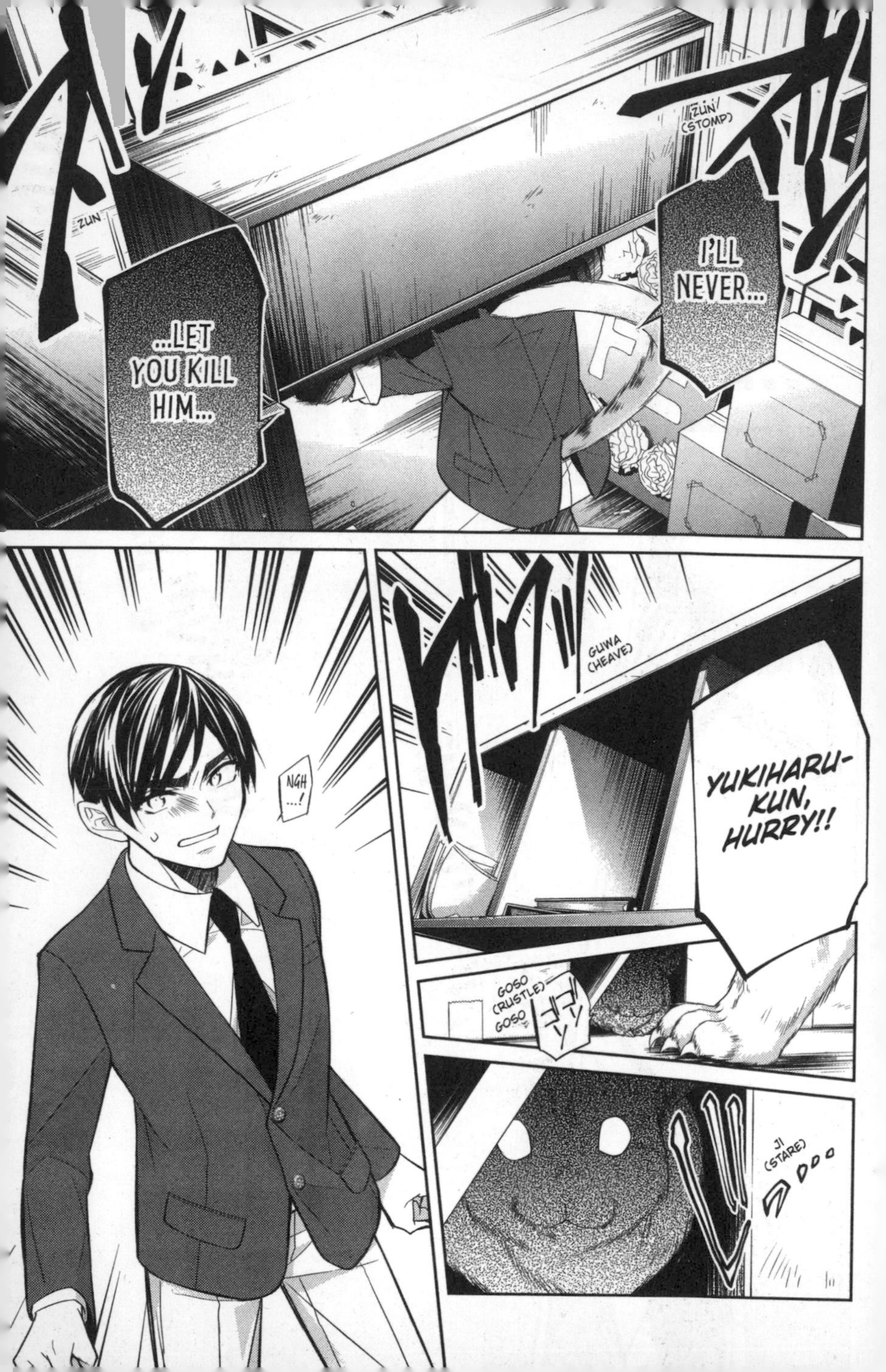
ZUN! (STOMP)
I'LL NEVER...
ZUN
...LET YOU KILL HIM...
GUWA (HEAVE)
YUKIHARU-KUN, HURRY!!
GOSO (RUSTLE) GOSO
JI (STARE)
NGH ...!

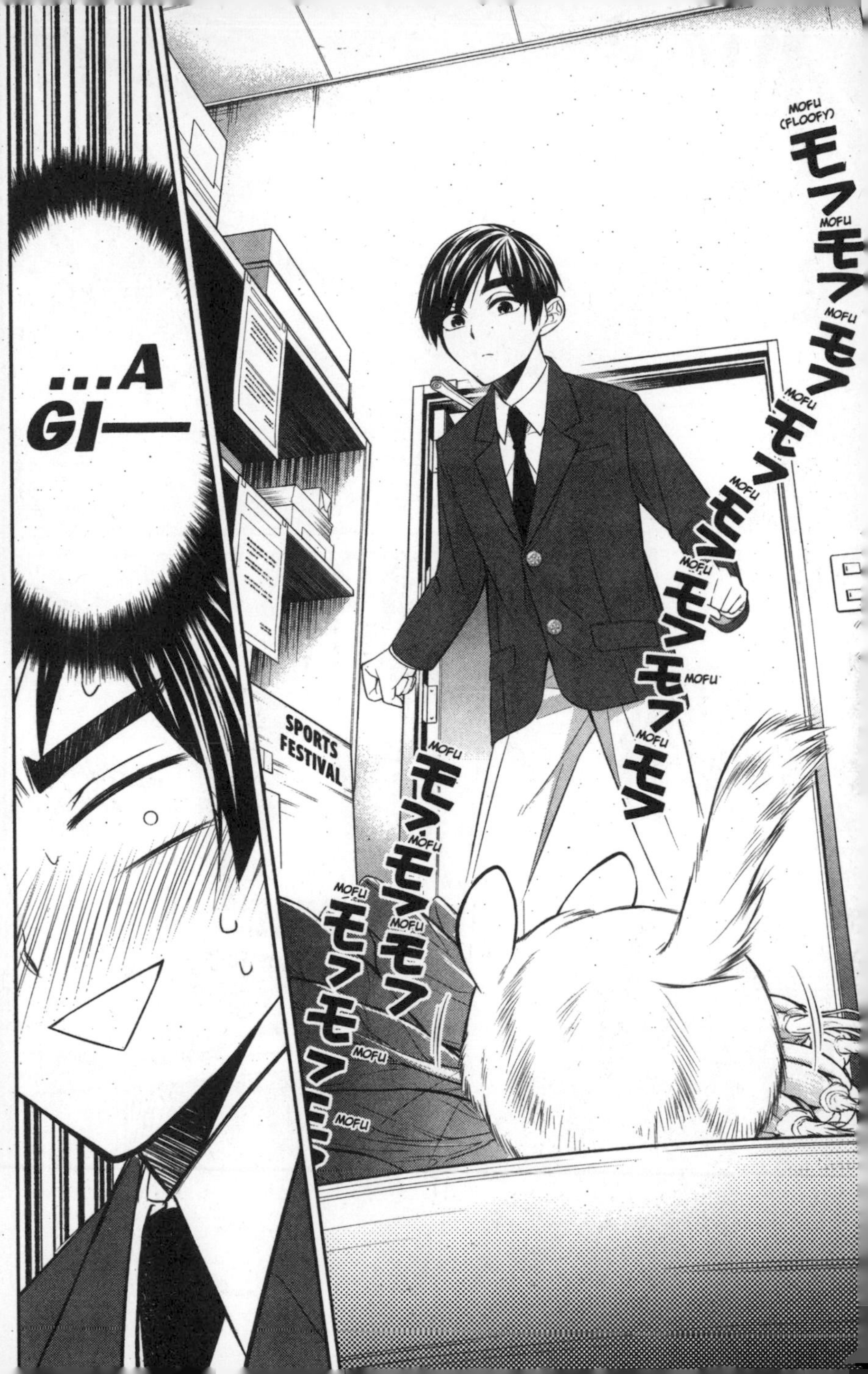
MOFU (FLOOFY)
モフ
MOFU
モフ
MOFU
モフ
MOFU
モフ
MOFU
モフ
MOFU
モフ
MOFU
モフ
MOFU
モフ
MOFU
モフ
MOFU
モフ
MOFU
モフ
MOFU
モフ
MOFU
モフ
MOFU
SPORTS FESTIVAL
...A
GI—

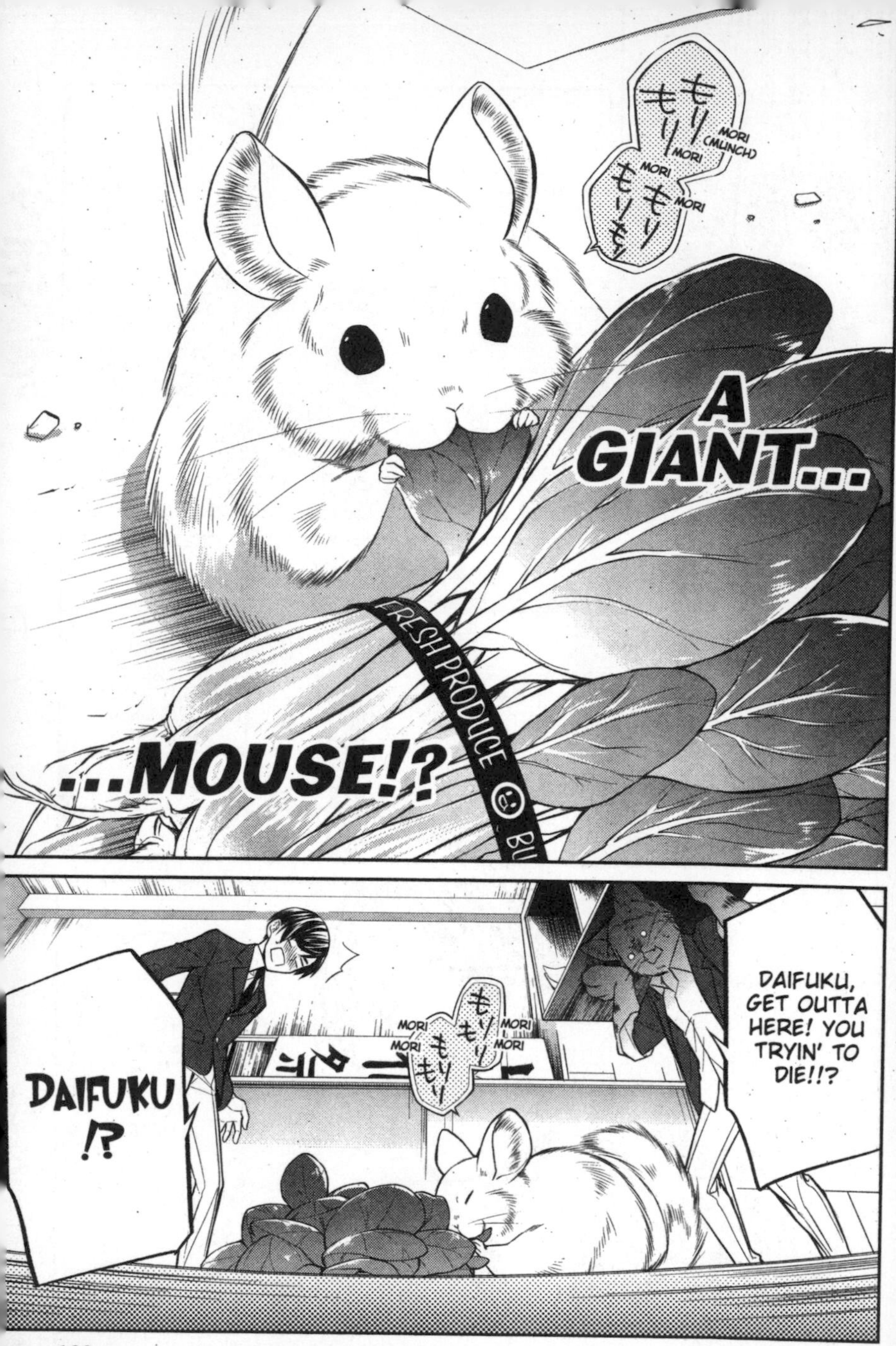
もりもり もりもり
MORI (MUNCH) MORI MORI MORI
A GIANT...
...MOUSE!?
FRESH PRODUCE
DAIFUKU, GET OUTTA HERE! YOU TRYIN' TO DIE!!?
もりもり もりもり
MORI MORI MORI MORI
DAIFUKU !?

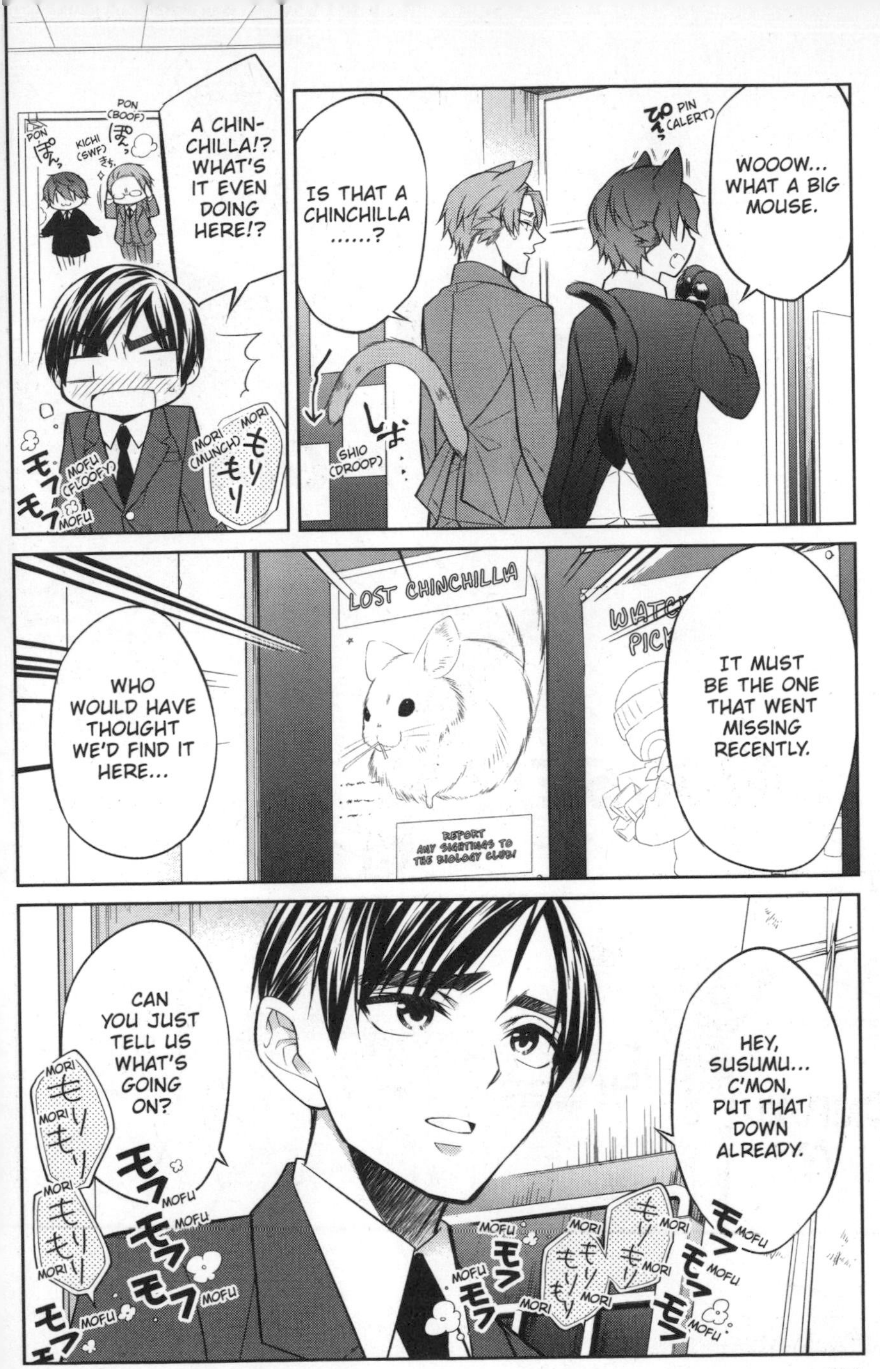

ぴくっ PIN (ALERT)
WOOOW... WHAT A BIG MOUSE.
IS THAT A CHINCHILLA ......?
しお SHIO (DROOP)
ぽんっ PON (BOOF)
ぽんっ PON
きゅ KICHI (SWF)
A CHIN-CHILLA!? WHAT'S IT EVEN DOING HERE!?
もりもり MORI MORI (MUNCH)
モフモフ MOFU (FLOOFY) MOFU
IT MUST BE THE ONE THAT WENT MISSING RECENTLY.
LOST CHINCHILLA
REPORT ANY SIGHTINGS TO THE BIOLOGY CLUB!
WHO WOULD HAVE THOUGHT WE'D FIND IT HERE...
HEY, SUSUMU... C'MON, PUT THAT DOWN ALREADY.
CAN YOU JUST TELL US WHAT'S GOING ON?
もりもり MORI MORI
モフモフ MOFU MOFU

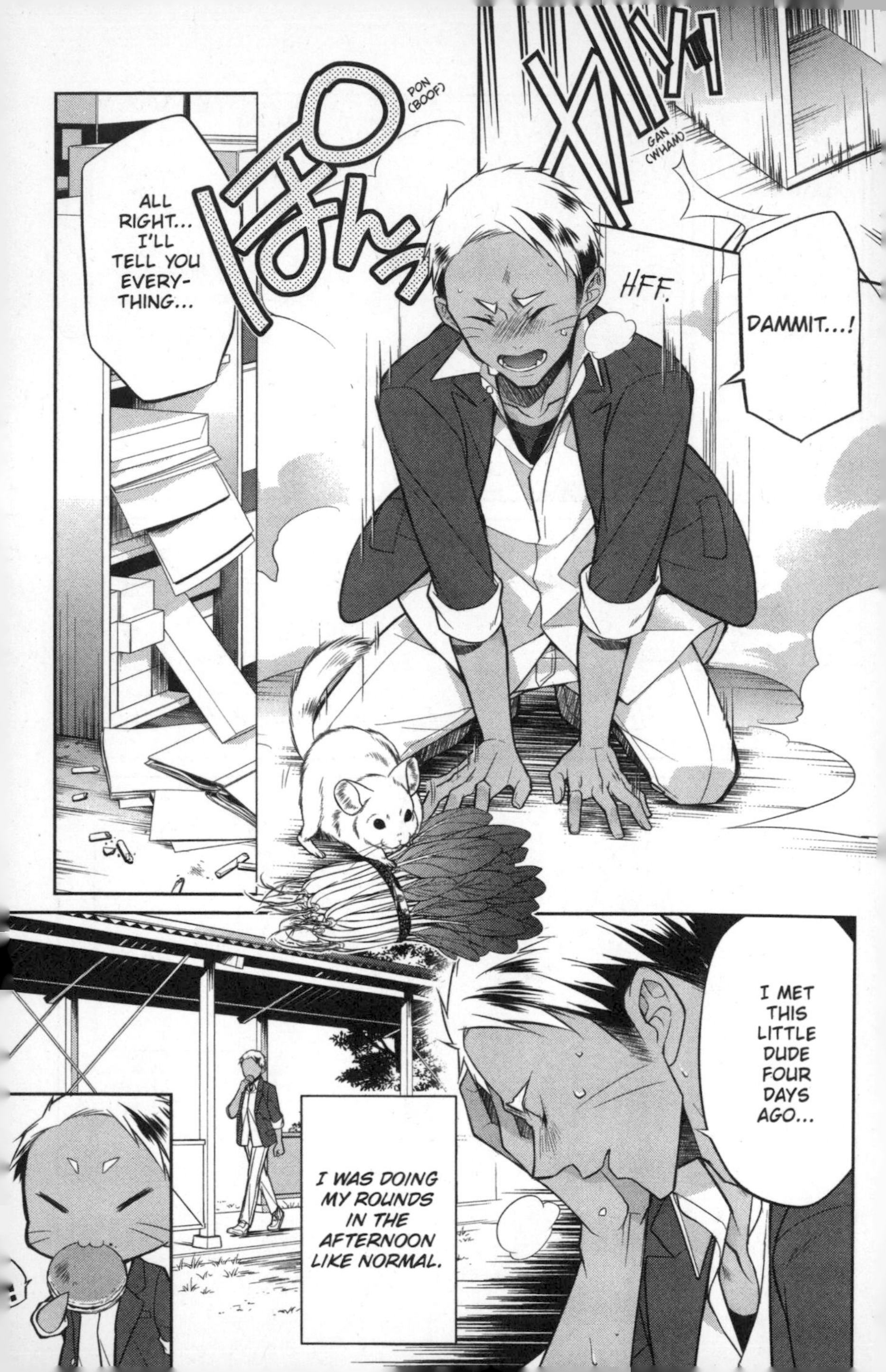
GAN (WHAM)
DAMMIT...!
HFF.
PON (BOOF)
ALL RIGHT... I'LL TELL YOU EVERY-THING...
I MET THIS LITTLE DUDE FOUR DAYS AGO...
I WAS DOING MY ROUNDS IN THE AFTERNOON LIKE NORMAL.

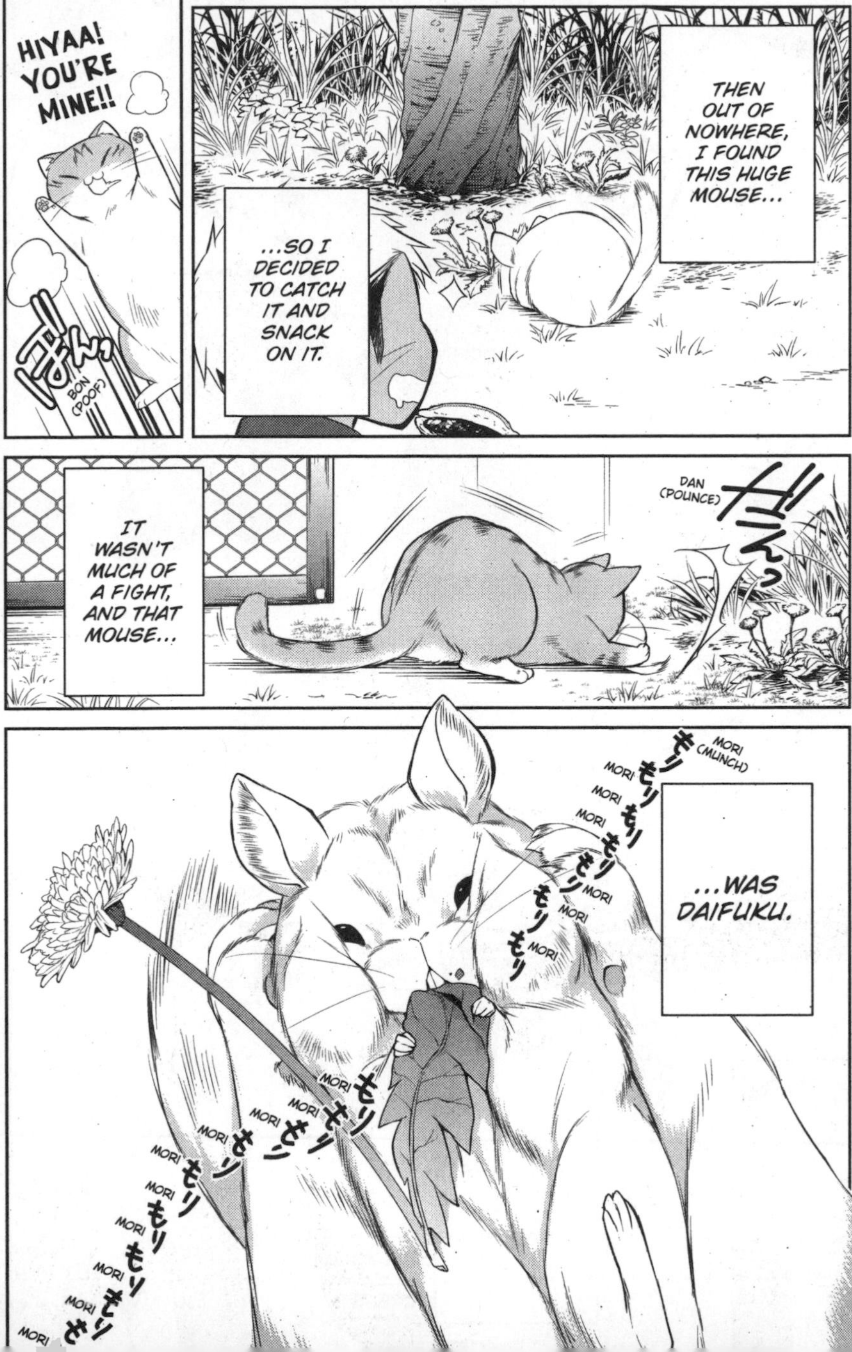
THEN OUT OF NOWHERE, I FOUND THIS HUGE MOUSE...
...SO I DECIDED TO CATCH IT AND SNACK ON IT.
HIYAA! YOU'RE MINE!!
ぼんっ
BON (POOF)
だんっ
DAN (POUNCE)
IT WASN'T MUCH OF A FIGHT, AND THAT MOUSE...
...WAS DAIFUKU.
もりもりもりもりもりもり
MORI (MUNCH) MORI MORI MORI MORI MORI MORI
もりもりもりもりもりもりもりもり
MORI MORI MORI MORI MORI MORI MORI MORI MORI

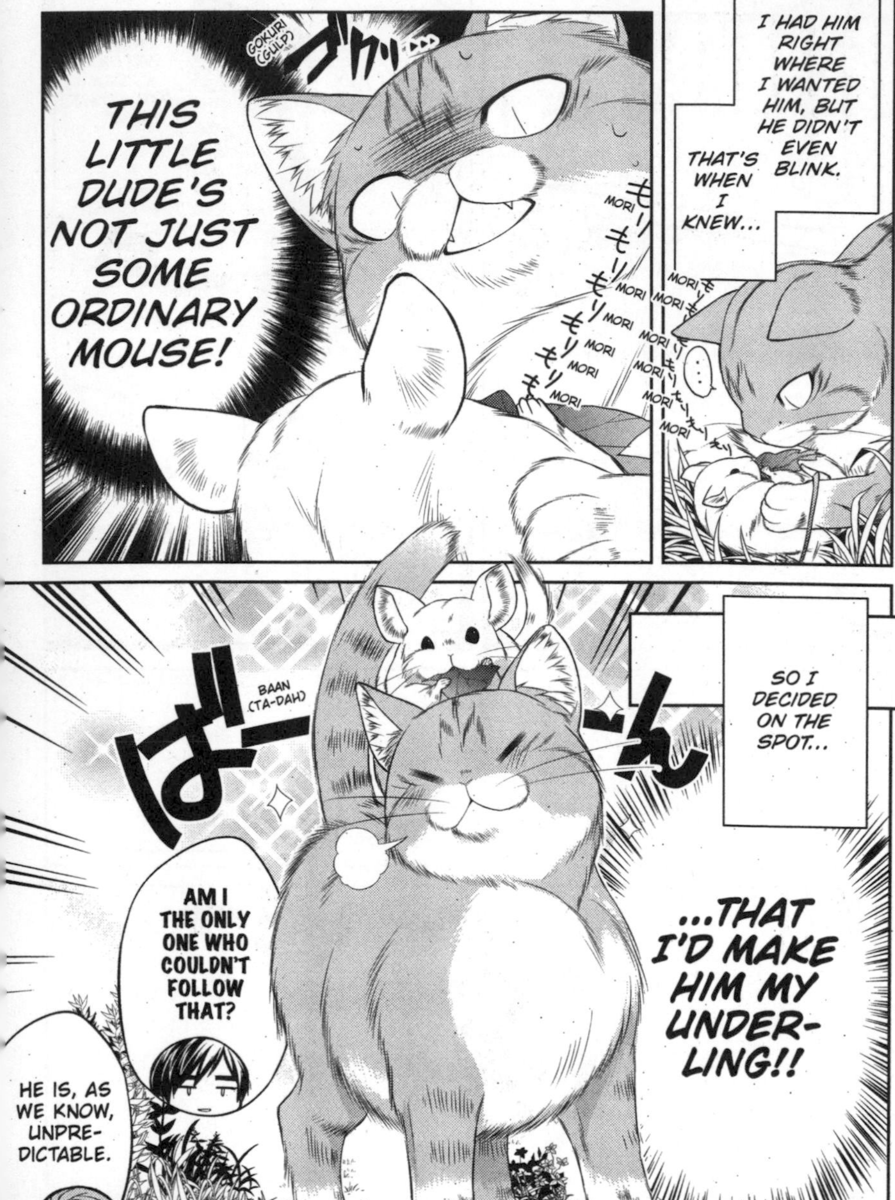
I HAD HIM RIGHT WHERE I WANTED HIM, BUT HE DIDN'T EVEN BLINK.
THAT'S WHEN I KNEW...
MORI MORI MORI MORI MORI
...
GOKURI (GULP)
THIS LITTLE DUDE'S NOT JUST SOME ORDINARY MOUSE!
MORI MORI MORI MORI MORI
SO I DECIDED ON THE SPOT...
BAAN (TA-DAH)
...THAT I'D MAKE HIM MY UNDER-LING!!
AM I THE ONLY ONE WHO COULDN'T FOLLOW THAT?
HE IS, AS WE KNOW, UNPRE-DICTABLE.

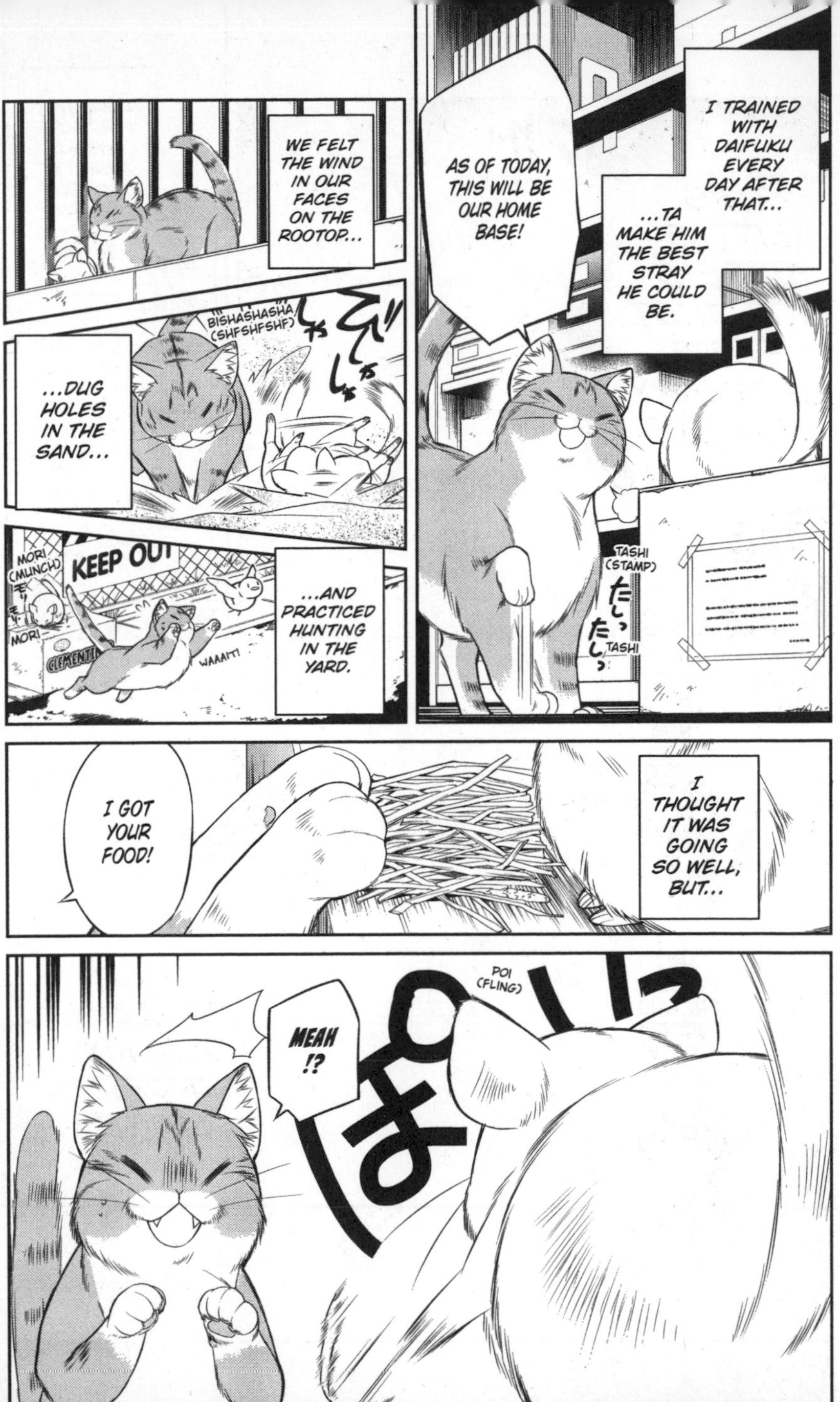
I TRAINED WITH DAIFUKU EVERY DAY AFTER THAT...
...TA MAKE HIM THE BEST STRAY HE COULD BE.
AS OF TODAY, THIS WILL BE OUR HOME BASE!
TASHI (STAMP)
たしっ
たしっ
TASHI
WE FELT THE WIND IN OUR FACES ON THE ROOTOP...
BISHASHASHA (SHFSHFSHF)
...DUG HOLES IN THE SAND...
...AND PRACTICED HUNTING IN THE YARD.
KEEP OUT
MORI (MUNCH)
MORI!
WAAAIT!
I THOUGHT IT WAS GOING SO WELL, BUT...
I GOT YOUR FOOD!
POI (FLING)
MEAH !?

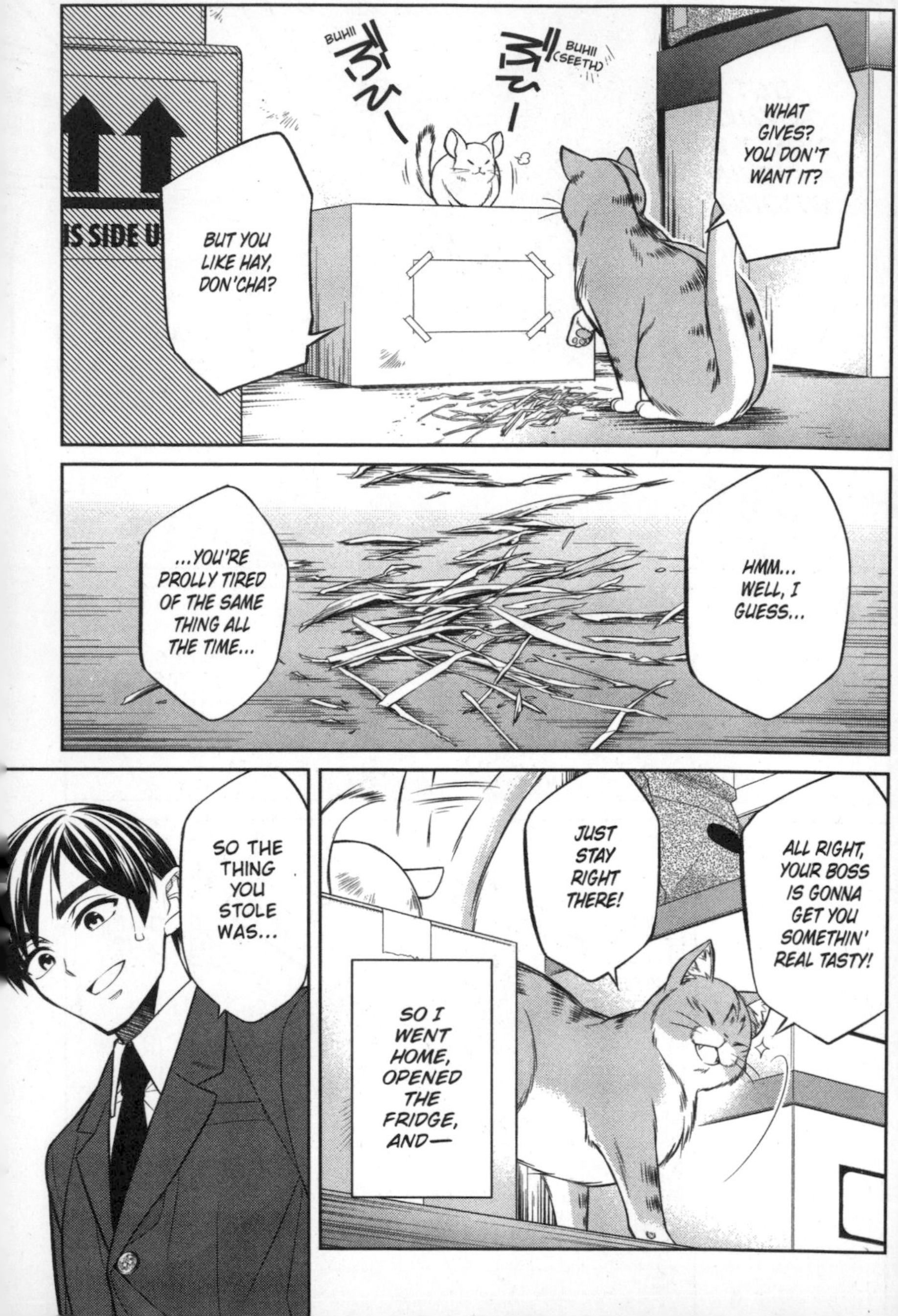
BUHII (SEETH)
BUHII
WHAT GIVES? YOU DON'T WANT IT?
BUT YOU LIKE HAY, DON'CHA?
IS SIDE U
HMM... WELL, I GUESS...
...YOU'RE PROLLY TIRED OF THE SAME THING ALL THE TIME...
ALL RIGHT, YOUR BOSS IS GONNA GET YOU SOMETHIN' REAL TASTY!
JUST STAY RIGHT THERE!
SO I WENT HOME, OPENED THE FRIDGE, AND—
SO THE THING YOU STOLE WAS...

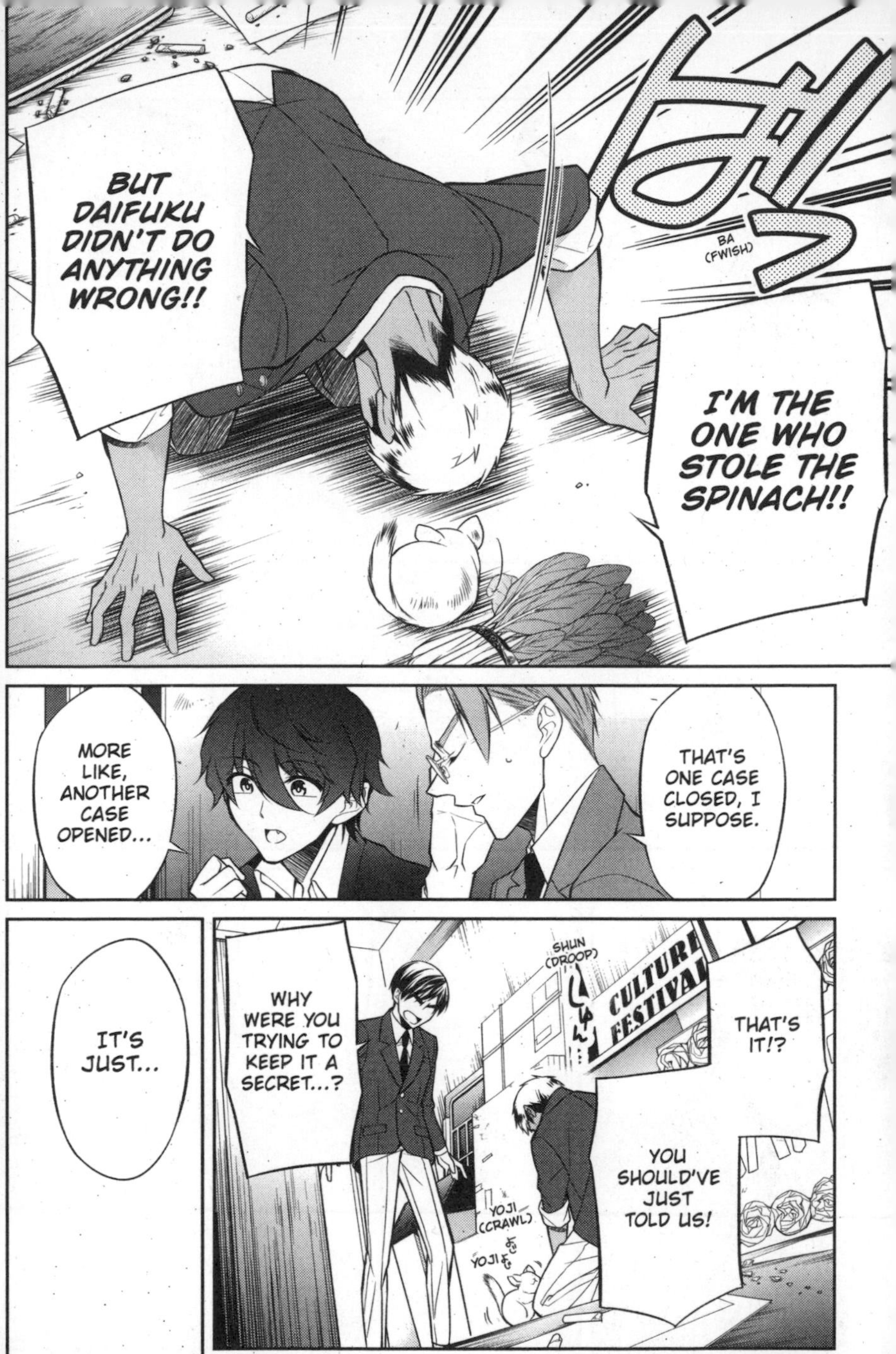
BA (FWISH)
I'M THE ONE WHO STOLE THE SPINACH!!
BUT DAIFUKU DIDN'T DO ANYTHING WRONG!!
THAT'S ONE CASE CLOSED, I SUPPOSE.
MORE LIKE, ANOTHER CASE OPENED...
THAT'S IT!?
CULTURE FESTIVAL
SHUN (DROOP)
WHY WERE YOU TRYING TO KEEP IT A SECRET...?
YOU SHOULD'VE JUST TOLD US!
YOJI (CRAWL)
YOJI
IT'S JUST...

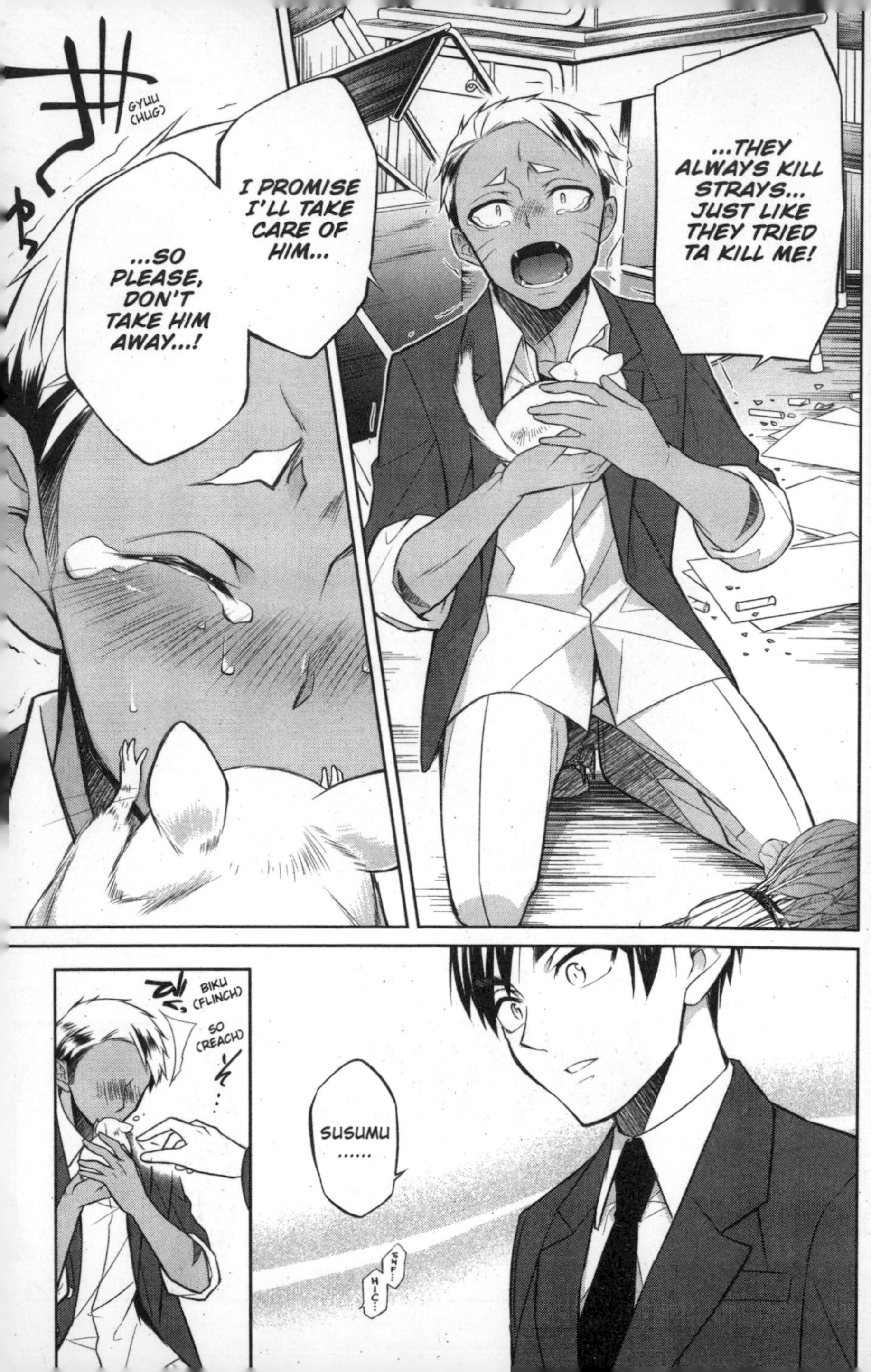
...THEY ALWAYS KILL STRAYS... JUST LIKE THEY TRIED TA KILL ME!
I PROMISE I'LL TAKE CARE OF HIM...
GYUU (HUG)
...SO PLEASE, DON'T TAKE HIM AWAY...!
SUSUMU ......
SNF... HIC...
BIKU (FLINCH)
SO (REACH)

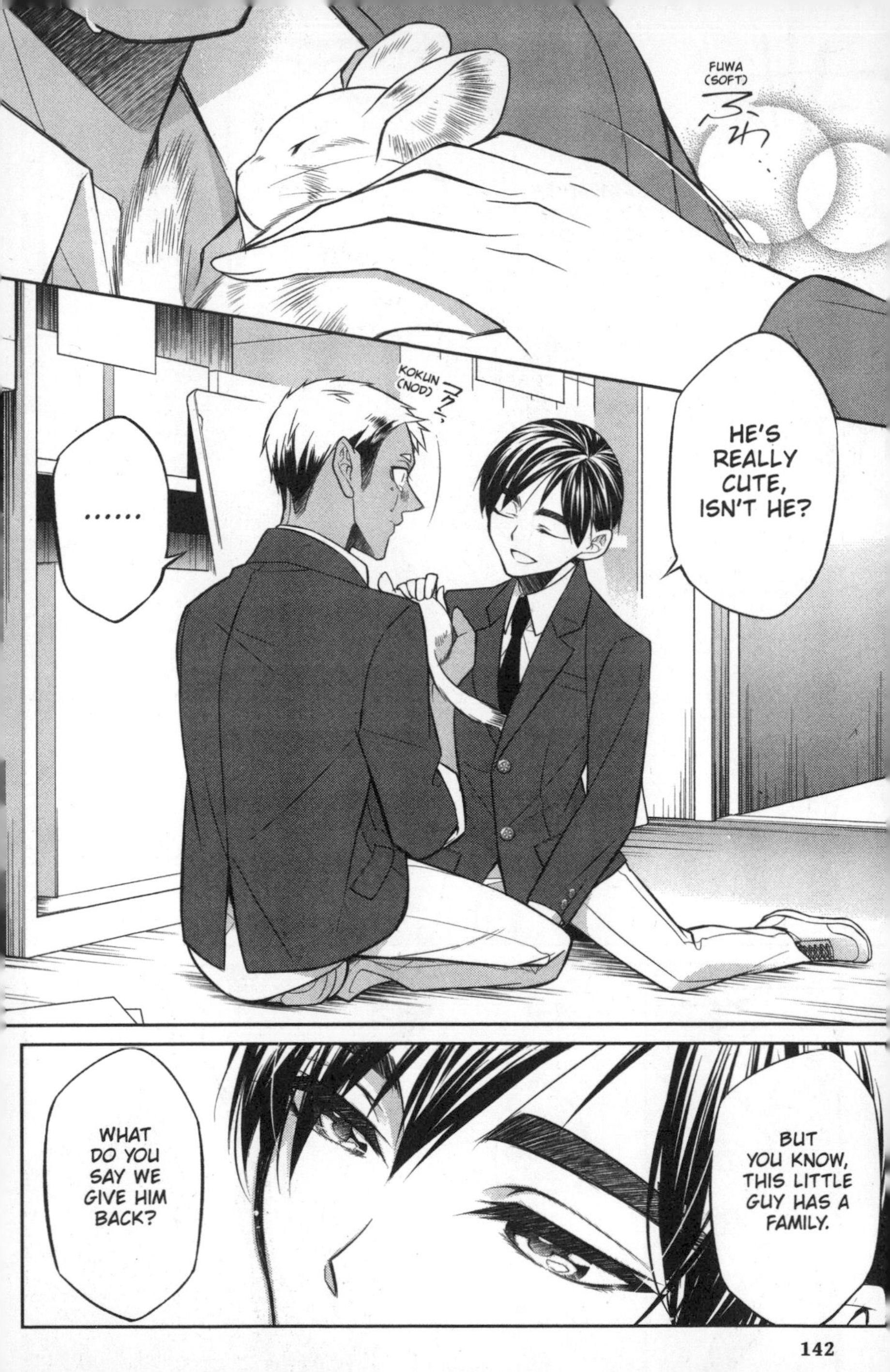
FUWA (SOFT)
HE'S REALLY CUTE, ISN'T HE?
KOKUN (NOD)
......
BUT YOU KNOW, THIS LITTLE GUY HAS A FAMILY.
WHAT DO YOU SAY WE GIVE HIM BACK?

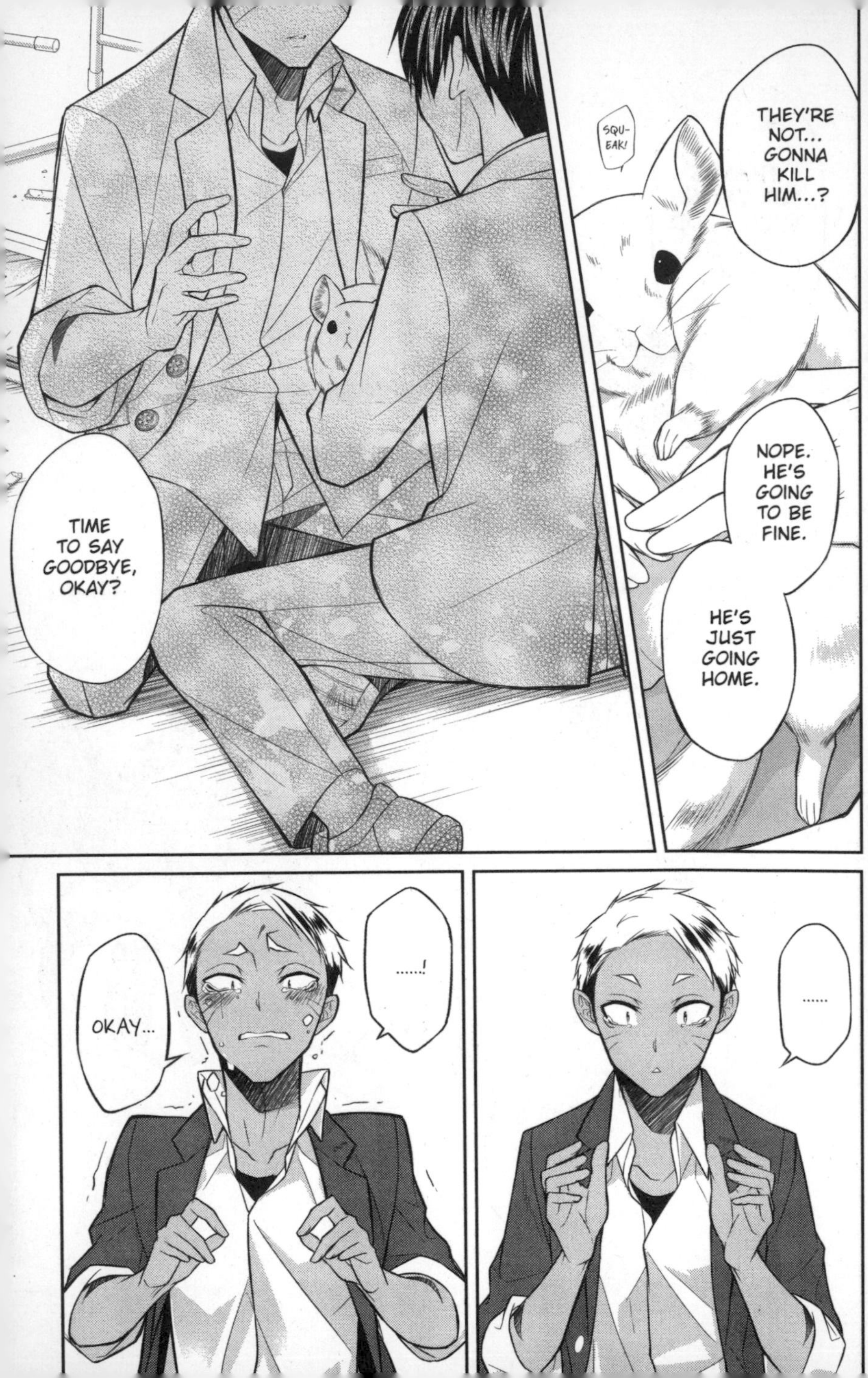
THEY'RE NOT... GONNA KILL HIM...?
SQU-EAK!
NOPE. HE'S GOING TO BE FINE.
HE'S JUST GOING HOME.
TIME TO SAY GOODBYE, OKAY?
......
......!
OKAY...

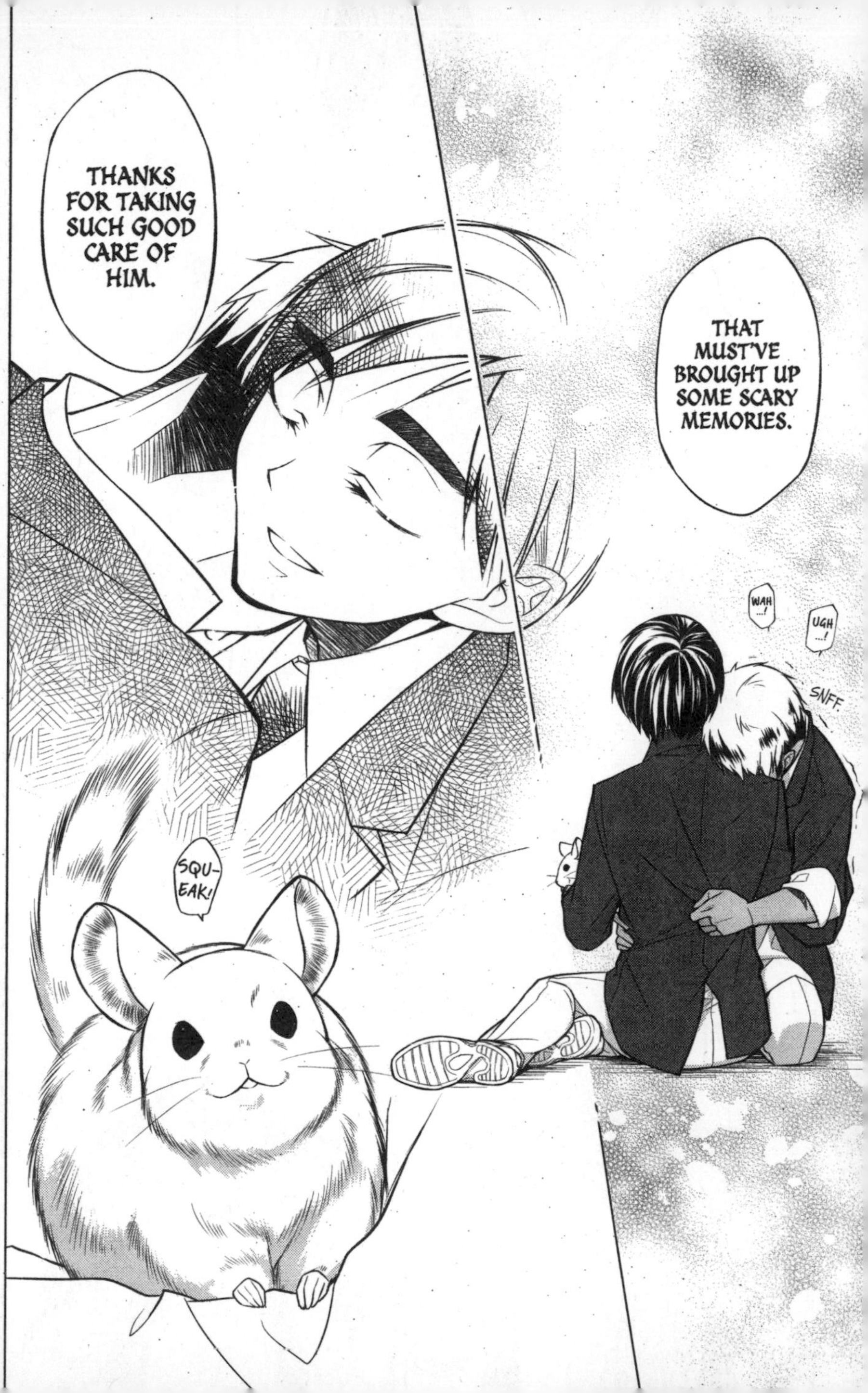
THAT MUST'VE BROUGHT UP SOME SCARY MEMORIES.
WAH ...!
UGH ...!
SNFF.
THANKS FOR TAKING SUCH GOOD CARE OF HIM.
SQU-EAK!

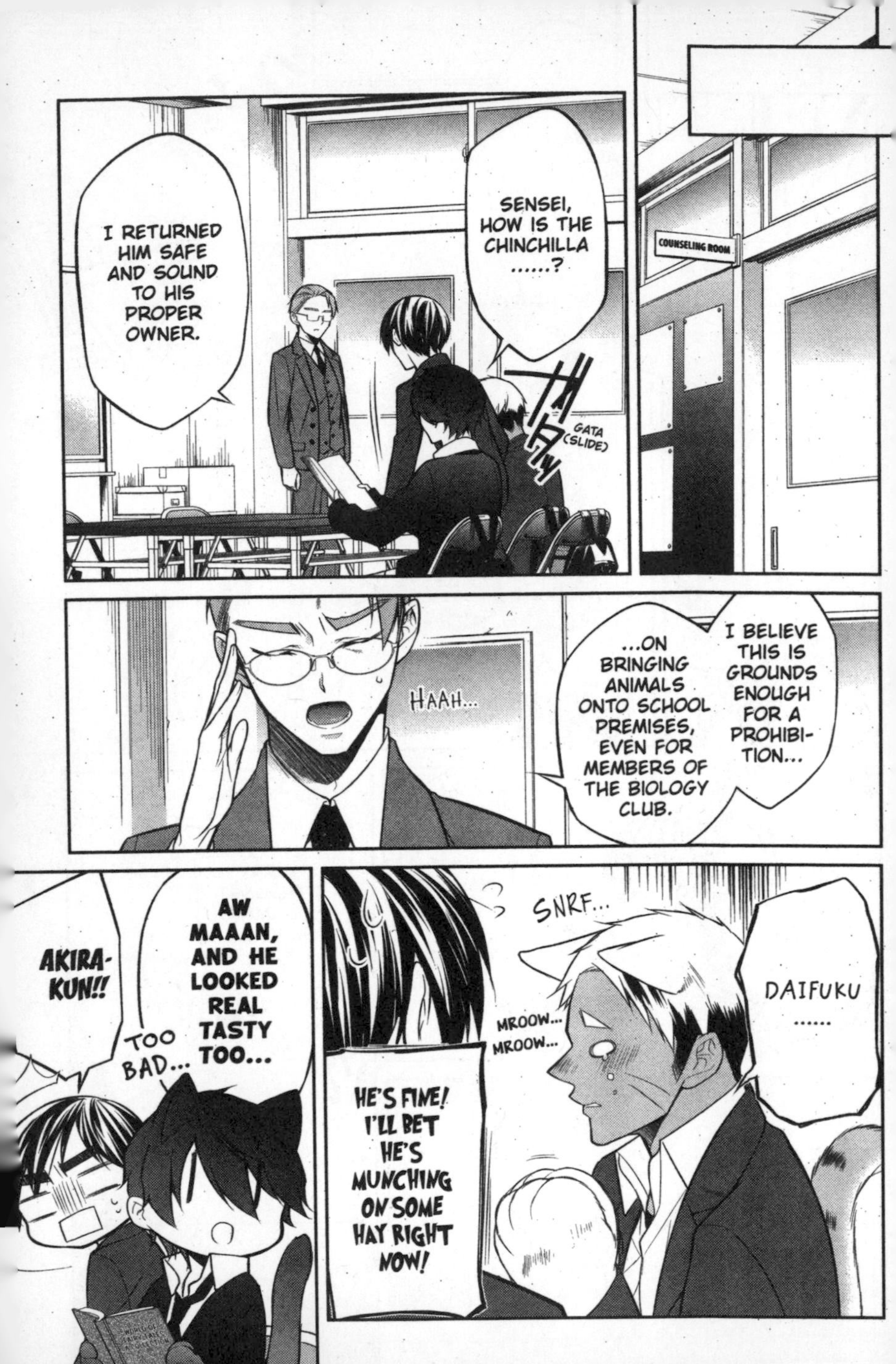
COUNSELING ROOM
SENSEI, HOW IS THE CHINCHILLA ......?
GATA (SLIDE)
I RETURNED HIM SAFE AND SOUND TO HIS PROPER OWNER.
I BELIEVE THIS IS GROUNDS ENOUGH FOR A PROHIBITION...
...ON BRINGING ANIMALS ONTO SCHOOL PREMISES, EVEN FOR MEMBERS OF THE BIOLOGY CLUB.
HAAH...
DAIFUKU ......
SNRF...
MROOW... MROOW...
HE'S FINE! I'LL BET HE'S MUNCHING ON SOME HAY RIGHT NOW!
AW MAAAN, AND HE LOOKED REAL TASTY TOO...
TOO BAD...
AKIRA-KUN!!

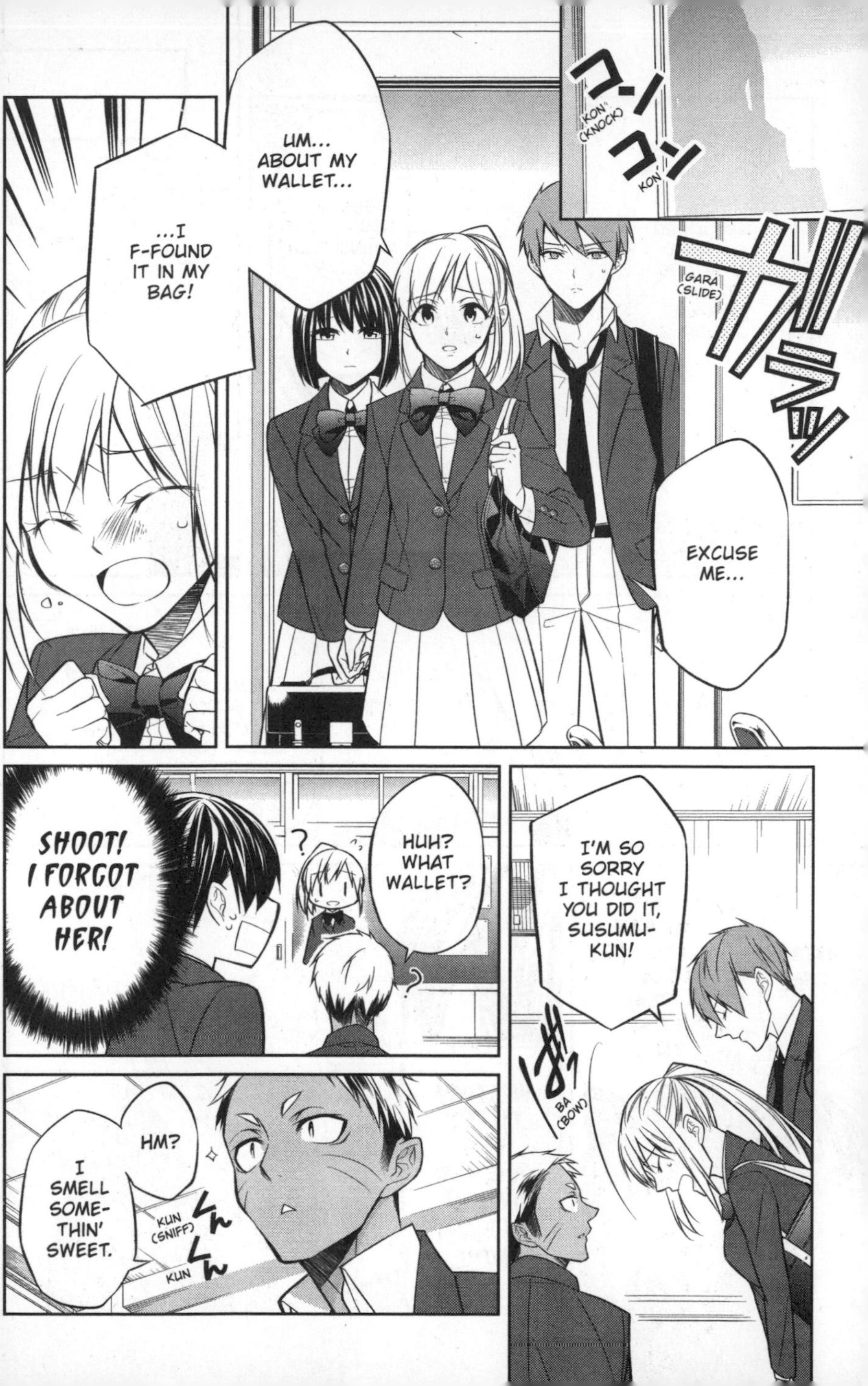

コン
KON (KNOCK)
コン
KON
ガラッ
GARA (SLIDE)
EXCUSE ME...
UM... ABOUT MY WALLET...
...I F-FOUND IT IN MY BAG!
I'M SO SORRY I THOUGHT YOU DID IT, SUSUMU-KUN!
BA (BOW)
HUH? WHAT WALLET?
SHOOT! I FORGOT ABOUT HER!
HM?
I SMELL SOME-THIN' SWEET.
KUN (SNIFF)
KUN

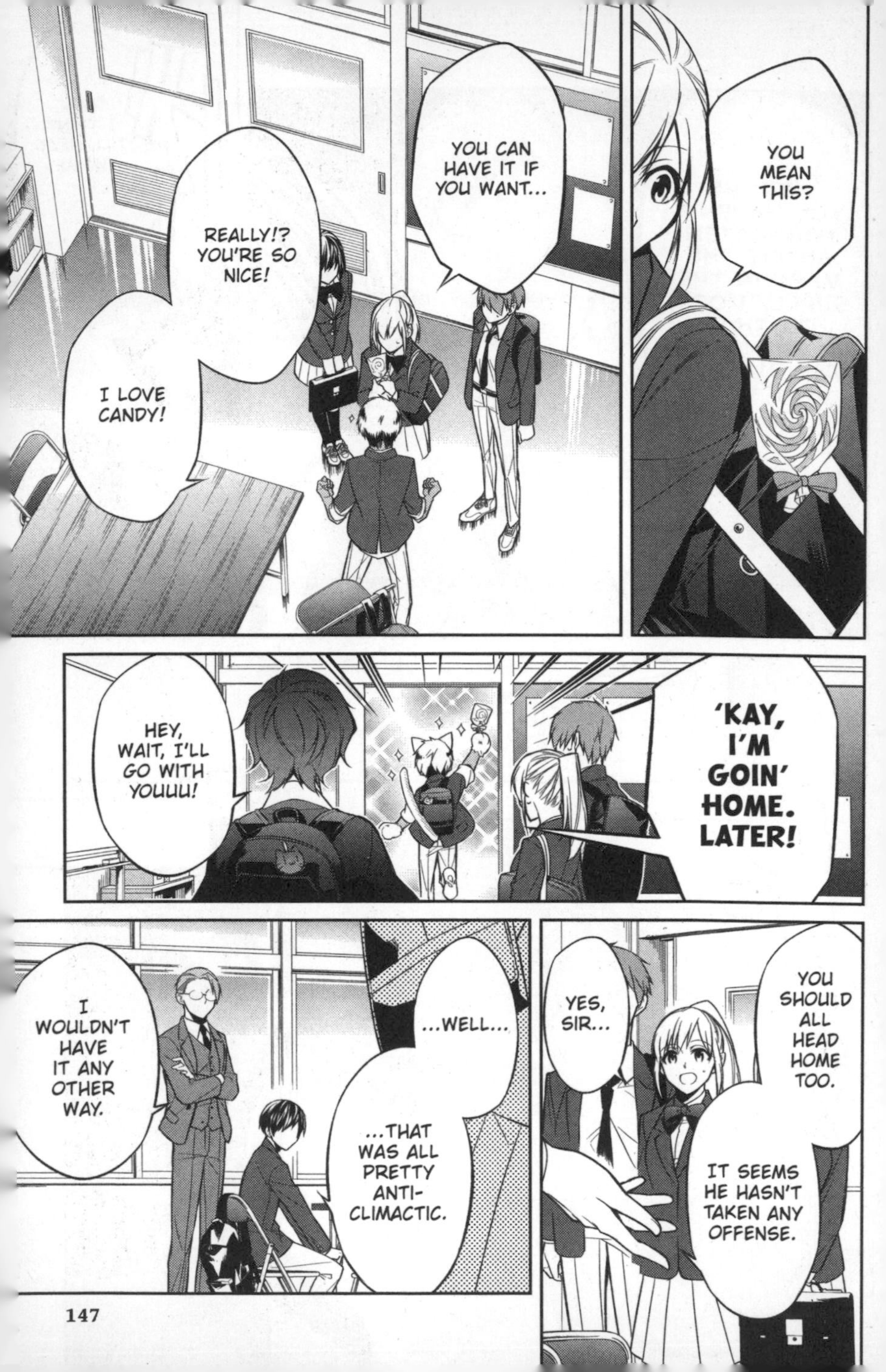
YOU MEAN THIS?
YOU CAN HAVE IT IF YOU WANT...
REALLY!? YOU'RE SO NICE!
I LOVE CANDY!
'KAY, I'M GOIN' HOME. LATER!
HEY, WAIT, I'LL GO WITH YOUUU!
YOU SHOULD ALL HEAD HOME TOO.
YES, SIR...
IT SEEMS HE HASN'T TAKEN ANY OFFENSE.
...WELL...
...THAT WAS ALL PRETTY ANTI-CLIMACTIC.
I WOULDN'T HAVE IT ANY OTHER WAY.

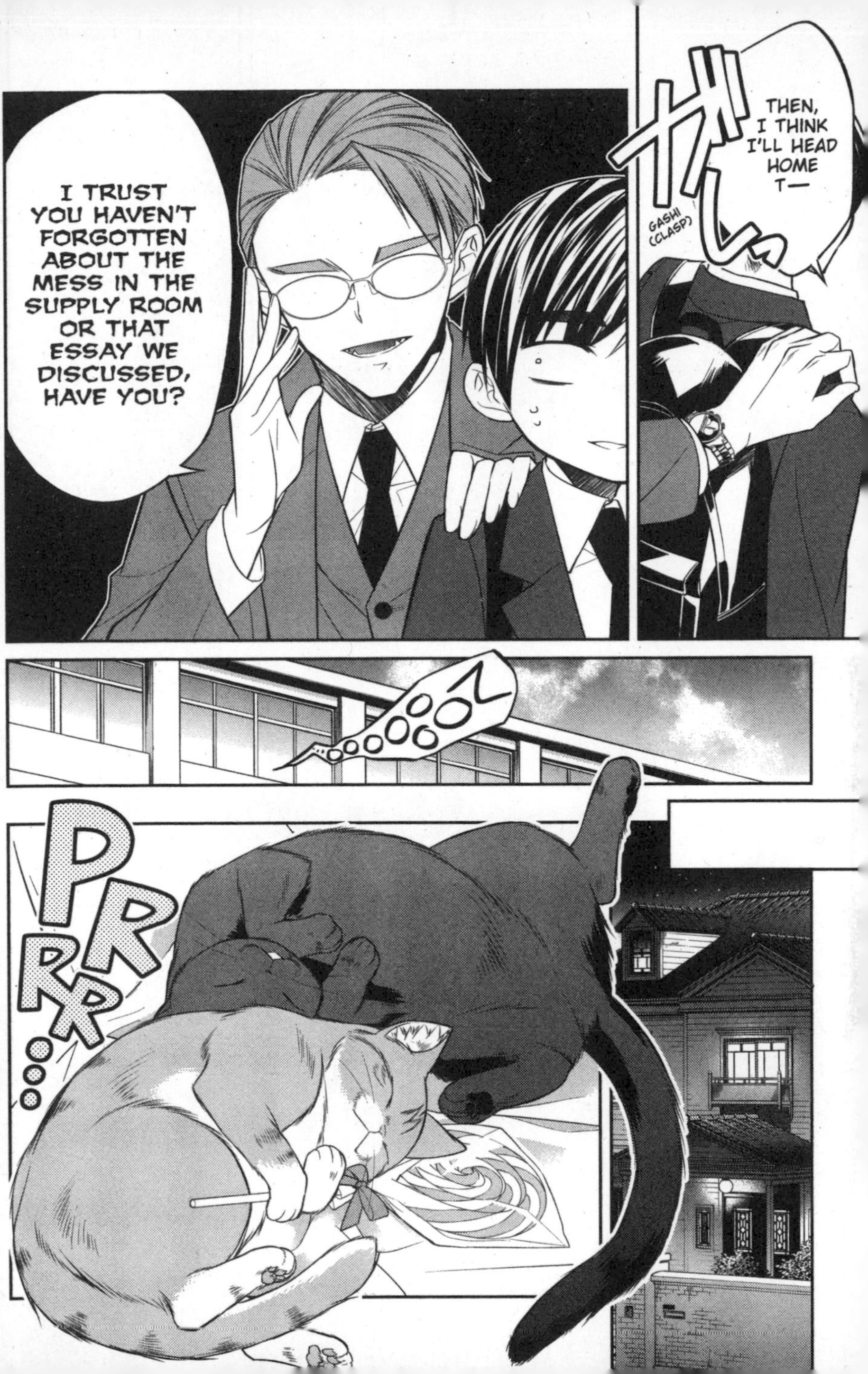
THEN, I THINK I'LL HEAD HOME T—
GASHI (CLASP)
I TRUST YOU HAVEN'T FORGOTTEN ABOUT THE MESS IN THE SUPPLY ROOM OR THAT ESSAY WE DISCUSSED, HAVE YOU?
NOOOOOOOO...
PRRR...

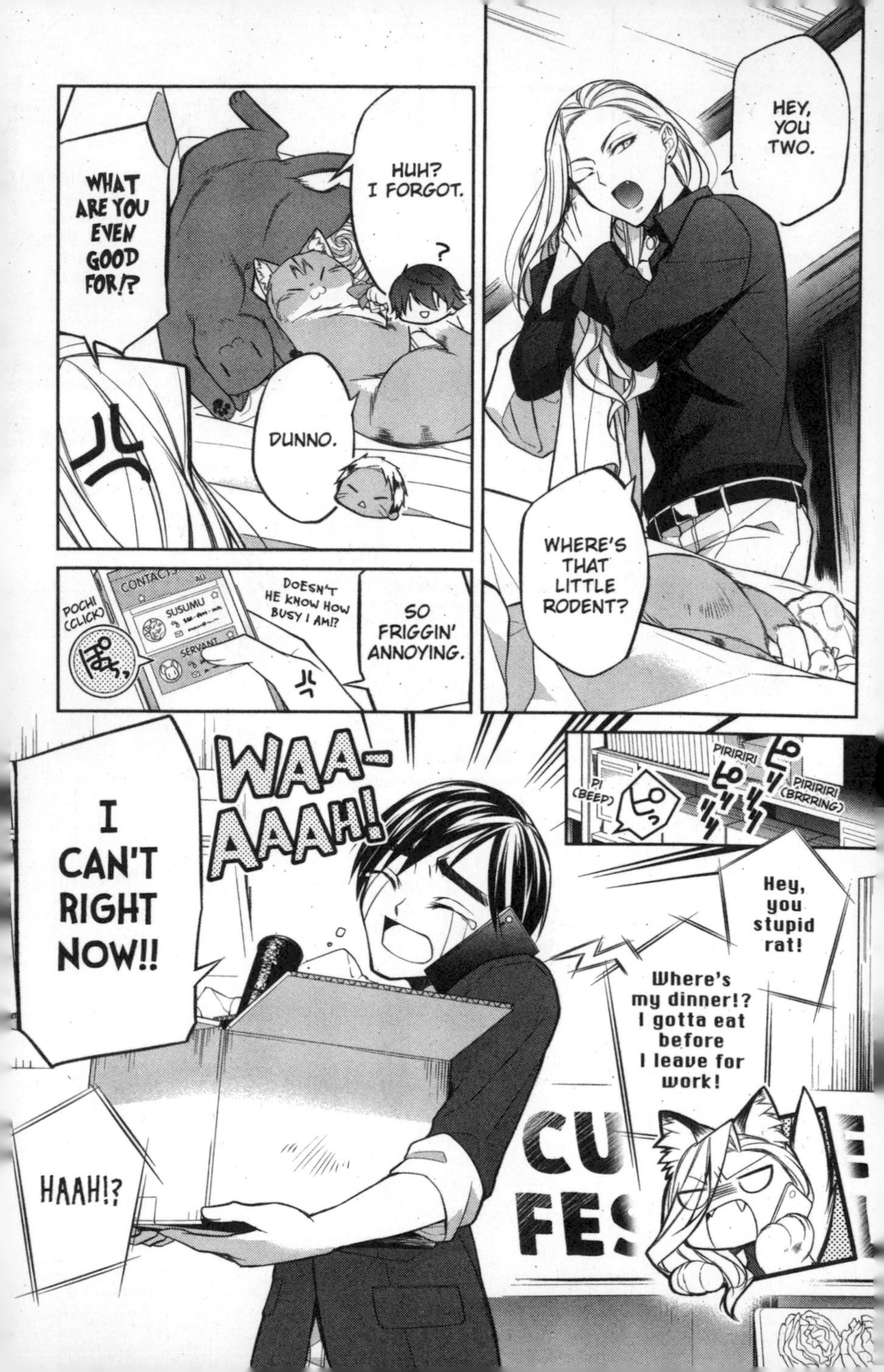
HEY, YOU TWO.
WHERE'S THAT LITTLE RODENT?
HUH? I FORGOT.
WHAT ARE YOU EVEN GOOD FOR!?
?
DUNNO.
SO FRIGGIN' ANNOYING.
DOESN'T HE KNOW HOW BUSY I AM!?
CONTACTS
ALL
SUSUMU
SERVANT
POCHI (CLICK)
PIRIRIRI (BRRRING)
PIRIRIRI
PI (BEEP)
Hey, you stupid rat!
Where's my dinner!? I gotta eat before I leave for work!
WAA-AAAH!
I CAN'T RIGHT NOW!!
HAAH!?

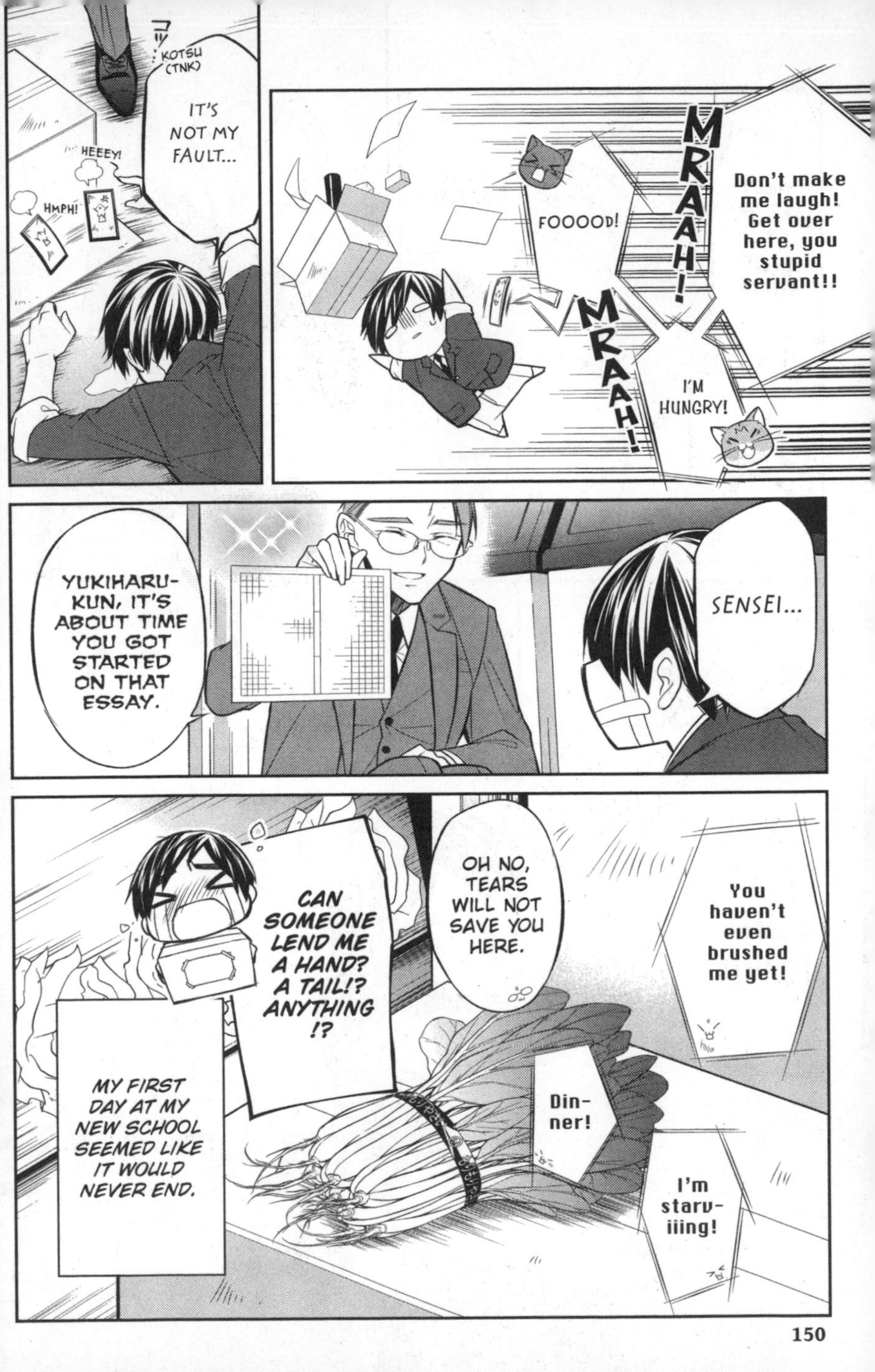
Don't make me laugh! Get over here, you stupid servant!!
MRAAH!
FOOOOD!
MRAAH!
I'M HUNGRY!
KOTSU (TNK)
IT'S NOT MY FAULT...
HEEEY!
HMPH!
SENSEI...
YUKIHARU-KUN, IT'S ABOUT TIME YOU GOT STARTED ON THAT ESSAY.
You haven't even brushed me yet!
OH NO, TEARS WILL NOT SAVE YOU HERE.
CAN SOMEONE LEND ME A HAND? A TAIL!? ANYTHING!?
Dinner!
I'm starviiing!
MY FIRST DAY AT MY NEW SCHOOL SEEMED LIKE IT WOULD NEVER END.

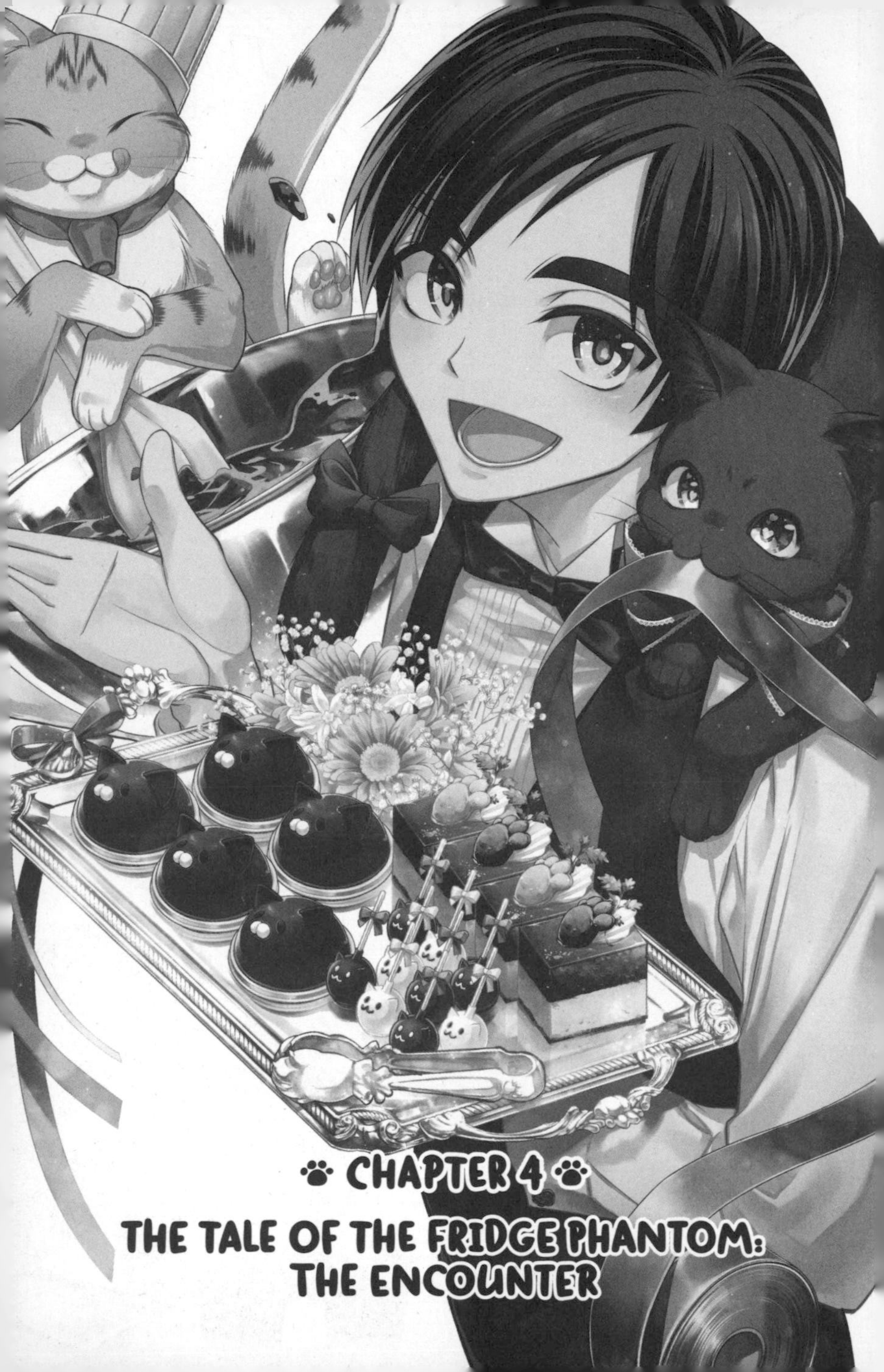
CHAPTER 4
THE TALE OF THE FRIDGE PHANTOM: THE ENCOUNTER

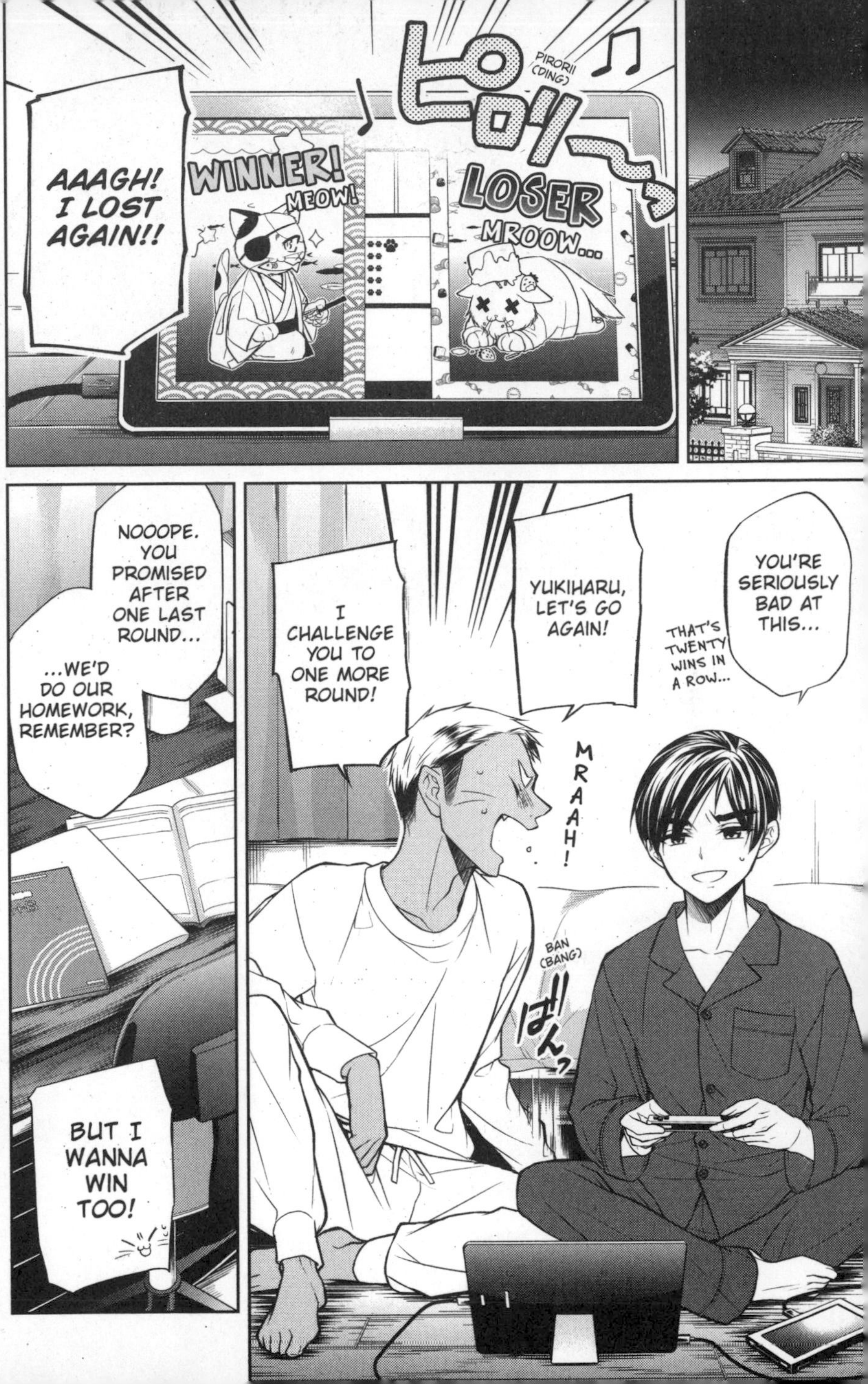
ピロリ～
PIRORII (DING)
WINNER!
MEOW!
LOSER
MROOW...
AAAGH! I LOST AGAIN!!
YOU'RE SERIOUSLY BAD AT THIS...
THAT'S TWENTY WINS IN A ROW...
YUKIHARU, LET'S GO AGAIN!
I CHALLENGE YOU TO ONE MORE ROUND!
MRAAH!
BAN (BANG)
ばんっ
NOOOPE. YOU PROMISED AFTER ONE LAST ROUND...
...WE'D DO OUR HOMEWORK, REMEMBER?
BUT I WANNA WIN TOO!

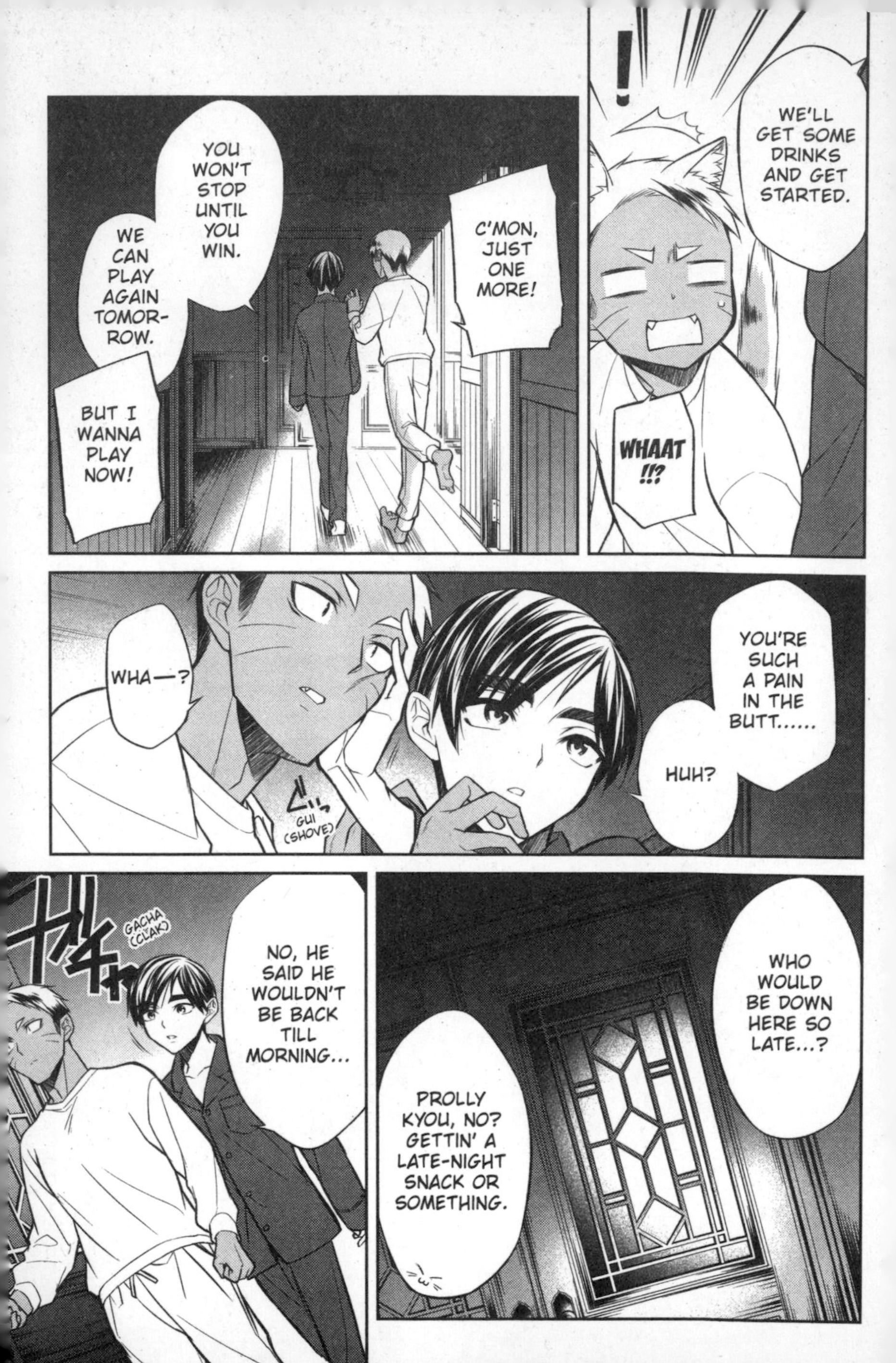
!
WE'LL GET SOME DRINKS AND GET STARTED.
WHAAT!!?
C'MON, JUST ONE MORE!
YOU WON'T STOP UNTIL YOU WIN.
WE CAN PLAY AGAIN TOMORROW.
BUT I WANNA PLAY NOW!
YOU'RE SUCH A PAIN IN THE BUTT......
HUH?
GUI (SHOVE)
WHA—?
WHO WOULD BE DOWN HERE SO LATE...?
PROLLY KYOU, NO? GETTIN' A LATE-NIGHT SNACK OR SOMETHING.
GACHA (CLAK)
NO, HE SAID HE WOULDN'T BE BACK TILL MORNING...

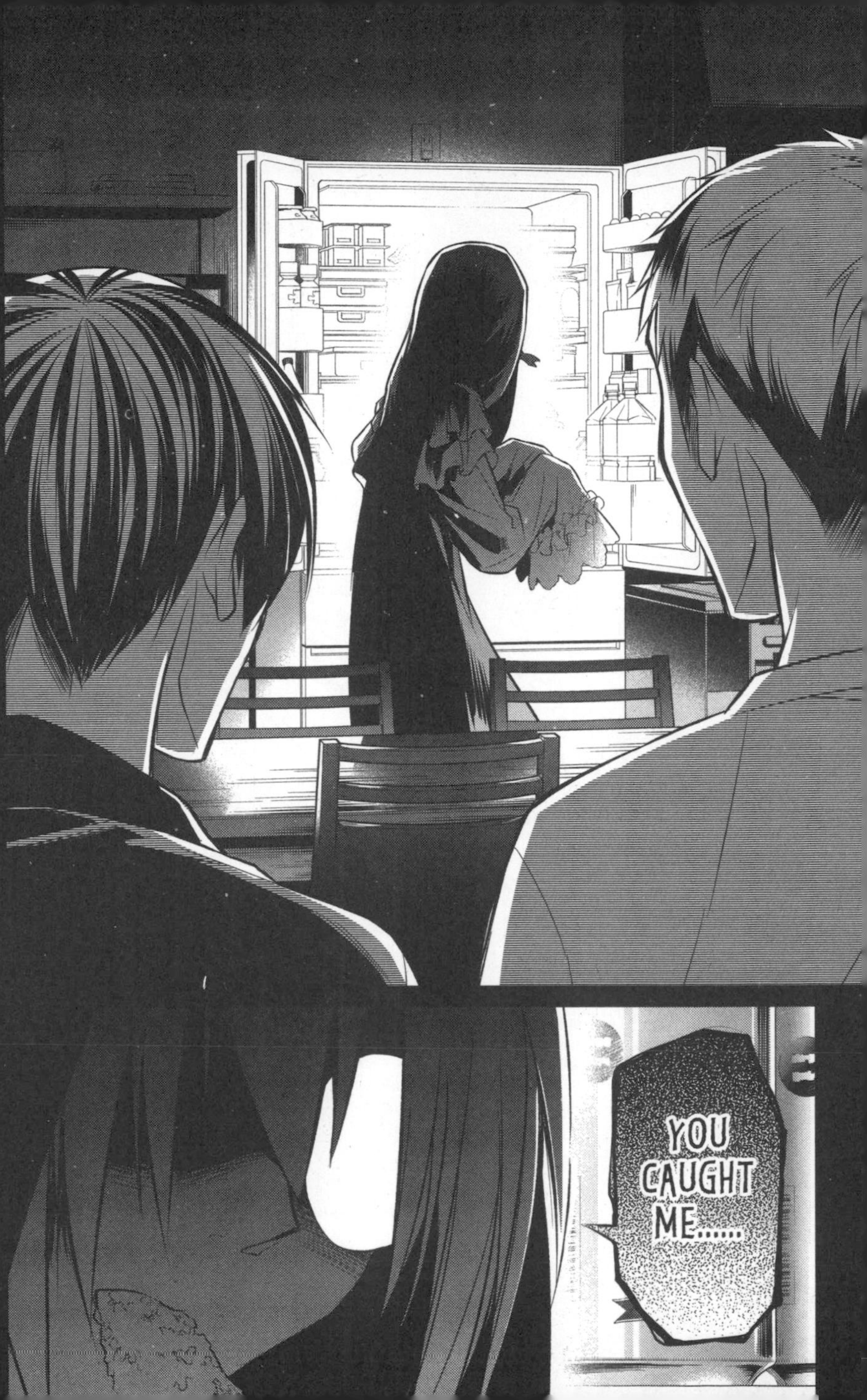
YOU CAUGHT ME......

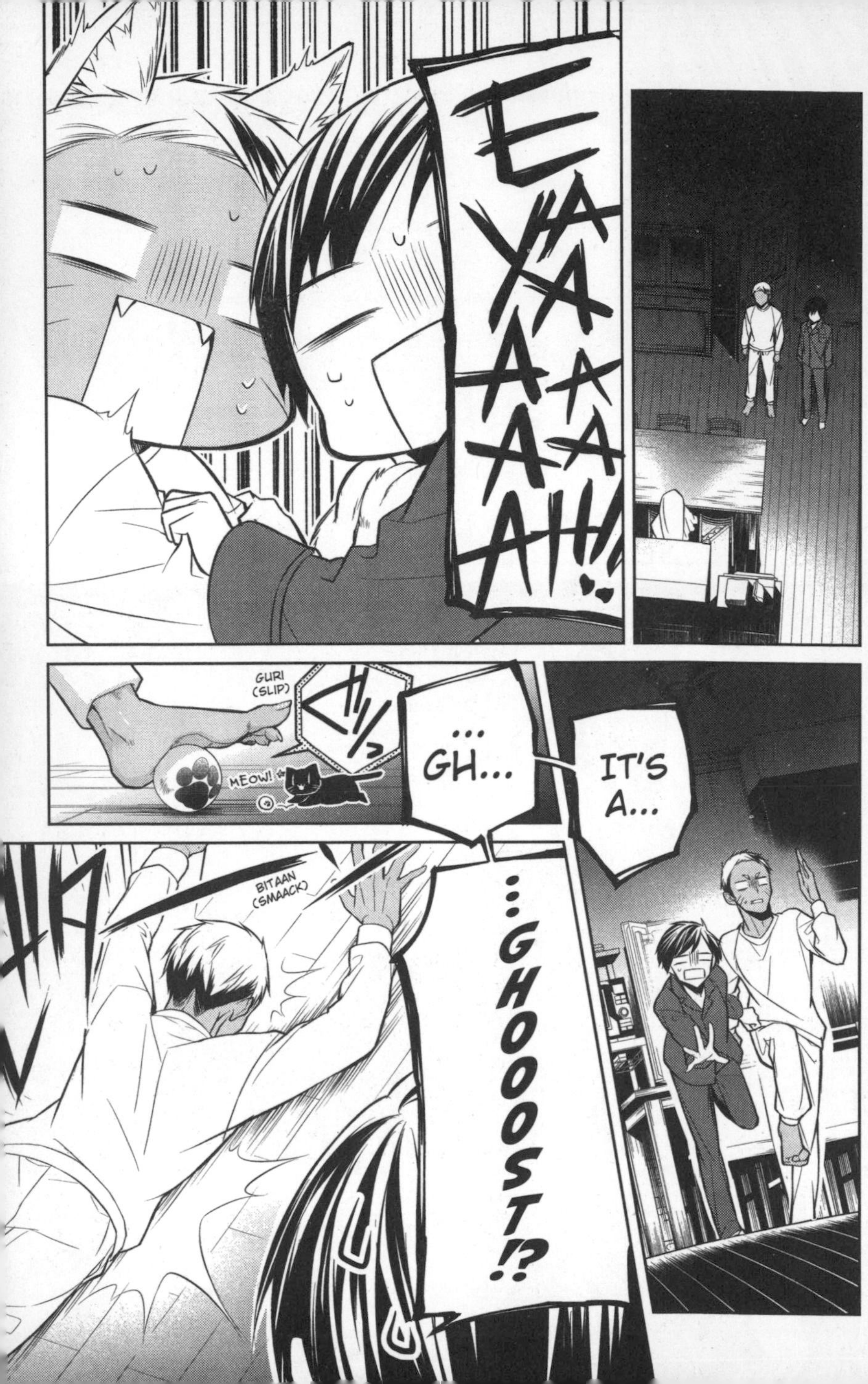

EYAAAAAAAAH!!
...GH...
IT'S A...
GURI (SLIP)
MEOW!
...GHOOOOST!?
BITAAN (SMAACK)

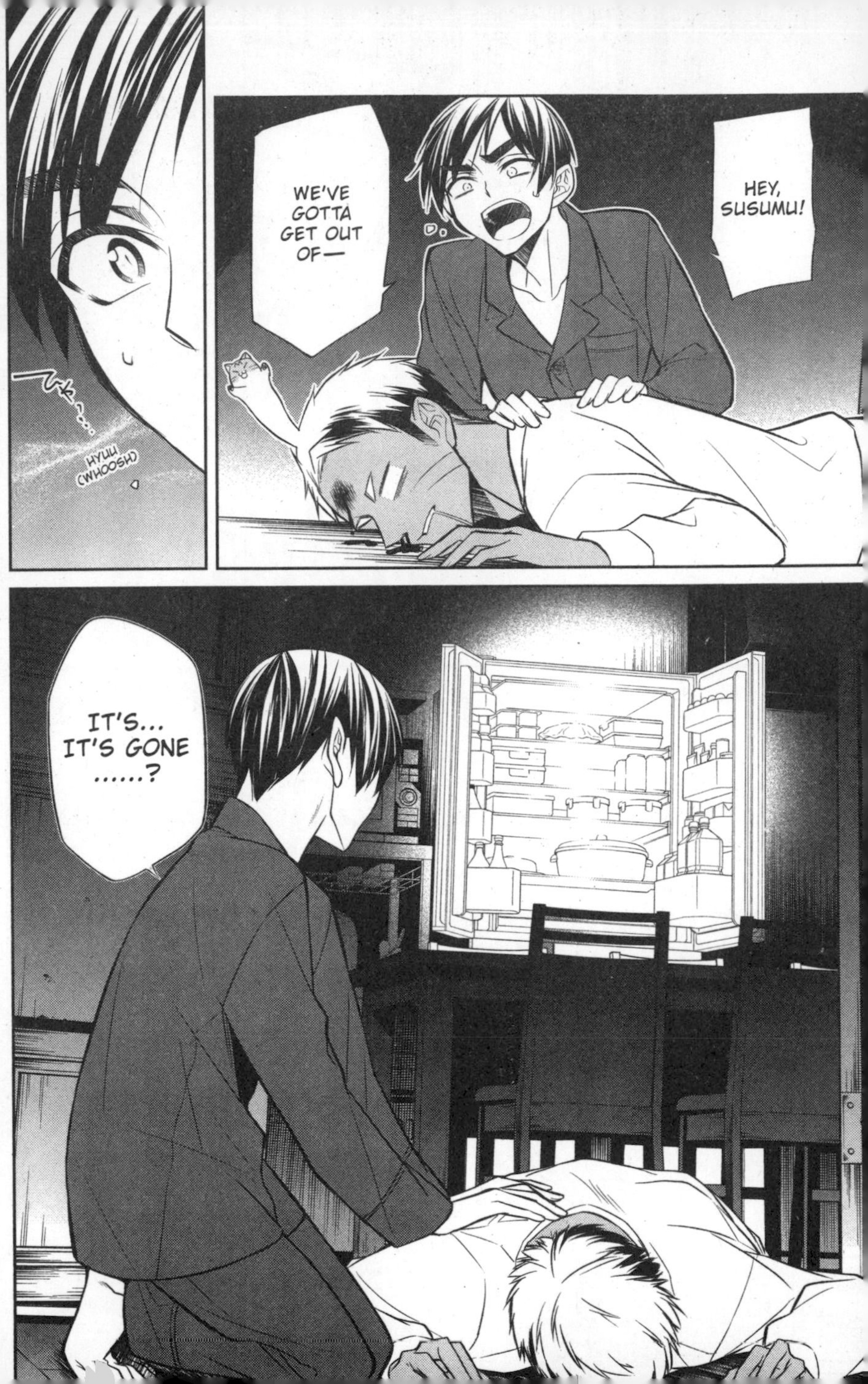
HEY, SUSUMU!
WE'VE GOTTA GET OUT OF—
HYUU (WHOOSH)
IT'S... IT'S GONE ......?

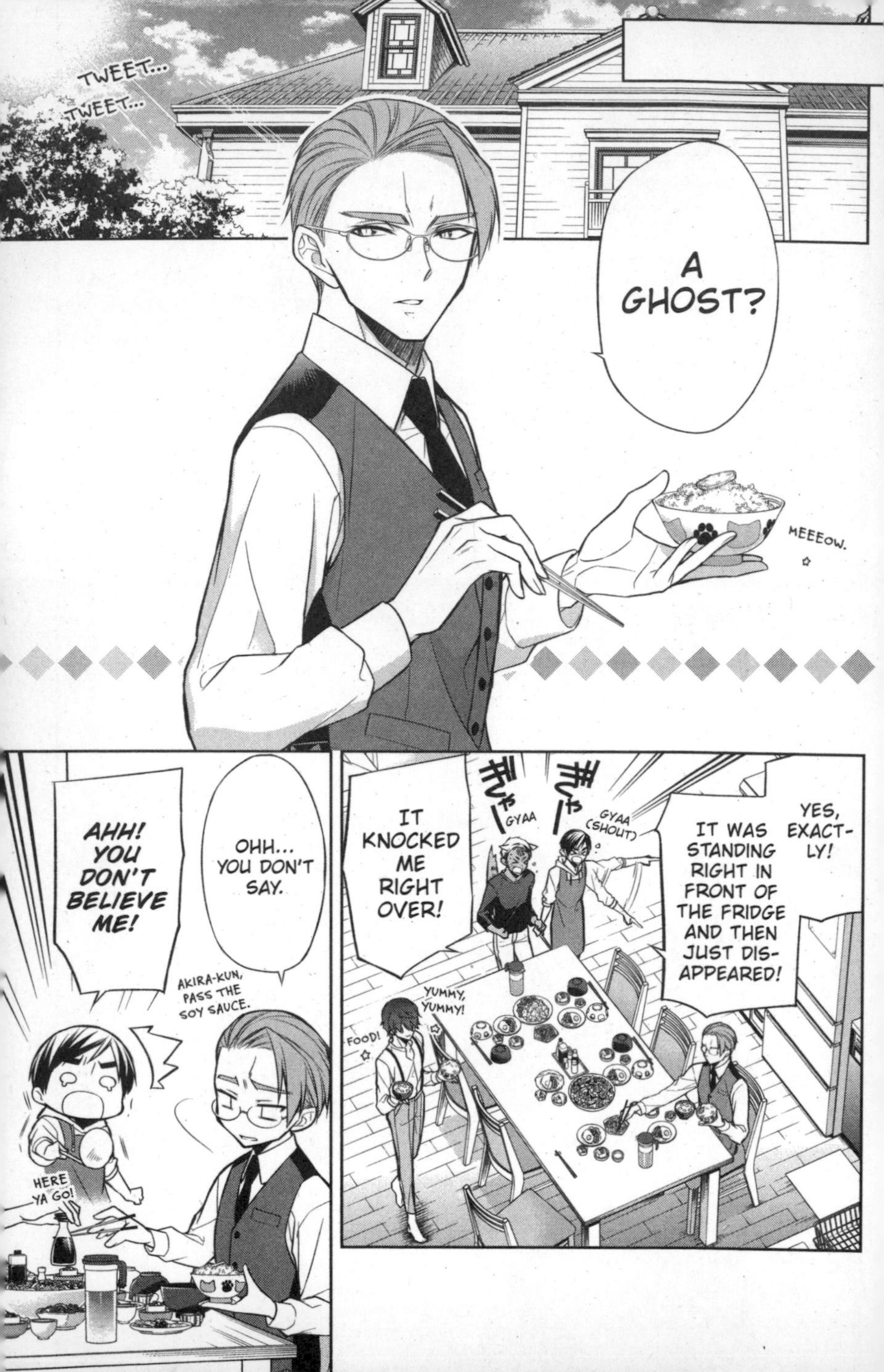
TWEET...
TWEET...
A GHOST?
MEEEOW.
YES, EXACT-LY!
IT WAS STANDING RIGHT IN FRONT OF THE FRIDGE AND THEN JUST DIS-APPEARED!
GYAA (SHOUT)
GYAA
IT KNOCKED ME RIGHT OVER!
YUMMY, YUMMY!
FOOD!
OHH... YOU DON'T SAY.
AHH! YOU DON'T BELIEVE ME!
AKIRA-KUN, PASS THE SOY SAUCE.
HERE YA GO!

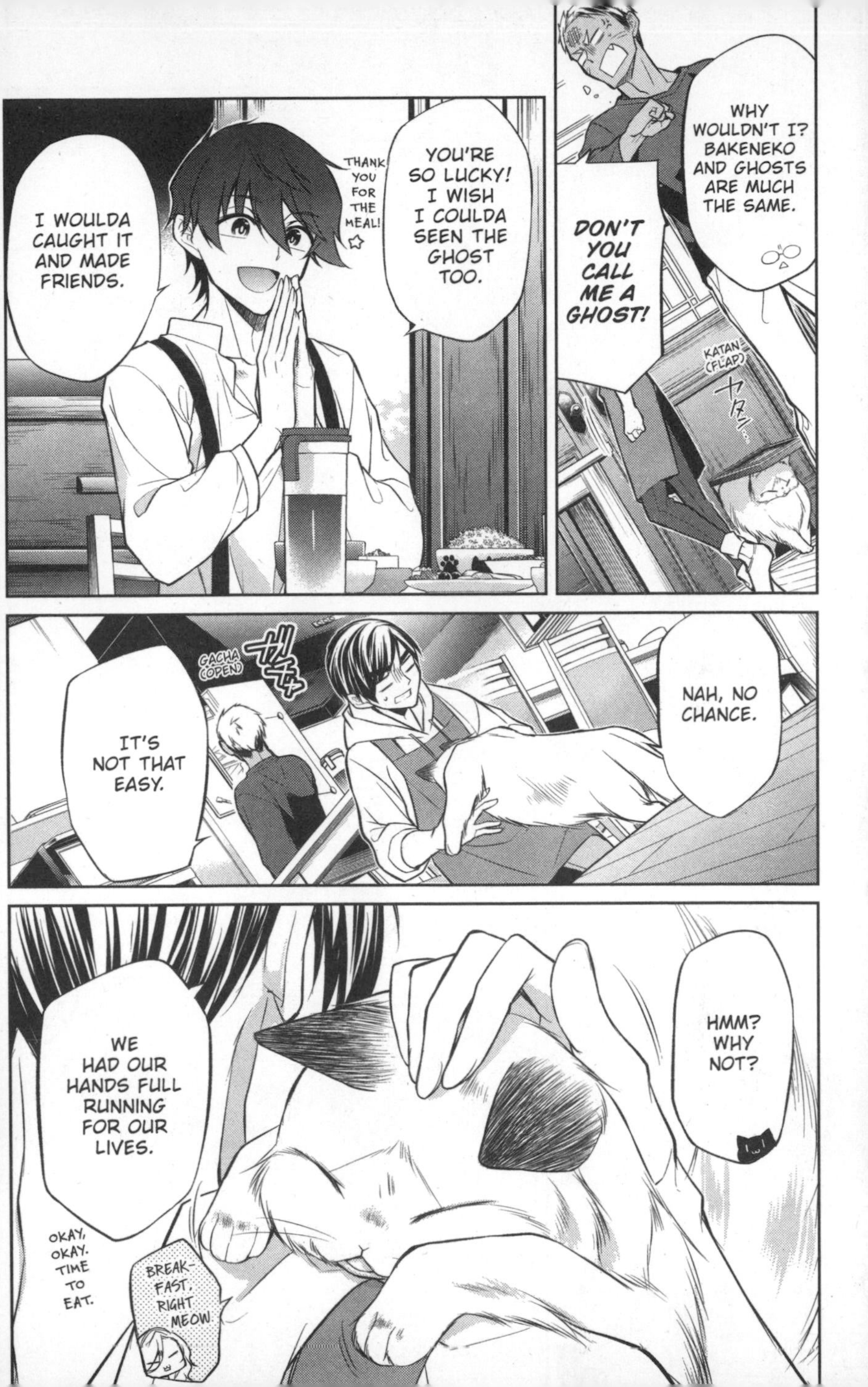
WHY WOULDN'T I? BAKENEKO AND GHOSTS ARE MUCH THE SAME.
DON'T YOU CALL ME A GHOST!
KATAN (FLAP)
YOU'RE SO LUCKY! I WISH I COULDA SEEN THE GHOST TOO.
THANK YOU FOR THE MEAL! ☆
I WOULDA CAUGHT IT AND MADE FRIENDS.
NAH, NO CHANCE.
GACHA (OPEN)
IT'S NOT THAT EASY.
HMM? WHY NOT?
WE HAD OUR HANDS FULL RUNNING FOR OUR LIVES.
OKAY, OKAY. TIME TO EAT.
BREAK-FAST, RIGHT MEOW.

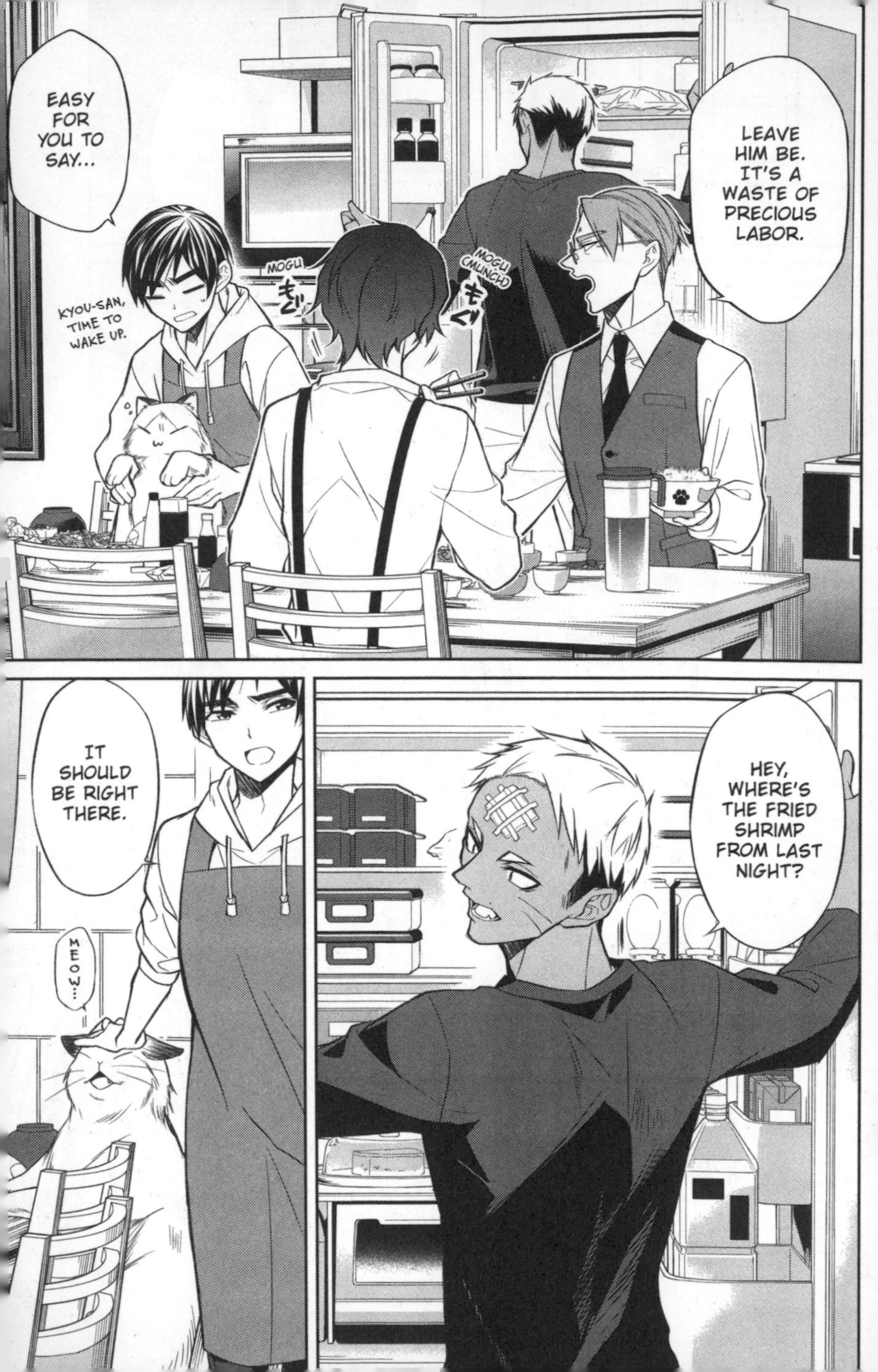
LEAVE HIM BE. IT'S A WASTE OF PRECIOUS LABOR.
MOGU (MUNCH)
もぐ
MOGU
もぐ
EASY FOR YOU TO SAY...
KYOU-SAN, TIME TO WAKE UP.
HEY, WHERE'S THE FRIED SHRIMP FROM LAST NIGHT?
IT SHOULD BE RIGHT THERE.
MEOW...

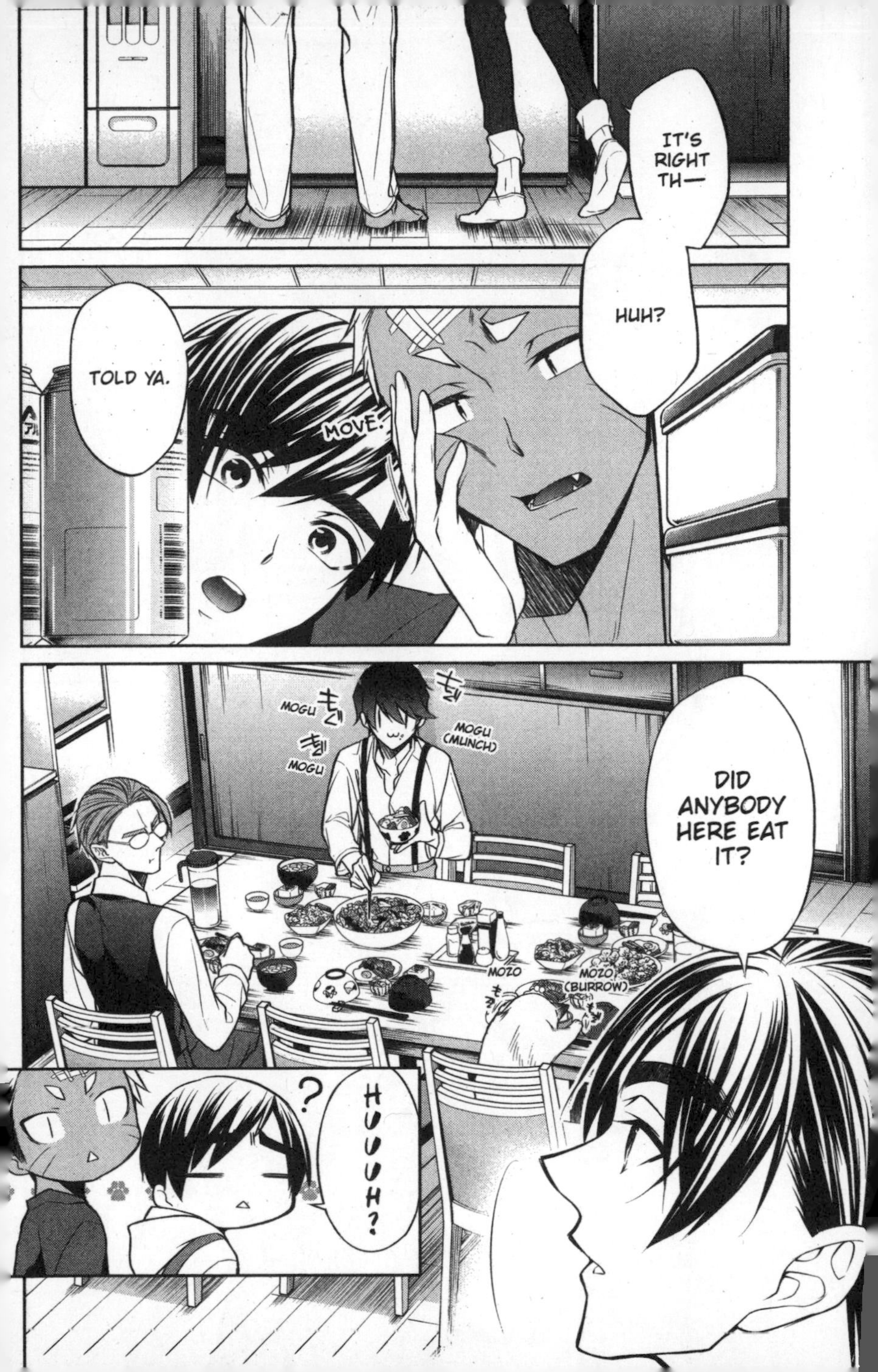
IT'S RIGHT TH—
HUH?
MOVE.
TOLD YA.
DID ANYBODY HERE EAT IT?
MOGU (MUNCH)
MOGU
MOGU
MOZO (BURROW)
MOZO
?
HUUUUH?

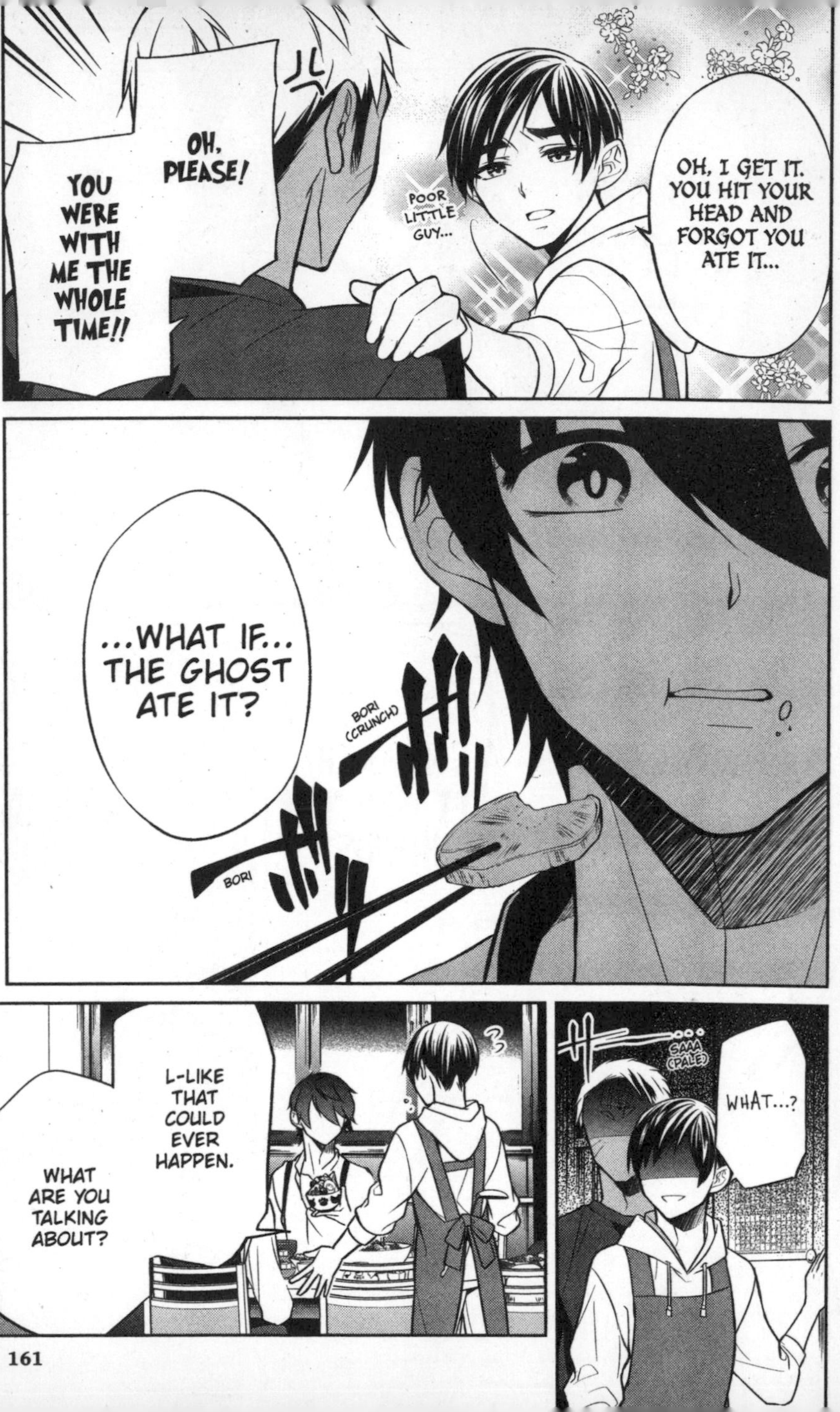
OH, I GET IT. YOU HIT YOUR HEAD AND FORGOT YOU ATE IT...
POOR LITTLE GUY...
OH, PLEASE!
YOU WERE WITH ME THE WHOLE TIME!!
...WHAT IF... THE GHOST ATE IT?
BORI (CRUNCH)
BORI
SAAA (PALE)
WHAT...?
L-LIKE THAT COULD EVER HAPPEN.
WHAT ARE YOU TALKING ABOUT?

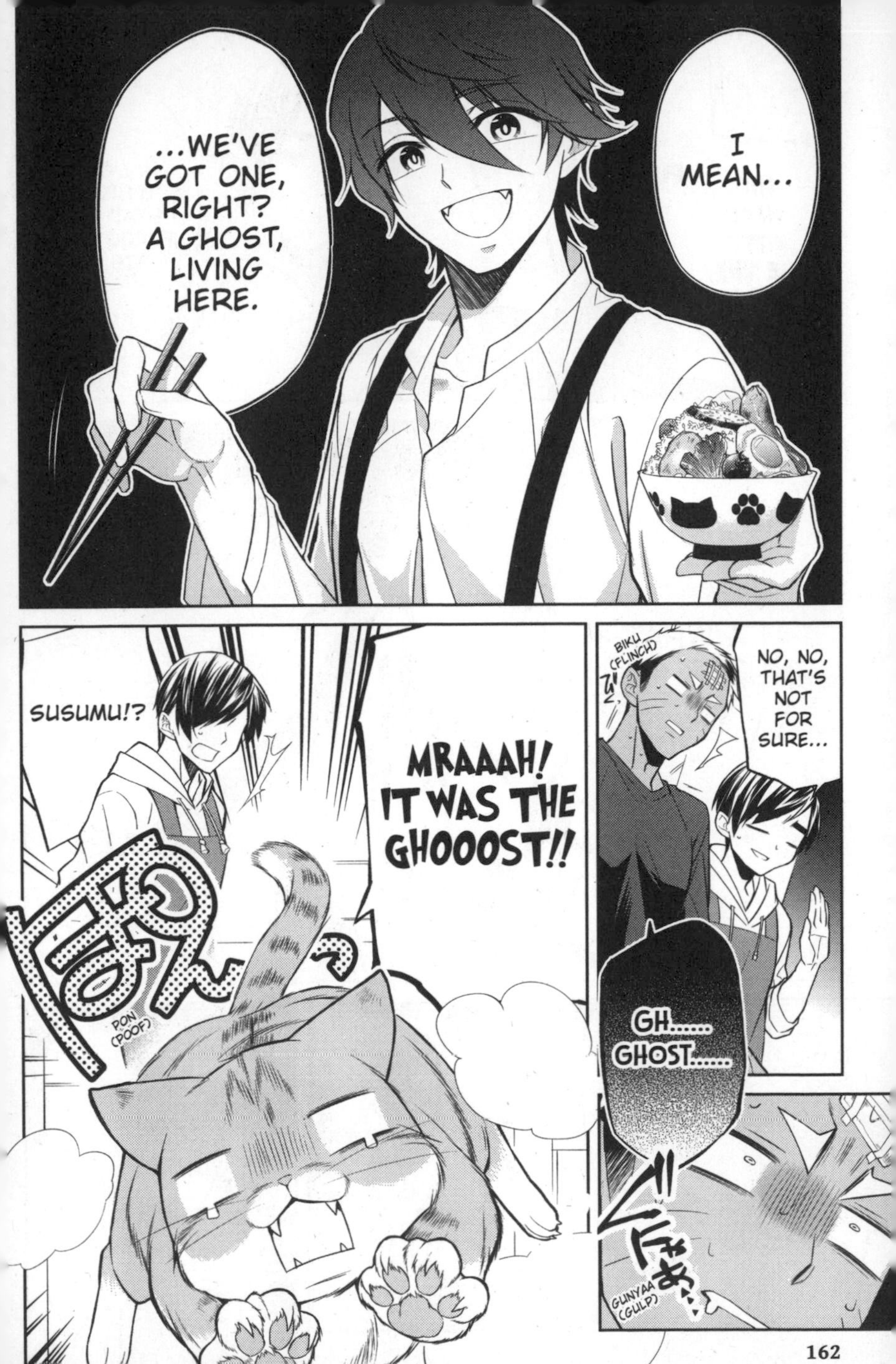
I MEAN...
...WE'VE GOT ONE, RIGHT? A GHOST, LIVING HERE.
BIKU (FLINCH)
NO, NO, THAT'S NOT FOR SURE...
GH...... GHOST......
GUNYAA (GULP)
SUSUMU!?
MRAAAH! IT WAS THE GHOOOST!!
PON (POOF)

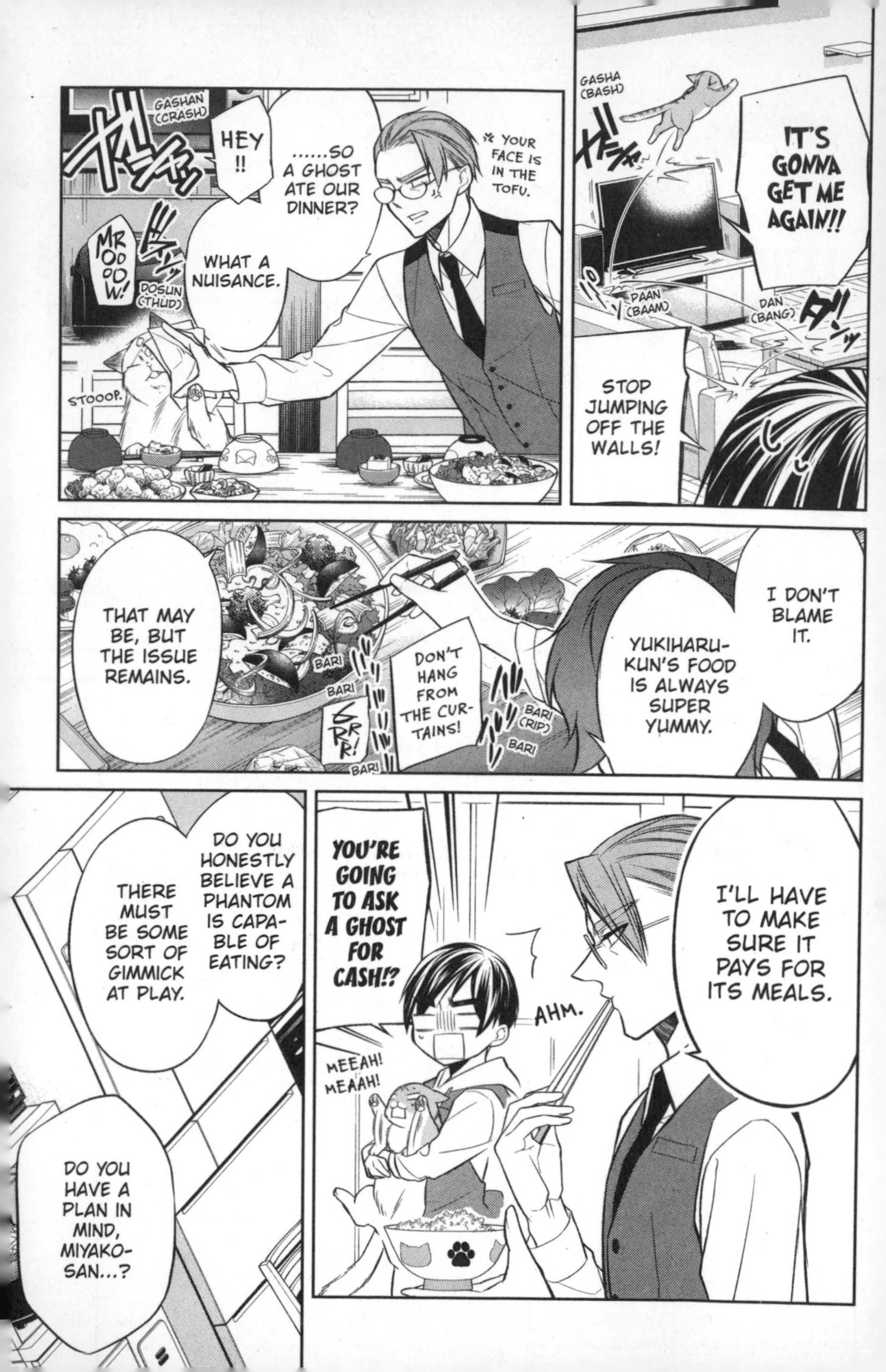
GASHA (BASH)
IT'S GONNA GET ME AGAIN!!
PAAN (BAAM)
DAN (BANG)
STOP JUMPING OFF THE WALLS!
※ YOUR FACE IS IN THE TOFU.
......SO A GHOST ATE OUR DINNER?
HEY !!
GASHAN (CRASH)
WHAT A NUISANCE.
MROOOOW!
DOSUN (THUD)
STOOOP.
I DON'T BLAME IT.
YUKIHARU-KUN'S FOOD IS ALWAYS SUPER YUMMY.
BARI (RIP)
BARI
DON'T HANG FROM THE CUR-TAINS!
GRRR!
BARI
BARI
BARI
THAT MAY BE, BUT THE ISSUE REMAINS.
I'LL HAVE TO MAKE SURE IT PAYS FOR ITS MEALS.
AHM.
YOU'RE GOING TO ASK A GHOST FOR CASH!?
MEEAH! MEAAH!
DO YOU HONESTLY BELIEVE A PHANTOM IS CAPA-BLE OF EATING?
THERE MUST BE SOME SORT OF GIMMICK AT PLAY.
DO YOU HAVE A PLAN IN MIND, MIYAKO-SAN...?

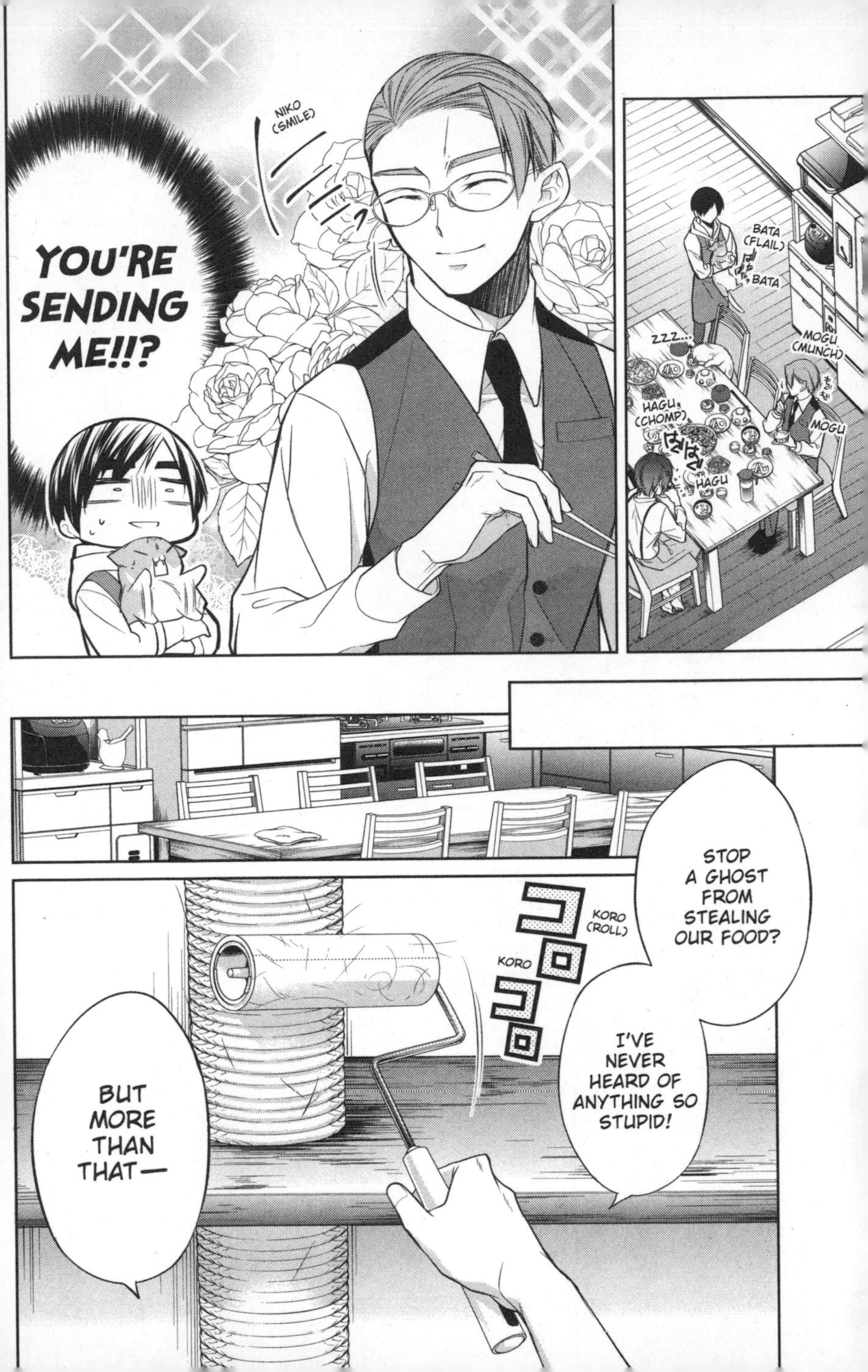
BATA (FLAIL)
BATA
ZZZ...
MOGU (MUNCH)
MOGU
HAGU (CHOMP)
HAGU
NIKO (SMILE)
YOU'RE SENDING ME!!?
STOP A GHOST FROM STEALING OUR FOOD?
I'VE NEVER HEARD OF ANYTHING SO STUPID!
KORO (ROLL)
KORO
BUT MORE THAN THAT—

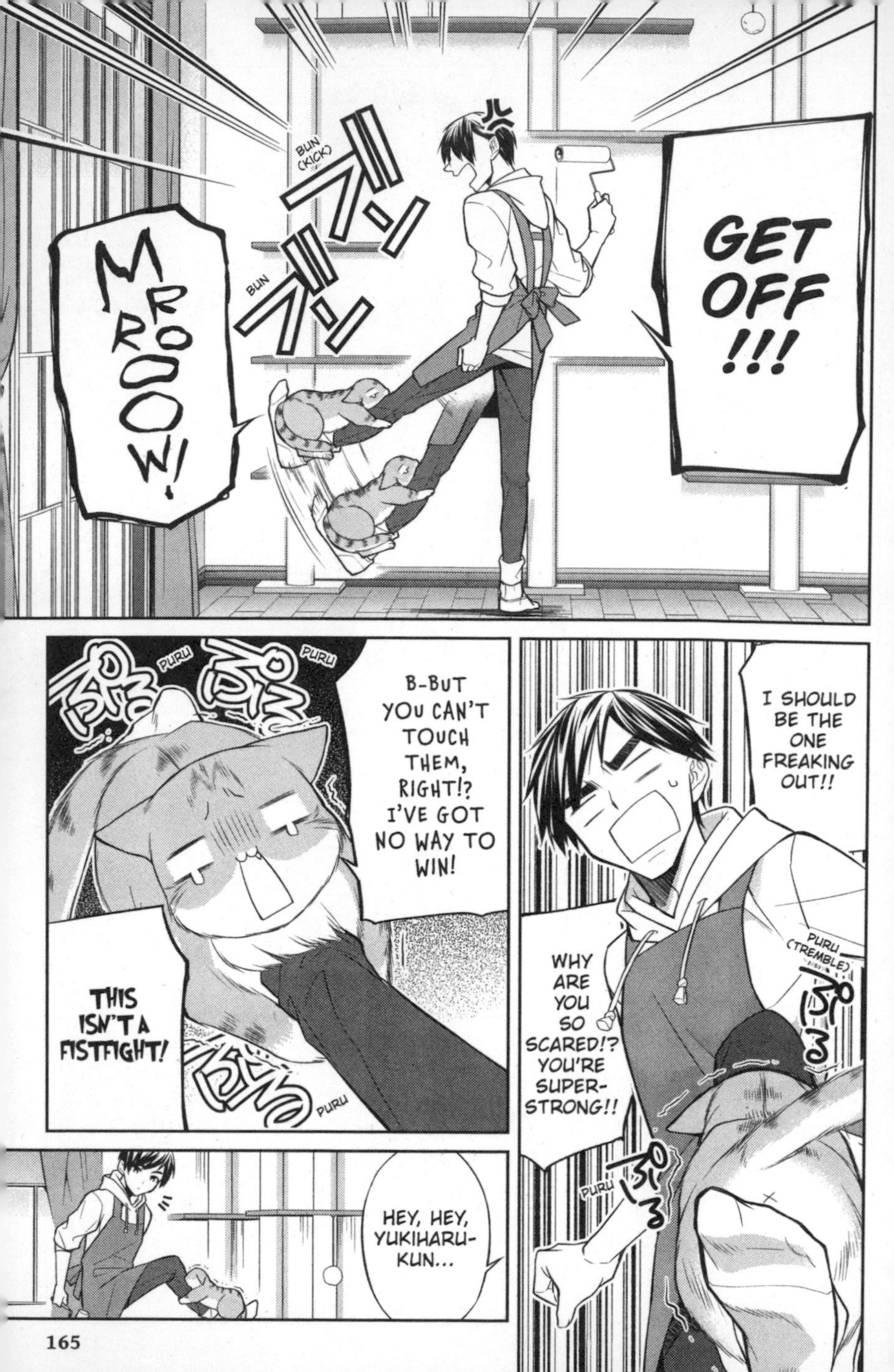
GET OFF!!!
BUN (KICK)
BUN
MRROOOOW!
I SHOULD BE THE ONE FREAKING OUT!!
WHY ARE YOU SO SCARED!? YOU'RE SUPER-STRONG!!
PURU (TREMBLE)
PURU
PURU
PURU
B-BUT YOU CAN'T TOUCH THEM, RIGHT!? I'VE GOT NO WAY TO WIN!
THIS ISN'T A FISTFIGHT!
PURU
HEY, HEY, YUKIHARU-KUN...

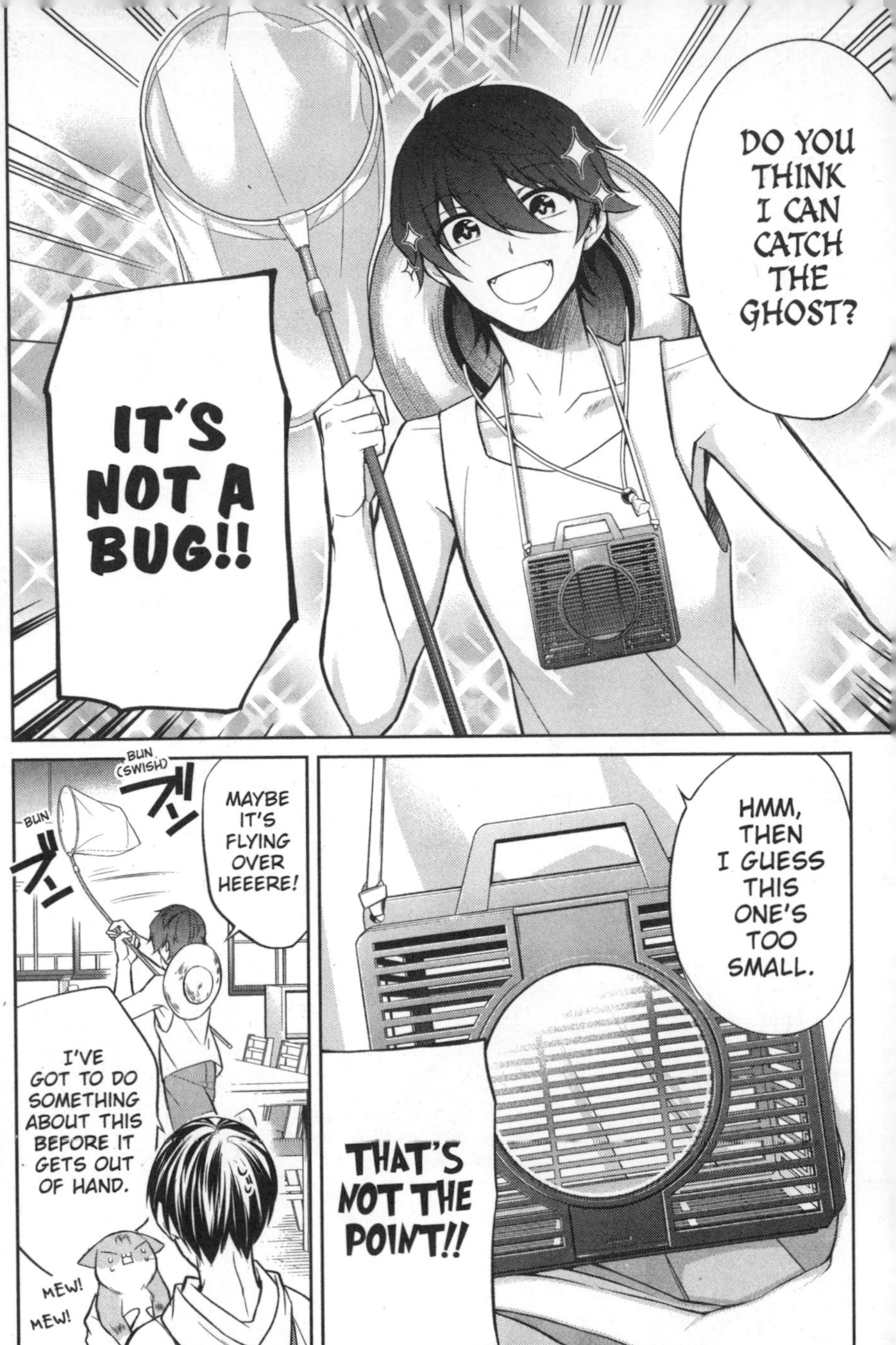
DO YOU THINK I CAN CATCH THE GHOST?
IT'S NOT A BUG!!
HMM, THEN I GUESS THIS ONE'S TOO SMALL.
THAT'S NOT THE POINT!!
BUN (SWISH)
MAYBE IT'S FLYING OVER HEEERE!
BUN
I'VE GOT TO DO SOMETHING ABOUT THIS BEFORE IT GETS OUT OF HAND.
MEW!
MEW!

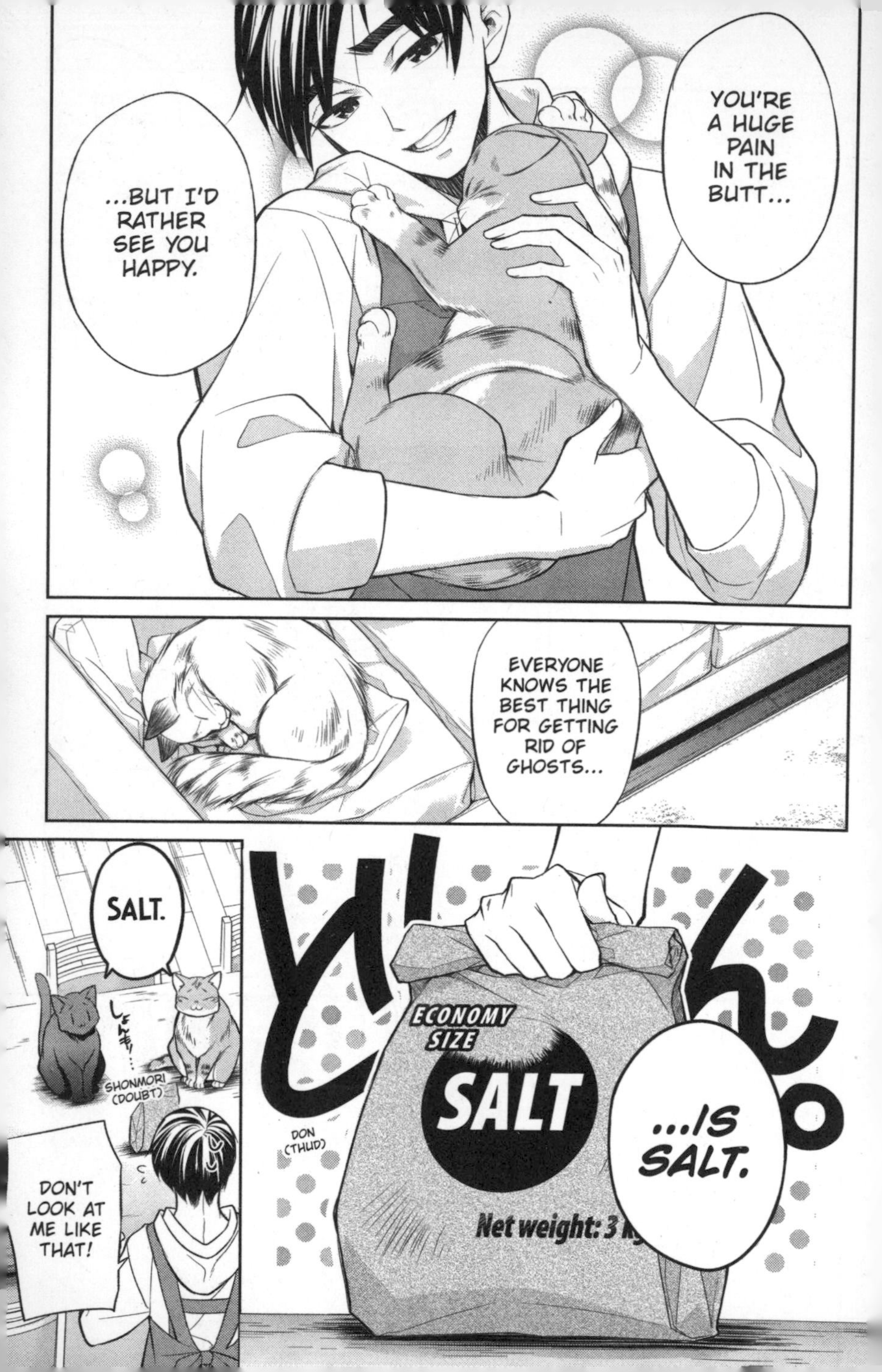
YOU'RE A HUGE PAIN IN THE BUTT...
...BUT I'D RATHER SEE YOU HAPPY.
EVERYONE KNOWS THE BEST THING FOR GETTING RID OF GHOSTS...
...IS SALT.
ECONOMY SIZE
SALT
DON (THUD)
SALT.
SHONMORI (DOUBT)
DON'T LOOK AT ME LIKE THAT!

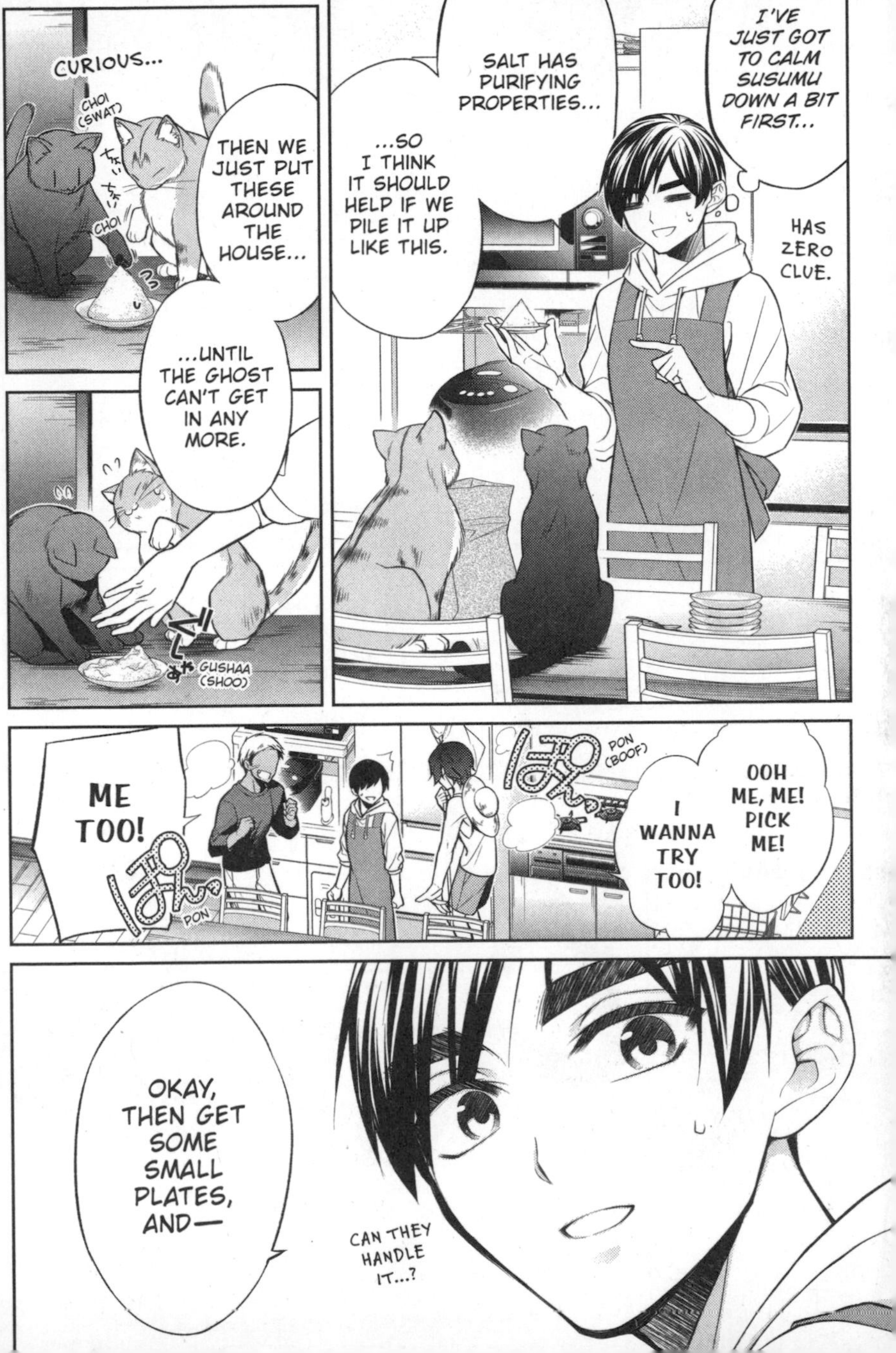
I'VE JUST GOT TO CALM SUSUMU DOWN A BIT FIRST...
SALT HAS PURIFYING PROPERTIES...
...SO I THINK IT SHOULD HELP IF WE PILE IT UP LIKE THIS.
HAS ZERO CLUE.
THEN WE JUST PUT THESE AROUND THE HOUSE...
CURIOUS...
CHOI (SWAT)
CHOI
...UNTIL THE GHOST CAN'T GET IN ANY MORE.
GUSHAA (SHOO)
OOH ME, ME! PICK ME!
I WANNA TRY TOO!
PON (BOOF)
ME TOO!
PON
OKAY, THEN GET SOME SMALL PLATES, AND—
CAN THEY HANDLE IT...?

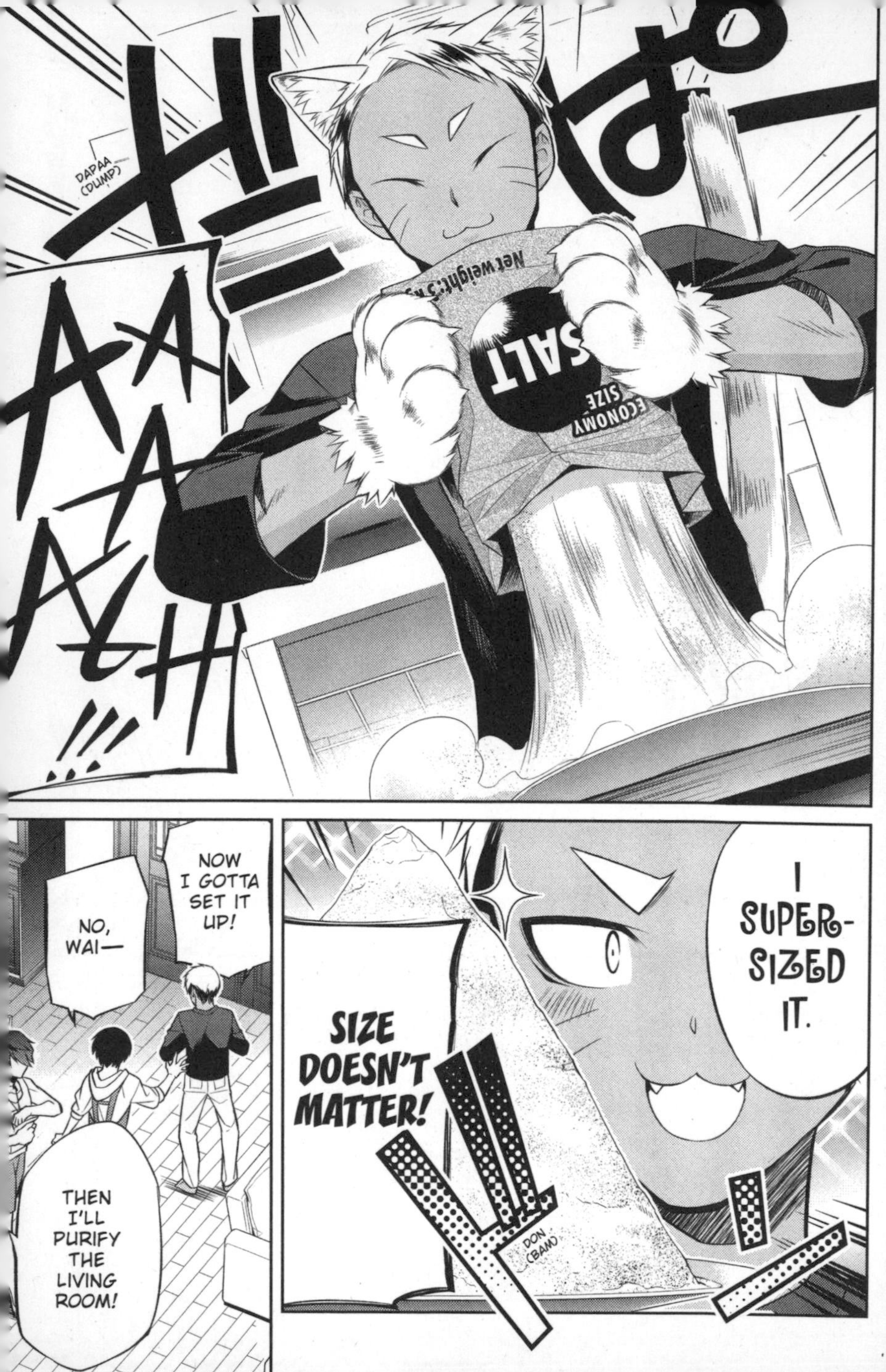
SALT
ECONOMY SIZE
AAAAAGH!!!
DAPAA (DUMP)
I SUPER-SIZED IT.
SIZE DOESN'T MATTER!
DON (BAM)
NOW I GOTTA SET IT UP!
NO, WAI—
THEN I'LL PURIFY THE LIVING ROOM!

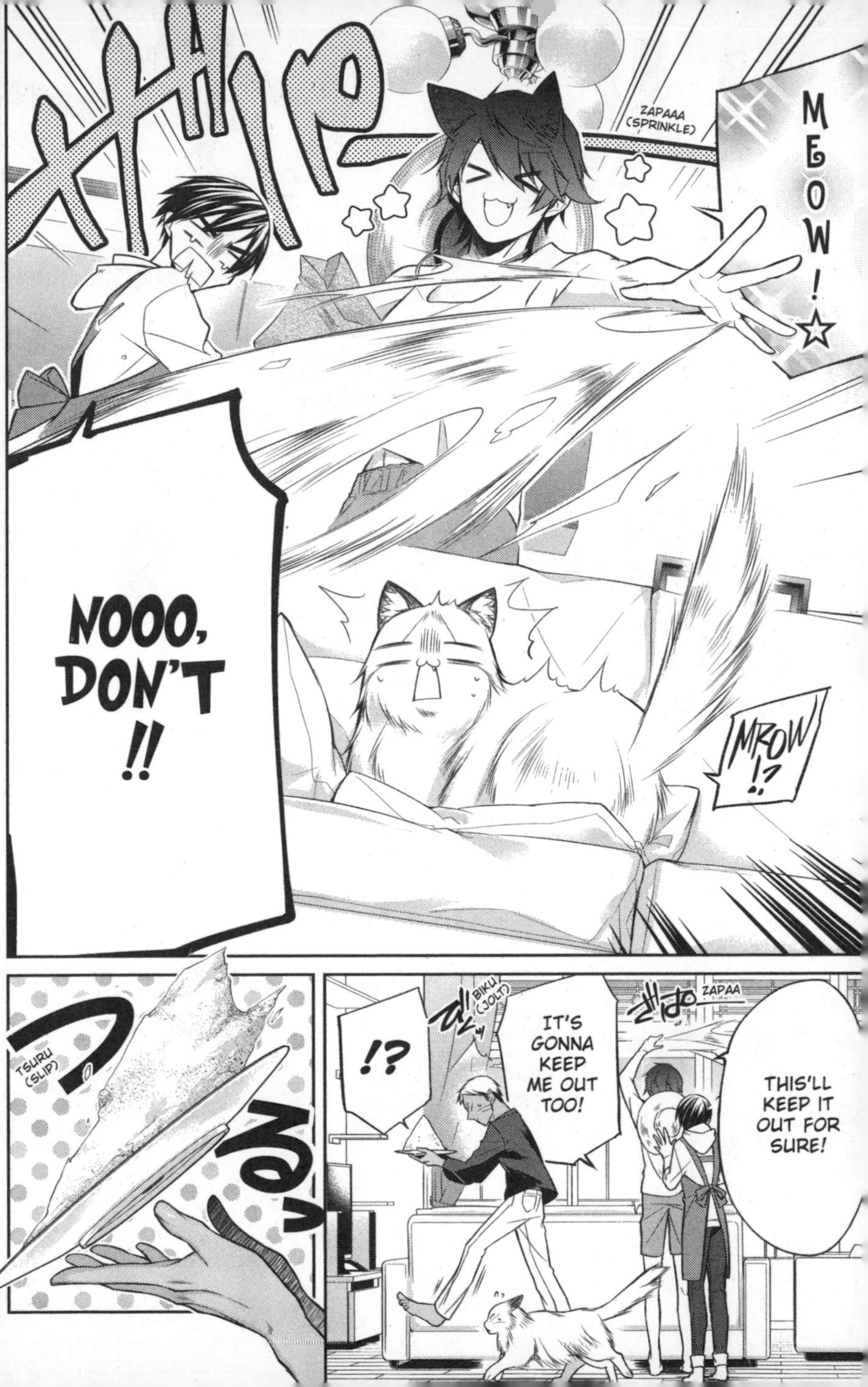
MEOW!☆
ZAPAAA (SPRINKLE)
WHIP
NOOO, DON'T!!
MROW!?
ZAPAA
THIS'LL KEEP IT OUT FOR SURE!
IT'S GONNA KEEP ME OUT TOO!
BIKU (JOLT)
!?
TSURU (SLIP)

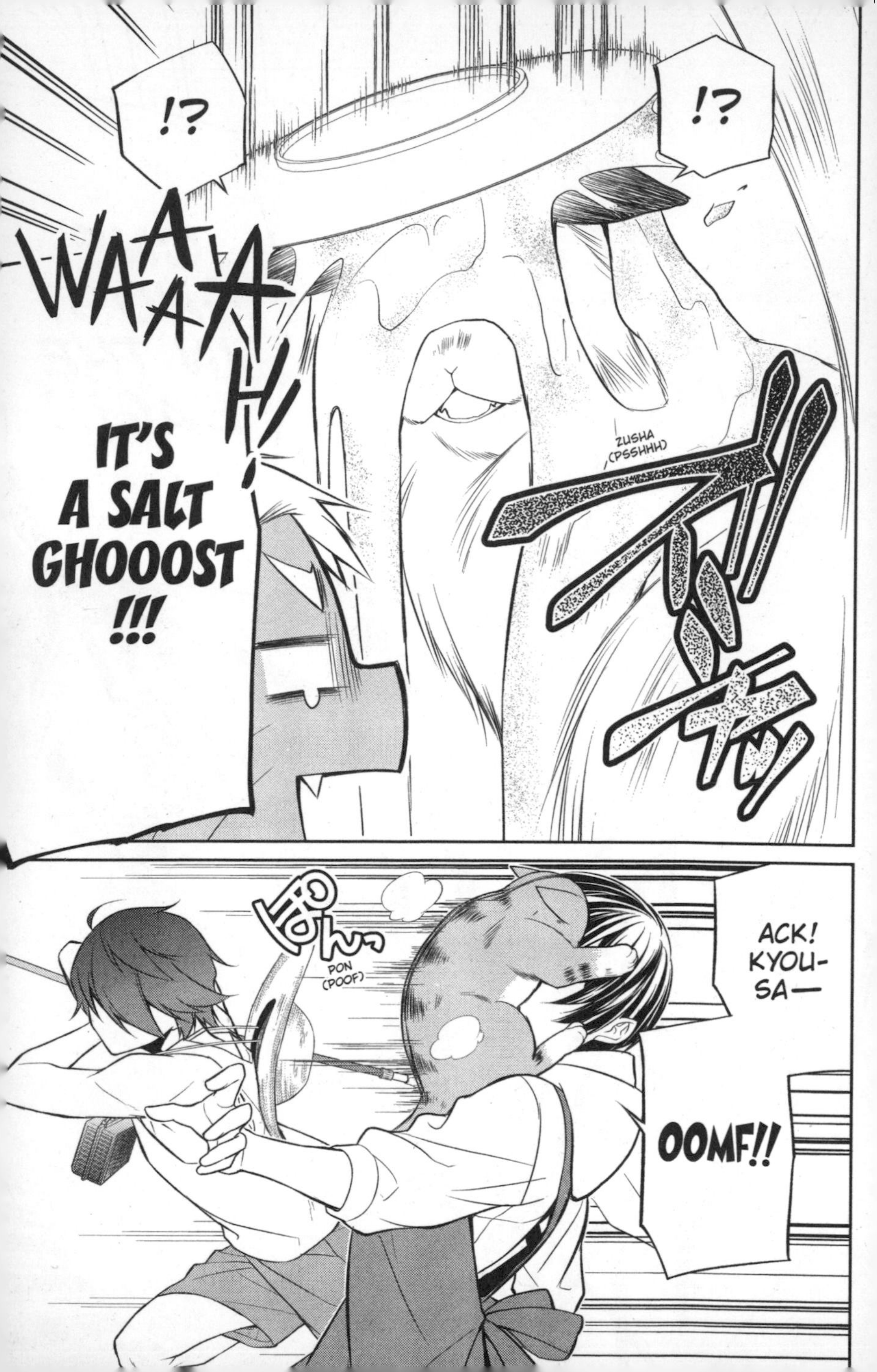
!?
!?
ZUSHA (PSSHHH)
WAAAAAH!
IT'S A SALT GHOOOST!!!
ACK! KYOU-SA—
OOMF!!
PON (POOF)

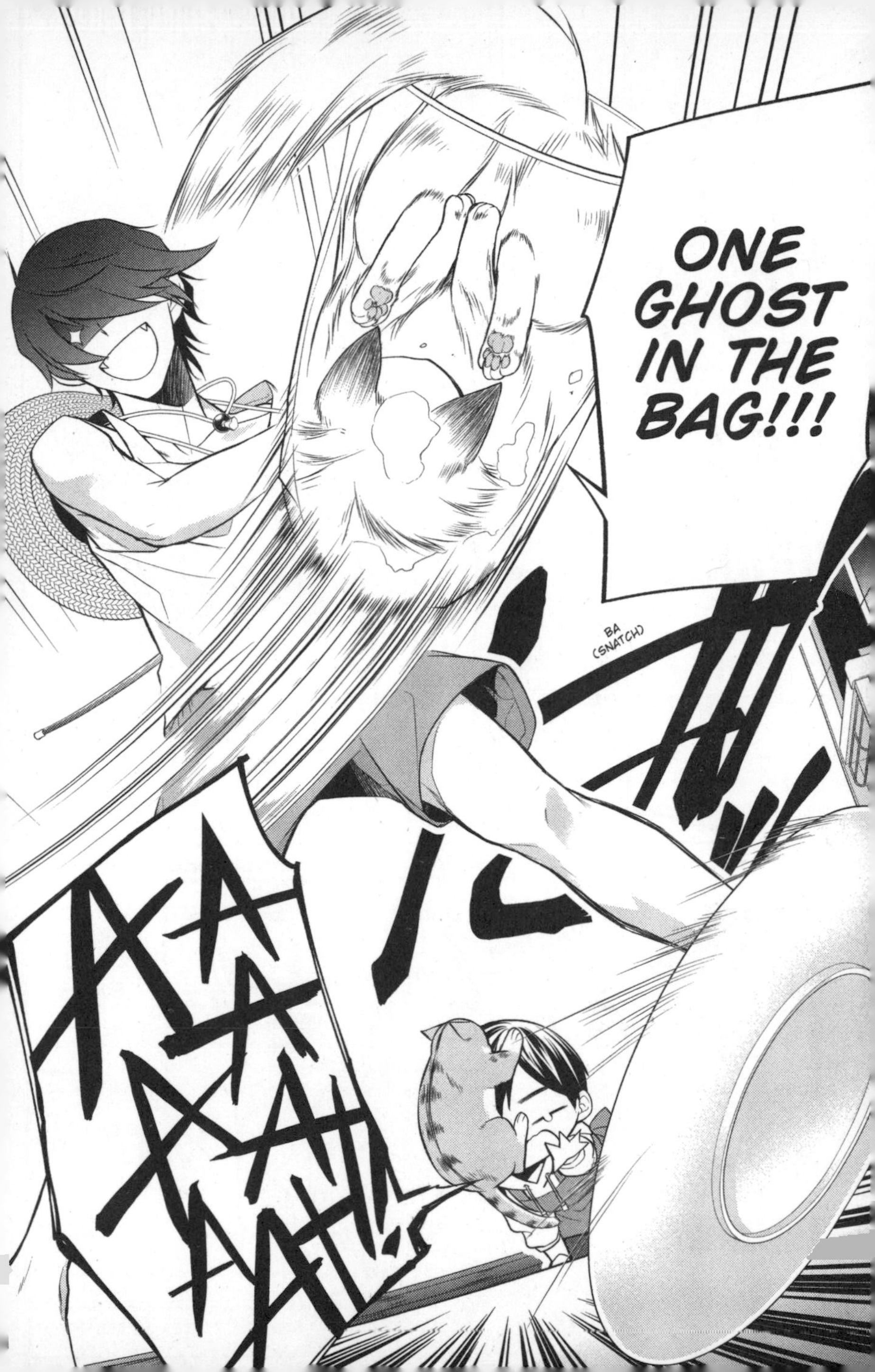
ONE GHOST IN THE BAG!!!
BA (SNATCH)
AA AAH AAH!!

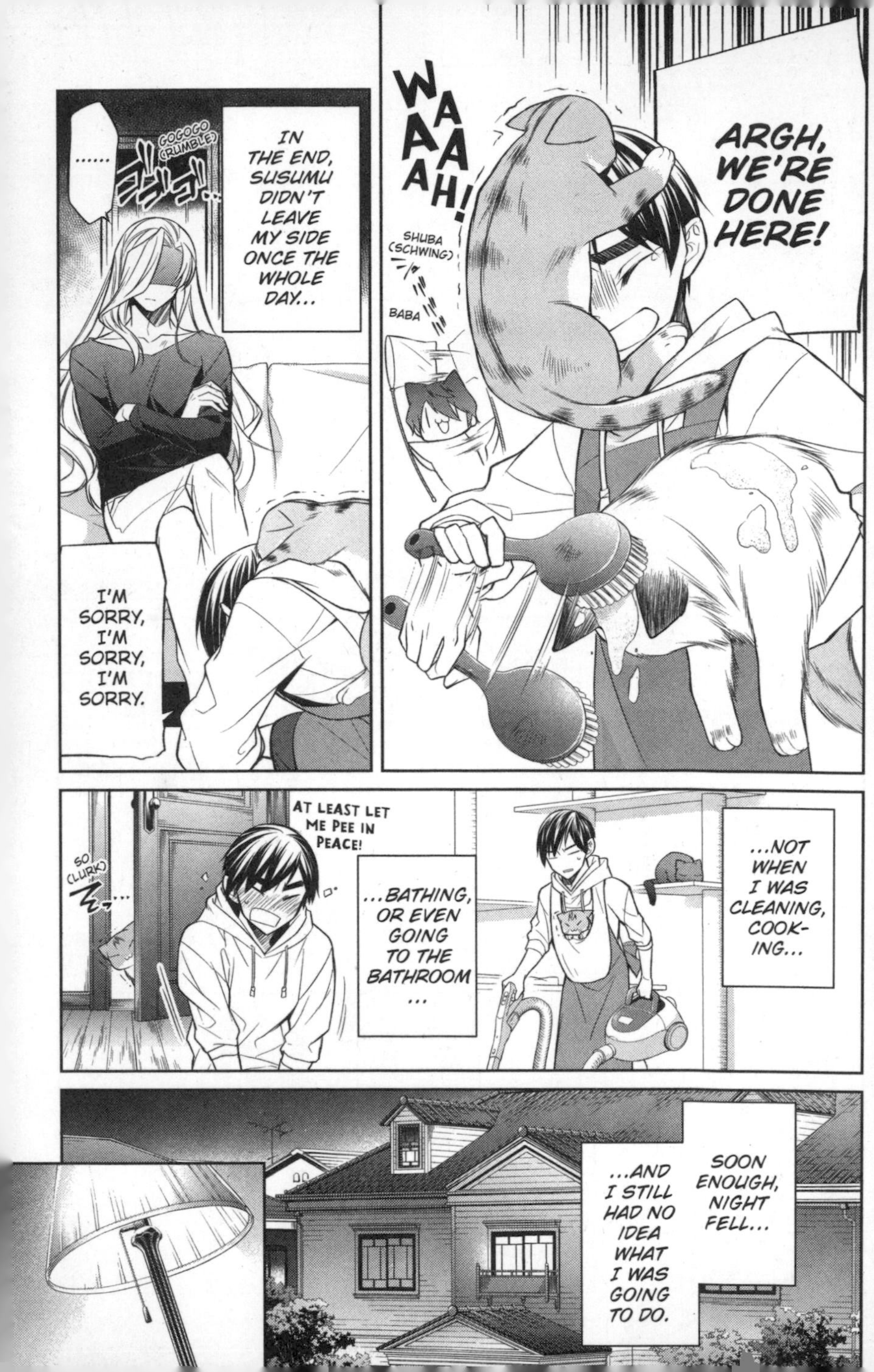
ARGH, WE'RE DONE HERE!
WAAAAAH!
SHUBA (SCHWING)
BABA
IN THE END, SUSUMU DIDN'T LEAVE MY SIDE ONCE THE WHOLE DAY...
GOGOGO (RUMBLE)
......
I'M SORRY, I'M SORRY, I'M SORRY.
...NOT WHEN I WAS CLEANING, COOK-ING...
...BATHING, OR EVEN GOING TO THE BATHROOM...
AT LEAST LET ME PEE IN PEACE!
SO (LURK)
SOON ENOUGH, NIGHT FELL...
...AND I STILL HAD NO IDEA WHAT I WAS GOING TO DO.

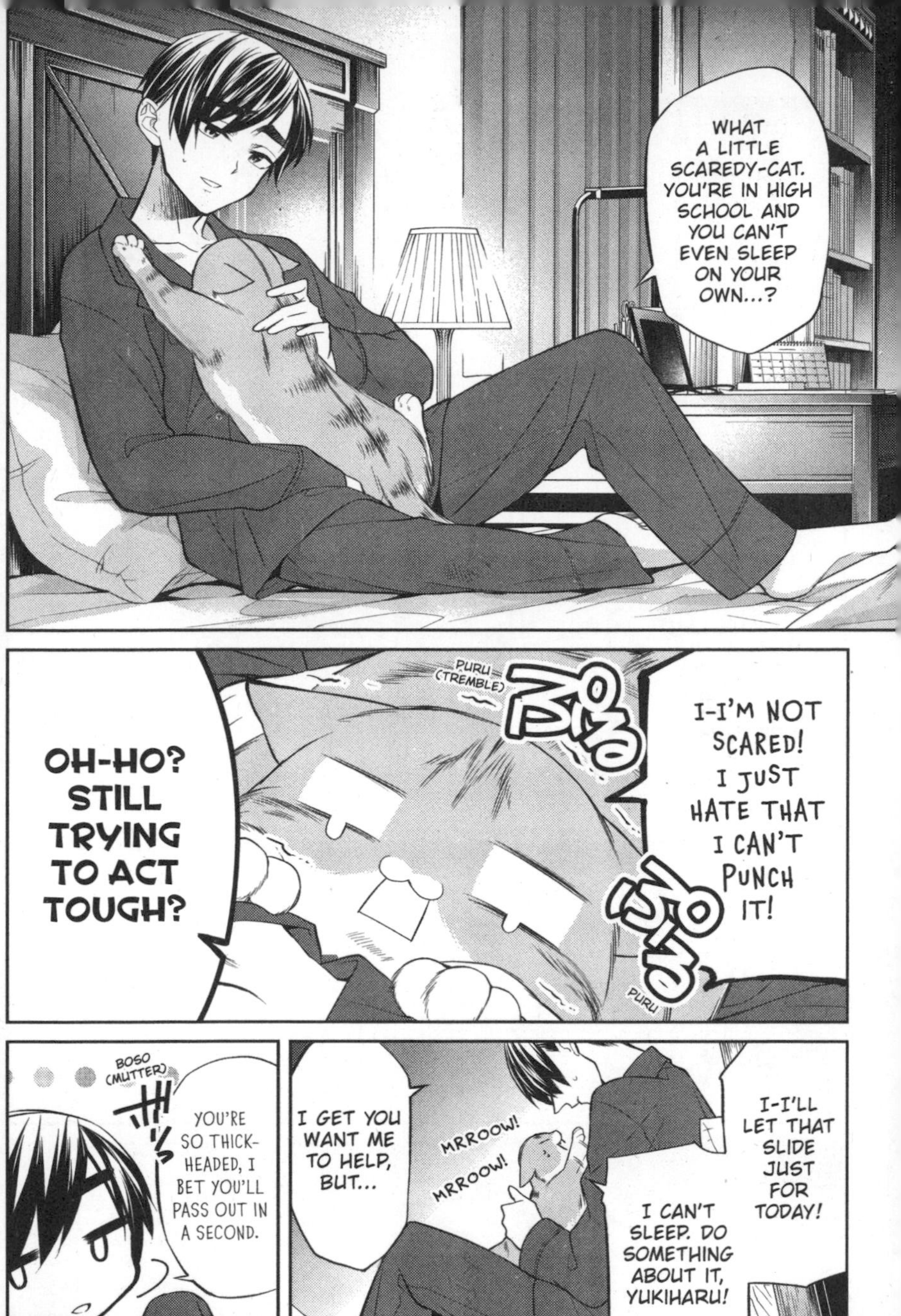
WHAT A LITTLE SCAREDY-CAT. YOU'RE IN HIGH SCHOOL AND YOU CAN'T EVEN SLEEP ON YOUR OWN...?
I-I'M NOT SCARED! I JUST HATE THAT I CAN'T PUNCH IT!
PURU (TREMBLE)
PURU
OH-HO? STILL TRYING TO ACT TOUGH?
I-I'LL LET THAT SLIDE JUST FOR TODAY!
I CAN'T SLEEP. DO SOMETHING ABOUT IT, YUKIHARU!
MRROOW!
MRROOW!
I GET YOU WANT ME TO HELP, BUT...
BOSO (MUTTER)
YOU'RE SO THICK-HEADED, I BET YOU'LL PASS OUT IN A SECOND.

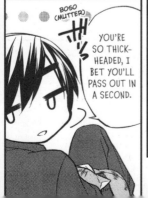

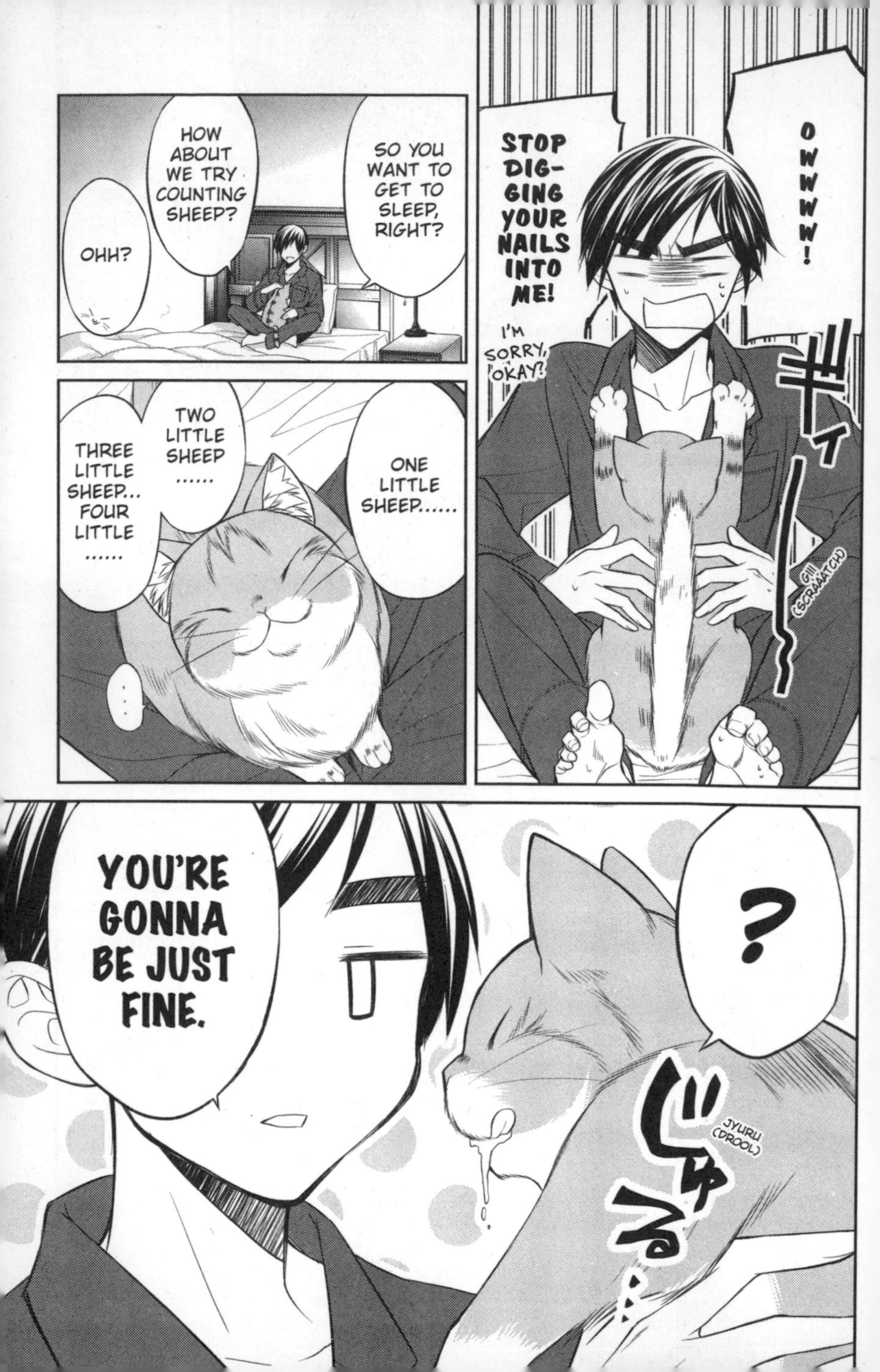
OWWWWW!
STOP DIG-GING YOUR NAILS INTO ME!
I'M SORRY, OKAY?
GIII (SCRAAATCH)
SO YOU WANT TO GET TO SLEEP, RIGHT?
HOW ABOUT WE TRY COUNTING SHEEP?
OHH?
ONE LITTLE SHEEP......
TWO LITTLE SHEEP......
THREE LITTLE SHEEP... FOUR LITTLE......
...
?
JYURU (DROOL)
YOU'RE GONNA BE JUST FINE.

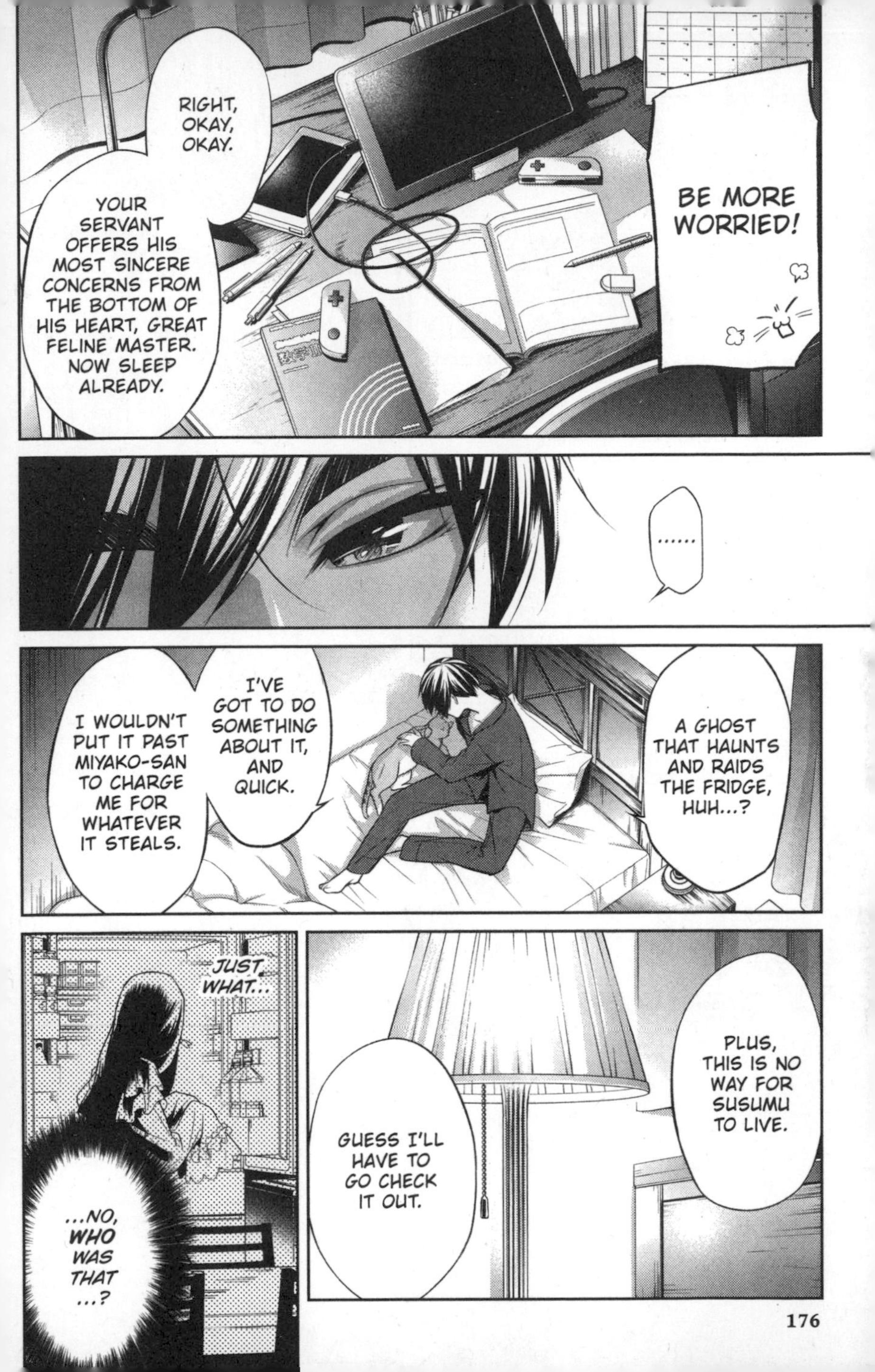
BE MORE WORRIED!
RIGHT, OKAY, OKAY.
YOUR SERVANT OFFERS HIS MOST SINCERE CONCERNS FROM THE BOTTOM OF HIS HEART, GREAT FELINE MASTER. NOW SLEEP ALREADY.
......
A GHOST THAT HAUNTS AND RAIDS THE FRIDGE, HUH...?
I'VE GOT TO DO SOMETHING ABOUT IT, AND QUICK.
I WOULDN'T PUT IT PAST MIYAKO-SAN TO CHARGE ME FOR WHATEVER IT STEALS.
PLUS, THIS IS NO WAY FOR SUSUMU TO LIVE.
GUESS I'LL HAVE TO GO CHECK IT OUT.
JUST WHAT...
...NO, WHO WAS THAT ...?

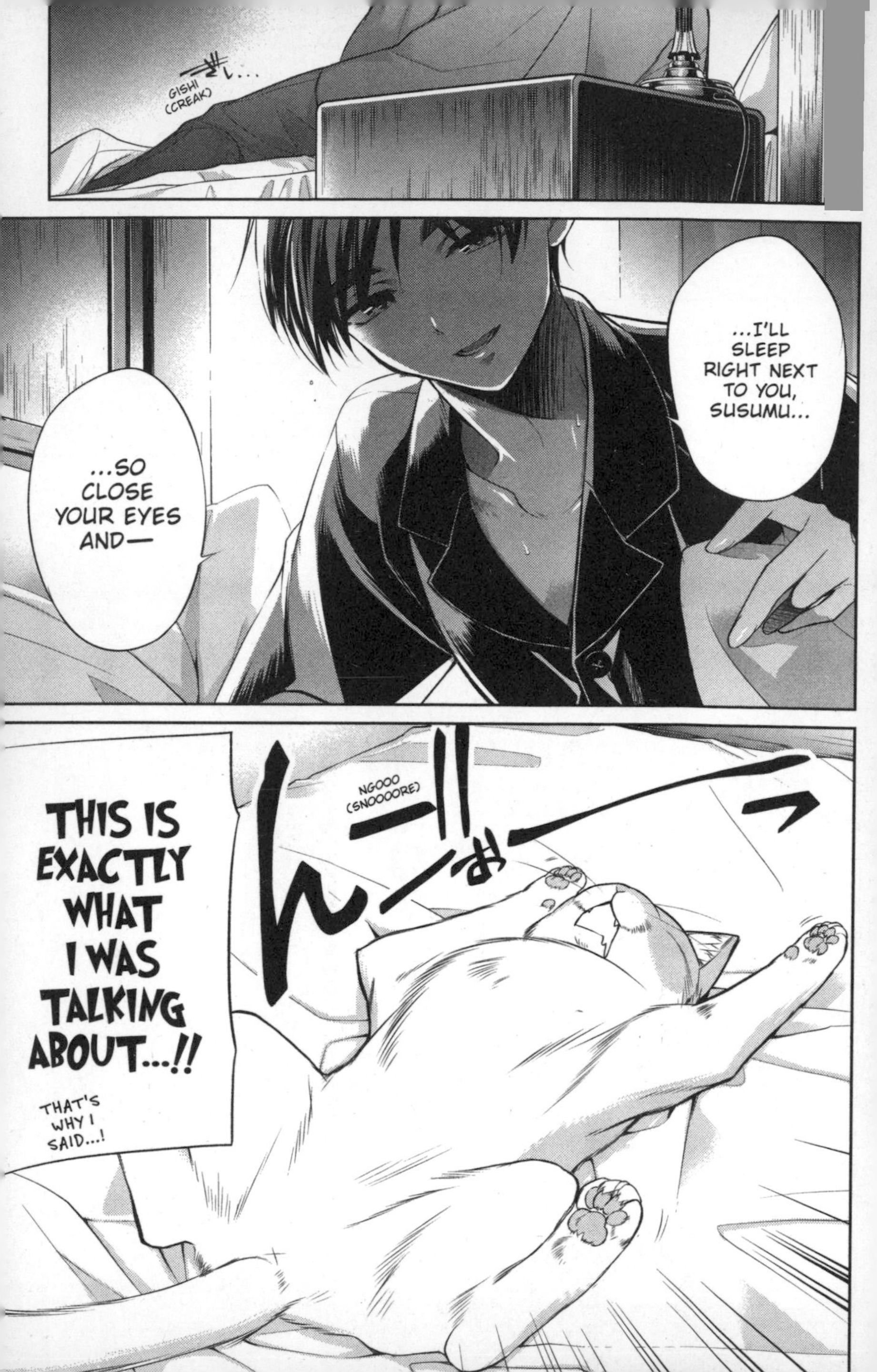
GISHI (CREAK)
...I'LL SLEEP RIGHT NEXT TO YOU, SUSUMU...
...SO CLOSE YOUR EYES AND—
NGOOO (SNOOOORE)
THIS IS EXACTLY WHAT I WAS TALKING ABOUT...!!
THAT'S WHY I SAID...!

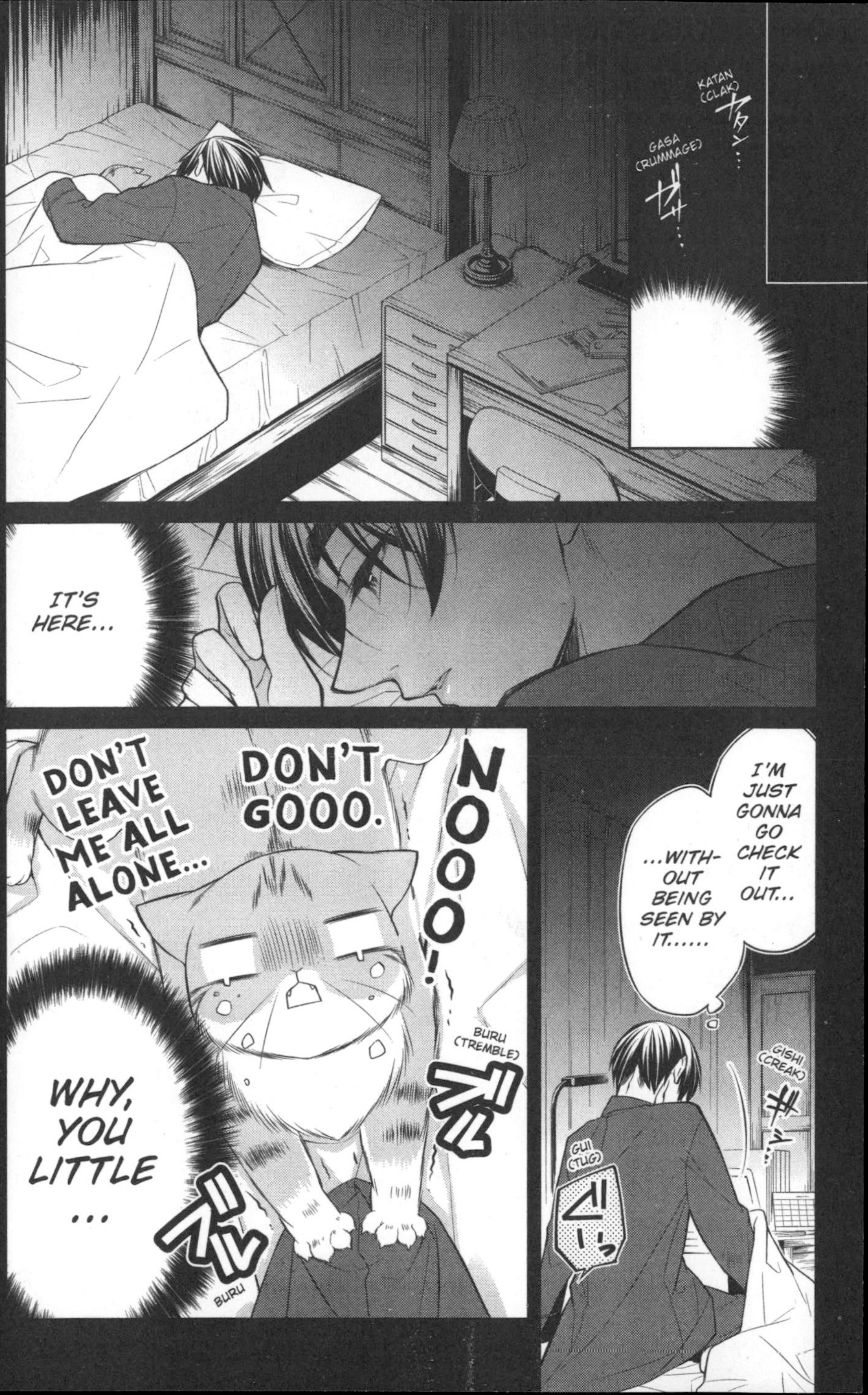
KATAN (CLAK)
GASA (RUMMAGE)
IT'S HERE...
I'M JUST GONNA GO CHECK IT OUT...
...WITH-OUT BEING SEEN BY IT......
GISHI (CREAK)
GUI (TUG)
NOOOO!
DON'T GOOO.
DON'T LEAVE ME ALL ALONE...
BURU (TREMBLE)
BURU
WHY, YOU LITTLE ...

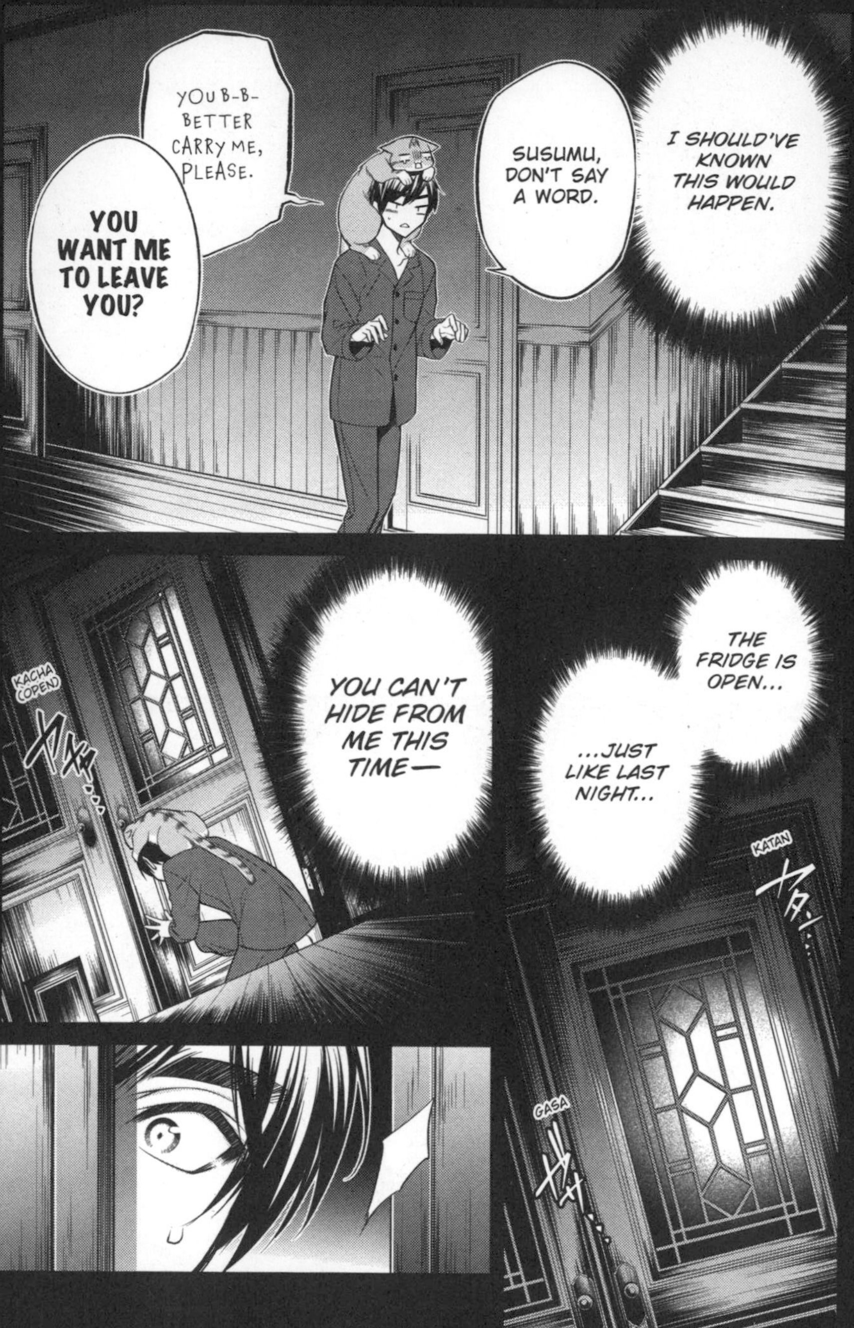
I SHOULD'VE KNOWN THIS WOULD HAPPEN.
SUSUMU, DON'T SAY A WORD.
YOU B-B-BETTER CARRY ME, PLEASE.
YOU WANT ME TO LEAVE YOU?
THE FRIDGE IS OPEN...
...JUST LIKE LAST NIGHT...
KATAN
GASA
YOU CAN'T HIDE FROM ME THIS TIME—
KACHA (OPEN)

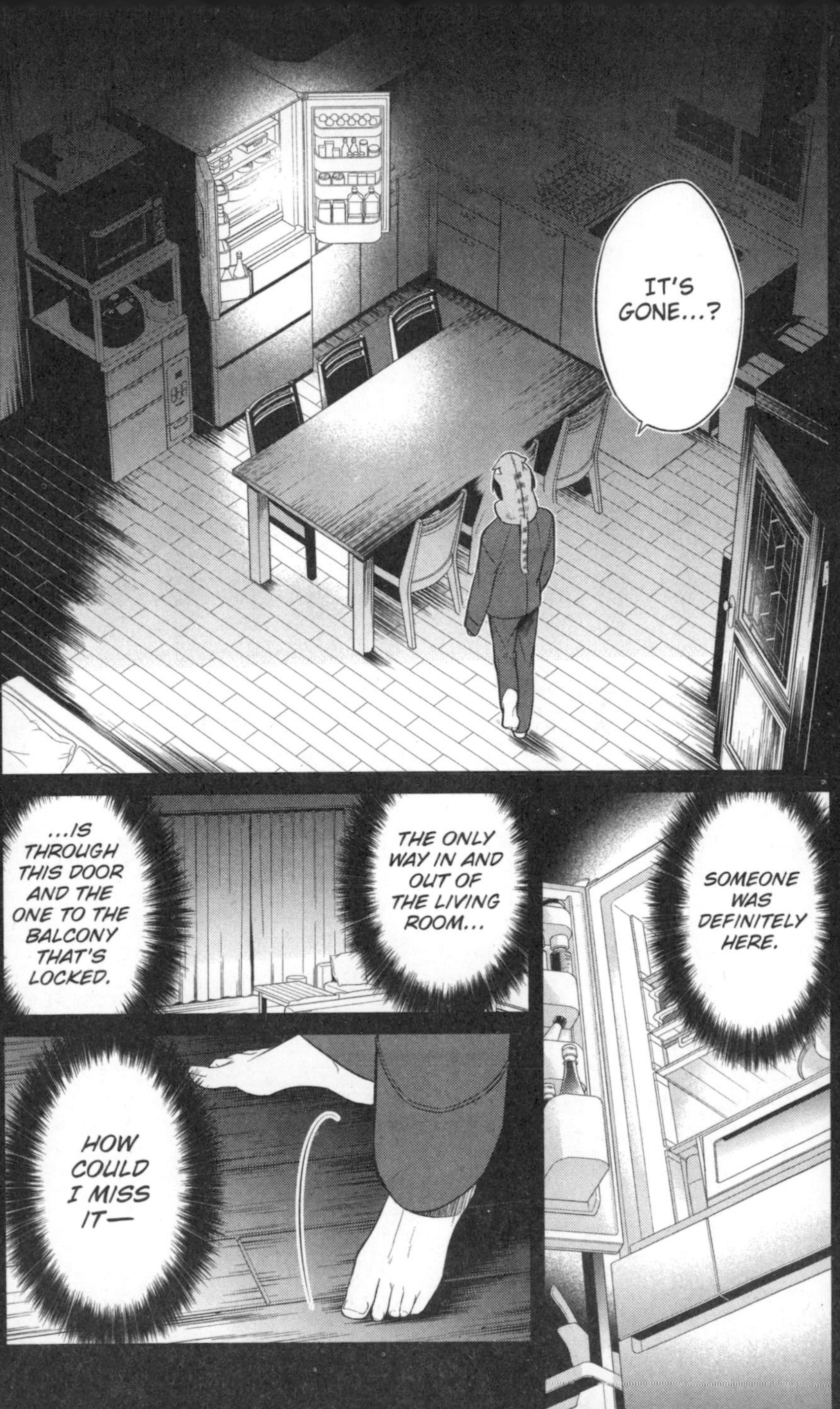
IT'S GONE...?
SOMEONE WAS DEFINITELY HERE.
THE ONLY WAY IN AND OUT OF THE LIVING ROOM...
...IS THROUGH THIS DOOR AND THE ONE TO THE BALCONY THAT'S LOCKED.
HOW COULD I MISS IT—

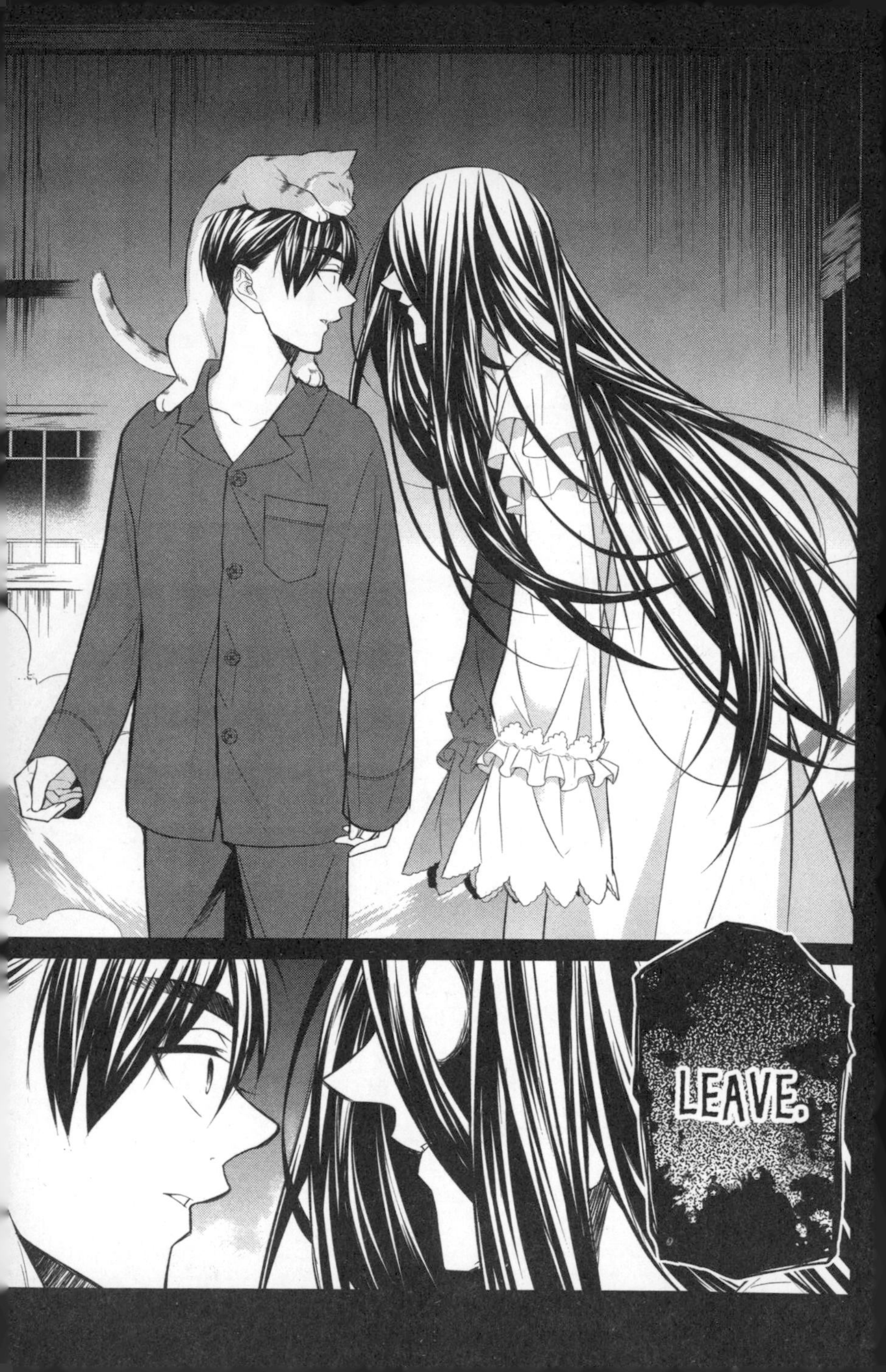
LEAVE.

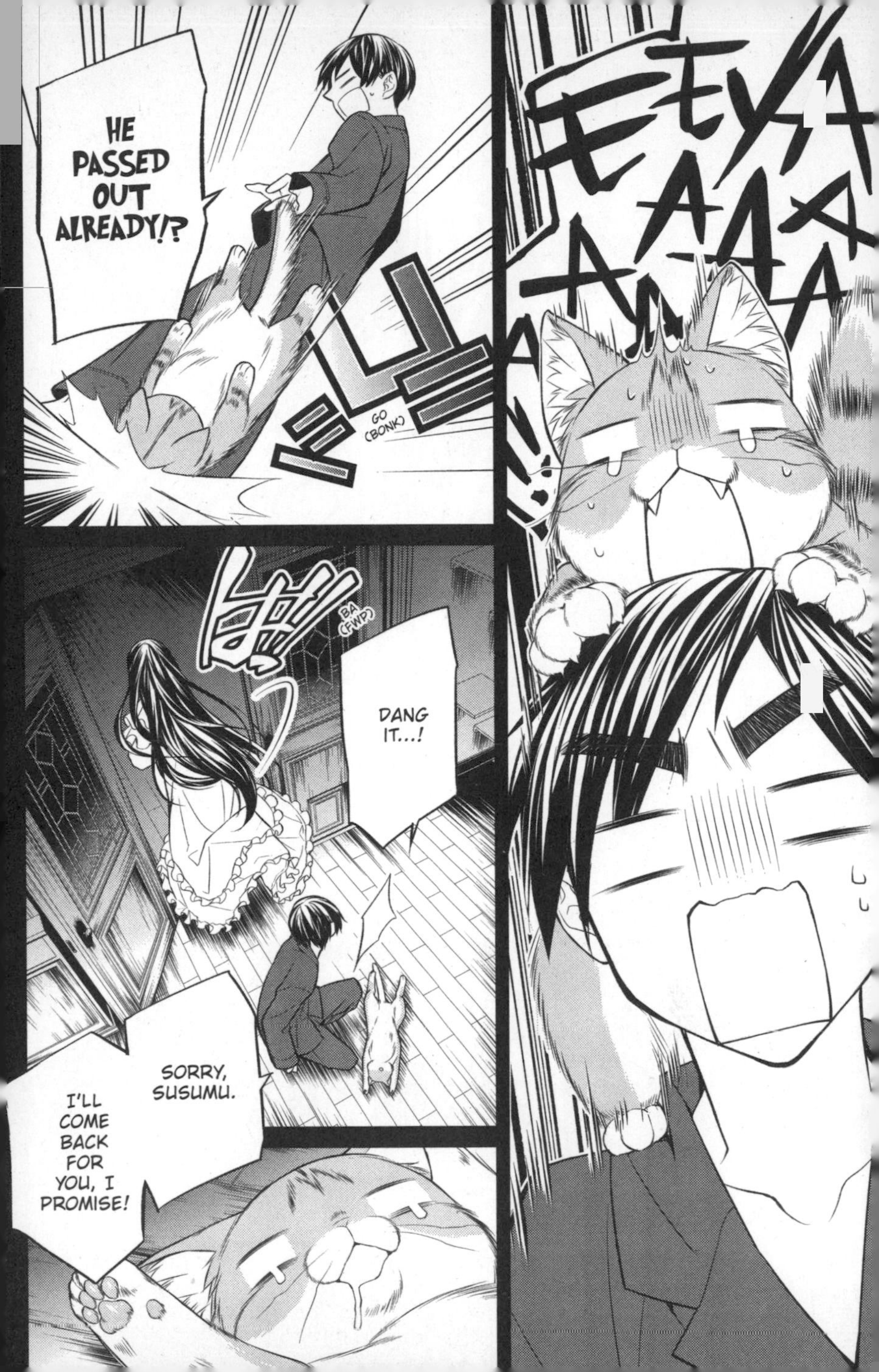
FEEYAAAAAAAA!!
HE PASSED OUT ALREADY!?
GO (BONK)
BA (FWP)
DANG IT...!
SORRY, SUSUMU.
I'LL COME BACK FOR YOU, I PROMISE!

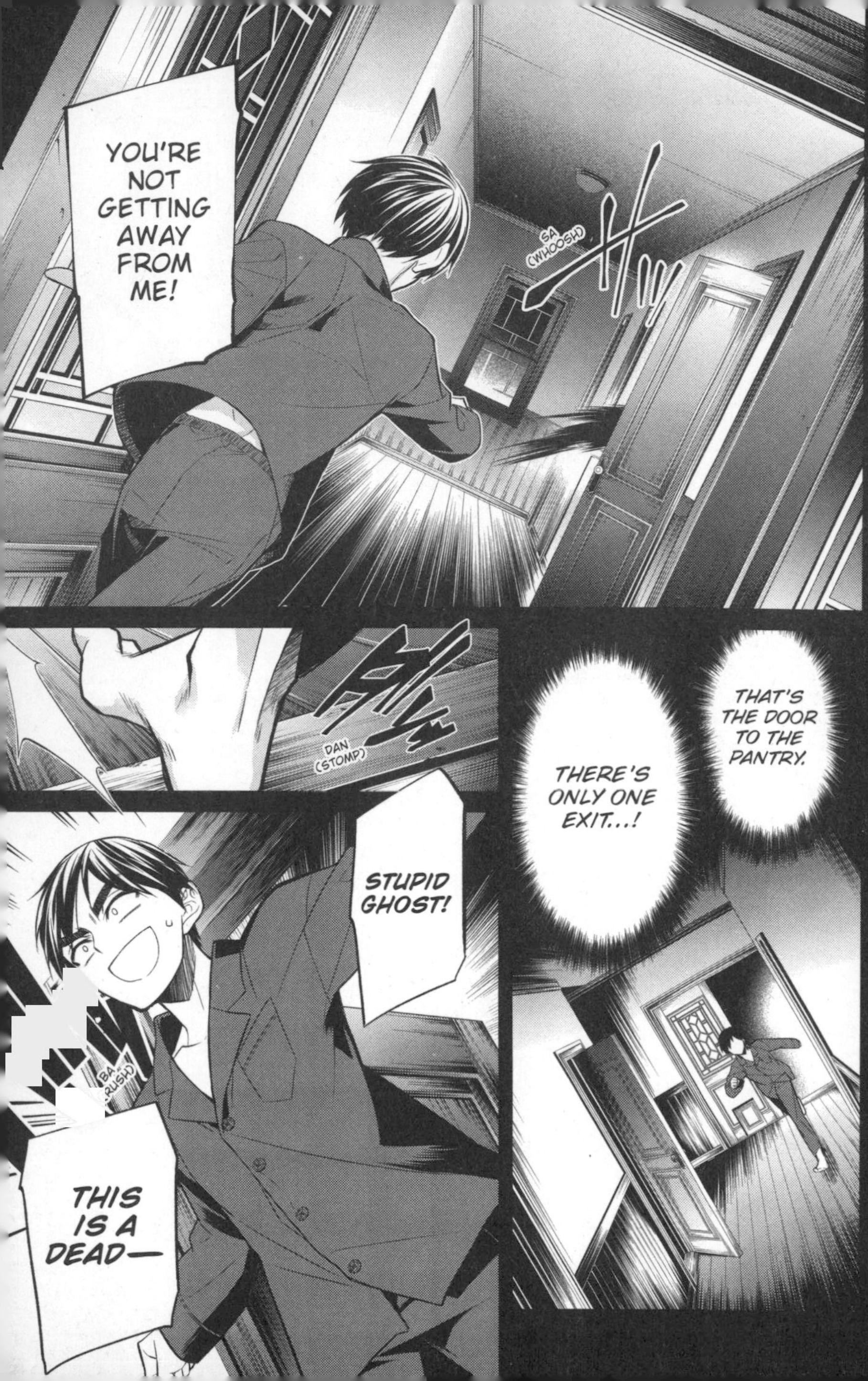
YOU'RE NOT GETTING AWAY FROM ME!
SA (WHOOSH)
THAT'S THE DOOR TO THE PANTRY.
THERE'S ONLY ONE EXIT...!
DAN (STOMP)
STUPID GHOST!
BA (RUSH)
THIS IS A DEAD—

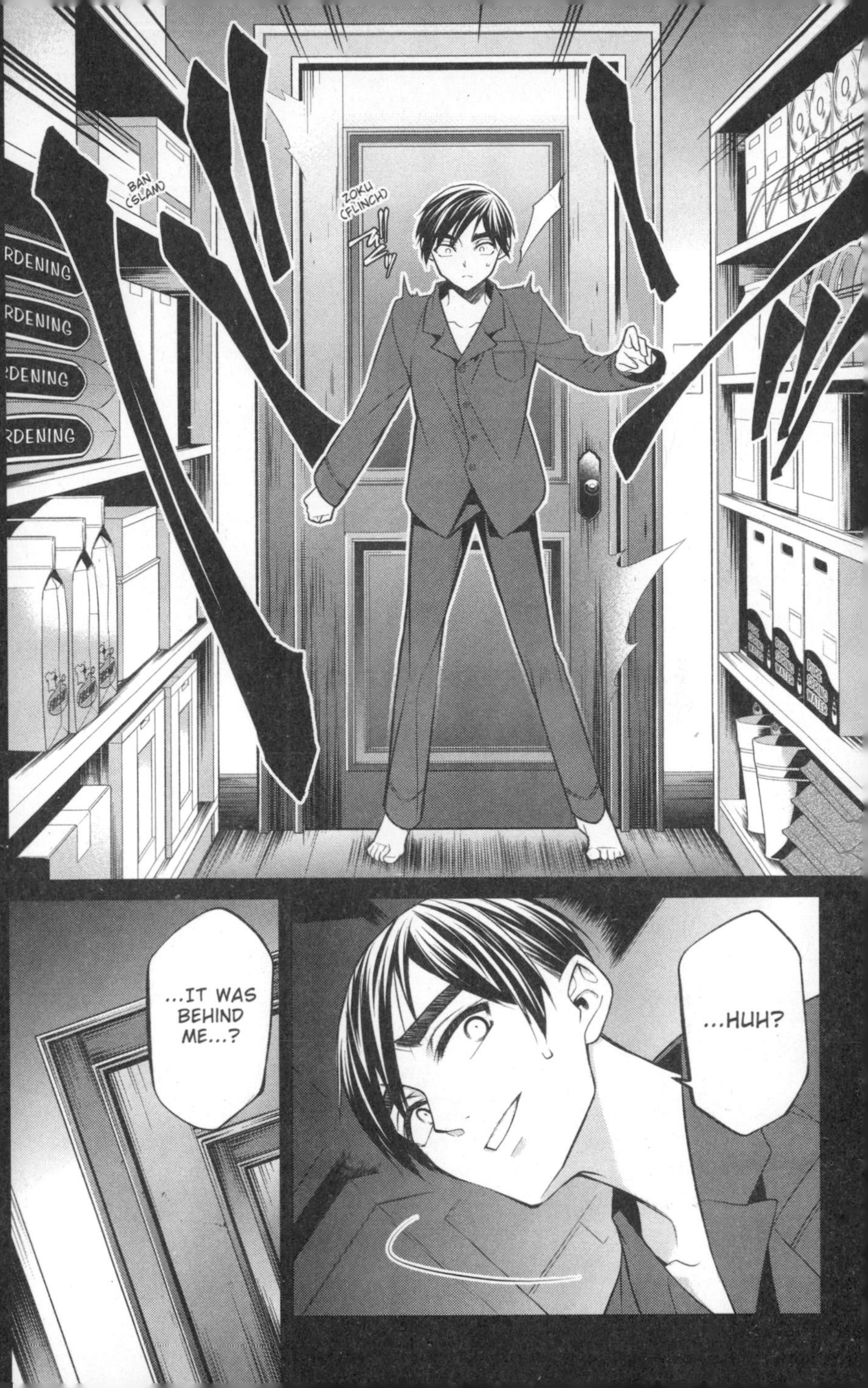
ZOKU (FLINCH)
BAN (SLAM)
...HUH?
...IT WAS BEHIND ME...?

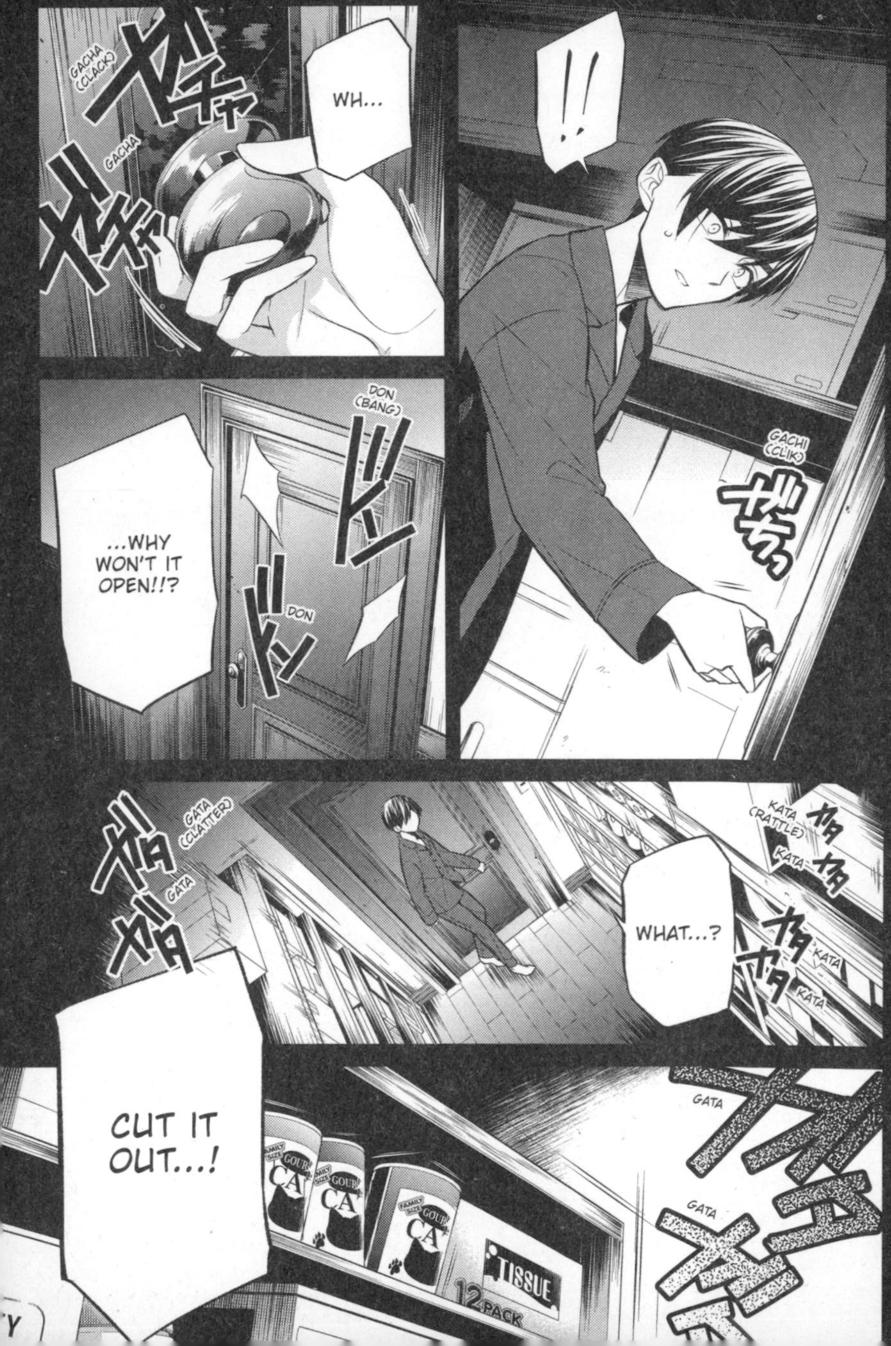

!!
GACHI (CLIK)
GACHA (CLACK)
GACHA
WH...
DON (BANG)
DON
...WHY WON'T IT OPEN!!?
KATA (RATTLE)
KATA
KATA
KATA
WHAT...?
GATA (CLATTER)
GATA
GATA
GATA
CUT IT OUT...!
TISSUE
12 PACK

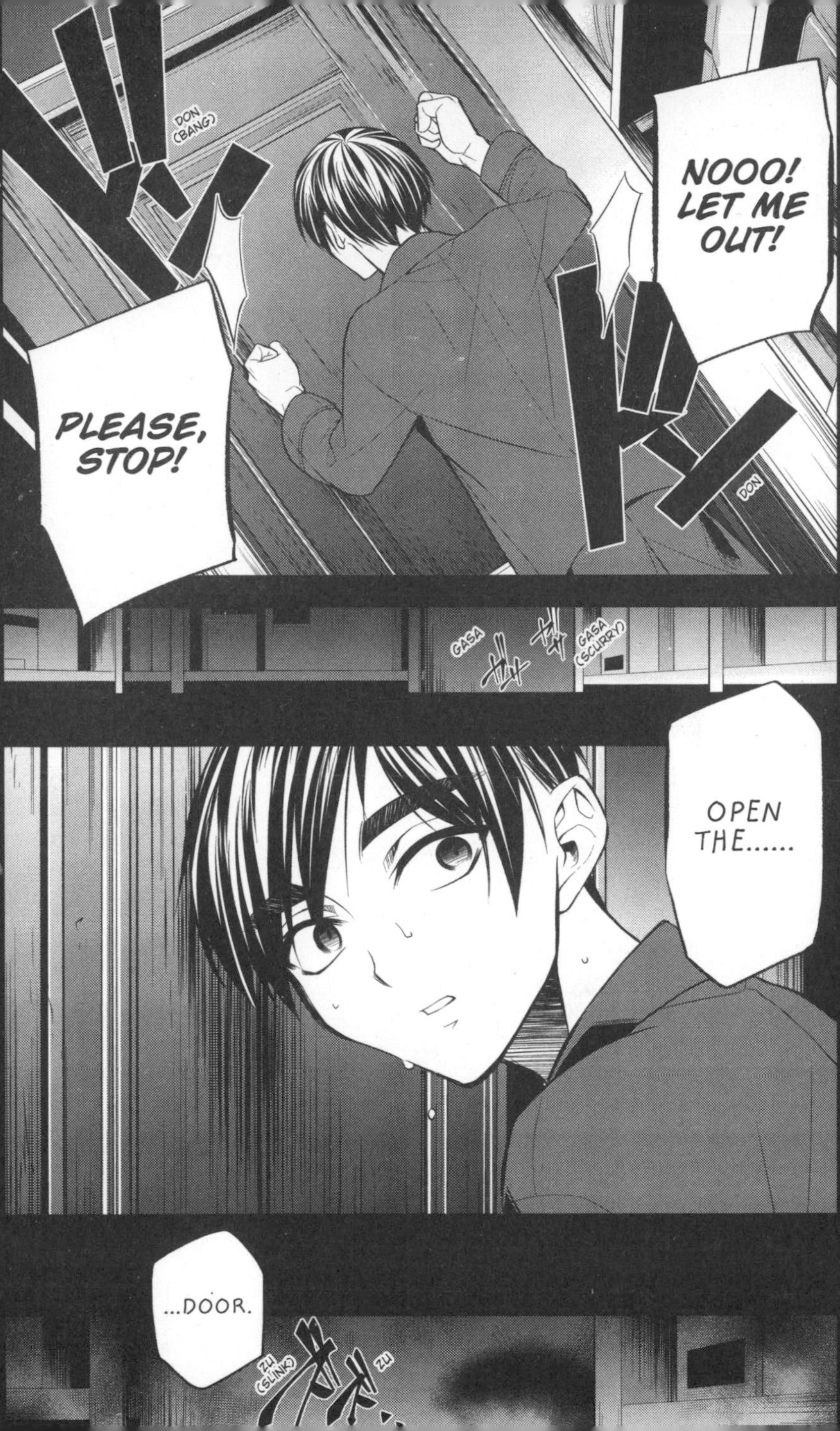
NOOO! LET ME OUT!
DON (BANG)
DON
PLEASE, STOP!
GASA (SCURRY)
GASA
OPEN THE......
...DOOR.
ZU
ZU (SLINK)

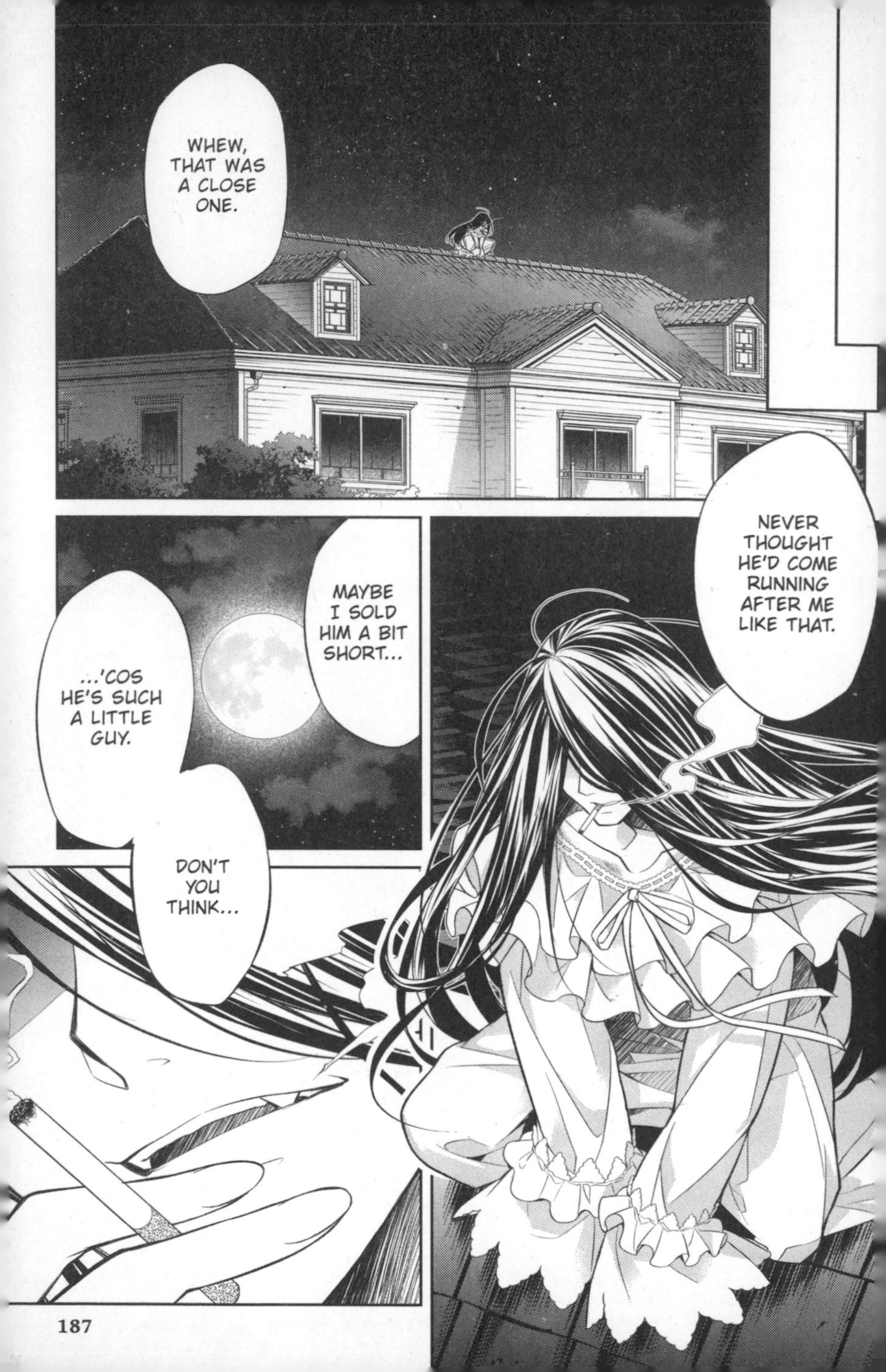
WHEW, THAT WAS A CLOSE ONE.
NEVER THOUGHT HE'D COME RUNNING AFTER ME LIKE THAT.
MAYBE I SOLD HIM A BIT SHORT...
...'COS HE'S SUCH A LITTLE GUY.
DON'T YOU THINK...

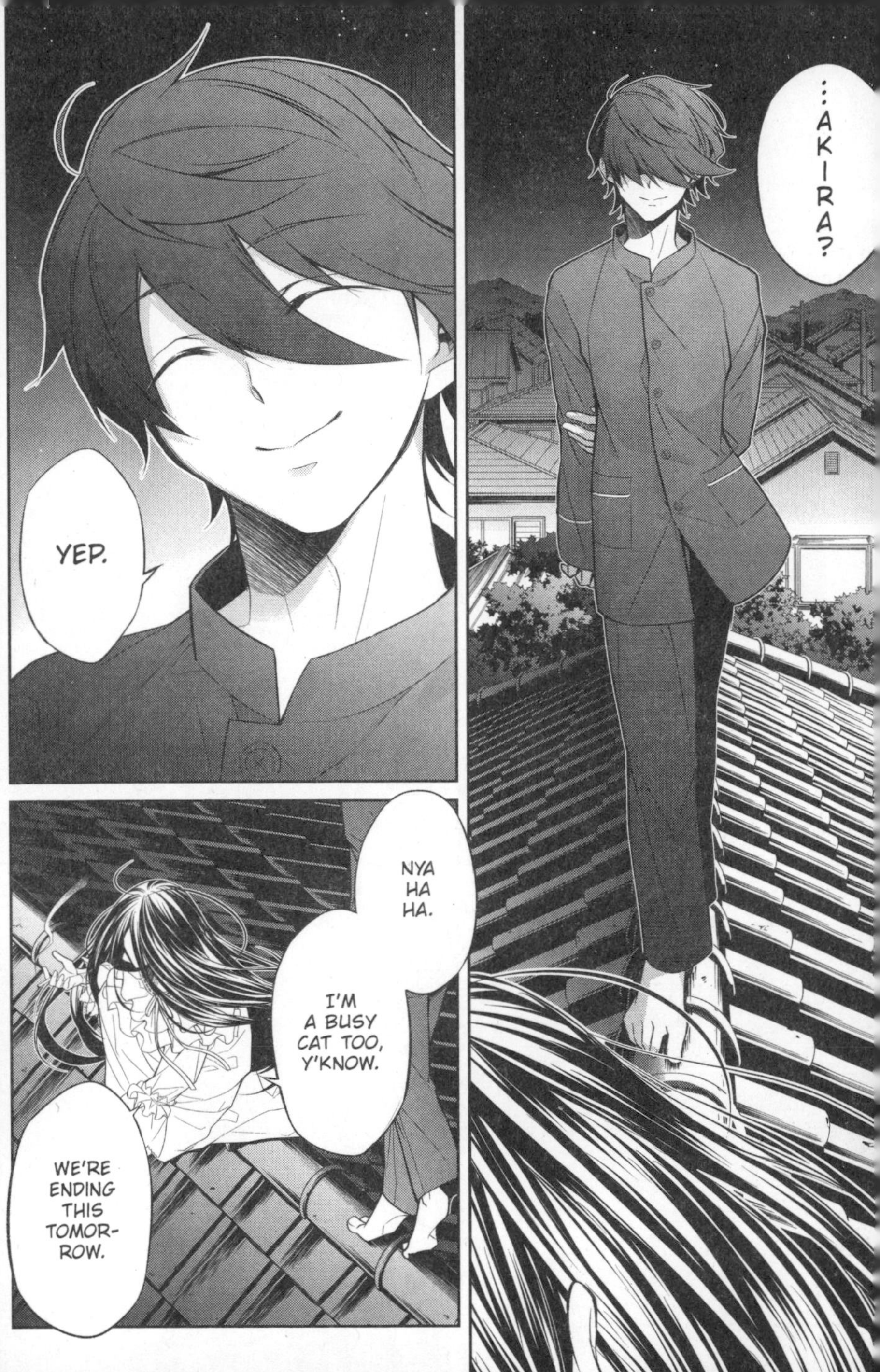
...AKIRA?
YEP.
NYA HA HA.
I'M A BUSY CAT TOO, Y'KNOW.
WE'RE ENDING THIS TOMOR-ROW.

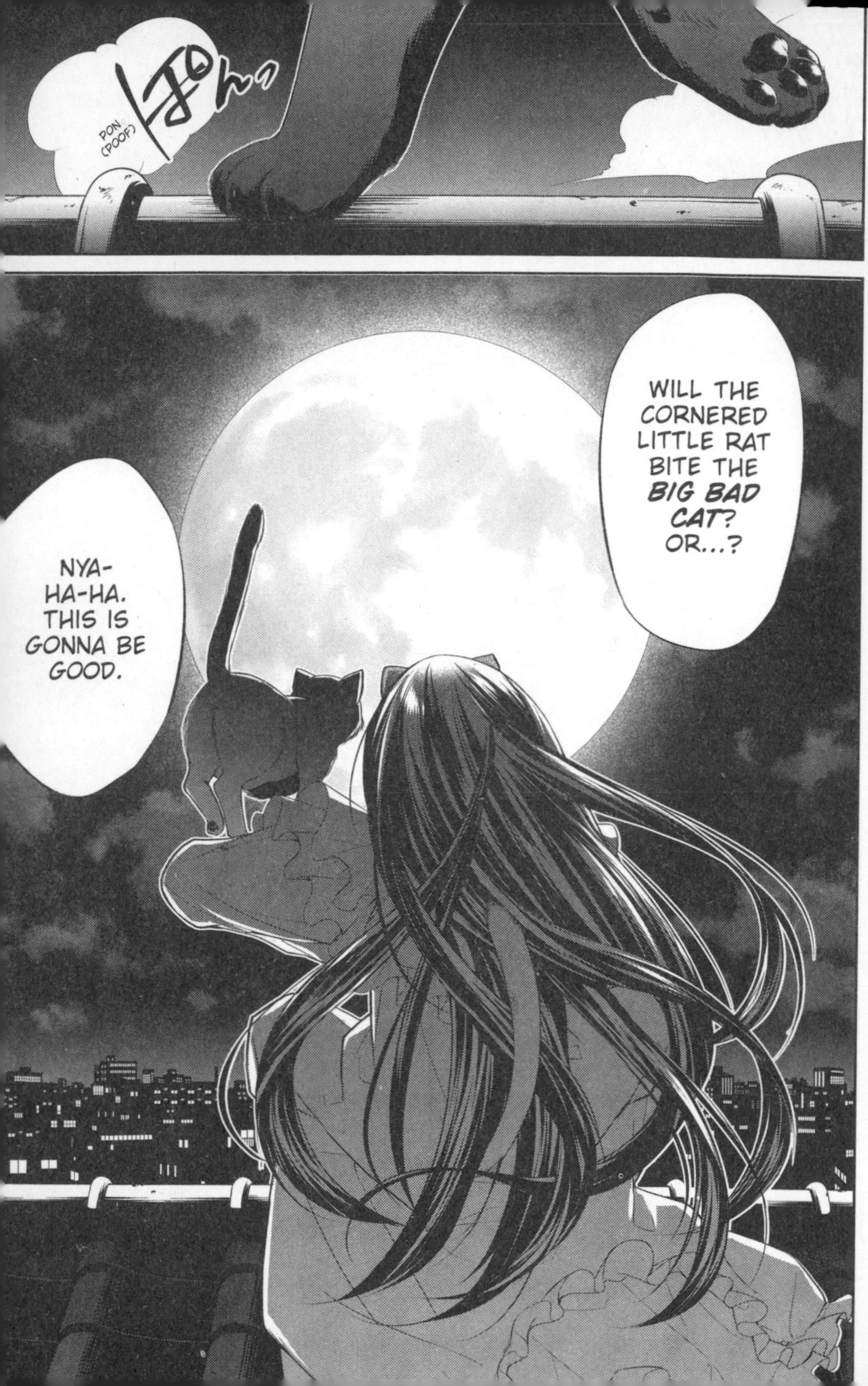
ぽんっ
PON (POOF)
WILL THE CORNERED LITTLE RAT BITE THE *BIG BAD CAT*? OR...?
NYA-HA-HA. THIS IS GONNA BE GOOD.

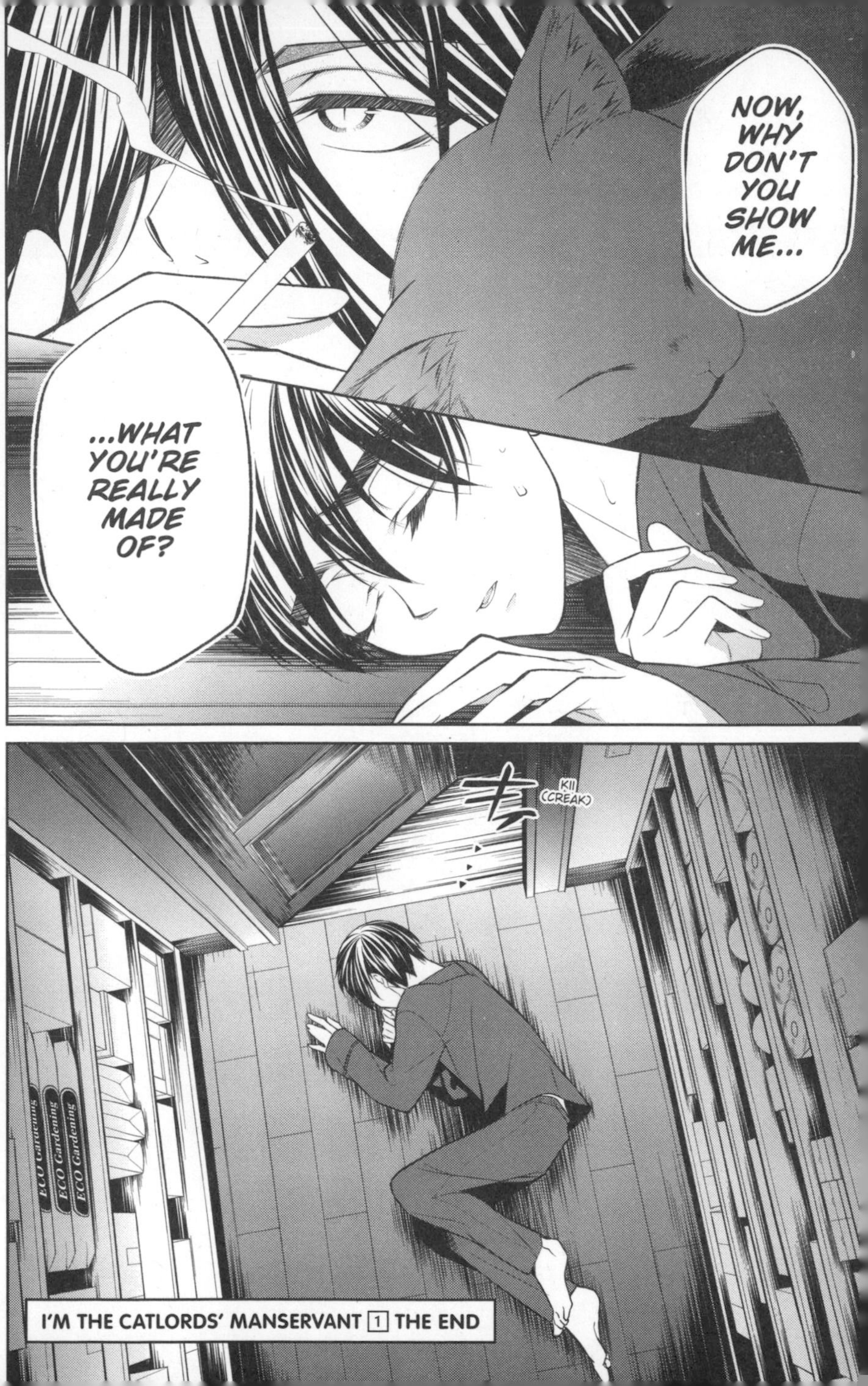
NOW, WHY DON'T YOU SHOW ME...
...WHAT YOU'RE REALLY MADE OF?
KII (CREAK)
ECO Gardening
ECO Gardening
ECO Gardening
I'M THE CATLORDS' MANSERVANT 1 THE END

Thank you very much for reading this volume. I'll put my all into the next ones too, so please look forward to it!

Rat Kitaguni

🐾 **STAFF** (No particular order)

🐾 Nitsuki Tachibana-san

🐾 Maruyama-san

🐾 Nogata-san

🐾 Saruka Satou-san

Thank you for all your support!

I'd like to thank my editor, my brother who manages my Twitter account, my family and friends who have supported me through everything, and all my followers and readers who write me messages and letters. You are the reason I was able to publish this book. Thank you very much!

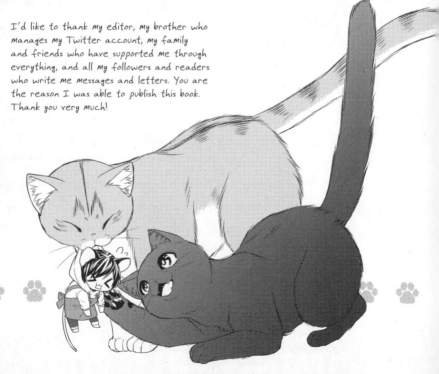

IN THE NEXT VOLUME

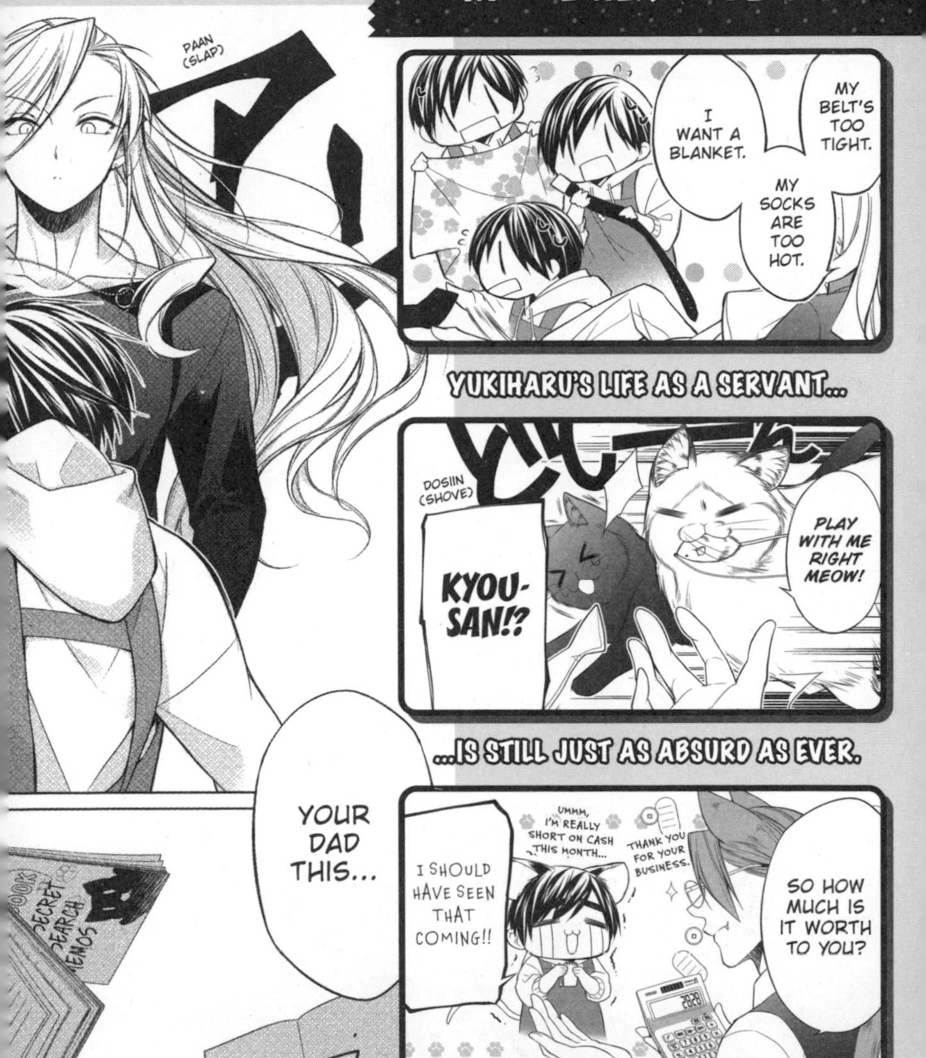

MY BELT'S TOO TIGHT.
I WANT A BLANKET.
MY SOCKS ARE TOO HOT.
PLAY WITH ME RIGHT MEOW!
DOSIIN (SHOVE)
KYOU-SAN!?
SO HOW MUCH IS IT WORTH TO YOU?
THANK YOU FOR YOUR BUSINESS.
UMMM, I'M REALLY SHORT ON CASH THIS MONTH...
I SHOULD HAVE SEEN THAT COMING!!
PAAN (SLAP)
YOUR DAD THIS...
SECRET SEARCH MEMOS

YUKIHARU'S LIFE AS A SERVANT...

...IS STILL JUST AS ABSURD AS EVER.

...IN VOLUME 2.

COMING FALL 2021

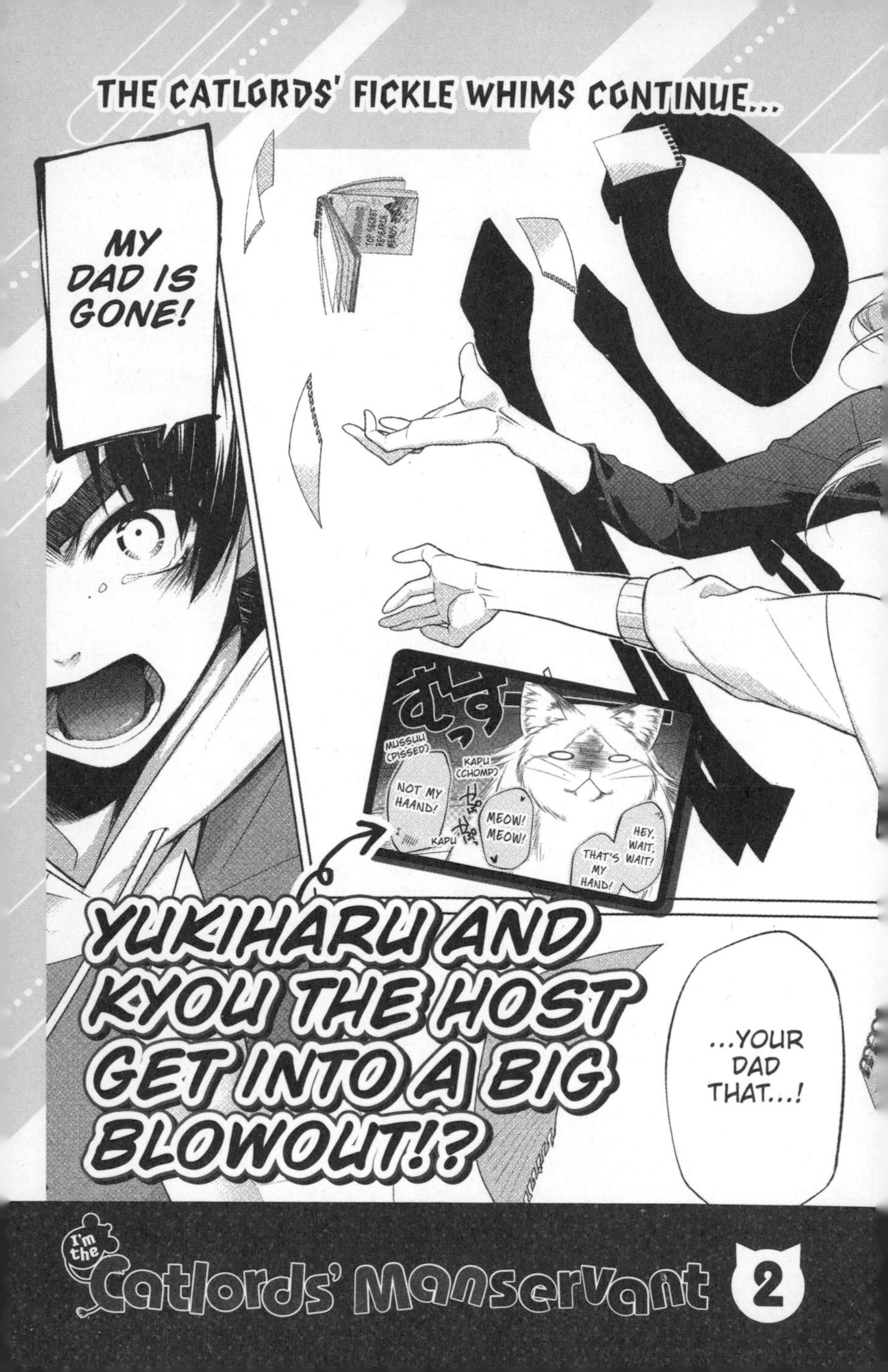
THE CATLORDS' FICKLE WHIMS CONTINUE...
MY DAD IS GONE!
TOP SECRET RESEARCH MEMOS
MUSSUU (PISSED)
KAPU (CHOMP)
NOT MY HAAND!
KAPU
MEOW! MEOW!
HEY, WAIT, WAIT!
THAT'S MY HAND!
YUKIHARU AND KYOU THE HOST GET INTO A BIG BLOWOUT!?
...YOUR DAD THAT...!
I'm the Catlords' Manservant 2

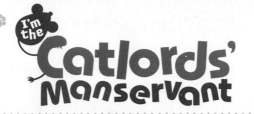

I'm the Catlords' Manservant 1

Rat Kitaguni

Translation:
Alexandra McCulloush-Garcia

Lettering:
Rochelle Gancio

BOKU WA ONEKOSAMA NO GEBOKU DESU Vol. 1
©2020 Rat Kitaguni/SQUARE ENIX CO., LTD.
First published in Japan in 2020 by SQUARE ENIX CO., LTD.
English translation rights arranged with SQUARE ENIX CO., LTD.
and Yen Press, LLC through Tuttle-Mori Agency, Inc., Tokyo.

English translation ©2021 by SQUARE ENIX CO., LTD.

Yen Press
150 West 30th Street, 19th Floor
New York, NY 10001

Visit us at yenpress.com
facebook.com/yenpress
twitter.com/yenpress
yenpress.tumblr.com
instagram.com/yenpress

First Yen Press Print Edition: April 2021

Yen Press is an imprint of Yen Press, LLC.
The Yen Press name and logo are trademarks of Yen Press, LLC.

The publisher is not responsible for websites (or their content) that are not owned by the publisher.

Library of Congress Control Number: 2021

ISBNs: 978-1-9753-2439-1 (paperback)
       978-1-9753-2440-7 (ebook)

10 9 8 7 6

TPA

Printed in South Korea

D0388485